Guns, Crime, and Punishment
in America

Guns, Crime, and Punishment in America

EDITED BY

Bernard E. Harcourt

New York University Press

NEW YORK AND LONDON

NEW YORK UNIVERSITY PRESS
New York and London

© 2003 by New York University

Library of Congress Cataloging-in-Publication Data
Guns, crime, and punishment in America /
[edited by] Bernard E. Harcourt.
p.   cm.
Includes bibliographical references and index.
ISBN 0-8147-3655-6 (alk. paper)
1. Gun control—United States. 2. Firearms—Law and
legislation—United States. 3. Crime prevention—United States.
I. Harcourt, Bernard E., 1963–
HV7436 .G8775 2002
363.3'3'0973—dc21   2002154636

New York University Press books are printed on acid-free paper,
and their binding materials are chosen for strength and durability.

Manufactured in the United States of America
10 9 8 7 6 5 4 3 2 1

Contents

Introduction

Bernard E. Harcourt

Media coverage, political debate, and public concern over firearm violence—and especially youth gun violence—have triggered a staggering number and a wide variety of public policy interventions aimed at reducing the availability of firearms to potential gun offenders and youths. The Bureau of Alcohol, Tobacco, and Firearms (ATF) has implemented a Youth Crime Gun Interdiction Initiative focused on tracing confiscated handguns from the manufacturer to the first point of retail sale, in order to develop intelligence about illicit gun markets and trafficking and to formulate supply-side interdiction strategies. Gun control advocates and legislators have proposed legislation extending *Brady*-type background checks to secondary gun markets, especially gun shows. Police departments in major urban areas have devised and implemented gun-oriented policing strategies, including aggressive stop-and-frisks and "hot spots" enforcement, aimed at reducing the number of firearms on the street. Community groups and religious leaders have organized neighborhood programs in an effort to leverage in some cases and to mitigate in others the impact of new policing techniques. Many states enacted statutes that facilitate the transfer of juvenile gun offenders to adult court—some states requiring automatic transfer for serious offenses, others lowering the age for discretionary transfers by the courts, and still others increasing the prosecutor's discretion to file juvenile cases directly in the adult system. Top federal law enforcement administrators have encouraged federal prosecutors to indict and prosecute state and local gun offenders on the model of Project Exile in Richmond, Virginia. More than forty counties and cities, including Chicago, Boston, Newark, Atlanta,

St. Louis, and San Francisco, have filed suit against gun manufacturers challenging their marketing and distribution practices. Numerous other gun control and safety measures are being debated and some implemented, including bans on particular weapons, gun licensing requirements, gun registries, limits on handgun purchases, straw purchaser laws, safe or negligent storage laws, nondiscretionary concealed weapons laws, and smart gun technology.

These measures have had wide-ranging repercussions in the criminal justice system and throughout society. They have redrawn traditional lines between federal and state enforcement of traditional police powers, reconfigured the ways that law enforcement agencies think about gun violence, fractured communities with charges of police racial profiling, challenged traditional notions of gun ownership, and virtually dismantled the juvenile courts in many jurisdictions. The measures raise a host of critical questions as we enter the twenty-first century: Do any of these policies reduce the flow of guns to the illicit gun market, to potential offenders, and to youths? Are they likely to reduce crimes committed with firearms? Have gun-oriented policing strategies reduced the extent of illegal gun carrying? At what cost? Have increased federal enhancements stemmed the tide of gun violence or unnecessarily overcrowded our prisons? How are federal prosecutions of state and local gun offenses affecting the distribution of law enforcement authority in this country? Will civil lawsuits alter the marketing and distribution practices of gun manufacturers?

Despite the salience of these questions, the great American gun debates remain some of the most ideological, visceral, polarized, ad hominem—and, often, ugly—debates in contemporary law and politics, matched only perhaps by the debates surrounding abortion and the death penalty. Meaningful engagement in the gun debates is most often rewarded with claims of bias and partiality. Scholarly and policy contributions are, more often than not, alleged to be tainted by links to the gun industry, the National Rifle Association, or the gun control lobby or are claimed to reflect pro- or antigun bias. Policy arguments devolve into character assassination. And, in all the mud slinging, it is practically impossible today for a concerned citizen, lawyer, social scientist, policymaker, or politician to trust anything she reads or hears. "For most Americans," Dan Kahan writes incisively in his contribution to this book, "the 'Great American Gun Debate' isn't particularly great."

To redress the situation, this book of collected essays brings together the nation's leading experts in a wide range of gun research, from a wide spectrum of perspectives, and with a wide variety of methodological approaches. The goal of the book is to present the most current research on a range of policy interventions in the gun area to enhance our shared understanding of the policy alternatives and to help promote dialogue between the various approaches to guns and gun violence.

While the authors take a variety of positions on the wisdom of specific policy interventions, there is a collective argument that unifies the book. It can be summarized as follows: The great American gun debates are presently polarized along two extreme positions for and against gun control measures. This polarization obscures, rather than clarifies, the debate. To move the conversation forward, it is essential that we focus on more nuanced and subtle discussions of particular policy interventions and on the relationship among the different approaches. We must develop first a better base of information about the specific public policies, as well as about gun markets, gun availability, and the connection between guns and violent crime. We must focus more closely on the specific measures that have been implemented, taking a *wide* view of the very idea of policy interventions to include not only the Brady bill and possible extensions to secondary markets but also numerous other measures such as gun tracing, gun-oriented policing, federal gun-law enforcement, and civil litigation against gun manufacturers. The overarching goal must be to link the policy research in order to promote more concrete and less polarized debates about guns.

The collective argument of this book is articulated well by Franklin Zimring, who writes in his contribution to this book: "What will improve the gun debate at the top end of the policy community is careful attention to the differences between types and intensities of firearms regulation. If experts start avoiding the silly overgeneralizations that come from assuming that all gun regulations were created equal, there is some hope that a more specific and pragmatic approach to reducing the harms of gun violence might trickle down the intellectual food chain to the powerful and powerfully confused citizenry that will shape gun policy in the fast approaching future."

In this essay, I briefly sketch the empirical landscape at the intersection of guns, crime, and punishment in America and outline the themes presented in this book as a way to lay a foundation for the individual essays included in this collection.

The Empirical Landscape

Guns

The total number of privately owned firearms in the United States stands roughly at 200 to 250 million, of which about 65 million, or one third, are handguns.[1] Approximately 80 percent of these privately owned firearms were acquired after 1974.[2] A large number of new firearms, approximately 4.5 to 5 million, are purchased every year.[3] Y2K fears helped make 1999 a banner year for gun sales: Smith and Wesson, the world's biggest manufacturer of handguns, saw its U.S. sales increase by about 15 percent in 1999.[4] Between 35 and 50 percent of households are estimated to have at least one firearm, and the personal adult firearm gun ownership rate is around 25 percent.[5]

Gun possession is not limited to adult ownership, however. Among adjudicated male youths, rates of possession and carrying can reach into the ninetieth percentile. A 1991 study of 835 male juveniles in correctional facilities in four different states—California, Illinois, Louisiana, and New Jersey—found that 86 percent of the young inmates had owned at least one firearm at some point in their lives. Seventy-three percent of the inmates had owned three or more types of guns. A 1995 study of forty-two male and twenty-one female juvenile offenders detained at five facilities in metropolitan Atlanta found that forty-one (or 97.6 percent) of the male and twelve (or 57 percent) of the female youths had owned handguns at some point in the past. Eighty-four percent of the youth who had handguns had acquired their first before the age of fifteen. A RAND study conducted in 1998, involving interviews of thirty-four youthful offenders ages sixteen and seventeen years detained in the Los Angeles Juvenile Hall, revealed that 75 percent had been threatened with a gun at least once, and 66 percent had been shot at least once. A 2000 study of thirty male youths detained at the Catalina Mountain School in Tucson, Arizona, revealed that twenty-six (or 87 percent) of the male youths had possessed guns at some point in their lives, twenty-three (or 77 percent) had carried one or more guns on their persons, and nineteen (or 63 percent) had significant histories of gun possession and carrying.[6] As a corollary, youths represent an increasing proportion of arrests for weapon offenses: whereas youths accounted for 16 percent of such arrests in 1974, they represented 23 percent of arrests for weapon offenses in 1993.[7]

These statistics, naturally, are only part of the story. Behind the numbers, there is in the United States an exceptional gun culture. It is a culture that reveres the gun as a liberator, a guarantor of freedom. At its heart lies a uniquely American belief. "I call it the 'Cowboy Corollary' to the Declaration of Independence," Richard Slotkin writes in this book. "It's a folk saying, dating from before the Civil War, which has many variations, all of which add up to this: 'God may have made *men,* but Samuel Colt made them *equal.*'"

For many Americans, guns are an integral and essential part of their identity. Among many young men, the gun can be a symbol of masculinity, status, aggressiveness, danger, and arousal. "Guns can perpetuate and refine the aesthetic of toughness, create an imminent threat of harm, help their users claim the identity of being amongst the 'toughest,' and act as an ultimate source of power in resolving disputes," Jeffrey Fagan suggests.[8] There is, in this country, a cult of the gun that has important implications for gun policies and debates.

Guns and Violent Crime

In 1993, in the United States, 1.3 million or 29 percent of victims of serious violent crime (rape, sexual assault, robbery, and aggravated assault) faced an offender with a firearm.[9] Handguns alone accounted for more than 900,000 nonfatal violent crimes in 1992.[10] Although the 1990s witnessed one of the most remarkable and consistent drops in crime in the twentieth century, made possible by an equally remarkable rise in crime during the 1960s, 1970s, 1980s and early 1990s, the amount of gun violence in America remains high. In 2000 alone, 533,470 victims of serious violent crimes said that they faced an offender with a firearm; in addition, approximately 66 percent of the 15,517 homicides in 2000 were committed with firearms.[11] Moreover, the proportion of gun homicides to total homicides has continued to increase with every crime peak. In New York City, for instance, the ratio of gun to nongun homicides has increased with each of the three homicide peaks, from 1.23 in 1972, to 1.76 in 1981, to 3.16 in 1991.[12]

Youth gun homicides remain proportionally high at the beginning of the twenty-first century. "The relative importance of youths in the national violence picture, which increased greatly during the epidemic, has remained relatively high by historical standards; killers under age 25 account for 60 percent of homicides in 1998, compared to 43 percent in 1982 (before the epidemic began)," Philip Cook and John Laub explain. There is, in their words, "a hangover from this binge of violence."[13]

Another element in the violent crime equation is the defensive use of guns. Estimates of the number of occasions in which guns are used defensively in America vary widely. On the conservative side, the National Crime Victimization Survey offers an estimate of approximately 65,000 defensive uses per year in the late 1980s.[14] The 1994 National Survey of the Private Ownership of Firearms (NSPOF) revealed that about 1.5 million adults used a gun defensively.[15] At the other extreme, Gary Kleck estimates from his research that guns are used defensively about 2.5 million times per year.[16]

On a related topic, John Lott has argued, in his provocative book *More Guns, Less Crime,* that nondiscretionary laws regarding the right to carry concealed weapons have significantly reduced the incidence of violent crime in this country. Using county-level data for the period 1977–1996, Lott finds that the adoption of nondiscretionary laws coincided with fewer murders, rapes, robberies, and aggravated assaults, as well as fewer property crimes, burglaries, larcenies, and auto theft.[17] These findings have been criticized on a number of empirical and theoretical grounds, and a panel of the National Academy of Sciences has been established to review the empirical evidence.[18]

Guns, Violent Crime, and Punishment

Punishment of gun offenders increased steadily during the last decades of the twentieth century. Beginning in 1968, Congress enacted several federal firearms statutes, including prohibitions on possession of a firearm by a previously convicted felon, gun possession in a gun-free school zone, and use of a firearm in the course of a predicate federal felony, among others. Over the years, Congress has consistently increased the sentences associated with these offenses. For example, while in 1968 the federal firearms enhancement statute, 18 U.S.C. Sec. 924(c), provided for an additional sentence of one to ten years (over and above the sentence for the predicate offense), Congress added a mandatory minimum five-year sentence in 1984 for crimes of violence and, since then, a mandatory term of thirty years for using or carrying a machine gun or assault weapon and a mandatory life sentence for those caught carrying a machine gun or assault weapon for a second time.

Under the federal firearms enhancement statute in force in 2000, the mandatory minimum consecutive sentence for use of a firearm ranges from five to thirty years depending on the type of firearm and on whether or not it was brandished or discharged. In the case of a second or subsequent conviction, the mandatory minimum ranges from twenty-five years to life, depending on the type of firearm.[19] States have similarly increased penalties for offenses committed with guns. At the state level, the average maximum length of prison sentences for weapons offenses was forty-seven months, almost four years, in 1994.[20]

Increased social control also pervades the streets of many urban areas, where police departments have implemented gun-oriented policing strategies that involve increased police-civilian contact. In New York City, Chicago, Boston, Indianapolis, Pittsburgh, and numerous other cities, police departments have begun targeting guns as a primary vehicle to reducing general crime levels. One of the most famous initiatives took place in New York City, where, in 1994, Mayor Rudolph Giuliani and Police Commissioner William Bratton began implementing an order-maintenance policing strategy emphasizing proactive and aggressive enforcement of misdemeanor laws against quality-of-life offenses, such as graffiti writing, loitering, public urination, public drinking, aggressive panhandling, turnstile jumping, and prostitution. The policy, which became known as "the quality-of-life initiative," was premised on the broken windows theory first articulated by James Q. Wilson and George L. Kelling in their 1982 *Atlantic Monthly* essay—the idea that toleration of minor infractions like graffiti writing, aggressive panhandling, public urination, and turnstile jumping encourages serious violent crime by sending a signal that the community is not in control. The strategy has significantly increased the punishment meted out by the criminal justice system, especially for what were considered minor disorderly conduct and misdemeanors.[21] Other cities and communities have adopted similar policing measures aimed at curbing the flow of guns among youths and criminals.

In addition, federal law enforcement administrators have turned increasingly to federal prosecutions of state and local gun offenders on the model of Project Exile, an initiative of the Eastern District of Virginia United States Attorney's Office.[22] The principal attraction of these federal law enforcement initiatives are the lengthier mandatory sentences and the more remote placement of federal penitentiaries.

Guns, Crime, and Punishment in America

In order to promote vigorous and constructive debate on these important issues, this book presents the most current and cutting-edge research on a wide variety of policy interventions in the gun area, ranging from ATF's gun-tracing initiative, to the extension of *Brady* background check requirements, gun-oriented policing, community interventions, Project Exile, and ongoing civil litigation against gun manufacturers. The book presents essays by the nation's leading experts on these different policies and places their research within the larger context of the history of the American gun debates and the recent heated controversy over the Second Amendment.

Part I of the book presents this larger context as a framework within which to place the different policy interventions. In a first section, titled *Perspectives,* the book explores how guns have been debated since the 1960s. Franklin Zimring, a leading scholar on firearms and violence for more than three decades, opens the section with a fascinating paper, "Continuity and Change in the American Gun Debate," that explores the trajectory of the American gun debates since the late 1960s. While Zimring observes some significant continuity, especially with regard to the dominance of symbolic preferences, the huge gap—or "gulch," as he calls it—in gun ownership between the sexes, and the centrality of handguns in the policy discussions, Zimring nevertheless emphasizes important changes in recent years. First, guns have changed from being episodically important to being chronically important as a public policy priority; second, empirical data on firearms, violence, and gun control, though still spotty, have increased tremendously since the 1970s; third, the Second Amendment has become a major topic of controversy; and fourth, the focus of citizen concern has shifted from general crime to lethal gun violence. Zimring calls for a more nuanced approach to gun policy analysis, an approach that distinguishes between specific policies rather than rely on the broad categories of pro- or anti–gun control.

Franklin Zimring emphasizes the dominance of symbolic preferences in the gun debates, and, in this regard, Dan Kahan, of Yale Law School, agrees. Drawing on these expressive and cultural dimensions, Kahan explores and deconstructs the rhetorical structure of the American gun debates in a provocative essay—or "manifesto," as he calls it—titled "The Tyranny of Econometrics and the Circumspection of Liberalism: Two Problems with the Gun Debate." Kahan argues forcefully that there are two distorting influences on the gun debates. The first is an excessive and numbing attention to empirical data. The best public opinion research demonstrates, Kahan argues, that individuals do not rely on empirical studies to formulate their positions regarding guns but instead base their opinions on their cultural interpretation of gun possession. It is not statistics but rather "cultural allegiances and outlooks that determine citizens' attitudes toward gun control," Kahan writes. The second distorting influence is our pervasive liberal discourse norm, which orients the public debate toward consequentialist arguments and away from appeals to cultural values. Yet it is precisely such appeals to values, Kahan suggests, that are needed to resolve expressive controversies. The result is devastating to the gun debates—but not necessarily or entirely paralyzing. Kahan urges the reader to construct a new, more respectful expressive idiom to debate guns. "In order to civilize the gun debate," Kahan writes, "*moderate* citizens . . . must come out from behind the cover of consequentialism and talk through their competing visions of the good life without embarrassment."

Richard Slotkin, author of an award-winning trilogy on the myth of the frontier in American cultural history, focuses our attention precisely on the rich and lengthy history to our present culture of guns. In his insightful essay "Equalizers: The Cult of the Colt in American Culture," Slotkin traces the historical roots of America's gun culture to a set of values that link equality, personal dignity, and status to the private ownership of guns and to the right of armed self-defense. What makes the United States exceptional in this regard is not simply the availability of guns or the high rate of gun violence, Slotkin argues, but an ideology that surrounds gun ownership—what he calls "powerful local, regional, and familial cultural traditions, which in turn have their roots deep in our communal history." Slotkin unearths the

geology of this unique gun culture, tracing it back to notions of equality and equal citizenship rooted in practices such as the dueling codes
of the late eighteenth and early nineteenth centuries, the right to serve
in the militia and later the military, the practices of vigilantism, especially after the Civil War, and the development of modern mass
media. In the process, Slotkin draws a sharp picture of today's gun
culture. "It is our permissive ethic of private violence—the 'Cult of the
Colt'—that has made Americans want not merely to own guns,"
Slotkin writes, "but to accumulate firepower in excess of need and has
given us a broad license to shoot each other."

One voice that is not often heard, but one that is centrally implicated in our gun culture and in the gun debates, is the voice of incarcerated males youths. Drawing on rich narratives from in-depth interviews with youths detained at the Catalina Mountain School in Tucson, Arizona, I investigate what handguns symbolize to adjudicated
male youths in an essay titled "'Hell no, you can't jack that fool. He
stays strapped. He's strapped all the time': Talking about Guns at an
All-Boy Correctional Facility in Tucson, Arizona." The essay explores
the language and registers of gun talk among adjudicated males in an
effort to develop a richer understanding of the environment within
which youths find themselves and strategically negotiate youth firearm possession. My purpose is not to present or advocate their views
on public policy but rather to decipher the rich symbolic dimensions
of guns to youths. What I discover in the process is that guns are a
deeply fascinating object of desire and hold a surprisingly powerful
grip over many of the youths at the Catalina Mountain School.

One of the major changes in the gun debate over the past two
decades, as Franklin Zimring emphasizes in his essay, is the newfound
importance of the Second Amendment. Sanford Levinson, a leading
constitutional scholar, triggered the most recent wave of legal scholarship with his essay "The Embarrassing Second Amendment," published in the *Yale Law Review* in 1989. Since then, a flurry of legal and
historical scholarship has emerged and flamed the debate between
the individual- and the collective-rights proponents of the Second
Amendment. The controversy has become all the more heated under
the administration of President George W. Bush and his attorney general, John Ashcroft. The Bush administration endorsed a broad individual-rights interpretation of the Second Amendment in pleadings
filed with the United States Supreme Court, prompting scores of crim-

inal defendants across the country to urge federal courts to dismiss their gun charges on Second Amendment grounds.[23] The second section of Part I addresses the contemporary debate over the meaning and implications of the Second Amendment.

In his stimulating essay "The Historians' Counterattack: Some Reflections on the Historiography of the Second Amendment," Sanford Levinson responds to the recent writings by historians, such as Saul Cornell, Michael Bellesiles, Don Higginbotham, Robert Shalhope, and Jack Rakove, who criticize the historical claims of individual-rights or "standard model" constitutional scholars. Levinson's overarching theme is that Second Amendment scholarship and historical research are in their infancy and that it is, at present, premature to make confident statements about the origins and implications of the Second Amendment or to speak about a "standard" interpretation. After addressing larger theoretical issues of historiography, including the tension between consensus and fragmented views of the Second Amendment and the role of ideas versus material circumstances in interpreting the Second Amendment, Levinson poses a number of sharp and insightful questions to historians: Who "proposed" the Second Amendment, and, more provocative, "Is James Madison a 'trickster' who gulled an easily fooled American public?" Is the history of state regulation relevant to the constitutional analysis of national powers? Should we focus on the Revolutionary Era or instead on 1868 and the ratification of the Fourteenth Amendment? In the process, Levinson makes clear that there remain important legal distinctions that need to be made in the constitutional law context, distinctions that are not necessarily resolved by historical evidence alone.

Carl Bogus, a leading proponent of the collective-rights interpretation and the editor of *The Second Amendment in Law and History: Historians and Constitutional Scholars on the Right to Bear Arms* (New York: New Press, 2000), takes the collective-rights argument one step further. In his challenging essay "What Does the Second Amendment Restrict? A Collective-Rights Analysis," Bogus addresses one of the leading criticisms of the collective-rights interpretation, namely that the interpretation renders the Second Amendment largely irrelevant. If the Second Amendment gives individuals the right to bear arms but only within the militia—an entity organized and controlled by the government itself—then isn't the Second Amendment in effect meaningless? Bogus responds to this criticism by exploring the kinds of constitutional situations where the Second Amendment might have been offended. He discusses three specific historical episodes that should have raised concern under a collective-rights interpretation. One example occurred on September 24, 1957, when President Dwight Eisenhower federalized the Arkansas National Guard to prevent Arkansas's governor, Orval Faubus, from using the state militia to prevent black students from enrolling at the Little Rock Central High School. "Eisenhower did not nationalize the Arkansas National Guard in order to use it to restore order," Bogus writes. "The main objective was to deprive Faubus of the Guard." Was this a violation of the Second Amendment under a collective-rights reading? Insofar as President Eisenhower was federalizing the militia in order to reduce the risk of hostile action with federal soldiers—the army had been sent to ensure peace and security in Arkansas—Eisenhower's actions may not have violated a collective-rights interpretation of the Amendment. But what is clear is that the Second Amendment would have been germane to the dispute and that, in other cases of state-federal conflict, there may indeed be a violation. "No one can foresee what those issues may be," Bogus contends. "Under a collective-rights interpretation, however, the Second Amendment remains a vital constitutional provision. It is a discrete but important element of federalism, guaranteeing the states not only a right but the capacity to provide for their own security."

Christopher Eisgruber, of Princeton University, author of *Constitutional Self-Government* (Harvard University Press, 2001), argues in his provocative essay that both the individual- and the collective-rights proponents have it all wrong. Constitutional interpretation of the Second Amendment should not turn on arcane historical trivia about "yeoman militia." "[W]hatever one's position about gun control," Eisgruber writes, "it is nutty to suppose that we should determine America's gun control policies today on the basis of arguments about, for example, how many Americans owned muskets in the late eighteenth century." Instead, the debate should address what scope to give the abstract moral principle concerning the right to bear arms. That principle provides, Eisgruber suggests, that "the American people shall enjoy those rights to gun ownership and military service which ought to belong to citizens of all free governments." In his essay "Moral Principle and the Second Amendment," Eisgruber urges us to debate the scope of this principle as a matter of moral and political theory.

"That is the right debate to have," Eisgruber contends, "and we should get on with it."

In Part II, the book explores, reviews, and evaluates five different categories of policy interventions in the gun area. The first is firearm tracing, a program promoted heavily under the administration of President Bill Clinton. Under this approach, law enforcement agencies are encouraged to submit confiscated guns to the Bureau of Alcohol, Tobacco, and Firearms so that it can attempt to trace the firearms from their manufacture in or import into the United States through their first sale by a retail firearms dealer. The goal of the program is to help identify and track the sources of guns to youths and criminals in order to attack the problem of illicit gun trafficking from the supply side. The program grew significantly during the 1990s, increasing threefold from 1993 to 1999 as measured by the number of guns submitted by law enforcement agencies for tracing.

Philip Cook, one of the nation's leading experts on guns and gun violence, and Anthony Braga, of the John F. Kennedy School of Government at Harvard University, explore the new data emerging from the ATF in a fascinating essay titled "New Law Enforcement Uses for Comprehensive Firearms Trace Data." Contrary to much popular opinion, the trace data reveal that guns reach the hands of criminals through narrower channels, especially through gun dealers and traffickers. "[N]ewer guns are overrepresented in crime even though criminal users are rarely among the first purchasers," Cook and Braga find. What this suggests is that "licensed dealers are playing a significant role in 'supplying the suppliers' of guns to criminals and that firearms trafficking may be one of the important channels by which guns reach criminals, especially in the tight-control states."

In their essay, Cook and Braga also explore the trace data to assess the effects of the Brady Act on interstate trafficking. Focusing on the city of Chicago, Cook and Braga find that *Brady* resulted in sharp declines in traceable firearms recovered in Chicago that were imported from Southern states (with more lax gun control regulations), replaced by an increase in the use of in-state sources. They conclude that implementation of *Brady* has impacted the flow of guns to illicit markets.

A second type of intervention in the gun area consists of police and community strategies aimed at reducing gun availability and gun violence. Jeffrey Fagan, of Columbia University, and Garth Davies, leading experts on gun-oriented policing, review the history and debates over the quality-of-life initiative in New York City, closely analyze the available studies, and present the results of their own research on the impact of order-maintenance policing on crime rates in New York City. In their groundbreaking essay "Policing Guns: Order Maintenance and Crime Control in New York," Fagan and Davies recount the development of aggressive arrest and stop-and-frisk policies in New York City during the administration of Mayor Rudolph Giuliani. They explore the existing social scientific evidence that supports the policing initiative, principally the recent study by George L. Kelling and William Souza Jr., titled *Do Police Matter? An Analysis of the Impact of New York City's Police Reforms,* and conclude that their "claims go well beyond the limits of the study and in fact are based on a shaky empirical and analytic foundation."[24] They then present the result of their own research, which finds that, "[f]or both violence arrests broadly and homicide arrests specifically, there is no single category of citizen stops by police that predicts where crime will increase or decrease in the following year." When they examine homicide fatalities, they observe different effects by type of stop and by victim race. "Stops for violence are significant predictors of reductions in both gun homicide deaths and overall homicide deaths, but only among Hispanics." In contrast, for African Americans, no type of arrests predicts homicide victimization a year later; for whites, the results are not reliable because of the low white homicide victimization rate. Why is it that there may be effects for Hispanics but not for African Americans? Fagan and Davies suggest that it may have to do with what they call "stigma saturation" in black communities: When stigma is applied in ways that are perceived as too harsh and unfair, it may have reverse effects. They write, "When legal control engenders resistance, opposition, or defiance, the opportunity to leverage formal social control into informal social control is lost. The absence of crime control returns from OMP policing may reflect just such a dynamic among African Americans, who shouldered much of the burden of OMP."

Christopher Winship, of Harvard University, and Jenny Berrien, who have studied extensively Boston's anticrime initiatives, report on the developments there. In their essay "Should We Have Faith in the Churches? The Ten-Point Coalition's Effect on Boston's Youth Violence," Winship and Berrien insightfully trace the history of the police efforts in Boston and the formation of the Ten-Point Coalition, a group of about forty ministers who organized to mobilize the community to combat the scourge of black-on-black violence. Although at first blush it is hard to imagine that the Ten-Point Coalition had a very significant impact on crime, Winship and Berrien tease out how it transformed police-community neighborhoods and in the process extended an umbrella of legitimacy over the police that significantly assisted them in carrying out their other crime-fighting techniques. "The key contribution of the Ten-Point Coalition and the efforts of other church-based groups," Winship and Berrien write, "lies perhaps not so much in their work with at-risk youth as in how they have changed the ways in which the police (and other elements of the criminal justice system) and Boston's inner-city community relate to each other. The coalition has done so by becoming an intermediary between the two parties." By becoming an intermediary, the ministers were able to support appropriate police activity and to restrain certain other practices in such a way as to extend legitimacy in the eyes of the community.

Jerome Skolnick, one of the leading experts on police practices in this country, and Abigail Caplovitz investigate the contemporary problem of racial profiling that is so often tied to gun-oriented policing strategies. In their excellent essay "Guns, Drugs, and Profiling: Ways to Target Guns and Minimize Racial Profiling," Skolnick and Caplovitz reexamine racial profiling in light of September 11 and the New Jersey's Supreme Court's decision in *State of New Jersey v. Carty*, which bans racial profiling.[25] Profiling is very different from a witness description, they argue. It is a type of modeling that depends for its accuracy on the kind of information fed into the model. Under certain specific conditions—with detailed information about location, behavior, and previous conduct—it may have some validity. But, for broad categories like "young black male," Skolnick and Caplovitz argue, it is likely to "increase the rate of false positives, disproportionately raising the social cost of policing to innocent nonwhites." Skolnick and Caplovitz offer solutions to minimize racial profiling. The key is to improve police accuracy, which can be achieved in three ways: first, police departments must engage in more sophisticated data collection, analysis, and management, tracking false positive rates as a way to identify problem officers and tracking problems over time. Second, there should be a greater emphasis on police management and leadership; "strong management can improve the accuracy of officers' searches," they write. Third, we should raise the cost of racial profiling; judicial and prosecutorial oversight and discipline can help turn these issues into problems that get addressed. These are the types of reforms, Skolnick and Caplovitz argue, that will help reduce profiling and the attendant harm of false positives.

A third type of intervention in the gun area is the approach taken by Congress with the passage in 1993 of the Brady Handgun Violence Prevention Act. *Brady* imposes on federally licensed firearms dealers the requirement to conduct background checks on handgun buyers to make sure that they are legally permitted to purchase a handgun and imposed, originally, a waiting period before transferring the handgun.

Philip Cook and Jens Ludwig, of Georgetown University, authors of *Gun Violence: The Real Costs* (Oxford University Press, 2000), thoroughly investigate the effect of the Brady bill on homicide and suicide rates in their essay "The Effects of the Brady Act on Gun Violence." Since the Brady Act effectively changed the legal requirements in only thirty-two states (given that eighteen states already met the *Brady* requirements), Cook and Ludwig brilliantly use the implementation of *Brady* as a natural experiment with a control group. They compare homicide and suicide patterns between the two category of states— those that required a change and the control group (those that already required background checks). Cook and Ludwig find that there is some evidence that the passage of *Brady* is associated with a decline in the firearm suicide rate, particularly among older residents, although the reduction is partly offset by an increased rate of nonfirearm suicide attempts. With regard to firearm homicides, and homicides more generally, Cook and Ludwig find no evidence of a greater decline in states that had to implement *Brady* versus the control states.

James B. Jacobs, of New York University, author of *Can Gun Control Work?* (Oxford University Press, 2002) explores the history and current state of the efforts to expand *Brady* to the secondary markets, especially to private sales of firearms at guns shows. The *Brady* background check requirements did not originally apply to casual gun sellers (non–federally licensed firearms dealers) at gun shows or in private sales. With more than four thousand per year in the United States, gun shows are a significant venue for guns transactions, and a lot of regulatory proposals have been made regarding gun shows and other secondary markets. Several congressional bills have been introduced, including the Gun Show Accountability Act in 1999, and the Gun Show Loop Hole Closing and Gun Law Enforcement Act in 2001. In his insightful essay "Gun Shows and Gun Controls," Jacobs evaluates the proposed regulation of gun shows. Jacobs finds that, given the size and dimensions of the secondary markets more generally, it makes little sense to regulate gun shows unless it represents a step toward regulating all secondary markets. "Otherwise," Jacobs writes, "private sellers could use the gun shows to display their guns and give out business cards. They could complete the sales later in the privacy of their homes, cars, or even on street corners." Jacobs observes that almost 50 percent of handgun transfers are made by casual sellers and that only a fraction of these take place at gun shows. In other words, regulating gun shows would likely have little effect on gun trafficking, especially since the regulations could so easily be evaded. Gun shows are just one small piece of the larger mosaic of unregulated secondary firearms sales. However, to effectively regulate the whole secondary market, Jacobs argues, would pose a prohibitive administrative and enforcement challenge.

The fourth type of policy intervention focuses on federal enforcement of gun laws. One important initiative in the federal arsenal has been the Eastern District of Virginia United States Attorney's Office Project Exile, which has targeted gun violence in the Richmond, Virginia, area by prosecuting, whenever possible, state and local gun arrests in federal court under federal firearms statutes. According to proponents, the increased federal sentences—the federal mandatory minimums and sentencing guidelines in the gun area—as well as federal preventative detention pending trial, and the "exile" of incarceration in a distant federal penitentiary, offer increased deterrence and break the cycle of social influence between gun offenders and their communities. Project Exile represents another type of intervention, focused on federal law enforcement and prosecution, that has been extremely popular under both Democrat and Republican administrations.

Daniel Richman, of Fordham University School of Law, a former Assistant United States Attorney in the Southern District of New York, subtly traces the intricate political genealogy of Project Exile and explores the implications of the initiative for the distribution of federal, state, and local enforcement authority. Project Exile, originally conceived late in 1996 during the administration of President Bill Clinton, was warmly received by Republican law makers and by all sides of the gun debates, from the NRA to Sarah Brady. The initiative eventually became the leading gun policy approach during the administration of President George W. Bush and has been extended nationwide

18 BERNARD E. HARCOURT

under a slightly new and more appealing rubric, Project Safe Neighborhood. In his essay "Project Exile and the Allocation of Federal Law Enforcement Authority," Daniel Richman argues that these developments "mark a new stage in the devolution of federal enforcement power." Whereas the federal government has, in the past, shifted control of crime from Washington, D.C., to the United States Attorneys' Offices throughout the country, this latest development represents an even further devolution to state and local agencies. This development, Richman argues, might "encourage and institutionalize the elimination of federal prosecutorial gatekeeping." "[T]he legacy of Project Exile," Richman writes, "may be a serious challenge to the idea of federal enforcement policy in the areas where federal, state, and local authority most overlap."

Sara Sun Beale, of Duke University Law School, a former Assistant to the Solicitor General and Attorney Adviser in the Office of Legal Counsel, explores the larger framework of enhanced gun penalties under the federal sentencing guidelines. Since the Gun Control Act of 1968, Congress has repeatedly and consistently increased the penalties for illegal firearm possession and use of a firearm in a federal crime. In her prescient essay "The Unintended Consequences of Enhancing Gun Penalties," Beale argues that congressional reform of the federal firearms statutes, as well as federal prosecutorial initiatives, have significantly altered the field of criminal law and prosecution. Though intended to shape the behavior of would-be criminals, the reforms have, Beale suggests, "created behavior-altering incentives for other actors in the criminal justice system, as well." Beale explores specifically how these legislative efforts have affected the behavior of judges and prosecutors. To begin with, the enhanced sentencing schemes have, Beale suggests, placed great pressure on the boundary of federal and state enforcement authority and provoked a judicial backlash against federal legislative efforts in this area, as evidenced by the Supreme Court's decision in *United States v. Lopez,* striking down the Gun-Free School Zones Act of 1990.[26] At the same time, federal prosecutors have been reluctant to actively pursue the superenhanced penalties and have either bargained away or declined to bring charges under the enhanced penalty provisions in most cases. As a result, the effect of enhancing the penalties applicable to gun-related crime, Beale concludes, has been to "enhance the prosecution's bargaining power and its unchecked discretion in a wide range of cases." This, Beale writes, may "result in greater inequity among defendants as a result of mandatory sentencing provisions. More subtle changes also may have been set in motion, as federal prosecutors seek to handle the crush of new gun cases by wholesale cross-designation of state prosecutors, setting a precedent for the delegation of federal prosecutorial authority to local actors."

The fifth type of policy intervention involves civil litigation against gun manufacturers. More than forty cities and counties have filed suit against gun manufacturers since 1998. Given the relatively small size of the gun industry—approximately $1.5 billion in revenues annually[27]—these civil suits have the potential of significantly affecting the gun debates. The suits have proceeded under a number of different theories, including public nuisance, negligence, and strict liability for abnormally dangerous activities or defective products.

The public-nuisance theory focuses principally on the marketing and distribution practices of gun manufacturers, which, it is alleged, make guns easily available for purposes of crime. Numerous cities and counties have invoked their public nuisance duties and powers and are seeking injunctive relief in the form of abatement and, in some cases, money damages. David Kairys, of Temple University, who formulated the public nuisance litigation strategy, traces the origin and development of these handgun cases in his forceful essay "The Cities Take the Initiative: Public Nuisance Lawsuits against Handgun Manufactures." As Kairys explains, the basic theory is that gun manufacturers have facilitated easy access to firearms among criminals and youths by means of their distribution and marketing policies and practices. The approach rests on the public-nuisance tort, a tort that focuses on the rights of the general public to be free of unreasonably harmful conduct, rather than on individuals rights. Kairys traces the subsequent history of the suits, including the passage by state legislatures of statutes prohibiting the lawsuits, and the litigation outcomes, especially the results of motions to dismiss the suits which have been evenly split, as well as Smith and Wesson's decision to settle with some of the government plaintiffs. The litigation is still young, and, as Kairys writes, "fuller assessment of the governmental handgun cases will have to await further developments."

Mark Geistfeld, of New York University, an expert in torts and product liability, carefully addresses the negligence and strict liability theories in his essay "Tort Law and Criminal Behavior (Guns)." With regard to negligence theories, Geistfeld suggests that there may not be a sufficiently strong causal connection between the negligent conduct of the manufacturers and the injury to sustain negligence suits. Even if most guns involved in crimes can be traced to negligent marketing practices, Geistfeld argues, it does not follow that the negligent marketing practices likely caused the criminal gun violence at issue; in all likelihood, the criminal would have gotten a gun anyway. With regard to strict liability for abnormally dangerous activities, Geistfeld concludes that the courts have reached the right result in denying liability, but for the wrong reason. Most courts have ruled that gun distribution is not an abnormally dangerous activity, because when everyone exercises reasonable care, there is no risk of criminal misuse. Geistfeld criticizes the reasonable-care assumption but ultimately defends the outcome. According to Geistfeld, tort law has already made the policy decision involved in the abnormally dangerous theory by sanctioning the right of self-defense of noncriminal gun holders. The end result, Geistfeld writes, is that, "although courts may have reached a defensible result in these cases, their poorly reasoned decisions have substantially undermined an important role of strict liability to enforce the duty of care. Even tort doctrine, it would seem, has been harmed by handguns."

David Kopel, research director of the Independence Institute and editor, with Andrew McClurg and Brannon Denning, of *Gun Control and Gun Rights: A Reader and Guide* (New York University Press, 2002), argues against court intervention in the gun debates principally on the ground of institutional competence—or lack thereof. In his provocative essay "Guns and Burglars," Kopel offers comparative evidence concerning "hot" burglary rates (burglaries committed while residents are in the home) in the United States versus those in Canada and in Great Britain, and suggests that the disparity is a large positive externality associated with gun possession in this country. Kopel argues that this social benefit is largely overlooked in the handgun suits and that courts are not equipped or competent to assess such externalities. For this reason, courts should not be involved in this type of litigation. "Courts," Kopel declares, "cannot properly assess the true socioeconomic costs and benefits of controversial products." Kopel concludes that, "while readers may agree or disagree about the exact degree to which U.S. firearms density deters hot burglaries, the very inability to come up with a precise answer suggests that resolution of the firearms cost/benefit issue is not appropriate for the judicial system."

Conclusion

The ultimate conclusions are for the reader to draw. The essays collected in this book have been commissioned not to present neutral summaries or disinterested reviews of the literature—as if that were possible—but instead to present the most current and cutting-edge research on guns, crime, and punishment in America. The essays collected here are situated. They take informed positions based on significant and substantial research. The reader will find in the pages of this book research and arguments for but also against *Brady*-type interventions; for but also against tort litigation. Conclusions and objectivity, in this sense, are to be achieved by taking the essays together, reading them as a whole, and evaluating the full panoply of research. This is made particularly enjoyable, I can attest, by the high caliber of the essays collected in this volume.

NOTES

1. The 1994 National Survey of the Private Ownership of Firearms (NSPOF) found that there were 192 million privately owned firearms, of which 65 million were handguns. See Philip J. Cook and Jens Ludwig, *Guns in America: Results of a Comprehensive National Survey on Firearms Ownership and Use: Summary Report 13* (Washington, D.C.: Police Foundation, 1996). The Bureau of Justice Statistics estimates that 223 million firearms entered circulation between 1899 and 1993. See Marianne W. Zawitz, *Firearms, Crime and Criminal Justice: Guns Used in Crime*, 2 (Washington, D.C.: Bureau of Justice Statistics Selected Findings, July 1995, NCJ–148201).

2. Cook and Ludwig, *Guns in America*, at 13.

3. See ibid. at 24–26 (stating that 4.4 million new guns were acquired annually on average in 1993 and 1994); *FBI Publications: Law Enforcement Bulletin*, September 1997 issue (available at http://www.fbi.gov/publications/leb/1997/sept297.htm) (9 million applications to purchase firearms submitted from March 1, 1994, through June 30, 1996).

4. See Erika Rasmusson, "A Company under Siege," *Sales and Marketing Management* 152:4 (April 2000): 90.

5. For household ownership, see Cook and Ludwig, *Guns in America,* at 14 (finding by NSPOF of 35 percent; 1993 Gallup Poll finding 49 percent; General Social Survey [GSS] of 1994 finding 40–43 percent during 1990s); Gary Kleck and Mark Gertz, "Armed Resistance to Crime: The Prevalence and Nature of Self-Defense with a Gun," *Journal of Criminal Law and Criminology* 86 (1995): 150 (reporting that a survey conducted in 1993 found 38 percent); see generally Gary Kleck, *Point Blank: Guns and Violence in America* (New York: A. de Gruyter, 1991) (finding that about 50 percent of households have at least one firearm, a consistent finding since polling began in the 1950s). For personal gun ownership rate, see Cook and Ludwig, *Guns in America,* at 12 (noting that Kleck and Gertz find 25.5 percent; GSS for 1994 finds 28.7 percent; NSPOF finds 24.6 percent).

6. Joseph F. Sheley and James D. Wright, *In the Line of Fire: Youths, Guns, and Violence in Urban America* (New York: A. de Gruyter, 1995), 40; Peter Ash et al., "Gun Acquisition and Use by Juvenile Offenders," *Journal of the American Medical Association* 275:22 (1996): 1754, 1755; Julie H. Goldberg and William Schwabe, *How Youthful Offenders Perceive Gun Violence* (Santa Monica: RAND, 1999), 11–12; Bernard E. Harcourt, "Measured Interpretation: Introducing the Method of Correspondence Analysis to Legal Studies," *University of Illinois Law Review* (forthcoming 2002).

7. Lawrence A. Greenfeld and Marianne W. Zawitz, *Firearms, Crime and Criminal Justice: Weapons Offenses and Offenders* (Washington, D.C.: Bureau of Justice Statistics Selected Findings, November 1995, NCJ–155284), 3.

8. Jeffrey Fagan, "Context and Culpability in Adolescent Crime," *Virginia Journal of Social Policy and Law* 6 (1999): 507, 529.

9. See Kathleen M. Quinn, *Guns and Crime Statistics Information Package,* Bureau of Justice Statistics, January 1997 (NCJ 161170); Zawitz, *Firearms, Crime and Criminal,* at 1.

10. Michael R. Rand, *Handgun Victimization, Firearm Self-Defense, and Firearm Theft: Guns and Crime* (Washington, D.C.: Bureau of Justice Statistics Crime Data Brief, April 1994, NCJ–147003), 1; see also U.S. Department of Justice, Bureau of Justice Statistics, *Firearms and Crimes of Violence: Selected Findings from National Statistical Series,* NCJ–146844 (February 1994); Jeffrey A. Roth, *Firearms and Violence,* National Institute of Justice Research in Brief, February 1994.

11. U.S. Department of Justice Bureau of Justice Statistics, *Firearms and Crime Statistics* (visited July 23, 2002) <http://www.ojp.usdoj.gov/bjs/guns.htm>.

12. See Jeffrey Fagan, Franklin Zimring, and June Kim, "Declining Homicide in New York City: A Tale of Two Trends," *Journal of Criminal Law and Criminology* 88 (1998): 1277; Jeffrey Fagan, *Social Contagion of Violence* (April 19, 1999) (paper presented at the Fortunoff Colloquium Series, Center for Research on Crime and Justice, New York University School of Law).

13. Philip J. Cook and John H. Laub, "After the Epidemic: Recent Trends

in Youth Violence in the United States," National Bureau of Economic Research, Working Paper 8571 (available at http://www.nber.org/papers/w8571) (2001): 4.

14. See David McDowall and Brian Wierseman, "The Incidence of Defensive Firearm Use by U.S. Crime Victims, 1987 through 1990," *American Journal of Public Health 1982* (1994) (for NCVS statistics).

15. Cook and Ludwig, *Guns in America,* at 57–76 (for NSPOF statistics).

16. See Gary Kleck, "Crime Control through the Private Use of Armed Force," *Social Problems* 35 (1988): 1; Gary Kleck, *Targeting Guns: Firearms and Their Control* (New York: A. de Gruyter, 1997), 150–152; Gary Kleck and Mark Gertz, "Armed Resistance to Crime: The Prevalence and Nature of Self-Defense with a Gun," *Journal of Criminal Law and Criminology* 86 (1995): 150.

17. See John R. Lott Jr., *More Guns, Less Crime: Understanding Crime and Gun-Control Laws* (Chicago: University of Chicago Press, 1998), 170–172 tbl. 9.1.

18. For criticisms of Lott's work, see, e.g., Ian Ayres and John Donohue III, "Nondiscretionary Concealed Weapons Laws: A Case Study of Statistics, Standards of Proof, and Public Policy," *American Law and Economics Review* 1 (1999): 436 (eliminating Maine and Florida data and using incarceration rather than arrest rates eliminates significant effect on crime rates); Dan A. Black and Daniel S. Nagin, "Do Right-to-Carry Laws Deter Violent Crime?" *Journal of Legal Studies* 27 (1998): 209 (removing Florida from the sample, no detectable impact on the rate of murder and rape); Jens Ludwig, "Concealed-Gun-Carrying Laws and Violent Crime: Evidence from State Panel Data," *International Review of Law and Economics* 18 (1998): 239 (finding discrepancies given the evidenced of similar juvenile crime reduction rates); Mark Duggan, "More Guns, More Crime" (October 2000) (SSRN Research Paper, on file with author) (finding that counties where gun ownership is highest did not see significant changes in crime with passage of concealed-weapons laws). For Lott's response, see Lott, *More Guns, Less Crime,* at 205–233; John R. Lott Jr., "More Guns, Less Crime: A Response to Ayres and Donohue" (September 1999) (SSRN Research Paper).

19. 18 U.S.C. § 924(c) (1994, Supp. IV. 1998 and Supp V. 1999).

20. See U.S. Department of Justice Bureau of Justice Statistics, *Sourcebook of Criminal Justice Statistics 1997,* 427 tbl. 5.53.

21. See generally Bernard E. Harcourt, *Illusion of Order: The False Promise of Broken Windows Policing* (Cambridge, Mass.: Harvard University Press, 2001).

22. See, e.g., Frank Bruni, "Citing the Drain of Violence, Bush Backs Increased Prosecution of Gun-Related Crimes," *New York Times,* May 15, 2001, at A16; see generally Daniel C. Richman, "'Project Exile' and the Allocation of Federal Law Enforcement Authority," *Arizona Law Review* 43 (2001): 369.

23. See generally Adam Liptak, "Revised View of 2nd Amendment Is Cited as Defense in Gun Cases," *New York Times,* July 23, 2002; Linda Greenhouse,

"Justices Reject Cases on Right to Bear Arms," *New York Times*, June 11, 2002, at A16.

24. For a similar argument, see Bernard E. Harcourt, "Policing Disorder: Can We Reduce Serious Crime by Punishing Petty Offenses?" *Boston Review* 27:2 (April–May 2002): 17–18.

25. *State of New Jersey v. Carty*, 2002 N.J. LEXIS 58 (March 4, 2002).

26. *United States v. Lopez*, 514 U.S. 549 (1995).

27. See Rasmusson, *Company under Siege*, at 90.

Part I

The Great American Gun Debates

A. Perspectives

Chapter 1

Continuity and Change in the American Gun Debate

Franklin E. Zimring

My license to survey the gun control debate is a tribute not to wisdom but to accumulated seniority: I have been associated with the study of firearms and violence for more than three decades now, and the hope was that experience of that length might generate perspectives useful in a debate not known for its awareness of history or sense of proportion. What has changed over thirty-five years in debates about firearms and violence? What is constant? Are there long-range trends so far, or just cyclical fluctuation? Is the great American gun policy debate heading toward any clear destination or dancing in circles?

This essay's path to addressing these questions involves three tasks. A brief first section provides my version of the debate on gun policy I came upon in 1967 and 1968. A second section discusses some of the characteristics of gun ownership, gun policy preferences, and the politics of guns that have remained constant over a generation. The third section identifies some changes in the gun debate and speculates on the impact of these changes on future policy. A concluding sermon addresses the current condition of the firearms debate as a prologue to future policy.

I. The Gun Debate in the 1960s

Prior to the late 1960s, guns and gun control had not been a major issue at any level of American government for a generation. State and local control efforts in the urban northeast were a product of the early decades of the twentieth century, most famously with New York's Sullivan law in 1911. Serious federal control proposals first appeared in the early years of the Roosevelt administration and produced two federal laws within five years, a 1934 act that all but banned automatic weapons and sawed-off shotguns and 1938 legislation that created a thin layer of regulation over firearms dealers and the sale of more popular firearms and prohibited minors, felons, and other disqualified classes of citizens from acquiring weapons.[1] What happened after 1938 in the United States on the legal regulation of firearms was practically nothing. The Second World War effectively ended federal anti-crime concerns until 1965. Rates of criminal homicide, after peaking in 1933, fell during the depression and war years and drifted downward thereafter until the early 1960s. Two New England senators, John F. Kennedy in the 1950s and Thomas Dodd in the 1960s, held hearings on the dangers of cheap foreign guns, but the threats that inspired this were as much to the domestic firearms industry as to the public health.

The mid-1960s witnessed a series of events that created concern about guns, beginning with the assassination of President Kennedy and the increases in urban violent crime reported from 1964 onward. Blue-ribbon commissions were appointed, first on crime, then on riots and on violence. Gun legislation proposals were taken much more seriously after 1965, and crime was, by 1967, an issue that attracted sustained national attention. Then came the watershed year of 1968. Whatever the slow progress toward federal firearms legislation from earlier events, a new dynamic emerged from the Martin Luther King Jr. and Robert Kennedy assassinations, the urban riots, and public anxiety about violent crime. The Congress that had passed no federal firearms legislation in thirty years passed two major acts in one year and created the new federal enforcement presence that the Bureau of Alcohol, Tobacco, and Firearms was to become. The year 1968 witnessed also the birth of the symbolic politics of gun control and the basic regulatory framework upon which the incremental politics of gun control would play out for the remainder of the twentieth century.

My concern here is more with the nature of the debate about guns that was generated in the late 1960s than with the details of the 1968 act.[2] The firearms control issue had taken the nation and the federal Congress by surprise. No agency of government had the responsibility for information about guns other than the Commerce Department, which maintained a census of manufacturers. There were no academic experts on firearms and violence in criminology in the United States or anywhere else in research universities. Prior to mid-1968, there were no published studies on the relationship between gun use and the death rate from assault. No credible estimate of the number and kind of firearms in the United States had been published. No taxonomy of firearms control laws had been attempted. No studies of the impact of various regulations of gun ownership and use had been attempted.

The politics of gun control was predictable and symbolic. Big-city liberals were procontrol and rural and small town conservatives were anticontrol—the specific nature of the control proposal did not matter much to the support and opposition elements. The only special firearms interest group in Washington was the National Rifle Association.

Violent death was the central concern of those who worried about guns and supported gun control, but there was no clear hierarchy of problems or choice of control tactics. In the first installment of the Gun Control Act of 1968, long guns and handguns were regulated equally, while in the second installment the handgun was the subject of special regulatory attention. As the focus shifted from political assassination to crime, and as data on firearms and violence were published, a priority concern with handguns settled in for a long run as the most serious of American's gun problems.

II. Constant Elements

There are five consistent elements of the gun debate over the generation since 1970 that I wish to nominate as significant influences on how policy has been selected: symbolic dominance, generality of preferences, the free-lunch syndrome, the gender gulch, and the centrality of handguns as the subject and object of the controversy.

The first three constant elements are interrelated and, jointly, quite influential in how gun policy gets debated in the United States. I address them together. While the specific content of proposals to regulate firearms vary over time and cross-sectionally, most citizens have a set of general attitudes about firearms and about laws to regulate firearms that is stable over time. I believe the debate about gun policy is one where these general sentiments are dominant in predicting citizen preferences on specific issues and in predicting the reasons citizens give for support or opposition to particular policies. This is the condition I call symbolic dominance.

A substantial majority of the public holds pretty strong sentiments either for or against gun control as a whole. Because the symbolic aspects dominate orientation toward specific policy proposals, the details of a program have little to do with the level of support or opposition to it. If most opponents of gun control are dominated by general attitudes, the type of control proposed and the type of gun involved will not explain or predict their opposition. Similarly, if most citizens who favor controls are motivated by a general sentiment, they will be disposed toward support of a wide variety of particular approaches.

One piece of evidence for this is that a wide variety of different proposals have quite similar levels of support and opposition, what Tom Smith called "the 75 percent solution."[3] This means that the same core constituencies of pros and antis will debate waiting periods for handgun sales, the requirement of licensing for sales at gun shows, and punitive damages against gun manufacturers and distributors. Further, because most of the values to be vindicated are symbolic, the intensity of support for large and small proposals will be nearly equal. Small changes in policy can be urged and opposed with the same degree of vigor as large changes. The heavy emphasis in 1999 and 2000 by both procontrol and anticontrol groups on what is called the gun show loophole in the Gun Control Act of 1968 is a clear illustration that intensity of commitment is not closely linked to operational importance in debates about gun control.

The general tendency for citizens to be for or against gun control proposals has definite limits. More substantial interventions that carry larger cost and restrict gun owners generate substantially lower levels of public support. The primary example of this in the 1980s and 1990s was proposals to "ban" handguns. And measures without any visible cost to most citizens—such as increased prison sentences for firearms criminals—can generate greater than 75 percent support. That there is some discrimination between control proposals is good news for the development of a more sophisticated public response to gun control. But if only the perceived costs of control proposals influence the level of public support, then support will cluster around proposals without regard to the potential benefits of the intervention.

This leads to a phenomenon of generality of preferences. People who favor "gun control" are positively disposed toward a general idea and will follow that general preference to support a wide variety of different proposals. It is the major premise—support in general—rather than the particular program that is the center of citizen concern. And anticontrol partisans seem willing to oppose any type of control, a general tendency that procontrol forces like to exploit by proposing bans on ammunition that is labeled "cop killer bullets" that nonetheless produces opposition from many gun owner groups, even at the price of substantial political embarrassment.

The Free-Lunch Syndrome

Since many of the central values that are in play are symbolic, and since almost any specific proposal can carry the symbolic colors of firearms control in congressional debate, there is a tendency for procontrol forces to pick on small and fairly uncontroversial control proposals but to invest these programs with the suggestion that their passage will have a substantial impact on rates of lethal violence. Pass a ban on cop killer bullets or impose a five-day waiting period on handgun sales, and the rhetorical suggestion is that major progress will be made in reducing the totality of firearms violence.

This tendency to push small policy increments as if they were major programs is what I call the "free-lunch syndrome," a tendency to couple small operational changes with the full weight of firearms control symbolism. Free-lunch rhetoric is good politics without question, but it removes realistic analysis of the impacts of specific control strategies from public discussion. There is nothing wrong with an incremental politics of gun control, but expecting large benefits from small investments is unreasonable.

The Gender Gulch

Forty-four percent of motorcycle owners are women. Forty-eight percent of truck owners are women. We even know a few who can wipe that stupid smirk off your face!
    —Oxygen advertisement, *The New Yorker*, October 16, 2000, p. 87

The generation after 1965 witnessed dramatic changes in the social, cultural, and economic status of women in the United States. In the wake of these shifts, activities and tastes formerly associated with men have become more evenly distributed by gender. That is the background to the surprising statistical claims of the recent ad about truck and motorcycle ownership that leads this section.

All the more remarkable, then, that the very great gender difference in rates of gun ownership continues to be the major dividing line between United States adults; gender is more important for predicting handgun ownership than region, politics, and income and usually more important than all those elements put together. When ownership rates by gender were first publically disclosed in the mid-1960s, about 7 percent of U.S. gun owners were identified as women in the crude manufacturers mail survey research we reviewed at the National Violence Commission. A precise ownership estimate could not be made from these data, but the female ownership was obviously quite low. Thirty years later, Tom Smith and Robert J. Smith reported their analysis of fifteen years of National Opinion Research Center General Social Survey data and found no evidence of any expansion in female ownership of either handguns or firearms generally during the period 1980–1994, while so much else was changing in the United States.

Smith and Smith found that, while just under half of all males own a firearm, the "any gun" ownership rate for females is one in eight, and four times as many men as women report handgun ownership.[4] The authors conclude:

> The ownership of firearms among women is not increasing, the gender gap is not closing, and the level of ownership is much lower than commonly stated, with about 11% to 12% of women owning a gun and 4.5 to 8% owning a handgun.[5]

Speculation that female ownership and attitudes might change has been recurrent during the period since 1970. Milestones in the anticipated increase in female demand include an advertising campaign for self-defense handgun ownership that was targeted on women (for the notorious "Lady Smith") in the 1980s by Smith and Wesson and books and articles about gun women; media coverage of women seeking self-defense handgun training has become a staple of National Rifle Association public relations and local television slow-news-week feature stories. But the ownership gap persists even as the number of female-headed household has sharply expanded, multiplying the number of instances where a woman's ownership decision determines the presence or absence of a gun in the house.

The huge gap in ownership is accompanied by two more subtle gender differences. Women are more likely to support legal restrictions on firearms, and, when men and women in the same household disagree about the wisdom of having a handgun, it is the woman who is more often antigun.

The gender differences in self-defense handgun ownership are important in the struggle for the moral high ground in the self-defense debate. If women, after all the traditional weaker sex, were aggressive in wanting and using handguns, the political pressure to allow and approve such usage would be substantial. But the refusal of most women to acknowledge the need for self-defense handguns undercuts male claims that the weapons are necessary. In this connection, Smith and Smith show very low rates of handgun ownership among single women (1.4 percent for the never married, 6.4 percent for the not currently married). In these head-of-household settings, the gender gap is greater than the overall 4:1 figure. Female need is, in such circumstances, a story that continues to be told by male gun owners.

The Handgun Focus

One further consistent strain in the gun policy debate of the past generation is the focus on handguns and special handgun regulation as the greatest priority in new policy. With the exception of short periods when semiautomatic firearms that could be either handguns or long guns attracted attention (the "assault weapon" issue), the handgun has held center stage in the American gun control debate for thirty years.

The case for special regulation of handguns is not a matter of firepower—both shotguns and rifles often have more destructive force, and long guns are also easier to use accurately from medium and long range. But the handgun, easy to conceal and transport, is nine times more likely than a long gun to be used in a homicide and is even more dominant than that in robbery with firearms. As the chief concern about firearms violence shifted from assignation to violent crime, the handgun became the focus of procontrol efforts by the early 1970s. While gun-owning organizations prefer not to distinguish between types of firearms, their general opposition to all control proposals is most often manifest in their opposition to proposed handgun regulation. And the focus of procontrol advocates on handguns has become a defining element of special interests organized to support firearms regulation. It is neither an accident nor a trivial detail that the major gun control lobby in the United States calls itself "Handgun Control."

Special attention to handguns is a common characteristic of legal systems throughout the developed world. Even nations with high rates of long gun usage, such as Switzerland and Israel, have low ownership and, usually, special restrictions on handguns. So the consistent emphasis on handguns is by no means an American invention. Nor is the debate about the special status of handguns an American exclusive. The tendency for anticontrol groups in all nations is to urge opposition to handgun controls because they threaten long guns, as well. But this effort to make common cause of all gun owners has been more successful in the United States than elsewhere.

III. What Changed?

Here are four important changes in the character of public debate about government and firearms. What used to be an issue that was only cyclically important has become a priority concern on a continuing basis. What used to be an undocumented dispute with few data and no specialist experts has become a debate between special interests that are well informed but often heavily biased by anti- or procontrol orientations. What used to be a debate in which the Second Amendment to the U.S. Constitution had no importance is now a debate in which the Second Amendment's implications are ambiguous. What used to be a debate about firearms and crime has been reframed, in expert and political areas, as a concern with firearms and violence.

1. From Episodic to Consistent Public Priority

In the first two decades after the Gun Control Act of 1968, public and political concern with the issue of firearms control was episodic. At the federal level, there was no further strong interest in firearms control until about 1975, and, after no laws passed in the mid-1970s, it was not until after the shooting of President Reagan in 1981 that serious attention was paid to a debate about further federal laws. Things were even quieter at the state and local level in most places. Concern with crime was a constant, but interest in the firearms issue was cyclical.

The long time gaps between high-visibility debates on guns was not a product of fickle public attitudes about the wisdom of gun control. Public support for most mainstream gun regulation was consistent over time, but the gun issue was not very important to most citizens most of the time. It was the salience of the gun control question, rather than attitudes about appropriate government action, that varied over time.

If the late 1990s were a sign of the new order, long gaps between high-visibility debates about guns will soon be regarded as an historical curiosity. In the late 1960s, the passage of a gun law like the Gun Control Act of 1968 was a signal for the federal Congress to ignore the field for a decade or so. In the aftermath of the Brady bill in 1993, however, there has not been any sustained period of time off from high-visibility gun policy debates. In 1998, 1999, and 2000, gun policy disputes at the federal level have been the single most important crime policy issue. At the state level, legislative proposals and legislation, running the gamut from efforts to ease restrictions on permits to carry concealed weapons to assault weapon and Saturday Night Special legislation, make gun proposals an annual event in big states. At the city level, a range of tactics, from municipal gun regulations to lawsuits against gun producers framed on the tobacco company litigation, are a hardy perennial. The gun question does not take time off from being a salient concern in the media, the political process, and public consciousness.

This essay cannot fully explore the reasons for this shift from cyclical to consistent public priority. In part, the vociferous energies of single-issue special interests on both sides of the gun debate fan the flames. In part, the usefulness to both political parties of guns as a wedge issue for different segments of the electorate keeps the pot boiling. Partisan tactics guarantee that gun politics will be spread among all levels of government. The National Rifle Association finds solace in state governments, particularly where rural and town representation is strong. Big cities are the home team for almost all forms of handgun restrictions. This has tended to make the gun issue into a levels-of-government version of a three-ring circus throughout the past decade. Consistent public and media attention, parallel markets for control and anticontrol new ideas in states and cities, and a longer public attention span for gun issues are markers of a brand-new era in the politics of gun control in the United States.

But how long will this era of intense interest continue? Two further elements of the 1990s contributed to the consistent priority of gun control at the federal level. One was the high level of public concern about life-threatening violence. At the beginning of the decade, public worries were linked to high rates of criminal homicide. By the end of the decade, the specific worry was school shootings.

A second element that maintained the public focus on gun control after 1992 was a two-term president who pushed firearms control proposals throughout his eight years in office. How much presidential leadership and public concern about particular violence problems has contributed to the public interest in gun control may soon be known. The current president of the United States has no strong interest in firearms control, and rates of lethal violence are at their lowest levels in thirty years. If consistent public interest continues, it will indicate that the issue of gun control has "legs" even when the political environment is unfavorable. In that sense, the George W. Bush presidency can be regarded as a natural experiment.

2. Information: From Ignorance to Special Pleading

The growth of information about firearms and their effects has been impressive but uneven over the past three decades. Any growth rate from a zero base will seem high, and guns are no exception. Official data on firearms manufacture, on gun use in crime and violence, and on patterns of regulation of firearms in the United States is far superior to the statistical base of thirty years ago. The number of university-based researchers who specialize more than half time in firearms probably exceeds fifty in the United States. There were none as recently as 1972.

The available data on firearms, violence, and firearms control are both abundant and spotty. Death statistics and some crime statistics are good. Production and import data are reliable, but the total stock of usable guns cannot be reliably estimated. The federal Bureau of Alcohol, Tobacco, and Firearms does a vast number of traces to first retail purchase of guns but little research on the flow of guns from that point on. Nobody knows the average use life of a handgun in the United States.

The information available on the effects of gun control policies on firearms deaths and injury are particularly spotty, in part because the legal changes to study in recent years have been of the modest "free-lunch" variety.

Many of the full-time researchers on the topic are organized into sectarian groups. Public health professionals put heavy emphasis on the impact of gun use in raising the death rate from assault and robbery and support most control efforts. Sociologists are split into "contra" factions (James Wright, Gary Kleck) and a larger number of procontrol partisans. In this contentious atmosphere, the margins for disagreement are not slight: Are guns used in 100,000 self-defense episodes each year or twenty times that many?[6] Do safe storage laws have little impact on violence or save the citizens of the fifteen states that passed them from an additional 250,000 violent crimes over five years?[7]

The known facts should produce a clean split in factional morale. The evidence that guns increase the death from violence is firm—this is the strong suit of the procontrol forces. The evidence that particular modest changes in legal regulation can make a dent in the gun violence toll is weak. This is the strong suit of the anticontrol partisans and skeptics.

3. The Second Amendment: From Irrelevance to Ambiguity

The Second Amendment's language describing a "right of the people to bear arms" has always played an important symbolic role in the rhetoric of opposition to gun controls, but the Second Amendment has been considered a dead letter as a potential obstacle to state and federal gun control laws. *United States v. Miller,* decided in 1939, was neither a closely reasoned nor a prominently publicized case, but it was widely considered to be a conclusive rejection of an individual's right to bear arms as a limit on the power of any level of government to regulate guns. Outside gun owner groups, the federal Constitution's Second Amendment was not regarded as an important part of American legal culture or history.

In recent years, academic interest in a personal right to bear arms has been growing, from a variety of different points of origin. There is,

of course, the gun interests, which have supported and publicized historical arguments about an expansive reading of the Second Amendment. There has also been at least one study of the English origins
of the Second Amendment that is consistent with individual claims
against governmental regulation and with a legal theory of personal
right based on personal rights to oppose tyranny.[8] What this work has
done so far is to put the possibility of a personal right to bear arms in
play in academic settings, where it had received neither attention nor
mention previously in constitutional scholarship. The increased
salience of the issue has in turn produced anti-personal-right historical
scholarship and legal argument.[9]

One Fifth Circuit panel has expressly endorsed a "personal right"
theory of the Second Amendment as dicta in rejecting a criminal defendant's attempt to challenge an indictment under one section of the
federal Gun Control Act.[10] In an era when judicial activism from the
right has already significantly reshaped constitutional law relating to
federal-state relations, the judicial recognition of a personal right in
the Second Amendment is by no means farfetched.

But the effect any personal right to bear arms would have on restricting regulation of guns is difficult to predict. The key questions
are, first, whether particular weapons (e.g., handguns, automatic firearms) would be covered and, second, what sort of balance between
personal and governmental interests would animate decisions. The
discussion of such questions has not been substantial to date, and, because the entire constitutional calculus would have to be created without any background in prior case reasoning, the impact of a personal
legal right on the field of choice for gun regulation is still a wide-open
question.

4. From Crime to Violence

One further shift in American sentiment occurred in the 1990s as a
result of several concurrent developments. While the public anxieties
most closely associated with the gun debate had traditionally been
thought of as centered around crime and criminals, the problem of
lethal violence emerged by the turn of the century as discrete from
general concerns about crime and its control.

The last eight years of the 1990s witnessed the broadest and most
sustained drop in crime rates that America had experienced in half a

century. But, just as the criminal stranger was seen as a smaller threat, the boy next door become a potential menace. A cluster of school shootings in the late 1990s culminated in the killing of twelve students and a teacher by two students at Columbine High School, in Littleton, Colorado. The Columbine shootings of 1999 provoked a shift in focus for American anxieties. The "trench coat mafia" of Littleton differed from Willie Horton not in degree but in kind. No longer was the threat associated with a distinct criminal class, nor could it be blamed on avarice. Columbine High was an inside job, not the work of aliens.

The justifying ideology of free availability of firearms in the United States is that lethal violence is the threat of a criminal class, a discrete and insular minority. When the children of good people are the enemy we fear, it is more than difficult to pretend that the millions of guns tolerated as home furnishings are not connected to the guns that kill schoolgirls in Jonesboro and Paducah and Littleton. The boundaries between legitimate and illegitimate arms were blurred in the minds of many when good people's guns went to school. And the violent outbursts of adolescent assassins seemed closer to suicide than to mercenary crime, far less comprehensible in terms of rational choice or pecuniary motivation than the actions of the criminal classes of previous public imagination. As the great cartoon character Pogo had prophesied a generation before, "We have met the enemy, and he is us." This clear focus on violence without a differentiating criminal identity is one of the primary causes of sustained attention to guns and gun control in the United States at the turn of a new century.

Conclusion

It turns out to be much easier to predict the volume of debate about changes in gun policy than either the magnitude or the direction of policy changes in the United States in the next decade. High levels of activity at the federal, state, and municipal government are a safe bet. But whether the sum of the changes will amount to a shift in substantive direction for gun policy, particularly handgun policy, is not at all clear. The symbolic politics of guns will play a prominent role in politics at all levels of government.

One reason the shape and net impact of new gun policies are difficult to predict is that there are no clear priorities among the new control activists. Citizens are still for or against gun control as a general sentiment, never mind the details. And most of the new academic experts on guns have done little to push the gun control debate toward specifics and priorities.

Yet, there are a huge number of different types of gun regulations being debated in the contentious American present. There are gun show permit requirements, "gun-free school zones," sharp restrictions on handgun ownership, mandatory minimum penalties for firearms crimes, tort suits against handgun manufacturers, buy-back schemes, and waiting periods. It would be an amazing coincidence if all these approaches were equally promising or futile. Just because gun use elevates the death rate from assaults does not mean that any law that concerns guns will save lives.

Indeed, when the symbolic politics of the issue produce chestnuts like the gun-free school law, the academic expert with sympathy for government efforts to control firearm violence should be the first to note the unlikely prospect that putting signs up by schoolyards will save the lives of children.

For similar reasons, the sweeping generalities of opponents of gun regulations are symptoms of analytic immaturity. The only reason gun regulations as a class could be excluded as a harm reduction technique would be if gun use did not influence the harms produced by violent assaults. Does any serious researcher believe this?

What will improve the gun debate at the top end of the policy community is careful attention to the differences between types and intensities of firearms regulation. If experts start avoiding the silly overgeneralizations that come from assuming that all gun regulations were created equal, there is some hope that a more specific and pragmatic approach to reducing the harms of gun violence might trickle down the intellectual food chain to the powerful and powerfully confused citizenry that will shape gun policy in the fast-approaching future.

NOTES

Reprinted with permission by the Brookings Institution Press.

1. Franklin E. Zimring,"Firearms and the Federal Law: The Gun Control Act of 1968," *Journal of Legal Studies* 4 (1975): Part I, 133–98.

2. See Zimring (1975) for the legislative details.

3. Tom W. Smith, "The 75% Solution: An Analysis of the Structure of Attitudes on Gun Control, 1959–1977," *Journal of Criminal Law and Criminology* 71 (1980): 300–16.

4. Tom W. Smith and Robert J. Smith, "Changes in Firearm Ownership among Women, 1980–1994," *Journal of Criminal Law and Criminology* 86 (1995): 147, Table 3.

5. Smith and Smith (1995): 145.

6. Philip J. Cook, Jens Ludwig, and David Hemenway, "The Gun Debate's New Mythical Number: How Many Defensive Uses per Year?" *Journal of Policy Analysis and Management* 16 (1997): 463–469; Gary Kleck and Marc Gertz, "Armed Resistance to Crime: The Prevalence and Nature of Self-Defense with a Gun," *Journal of Criminal Law and Criminology* 86 (1995): 150–87.

7. John R. Lott and John E. Whitley, "Safe Storage Gun Laws: Accidental Deaths, Suicides and Crime," Yale Law School, Programs for Studies in Law, Economics and Public Policy, Working Paper No. 237 (2000). Available at: <http://papers.ssrn.com/paper.taf?abstract_id=228534>.

8. Joyce Lee Malcolm, *To Keep and Bear Arms: The Origins of an Anglo-American Right* (Cambridge, Mass.: Harvard University Press, 1994); Sanford Levinson, "The Embarrassing Second Amendment," *Yale Law Journal* 99 (1989): 637–59.

9. Carl T. Bogus, "The Hidden History of the Second Amendment," *U.C. Davis Law Review* 31 (1998): 309–408.

10. *U.S. v. Emerson* 270 F. 3d 203 (2001).

Chapter 2

The Tyranny of Econometrics and the Circumspection of Liberalism
Two Problems with the Gun Debate

Dan M. Kahan

For most Americans, the "Great American Gun Debate" isn't particularly great. The question of how strictly to regulate firearms has convulsed the national polity for the better part of four decades without producing results satisfactory to either side. Drowning in a sea of mind-numbing statistics, ordinary citizens stand little chance of even understanding their opponents' arguments, much less being persuaded by them. Battered by procontrol forces in one election and by anticontrol ones in the next, moderate politicians say as little as they can get away with. The organizers of relatively extreme interest groups, in contrast, say—indeed, scream—as much as they possibly can, symbiotically nurturing a divided public's anxiety that one side or the other is poised to score a decisive victory.

My objective in this short essay—*manifesto* might be a better description—is not to take any particular position on gun control but instead to take issue with the terms in which the gun control debate is cast. That debate, I want to suggest, has been disfigured by two distorting influences on the rhetoric of both sides. I'll call one the *tyranny of econometrics* and the other *circumspection of liberalism*. Counteracting these influences almost certainly won't dispel Americans' differences of opinion on guns. But it will go a long way to making our public discussion of this issue into one that honors rather than mocks our pretension to be a well-functioning deliberative democracy.

The *tyranny of econometrics* refers to the inordinate emphasis that both sides of the gun control debate place on the tools of social science. Advocates of control use a diverse array of methods—not just econometrics, in fact, but contingent valuation studies, public health risk-factor analyses, and the like—to quantify the physical and economic harm that guns inflict on our society.[1] Control opponents, however, use the same methods to show that gun control creates even more such harm by making it harder for potential victims to defend themselves from violent predation.[2]

I, at least, am not sure who has the better argument here. Indeed, I don't think anyone can say definitively, on the basis of the extant social science data, whether "more guns" produce "more crime" or "less."

But one thing we *are* in a position to say with confidence is that empirical studies of this sort—whatever conclusion they generate—have precious little impact on how ordinary citizens think about gun control. From a sociology-of-knowledge point of view, it's hard to see how they possibly could. Very few members of the public, after all, possess the technical training necessary to evaluate the quality of these conflicting studies for themselves. Consequently, they must trust the experts to tell them which studies are persuasive and which not. But which experts are ordinary members of the public most likely to trust? The ones, obviously, who espouse the positions that these citizens already hold, or who at least demonstrate their trustworthiness by showing they share ordinary citizens' basic cultural orientation and values.

Indeed, according to a wealth of public opinion research, it's precisely these sorts of cultural allegiances and outlooks that determine citizens' attitudes toward gun control. Gun control positions vary across social groups, the members of which attach competing social meanings to guns. Control opponents tend to be rural, southern or western, Protestant, male, and white.[3] For them, guns symbolize a cluster of positive values, from physical prowess and martial virtue to honor to individual self-sufficiency.[4] Control proponents, in contrast, are disproportionately urban, eastern, Catholic or Jewish, female, and African American.[5] They find the cultural significations of guns to be abhorrent and alarming; they see gun control as symbolizing a competing set of positive values, including civilized nonaggression, racial and gender equality, and social solidarity.[6] Once cultural variables are controlled for, there appears to be no significant correlation between attitudes toward gun control and the types of experiences, beliefs, or attitudes that one would expect to incline individuals either to support or oppose gun control as a simple policy for reducing crime.[7]

Often, disputes in criminal law that seem empirical or instrumental are really expressive in nature. In such disputes, citizens care less about how a particular law will affect behavior than they do about what the adoption of that law will say about the authority of contested moral values and about the relative status of the social groups and cultural styles associated with those values. The century's long dispute over temperance, for example, can be understood as an attempt by America's traditional agrarian elite to repel the challenge to their cultural preeminence posed by a commercial ethos associated primarily with immigrant urban Catholics.[8] Today's dispute over the death penalty has been described as an essentially "symbolic" one, too, in which citizens "choose sides" consistent with their cultural allegiances[9] and on which legislators vote consistent with their desire to apportion status among competing cultural styles.[10] Proposals to ban flag desecration ignite intense passions because they are understood to be tests of the national commitment to patriotism and accordingly of the status of those for whom patriotism is an unproblematic virtue.[11] The rule affording mitigation to cuckolds who kill their unfaithful wives, a staple of criminal law for centuries, now provokes intense disagreement because of contemporary contestation over the patriarchal norms that that rule expresses.[12]

Gun control fits the same expressive pattern. As one southern Democratic senator recently put it, in urging his party to back off the issue, the gun debate is "about *values*"—"about who you are and who you aren't."[13] Those who share an egalitarian and solidaristic worldview, on the one hand, and those who adhere to a more hierarchical and individualistic one, on the other, both see the extent of gun regulation as a measure of their (and their social groups') relative status in American society.[14] What makes the gun control debate so intense isn't a disagreement about the facts—does private ownership of guns promote or deter violent crime?—but a disagreement about "alternative views of what America is and ought to be."[15]

Because the gun control controversy is an expressive one, empirical methods of analysis offer little prospect for resolving it. This is so, in part, for cognitive reasons. As they do with do with respect to other expressive issues, such as the death penalty,[16] individuals can be expected to resolve empirical doubts about the consequences of gun control consistently with the position suggested by their cultural orientations.[17] But an even bigger problem for the empirical idiom in which the gun control debate is carried on is normative or moral in nature. Econometrics, contingent valuation, and the like simply ignore what participants in the gun control controversy really care about.

In this respect, it might be helpful to draw an analogy between political conflict over gun control and political conflict over environmental regulation. Disputes over technological risks turn out to be largely expressive in nature. For example, experts disagree with members of the public, and members of the public with one another, over nuclear power not primarily because they have different appraisals of the *magnitude* of the risks involved but rather because they attach different *meanings* to them. For nuclear proponents, the acceptance of those risks conveys appropriate deference to political authority, respect for human technical acumen, and confidence in the resilience of nature to accommodate the byproducts of free trade and industrial expansion. For opponents, in contrast, those same risks convey collective hubris, generational selfishness, and disrespect for the sacredness of nature.[18] Because positions on nuclear power are shaped by these meanings, it would be obtuse to try to resolve the dispute with a mode of empirical risk assessment that excludes cultural values from its analysis of nuclear power's costs and benefits.[19]

The idea that we can solve the gun control debate with modes of empirical analysis that abstract from cultural values is just as obtuse. Those involved in gun control debate aren't really arguing about whose position is more grounded in empirical reality; they are arguing about what it would say about our society's values to credit one or the other sides' fears in our law. For the opponent of gun control, it would be a cowardly and dishonorable concession to our own physical weaknesses for us to disarm all private citizens in the interest of public safety. For the proponent of control, it would send an unacceptable message of mutual distrust in one another's intentions, of collective indifference to one another's welfare, and of the glamorization of power and violence to rely on each citizen's decision to arm himself as a means of keeping the civil peace.

No amount of econometrics or contingent valuation analysis can settle a disagreement of this sort. The only philosophically cogent way to resolve the gun control debate is to confront head on the competing cultural visions that animate the gun debate. Can they be reconciled, expressively, in public policy? Should they be? If they can't be reconciled, or if it would be morally wrong to build one or the other into the law, whose vision—the control proponent's or the control opponent's —should prevail?

This, however, is exactly the sort of question that liberalism—the second distorting influence on the gun control debate—insists we not address through democratic deliberation. American political culture is heavily influenced by liberal discourse norms, which direct those engaged in public debates to disclaim reliance on contested visions of the good life and instead base arguments on grounds acceptable to citizens of diverse moral outlooks.[20] Consequentialist modes of decision making seem to satisfy this standard. Furnishing apparently "objective procedures and criteria" for policy making, econometrics, cost-benefit analyses, contingent valuation studies, and the like are "decidedly divorced from statements about morality."[21] Because they elide contestable judgments of value, instrumental arguments are the "don't ask, don't tell" solution to cultural disputes in the law—not just over gun control, but over policies like the death penalty, hate crimes legislation, welfare reform, environmental regulation, and a host of other controversial policies.[22]

Of course, it isn't really the case that we *never* see appeals to contested cultural values in such controversies. We are all perfectly familiar, for example, with what culturally partisan appeals sound like in the gun control debate: excruciatingly judgmental and intolerant. Control partisans ridicule their adversaries as "hicksville cowboy[s]," members of the "big belt buckle crowd"[23] whose love of guns stems from their "macho Freudian hangups,"[24] while the NRA president Charlton Heston declares "cultural war" against "blue-blooded elitists" who threaten an "America . . . where you [can] . . . be white without feeling guilty, [and] own a gun without shame."[25]

Most citizens undoubtedly find this culturally chauvinistic style of debate exceedingly unpleasant. Indeed, it is precisely the judgmental tone of expressive condemnation, we believe, that explains the appeal of public safety arguments in the mainstream gun debate.

But the hope that the gun control debate can be made less contentious by confining it to empirical arguments is in fact an idle one. On the contrary, the unwillingness of most academics, politicians, and ordinary citizens to engage in a frank airing of their cultural differences ultimately deepens the acrimonious quality of the gun debate. Most Americans are not cultural imperialists, but, as the gun debate starkly illustrates, at least some *are*. For them, the liberal norm against public moralizing lacks any constraining force. By speaking in the muted tones of deterrence in a (vain) effort to avoid giving offense, moderate commentators, politicians, and citizens cede the rhetorical stage to these expressive zealots, who happily seize on the gun debate as an opportunity to deride their cultural adversaries and stigmatize them as deviants.[26]

In order to civilize the gun debate, then, *moderate* citizens—the ones who are repulsed by cultural imperialism of all varieties—must come out from behind the cover of consequentialism and talk through their competing visions of the good life without embarrassment. They must, in the spirit of genuine democratic deliberation, appeal to one another for understanding and seek policies that accommodate their respective worldviews. An open debate about the social meanings the law should express is not just the only *philosophically cogent* way to resolve the gun debate; it is also the only *practical* way to resolve it in terms that embody an appropriate dedication to political pluralism.

This conclusion presupposes that expressive debate in law can be simultaneously pertinent and tolerant. The liberal anxiety that it can't be—that the only way to avert "the domination of one cultural and moral ethos over all others"[27] is to cleanse public discourse of appeals to contested cultural views altogether—is far too pessimistic. Anthropologists, sociologists, and comparative law scholars have in fact cataloged many examples of communities successfully negotiating culture-infused controversies—ones between archaeologists and Native Americans over the disposition of tribal artifacts;[28] between secular French educators and Muslim parents over the donning of religious attire by Muslim school children;[29] between the supporters and opponents of abortion rights in France and Germany.[30] Rather than hide behind culture-effacing modes of discourse, the individuals involved in these disputes fashioned policies that were expressively rich enough to enable *all* parties to find their cultural visions affirmed by the law.[31]

I do not mean to understate the difficulty of adapting this strategy of pluralistic expressive deliberations to the gun control issue. Our society has grown so accustomed to the constraints that liberalism places on political discourse that we seem to lack the vocabulary and habits necessary for debating cultural issues in a constructive way.[32] When the constraining force of liberal discourse norms break down, as it inevitably does, we lapse into acrimony and contempt.

This is the problem that scholars and others who want to make a constructive contribution to the gun debate should dedicate themselves to solving. The construction of a pertinent yet respectful expressive idiom for debating gun control is a task that will require at least as much energy and creativity as has been invested so far in the study of gun control's consequences. It is a project, however, in which anthropologists, sociologists, and philosophers are likely to have a larger role to play than economists.

NOTES

1. See, e.g., Mark Duggan, "More Guns, More Crime," *J. Pol. Econ.* 109 (2001): 286; Philip J. Cook and Jens Ludwig, *Gun Violence: The Real Costs* (New York: Oxford University Press, 2000); Dan Black and Daniel Nagin, "Do 'Right to Carry' Laws Deter Violent Crime?" *J. Legal Stud.* 27 (1998): 209; Arthur L. Kellermann et al., "Gun Ownership as a Risk Factor for Homicide in the Home," *New Eng. J. Med.* 329 (1993): 1084.

2. John R. Lott Jr., *More Guns, Less Crime: Understanding Crime and Gun Control Laws* 23–24 (Chicago: University of Chicago Press, 2d ed., 2000).

3. See Gary Kleck, "Crime, Culture Conflict, and the Sources of Support for Gun Control," *Am. Behavioral Sci.* 39 (1996): 387, 390, 398; Tom W. Smith, *1999 National Gun Policy Survey of the National Opinion Research Center: Research Findings* 19–20b (Chicago: University of Chicago Press, 2000) [hereinafter *National Gun Policy Survey 1999*]; Tom W. Smith, *1996 National Gun Policy Survey of the National Opinion Research Center: Research Findings* 5 (Chicago: University of Chicago Press, 1997) [hereinafter *National Gun Policy Survey 1996*].

4. See, e.g., B. Bruce-Briggs, "The Great American Gun War," *Pub. Int.*, Fall 1976, at 61 ("[The gun culture's] model is that of the independent frontiersman who takes care of himself and his family with no interference from the state"); William R. Tonso, *Gun and Society: The Social and Existential Roots of the American Attachment to Firearms* (Washington, D.C.: University Press of America, 1982) ("'Just to hold [a Colt Model 'P'] in your hand produces a feeling of kinship with our western heritage—an appreciation of things like courage and honor and chivalry and the sanctity of a man's world'" [quoting gun collector]); James D. Wright, Peter H. Rossi, and Kathleen Daly, *Under the Gun: Weapons, Crime, and Violence in America* (New York: Aldine Pub. Co., 1983), 113 ("The values of th[e] [progun] culture are best typified as rural rather than urban: they emphasize independence, self-sufficiency, mastery over nature,

closeness to the land, and so on"); James D. Wright, "Ten Essential Observations on Guns in America," *Society,* Mar./Apr. 1995, at 68 (for control opponent, the gun "symbolizes manliness, self-sufficiency, and independence, and its use is an affirmation of man's relationship to nature and to history"). See generally Richard Slotkin, *Gunfighter Nation: The Myth of the Frontier in Twentieth-Century America* (New York: Maxwell Macmillan International, 1998) (examining historical evolution of progun meanings in American culture).

5. See Kleck, supra note 3; *National Gun Policy Survey 1999; National Gun Policy Survey 1996.*

6. See H. Taylor Buckner, "Sex and Guns: Is Gun Control Male Control?" (unpublished manuscript, Aug. 5, 1994) (finding that aversion to "macho" style and tolerance of homosexuality predict support for gun control); Lee Kennett and James La Verne Anderson, *The Gun in America: the Origins of a National Dilemma* (Westport, Conn.: Greenwood Press, 1975) (noting historical centrality of gun control to women's movement); Wright, supra note 4, at 68 (for procontrol individuals, the gun "symbolizes violence, aggression, male dominance"); Richard Hofstadter, "America as a Gun Culture," *Am. Heritage* 21 (1970): 84 (noting that the gun has historically been "an important symbol of white male status").

7. See Kleck 1996; see also Donald Braman and Dan M. Kahan, "More Statistics, Less Persuasion" (unpublished manuscript, June 2002) (finding strong positive correlations between attitudes toward gun control and individual cultural orientations).

8. See generally Joseph R. Gusfield, *Symbolic Crusade: Status Politics and the American Temperance Movement* (Urbana: University of Illinois Press, 2d ed., 1986).

9. Phoebe C. Ellsworth and Samuel R. Gross, "Hardening of the Attitudes: Americans' Views on the Death Penalty," *J. Soc. Issues* 50 (1994): 19, 23.

10. See Barbara Ann Stolz, "Congress and Capital Punishment: An Exercise in Symbolic Politics," *L. and Pol. Q.* 5 (1983): 157.

11. See generally Robert Justin Goldstein, *Burning the Flag: The Great 1989–1990 American Flag Desecration Controversy* (Ohio: Kent State University Press, 1996).

12. See Dan M. Kahan and Martha C. Nussbaum, "Two Conceptions of Emotion in Criminal Law," *Colum. L. Rev.* 96 (1996): 269, 346–50.

13. Zell Miller, "The Democratic Party's Southern Problem," *N.Y. Times,* June 4, 2001, at A17.

14. See Braman and Kahan 2002.

15. B. Bruce-Briggs 1976: 61.

16. See Julian V. Roberts and Loretta Stalans, *Public Opinion, Crime, and Criminal Justice* (Boulder, Colo.: Westview Press, 1997), 239, 242–43.

17. See generally Mary Douglas, *Risk Acceptability According to the Social*

Sciences (New York: Russell Sage Foundation, 1985), 60 (suggesting that cultural orientations operates to accentuate perception of certain physical risks and mute others).

18. See generally Ellen Peters and Paul Slovic, "The Role of Affect and Worldviews as Orienting Dispositions in the Perception and Acceptance of Nuclear Power," *J. Applied Soc. Psych.* 26 (1996): 1427.

19. See Mary Douglas and Aaron Wildavsky, *Risk and Culture* (Berkeley: University of California Press, 1982), 73, 80–82.

20. See John Rawls, *Political Liberalism,* Lecture VI (Cambridge, Mass.: Harvard University Press, 1993); Bruce A. Ackerman, *Social Justice and the Liberal State* (New Haven: Yale University Press, 1980), 8–12; Amy Gutmann and Dennis Thompson, *Democracy and Disagreement* (Cambridge, Mass.: Harvard University Press, 1996), ch. 2.

21. Martin Rein and Christopher Winship, "The Dangers of 'Strong' Causal Reasoning in Social Policy," *Society,* July/Aug. 1999, at 39.

22. See Dan M. Kahan, "The Secret Ambition of Deterrence," *Harv. L. Rev.* 113 (1999): 413; Rein and Winship 1999; Note, "The CITES Fort Lauderdale Criteria: The Uses and Limits of Science in International Conservation Decisionmaking," *Harv. L. Rev.* 114 (2001): 1769.

23. Margery Eagan, "Rally Proves Gun Lovers Are Still Out There," *Boston Herald,* May 18, 1999, at 4; see also Richard Cohen, "The Tame West," *Wash. Post,* July 15, 1999, at A25 ("[Republican control opponents] all pretend to be upholding American tradition and rights, citing in some cases an old West of their fervid imagination and suggesting remedies that can only be considered inane."); Ted Flickinger, "Dodge City" (Letter to the Editor), *Pittsburgh Post-Gazette,* June 1, 1999, at A-10 ("The widespread availability of guns in a society in which many so-called adult males still embrace the frontier mentality makes it a certainty these periodic adolescent outbursts will be tragically repeated. It's still Dodge City out there, boys. Wahoo."); Perry Young, "We Are All to Blame," *Chapel Hill Herald,* April 24, 1999, at 4 ("[W]e seem crippled by a mythological 'tradition' (a frontier gun world that ceased to exist 100 years ago and was wrong even then) and bullied into submission by a ridiculous minority of airheads like B-movie actor Charlton Heston and the National Rifle Association.").

24. Norman W. Nielsen, "Letter to Editor," *L.A. Times,* Apr. 30, 1999, at B6. See also Robert Reno, "NRA Aims but Shoots Self in Foot," *Newsday* (New York, N.Y.), May 9, 1999, at 5H (sign at gun control rally: "Gun owners have penis envy.").

25. See Charlton Heston, "The Second Amendment: America's First Freedom," in *Guns in America: A Reader* 203, Jan E. Dizard et al., eds. (New York: New York University Press, 1999) (exhorting those who "prefer the America . . . where you [can] pray without feeling naïve, love without being kinky, sing

without profanity, be white without feeling guilty, own a gun without shame" to join and "to win a cultural war"); David Keim, "NRA Chief Proves Big Draw at Vote Freedom First Rally," *Knoxville News-Sentinel* (Knoxville, Tenn.), Nov. 2, 2000, at A1 ("'Our country is in greater danger now than perhaps ever before,'" Heston warned. "'Instead of Redcoats, you're fighting blue-blooded elitists.'").

26. Cf. James Davison Hunter, *Culture Wars: The Struggle to Define America* (New York, Basic Books, 1991), 321 ("A . . . condition . . . essential for rationally resolving morally grounded differences in the public realm would be the rejection by all factions of the impulse of public quiescence. . . . [T]here is a tendency among those Americans in the middle of these debates to hesitate from speaking at all.").

27. Ibid. at 42.

28. See Jack F. Trope and Walter R. Echo-Hawk, "The Native American Graves Protection and Repatriation Act: Background and Legislative History," *Arizona L. J.* 24 (1992): 35; Gene A. Marsh, "Walking the Spirit Trail," *Arizona L. J.* 24 (1992): 79; see also Robert Winthrop, "Resolving Culturally Grounded Conflict in Environmental Change" (unpublished manuscript, Aug. 1999) (describing cultural dispute resolution techniques used to resolve conflicts over development of sacred Native American lands).

29. See Marc Howard Ross, *The Management of Conflict* (New Haven: Yale University Press, 1993), 5–7.

30. See Mary Ann Glendon, *Abortion and Divorce in Western Law* (Cambridge, Mass.: Harvard University Press, 1987), ch. 1.

31. See ibid. at 33–50; Ross 1993: 167–93; Winthrop 1999: 9.

32. See Hunter 1991: 34.

Chapter 3

Equalizers
The Cult of the Colt in American Culture

Richard Slotkin

It is a fundamental principle of American politics that a democracy is a government of laws and not of men. Belief in this principle has sustained our remarkably durable faith in a Constitution that is now among the oldest such instruments still operative and has allowed us, for most of our history, to see the government not as a threat to the people's liberties but as a credible instrument for safeguarding and expanding those liberties. Yet, there is another uniquely American belief, to which we hold with equal stubbornness, which might be called the "Cowboy Corollary" to the Declaration of Independence: "God may have made *men,* but Samuel Colt made them *equal.*" The same culture that reveres the Constitution as a form of Holy Writ and that prides itself on its faith in law also sanctions the private use of deadly force with a permissiveness unknown in any other industrial democracy and experiences a murder rate that annually produces the kind of casualties that in other lands are associated with civil insurrections or guerrilla wars.

The widespread private ownership of guns is often cited as a cause of this murder rate—and it is certainly a contributing cause. But other societies have similar rates of gun ownership without commensurate experience of private violence. Both Israel and Switzerland are "militia republics," in which all male (and many female) citizens are required to serve in the armed forces and are also required to keep their weapons in their homes, in good order and ready for use when a call-up comes. In Israel, such weapons may figure in intercommunal violence between Jews and Arabs but they are rarely used to commit or defend against crimes or to settle personal disputes.[1]

What makes the difference is not simply the availability of weapons but the social ethic or ideology that teaches people how weapons may be used. American mass media have been particularly cited as promoters of a culture of violence, because of their sensationally appealing portrayals of violence and there is some evidence that excessive TV-watching correlates with violent behavior among young children. But the number of Americans who act out media-based scenarios of violence is infinitesimal compared with the number who treat fantasy *as* fantasy. European and Japanese audiences consume violent American films as avidly as we do, and their film industries have their own highly successful genres of ultraviolent cinema. But the spectacular mythologies of violence purveyed by mass media are supported, in this country, by powerful local, regional, and familial cultural traditions, which in turn have their roots deep in our communal history.

All cultures, whatever their supposed level of advancement, sanction particular forms of violence. The difference between the United States and Europe is that our culture grants a far broader license to private individuals to use violence for private ends. In contrast, the forms of violence sanctioned by European and Japanese culture are political and social, rather than personal. Europeans and Japanese are justly scandalized by American murder rates, and by our history of lynching and race riots. But, if we consider social violence in its totality, the balance shifts. There is no U.S. equivalent of the European and prewar Japanese police states, of the Gulag, or of the government sponsored violence of the Shoah, the Rape of Nanking, and the atrocious conduct of the Spanish or Russian civil wars. The postwar violence of American "militias" and the KKK is more than matched by the murderous work of the Red Brigades, the Japanese Red Army Faction, Bader-Meinhoff, the Basque ETA, and the IRA and its Protestant counterparts, and American terrorists cannot claim connection with mainstream political parties.

This peculiarity of American violence is often attributed to the large number of weapons in private hands. But the current widespread ownership of firearms—particularly those designed as man-killers— is itself an artifact of pre-existing cultural traditions. It is our permissive ethic of private violence—the "Cult of the Colt"—that has made

Americans want not merely to own guns but to accumulate firepower in excess of need and has given us a broad license to shoot each other.

The origins of America's gun culture are usually traced to the colonial settlements, when hunting was necessary to survival and every man was nominally required to present himself (with firelock) for militia service. Recent research has shown that most Americans made only perfunctory attempts to meet this militia obligation.[2] But if militia service was nominal as a social fact, the right to serve in the militia was one of the hallmarks of equal citizenship. Colonial militias excluded from service those residents who were not classed as freemen, a category that included poor whites and such disenfranchised groups as slaves, indentured servants, women, and (sometimes) non-Protestants. The expansion of citizenship rights from 1776 through the Age of Jackson extended the franchise and the right and obligation of militia service to the white male portion of the excluded classes. But most blacks were excluded from militia service, even in the free states, until the Civil War. The enlistment of blacks during the Civil War signaled the transformation of their status as citizens and the disarming of black militias after Reconstruction signaled their reduction to second-class citizenship. Thus, the right to bear arms came to be commonly recognized as a hallmark of citizenship, manhood, and racial identity.

Nineteenth-century American law and custom also developed unique rationales for defining the legitimate use of force by private individuals. In English law, if a person menaced with deadly force is able to flee without killing his assailant, he is obliged to do so. American laws of self-defense have (since the Jacksonian period) typically declared that a "true" man may defend himself with deadly force when he has a credible belief that he is menaced with deadly force.[3] Under this rule, a Louisiana man was acquitted in 1992 of having shot an unarmed Japanese exchange student who came to his door playing trick-or-treat. The jury found that the man had had a genuine and reasonably founded fear of harm.

In practice, custom and tradition broaden still further the already liberal sanction of violence provided by statute law. Judges and juries have customarily treated certain types of personal and social grievance as legitimate reasons for homicide, even when the victim posed no threat of bodily harm. Throughout our national history, levels of personal and social violence have always been highest in regions or communities divided along racial lines. In the Jim Crow era (which in some states lasted until the 1950s), whites who murdered African Americans for such offenses as refusing to step aside in the street, acting uppity, or looking at white women were typically let off by white juries. In effect, the victims were perceived as having traduced or abused the perpetrator by asserting their equality—thereby "degrading" the white man before his equals, threatening his social identity. In modern times, race-based jury nullification also works against whites —as, for example, in the O. J. Simpson and the Los Angeles riot cases. The physical abuse and even murder of women has historically been treated with similar tolerance. Juries responsive to the so-called unwritten law have often freed men who kill adulterous spouses. It remains part of our cultural tradition to regard certain kinds of grievance as legitimate reasons for committing or condoning acts of extra-legal violence.

The codes and myths that inform "grievance" killing can be traced to the dueling codes that developed in the United States between 1755 and 1850. Americans learned to associate dueling with social status from aristocratic British officers serving in the colonies during the French and Indian Wars. A gentleman was defined as a man of "honor," one whose standing was not to be questioned and whose word was to be accepted as given—and, if questioned by a person of comparable standing, the gentleman had the right (and the moral obligation) to duel. Aristocratic status was thus defined as the entitlement to "resent an insult" by issuing a challenge, and this distinction was preserved and elaborated in antebellum Southern society as a way of distinguishing between "gentlemen" and other classes of whites. But the democratizing tendencies of American life gradually extended the right to challenge, poorer whites could not accept their exclusion from the right to fight without acknowledging subordination and (by implication) their likeness to Negro slaves—the one class of Americans deemed to be intrinsically "without honor," whose word (even when sworn) was never acceptable. This Southern code was carried north of the Ohio after the War of 1812, and into the West after the Civil War.[4] So, the "right to fight," like the right to participate in the common defense, became a hallmark of equal citizenship, manhood, and racial identity.

The invention of the repeating revolver by Samuel Colt in 1836 has been seen as contributing to, and profiting from, this democratization of the right to fight. Even as good a historian as Daniel Boorstin has represented the Colt as a true "equalizer," which democratized American justice by "put[ting] 'law enforcement' in the reach of any trained arm." He sees the classic gunfight as a model of economic practice: two individuals compete with equal weapons, and the most effective producer of firepower wins the field. As long as each party has had "an even break," the outcome can be accepted as morally just and socially beneficial, as well as economically sound. Boorstin even suggests that the outcome of such competition favors better moral characters and that "the men who are killed generally deserve their fate." That the victory goes to the fastest draw is, for Boorstin, merely an extension of traditional American concepts of preemption and squatters rights, which give "the law and the right to the man who 'got there first.'"[5]

There are two problems with Boorstin's account of what we might call the moral economy of gunfighting. First, it is historically false. Boorstin seems to have gotten his information about Western gunfights from Western novels like Owen Wister's *The Virginian* or movies like *Shane* and *High Noon*. In fact, the walk-down and shootout between matched quick-draw artists was a rarity. Most Western gun battles took place in a flash of temper at card-table distances and were often more dangerous to bystanders than to the principals. In most deliberate killings, the shooter made sure to take his intended victim at a disadvantage wherever possible.[6] The whole point in having a weapon is to gain an edge; in using one against another armed man, it is vital that one have an additional advantage—a better angle, a faster draw, a better gun. Moreover, in the classic range wars that are Boorstin's historical reference point, the typical shootouts were not gunfights between individuals but pitched battles between mercenaries hired by well-capitalized big ranchers and citizen posses formed by small ranchers to protect their communities.

But the fundamental error at the heart of Boorstin's gunfighter economics is his equation of the right to use man-killing weapons as just another form of private property rights and his assumption that such rights must always be given the widest conceivable freedom to operate without regulation. And his error is characteristic of American culture: Whenever Americans consider the regulation of firearms, they associate the right to buy and use weapons with the right to buy and use *anything*.

In the classic Western *Shane* (1953), the hero tells the leading lady:

"A gun is just a tool, Marion. Like an axe or a plow. It's as good or as bad as the man that uses it." The handgun *is* a tool, a piece of private property; our national commitment to private enterprise makes it seem logical to treat it like any other piece of property and to grant the owner the right to use and enjoy it with maximum freedom. But a gun is a peculiar sort of tool: an instrument of power—a tool through which an individual can punish crime, defend his home, and—above all—impose his will on others. Unlike an axe or a plow, or a combine or a sewing machine, a revolver is never *merely* a tool. In private hands, unfettered by regulation, the gun allows an individual to do what in other countries only the state can legitimately do. It is always, by nature, a political instrument, because its use is *always* an exercise of power.

Moreover, the peculiar advantage of owning a repeating firearm like the Colt is not realized in a gunfight against an equally armed opponent. Rather, it lies in the capacity of a technologically advanced weapon to enable its user to defeat larger numbers of less well-armed adversaries. Colt recognized this in his early marketing, which was directed toward outfits like the Texas Rangers (whose enemies were Indians armed with bows or single-shot muskets) and toward Southern planters. In one of his earliest promotional statements, published in 1838 in the *Journal of the American Institute,* Colt gave the following account of the genesis of his idea:

> Mr. Colt happened to be near the scene of a sanguinary insurrection of negro slaves, in the Southern district of Virginia. He was startled to think against what fearful odds the white planter must ever contend, thus surrounded by a swarming population of slaves. What defense could there be in one shot, when opposed to multitudes, even though multitudes of the unarmed? The master and his family were certain to be massacred. Was there no way, thought Mr. Colt, of enabling the planter to repose in peace? no longer to feel that to be attacked, was to be at once and inevitably destroyed? that no resistance could avail, were the negroes once spirited up to revolt? . . . The boy's ingenuity was from that moment on the alert.[7]

There is reason to doubt this account of Colt's inspiration. Colt had made his first model of the pistol in 1830, as a sailor on a voyage to Singapore, and one presumes he had given the idea some thought before that. The "negro insurrection" to which the 1838 article refers is almost certainly Nat Turner's insurrection of 1832—the year in which Colt applied for his first patent. Colt was probably rewriting the history of his invention in order to create a market for his pistol among worried planters. In so doing, he also necessarily constructed an ideological paradigm, a set of social values and presumptions, which defined and gave political direction to the use of his invention: not as an equalizer between matched competitors, but as an instrument through which a small number of men could dominate a discontented mass.[8]

A similar logic lay behind the first great success of the Colt revolver: its use by Samuel Walker's Texas Rangers in mounted combat with Comanche Indians in 1836. The Comanche bow had an effective range comparable to the Rangers' single-shot carbine, and a higher potential rate of fire. Moreover, since the Rangers were attacking a tribal people operating within range of their home villages, they were likely to be outnumbered by the Comanche in most engagements. In that kind of combat, a repeating pistol was indeed an "equalizer."[9]

Through its use in the Indian wars, the Colt acquired a larger symbolic significance as the instrument of progress, the gun that won the West. Thus, in 1859, the author of *Hero-Martyr*, a collection of short biographies celebrating the prime exemplars of American virtue, hailed Samuel Colt as one whose invention had advanced the cause of civilization. "War appears to have been one of the principal occupations of our race," and, through war,

> the less cultivated races are conquered by the more intelligent, who introduce the knowledge of their own arts to the vanquished, and thus in the end bless them, through an introductory suffering and defeat.[10]

Colt's repeating pistol is an "instrument of civilization," because its fearsome capability for multiple killing instantly demonstrates the superiority of civilization and shortens the conquered race's "introductory" period of suffering. The author of *Hero-Martyr* follows his logic to the end, praying that Colt's principle will be further developed to create a true weapon of mass destruction. For,

> If a machine were invented and could be readily used, by which a few men could instantly and unfailingly, at once destroy a thousand lives,

wars among civilized nations would cease forever, and nations low in the scale would more speedily, and with comparatively little suffering, be brought under pupilary subjection. The inventor of such a machine would prove a greater benefactor of his race, than he who should endow a thousand hospitals.[11]

But the external imperial struggle between civilized nations and those "low in the scale" has its counterpart in the internal social conflicts between what the nineteenth century called "the enlightened classes" and those "lower in the scale." Within the industrializing United States were large groups of people bent on resistance, often violent, to the advance of corporate industrialism. These included "primitive" white trash like the Populists, or the former slaves in the South, or the hordes of non-English-speaking immigrants who flocked to American cities and industrial and mining districts after 1877, people who, in the words of E. L. Godkin, of *The Nation*, "carry in their very blood, traditions which give universal suffrage an air of menace to many of the things which civilized men hold most dear."[12]

When such metropolitan savages rise up against order, the ideological paradigm of frontier warfare suggests that they be treated like Indians: that is, treated as objects of coercion, not consenting citizens. And, since they are numerous, perhaps even a local majority, the necessary instruments of coercion must enable a minority of law enforcers to control the more numerous "dangerous classes."[13]

The social, economic, and demographic upheavals of the Reconstruction era after the Civil War, and of the era of industrialization that followed, augmented the motives for social violence. Industrialization threatened the status and well-being of workers and farmers; worker discontent seemed to businessmen and conservatives to threaten revolution; and the demographic revolution produced by the new immigration and by the outmigration of Southern blacks threatened social hierarchies and the traditions of American culture. In response, cultural and political leaders at both the national and the local level began to advocate a new approach to the administration of violence in American life. They called for more coercive measures against the new forces of disorder, from restricting the ballot for immigrant and racial minorities to an increased use of the military against organized labor.

Gunmakers like Colt used the new technologies of this industrial age to produce more and cheaper guns and to market them through the new mass media, with ads that alternately invoked the fear of crime or social upheaval and the mythic appeal of the Wild West. By the turn of the century, gun toting was common enough that Sears Roebuck catalogues marketed mass-produced pants with pistol pockets. Even so, most Americans did not own pistols. But, so many did go armed (by comparison with Europeans) that European travelers cited this as one of the distinctive features of American life.[14] To the public, gun manufacturers marketed pistols for self-protection in a time of fear. But, to governments and corporations, they offered a new weapon, the machine gun, which took the Colt revolver's principle, the "serial production of fire, to a level that would allow a small professional force to out-gun a conventionally-armed 'mob'—even if that mob was wielding Colt repeaters."[15]

The Colt repeating pistol enables the few to kill the many; the ideology of vigilantism gives the few the moral license to do so. Vigilantism is the extralegal use of deadly force by an organization of private individuals to achieve some public or political goal. Vigilante or "Regulator" movements figured periodically in the development of frontier settlements before 1850, and there were two urban vigilance movements with important political agendas: the abolitionist Vigilance Committee, in Boston, in the 1850s, and the San Francisco vigilantes of 1856. But after 1865, vigilance organizations became the cutting edge of social conflict in a wide variety of settings, usually with the sponsorship of local elites or businessmen, sometimes with the support of legal or government authorities. A modern wrinkle on traditional vigilantism was the development of professional vigilantes, "detectives" hired to disrupt or intimidate organizations of workers and small farmers or to assassinate organizers. The largest vigilance movements were those mounted by the KKK and similar organizations during Reconstruction, during the Jim Crow era, and again in the Civil Rights era. But vigilance-type movements were also mounted against urban political machines (San Francisco, 1856); against Asian immigrants (1850–1880); in land disputes and range wars (e.g., the Mussel Slough conflict of 1880 and the Johnson County War of 1892); and against labor unions during periods of industrial strife (1874–1877, 1885–1895, 1903–1925).[16]

It is worth noting that the turn of the century also saw the beginnings of modern mass media, especially movies. Popular writers like Zane Grey and Owen Wister, and early filmmakers like D. W. Griffith and W. S. Hart, drew on relatively recent vigilante violence to create the images and story forms that would become the basis for national popular-culture mythology in the twentieth century.

But to license coercion of this kind, on this scale, requires a radical revision of the Cowboy Corollary, to state that the privilege of using private violence for public good can be entrusted only to men of good character and standing—to morally and, if possible, socially superior classes or individuals. Whatever it may seem to be in theory, in practice the reliance on private firearms as a social and political equalizer produces not democracy but an aristocracy of violence.

In arguing for the unlimited privatization of firepower, the contemporary "gun-rights" movement—as exemplified by the gun manufacturers, the NRA, and other gun lobby organizations—invokes both the mantras of late Victorian laissez-faire capitalism and the heroic mythology of classic turn-of-the-century vigilantism. The first allows them to reduce weapons law to simple matters of property rights. But the appeal to vigilante traditions provides a model of political action, which, if carried to its logical conclusion, poses a serious threat to the nation's civil peace. The essence of vigilantism is the idea that civil liberty rests ultimately on the individual citizen's right and ability to defend himself with private arms against the agents of an elected government. Given the state's advantages of numbers and firepower, such a right would be moot unless the individual could possess advanced weaponry. Thus, the weapons that the manufacturers promote, and the gun lobby seeks to protect from regulation, are not only the hunter's rifle and the shopkeeper's .38 but also military weapons, capable of killing large numbers of people very rapidly. One of the most attractive marketing trends in the 1990s was the selling of "street sweepers" and "pocket rockets" (high-caliber, high-velocity hand weapons), .50-caliber "sniper rifles," and armor-piercing "cop killer" munitions, developed originally for the military. The right they seek to establish is the private individual's entitlement to wage social war, at will, against "government tyranny," as represented by the FBI or the Bureau of Alcohol, Tobacco, and Firearms—or against those classes of people deemed "dangerous" to public safety.[17] In the words of the NRA spokesman Fred Romero:

> The Second Amendment is not there to protect the interests of hunters, sports shooters, and casual plinkers. . . . The Second Amendment

is there as a balance of power. It is literally a loaded gun in the hands
of the people held to the heads of government.[18]

In the past few years, NRA spokesmen have moderated the vigilante
aspect of their rhetoric, though Charlton Heston still challenges the
BATF to come and take the flintlock from his cold dead hands. The
fears the NRA invokes are the classic terrors of vigilantism: an attack
on personal safety by the lower orders, an assault on vital interests by
government officials.[19] But, other organizations act out vigilante scenarios. Self-styled "militias" and the various "common law" sects typically operate like vigilance organizations, using weapons to intimidate their neighbors or to gain some advantage or immunity: to evade
taxes or debts, to win boundary disputes with neighbors or the Bureau
of Land Management, to evade or nullify government regulations
and policies that offend them, such as school integration or laws
against spousal and child abuse. White supremacist organizations like
Aryan Nations, WAR, Christian Identity, World Church of the Creator,
the Phineas Priesthood, and The Order see themselves as revolutionary political organizations and engage in terrorist acts beyond their
local communities. But, like vigilantes, they are private enterprises,
founded by charismatic leaders or organized around a single armed
and alienated family, dependent for safety on the sanctuary offered by
a particular locality.

The beliefs and practices that underlie American violence are
deeply embedded in the culture. Any attempt at reform must take this
into account and recognize that change cannot come easily or everywhere all at once. But history also points us toward the critical junc-
tures in the cultural system that shape the codes that govern violence.

The most critical venue for cultural change is the law. Public law,
local and national, is the register of existing values and may be the ful-
crum for shifting public ideology. The codes of the duel, of vigilante
justice, of Jim Crow justice, would not have developed as they did
without either statutory recognition (i.e., the laws of self-defense),
judicial toleration, or jury nullification. In recent years, changes in
statute law and newly stringent judicial enforcement have produced
remarkable reforms in two of the most ingrained patterns in American
culture: racial and sex discrimination and drunk driving.

A similar approach can change the culture of violence in the United
States. We need to rebalance our way of evaluating crimes, to weigh

violent crime more heavily than we now do. The free market in guns must be regulated and limited in ways consistent with the public safety. While "total disarmament" is neither possible nor desirable, we ought to prohibit absolutely the manufacture for private sale and possession of weapons designed for war fighting, rather than personal protection or hunting. All guns now privately held ought to be registered, in recognition of the inherent danger they represent. The recently published report of the Surgeon General on youth violence indicates that even the rudimentary efforts made so far to regulate and limit gun possession can have a substantial effect; while the overall level of youth violence has remained high, the levels of *lethal* violence have dropped substantially since 1994—and the change is attributable to "declining firearm use."[20]

We need to see to it that the system of laws, and the exercise of democratic politics, offers viable ways for citizens to redress the inequalities and injustices they experience. If we, as individuals, have to depend on our own guns as equalizers, then what we will have is not a government of laws but a government of *armed* men. In such a government, our individual equality will cease the moment we meet someone faster on the draw and more ruthless than we are, and politics will become a matter of which corporation can hire the most proficient and fear-inspiring gunslingers.

NOTES

1. Lee Kennett and James L. Anderson, *The Gun in America: The Origins of a National Dilemma* (Westport, Conn.: Greenwood Press, 1975), 249; Deborah Prothero-Stith, with Michael Weissman, *Deadly Consequences: How Violence Is Destroying Our Teenage Population and a Plan to Begin Solving the Problem* (New York: HarperCollins, 1991), 15.

2. Michael A. Bellesisles, "The Origins of Gun Culture in the United States, 1760–1865," *J. Am. Hist.* 83 (Sept. 1996): 425–455; Lawrence Delbert Cress, "An Armed Community: The Origins and Meaning of the Right to Bear Arms," *J. Am. Hist.* 71 (1984): 22–42; Robert Reinders, "Militia and Public Order in Nineteenth Century America," *J. Am. Stud.* 11 (1977): 81–102. Kennett and Anderson, *Gun in America*, 73–76; Stephen P. Halbrook, *A Right to Bear Arms: State and Federal Bills of Rights and Constitutional Guarantees* (New York: Greenwood Press, 1991), esp. Epilogue, 110; Allen R. Millett and Peter Maslowski, *For the Common Defense: A Military History of the United States of America* (New York:

Free Press, 1984), 247–49, 312–14; John K. Mahon, *History of the Militia and the National Guard* (New York: Macmillan, 1983).

3. Richard M. Brown, *No Duty to Retreat: An American Theme* (New York: Oxford University Press, 1992), esp. chs. 1, 4.

4. Kenneth S. Greenberg, *Honor and Slavery, Lies, Duels, Noses, Masks, Dressing as a Woman, Gifts, Strangers, Humanitarianism, Death, Slave Rebellions, the Proslavery Argument, Baseball, Hunting, and Gambling in the Old South* (Princeton: Princeton University Press, 1996), esp. ch. 1; Bertram Wyatt-Brown, *Southern Honor: Ethics and Behavior in the Old South* (New York: Oxford University Press, 1982), esp. Part III.

5. Daniel Boorstin, *The Americans: The Democratic Experience* (New York: Random House, 1973), 37; Phil Patton, *Made in USA: The Secret Histories of the Things That Made America* (New York: Penguin Books, 1991), ch. 3 and esp. 46; Wendy Kaminer, "Second Thoughts on the Second Amendment," *Atlantic Monthly*, March 1996, 32–45.

6. Joseph G. Rosa, *The Gunfighter: Man or Myth?* (Norman: University of Oklahoma Press, 1964), chs. 1, 3, 8, 9, 13; Brown, *No Duty to Retreat*, ch. 2.

7. Quoted in James E. Serven, *Colt Firearms from 1836* (Santa Ana, Calif.: Foundation Press, 1954), 4–5.

8. William Hosley, *Colt: The Making of a Legend* (Amherst: University of Massachusetts Press, 1996), 10–25, 66–97.

9. Walter Prescott Webb, *The Great Plains* (New York: Grossett and Dunlap, 1957 [1931]), 171–72, 176, 179, 214–15.

10. H— H—, *Hero-Martyr* ([n.p.], 1859), 149.

11. Ibid., 149–50.

12. E. L. Godkin, "The Late Riots," *The Nation*, August 2, 1877, 68–70; Richard Slotkin, *The Fatal Environment: The Myth of the Frontier in the Age of Industrialization* (New York: Atheneum, 1985), ch. 19.

13. Richard Slotkin, *Gunfighter Nation: The Myth of the Frontier in Twentieth-Century America* (New York: Atheneum, 1992), 89–106; Frederic Remington, "The Affair of the —th of July," *The Collected Writings of Frederic Remington*, ed. Peggy Samuels and Harold Samuels (Garden City, N.Y.: Doubleday, 1979), 176–83.

14. Kennett and Anderson, *Gun in America*, ch. 6.

15. John Ellis, *The Social History of the Machine Gun* (New York: Pantheon Books, 1975), 21–29, 42–45, and ch. 4; Patton, *Made in USA*, ch. 3.

16. Slotkin, *Gunfighter Nation*, ch. 5; Richard M. Brown, *Strain of Violence: Historical Studies of American Violence and Vigilantism* (New York: Oxford University Press, 1975), Part III.

17. See for example Wayne LaPierre, *Guns, Crime, and Freedom* (Washington, D.C.: Regnery, 1994), ch. 17.

18. Quoted in Josh Sugarmann, *National Rifle Association: Money, Firepower, Fear* (Washington, D.C.: National Press Books, 1992), 14.

19. Osha Gray Davidson, *Under Fire: The NRA and the Battle for Gun Control* (New York: Henry Holt, 1993), passim.

20. *Executive Summary: Youth Violence: A Report of the Surgeon General* (2001), 6, available at: www.mentalhealth.org/youthviolence/sgsummary/ summary.htm.

Chapter 4

"Hell no, you can't jack that fool. He stays strapped. He's strapped all the time"

Talking about Guns at an All-Boy Correctional Facility in Tucson, Arizona

Bernard E. Harcourt

> We were by the Tohono Center down in the wash.
> And we were just sitting there. . . . They were walking
> by. . . . We were just like sitting there. They kept on
> dogging me. . . . Staring down. Like not saying any-
> thing. Just staring . . . hard . . . [And they] started talk-
> ing crap. Like, you know, your instinct is to talk crap
> back. . . . Like, "You're a pussy." "No, you're a bitch."
> "I'm gonna kick your ass." Just talking. "Fuck your
> mother." They get mad. "Yeah whatever." "Fuck
> you." "You ain't down." . . . So we were talking crap
> and then like, "Yeah, whatever, whatever," he was all,
> "I'll shoot you." I said, "Do it then." So he pulled out
> a gun. And I pulled out mine really quick. And then
> we just stood there and I said, right at the end, I was
> all like, "You know both you and me aren't gonna
> pull the trigger so why don't you shut up and leave."[1]

The Catalina Mountain School is nested in the shadow of the scenic
Catalina Mountain foothills, approximately twelve miles north of Tucson, Arizona. The school is surrounded by the Sonoran desert. Tall
saguaros, lanky ocotillos, agaves, palo verde, and low mesquite trees
envelop the school grounds. A little further away, several sprawling

suburban subdivisions, complete with mini-shopping malls, Walgreens, Targets, and McDonalds, have begun to crop up, all within a three- to five-mile radius of the school.

The school is well maintained. There is a sense of order. It is attractive, in its way. The campus consists of approximately ten buildings, including the administrative office and a number of cottages where the students live. The grounds are kept neatly with desert landscape and give the appearance of a summer camp. Picnic tables, paths, and the desert sounds of cactus wren, grasshoppers, and the occasional roadrunner welcome the visitor. The air-conditioned lobby in the administration building provides shelter from the beating sun.

Inside, the students are in uniform, wearing state-issued T-shirts and grey dungarees. They are escorted by security or teaching staff whenever they leave their cottage. Some students—"upper-level" students who have earned privileges for good behavior—are allowed to walk unescorted on the premises, so long as they inform security of their whereabouts. The perimeter of the school is demarcated by tall barbed-wire fencing. A security pickup truck patrols the periphery, continuously driving around and around the barbed-wire fence.

The Catalina Mountain School is owned and operated by the Arizona Department of Juvenile Corrections, and it is home to more than 150 young males of various ages ranging from twelve to seventeen. These youths have run afoul of the law on repeated occasions for crimes such as burglary, robbery, auto theft, drug possession and sale, firearm possession, criminal damage, running away, and curfew violations. They have been warned many times but, apparently, have failed to heed the warnings. They have not, though, been convicted of the most violent offenses, such as murder or armed robbery, for which they would automatically have been transferred to the adult system, tried as adults, and sentenced to terms into their majority. At eighteen, these youths at the Catalina Mountain School regain their freedom.

It is here that I came in the fall of 2000 to conduct a semiotics of the gun: to explore the symbolic meaning of guns among youths; to hear their language, their voices, their cadence, and to listen to their experiences; to decipher what youths associate with guns and investigate how the symbolic dimensions of guns shape their lives. Not, I must emphasize, to record and advocate their views on public policies, but rather to collect data that might be useful in thinking about, or rethinking, the conventional ways in which we approach public policies

that address youth gun carrying—a phenomenon that has so fundamentally altered the way we administer and enforce the criminal laws
in the United States in the twenty-first century.

Using systematic random sampling, I conducted in-depth, semi-
structured interviews of thirty of the youths detained at the Catalina
Mountain School. I began each interview with a set of free-association
prompts. I showed the youths three color pictures of handguns taken
from articles in the November–December 2000 issue of the *American
Handgunner* magazine: the first, an HS 2000 full-size 9-mm service pistol from I.M. Metal of Croatia (page 60). This is a polymer semiautomatic, black plastic-looking pistol that resembles closely a Glock or
SIG 9-mm. Second, a Para-Ordinance P-14 LDA. This is a full-size .45
semiautomatic pistol with a five-inch barrel (page 42). Third, a Smith
and Wesson .45 Colt CTG revolver (page 68), the traditional-looking
.45-caliber revolver. Before giving the youths time to place the pictures
within the interview framework, I asked each one, "What are you
thinking of right now?" I followed up with further free-associational
prompts such as "What are the first experiences that these guns remind you of?" and "What do these guns make you think of?" I then
asked a number of other questions about their gun-carrying history
and practices, their experiences at both ends of guns, peer attitudes,
gun sources, and myriad other topics that might offer insight into the
symbolic realm of guns and gun carrying.

I encountered a significant amount and extensive histories of gun
carrying among the youths at the Catalina Mountain School. Although
they were incarcerated on various types of charges, mostly nongun offenses, twenty-six (or 87 percent) of the male youths had possessed
guns at some point in their lives, twenty-three (or 77 percent) had carried one or more guns on their persons, and nineteen (or 63 percent)
had significant histories of gun possession and carrying.[2] More important, though, what I discovered through the Catalina interviews is a
distinct language of guns shared by these incarcerated male youths. I
encountered recurring patterns of ways in which they talk about
guns—repeat associations with the photographs, recurring symbolic
references, multiple parallel scripts of experiences with firearms.
Using map analysis, I coded the transcripts of the interviews and deci-
phered nineteen identifiable and recurring meanings associated with
guns—what I call "primary associations." Then, using correspondence
analysis, I analyzed the nineteen primary associations to determine,

first, their relationship to each other and, second, their relationship within varying contexts, such as gun carrying and gang membership. The goal was to explore which primary meanings were more likely to go together and how these relations differ in specific youth contexts.[3] What I discovered is that there is, in addition to a language of guns among youths, certain distinct registers in which youths speak the language of guns. Let me begin here by relating the nineteen primary associations. They are in themselves so rich.

The Primary Associations with Guns

Protection and, Separately, Self-Defense

"My momma always said that guns, they bring trouble automatically. I don't know. I guess it was true. But I still had to protect myself whether it did or not. *Trouble come automatically when you don't have a gun*" (CMS–13:26). The most frequent association with guns is protection in an aggressive, confrontational manner. Under the protection rubric, guns are seen as a way to avoid being victimized in everyday encounters with other youths—to avoid getting "jumped," being "punked," or getting "disrespected." Of the thirty youths interviewed, almost half of the youths—fourteen, to be exact—mention protection as a primary association in discussing guns, five of them repeatedly.[4]

The word "strap," the most frequently mentioned slang term used to refer to guns, means precisely this notion of protection. A sixteen-year-old school dropout who carries all the time explains that the term refers to "the sheriff's holster." To call a gun a "strap" is to say that it's "just for protection." "Because," he explains, "if, out there, you don't have a strap, you're going to get killed. Because fools shoot at you and you don't have a gun, what are you going to do? Are you just going to sit there and party? Hell no. What are you going to do? You going to run? You're going to get shot in the back. That's pretty much why I had a gun" (CMS–2:12).

In this sense, gun possession is part of an image youths project to avoid being victimized. CMS–16 is a seventeen-year-old Mexican-Yaqui youth who began carrying a gun when he was eight or nine, hanging out at the neighborhood park holding drugs for older dealers. He started carrying, he explains, to protect himself from his peers:

When I was younger, I used to kick with those fools and I was looking, "There's a bad mother fucker right there. Look at that shit. Nobody fucks with that fool." And in the movies, "Man, that's a bad
mother fucker." And I just wanted to be a bad mother fucker. . . . Like,
nobody, nobody crosses him. . . . Fools just always trying to start shit
with you. Everybody always trying to like, I don't know, kinda like
trying to like, punk you, or whatever. . . . Like tell you, or just punk
you, like, "Fool, you ain't this, you ain't that, blah, blah, blah. . . ."
And then, when you, probably especially when you're younger, that's
when you got to fight back the most, because you got, once you start a
reputation, you got to keep it, I guess. If you start off as being, getting
punked and stuff, it's not good. Cuz then everybody tries to punk
you. And then if you, and then one day, somebody's punking you and
you get tired of it, and you scrap them, then it's like, it's looked at as
being forced into a fight. Like you were forced to fight. Like, even
though you beat him up, you like, still, fool, you were forced to fight,
you didn't fight that fool on your own. . . . If you get a reputation for
being forced to fight, that's a bad, that's a bad thing. (CMS–16:35–36)

Protection, for many youths, revolves precisely around this idea of not
being harassed, intimidated, or "punked."

What is particularly interesting about this notion of protection is
how it differs from the more conventional meaning of self-defense—
the need to have a gun in order to defend yourself against an armed
intruder in your home or a carjacker. Under this self-defense rubric,
youths speak about needing a gun if they ever own a nice house or
car. A sixteen-year-old European-American youth, himself incarcerated on a burglary charge, explains: "If I had my own house I would
[want a gun]. . . . But I wouldn't carry it around with me. I'd leave it in
the house" (CMS–69:13). These youths are referring to a more conventional, propertied rationale for owning a gun. The self-defense association appeared as a primary meaning in only three separate interviews.

Danger and, Separately, Death

Guns also symbolize danger to many youths—the danger of accidental shootings, or even of accidentally killing a young sibling or
friend. Here guns are associated with injuries and mistakes, sometimes fatal. One youth, a seventeen-year-old European of Irish de-

scent, immediately thought of the time he accidentally grazed his toe with a .38. He used to take his guns apart to clean then. Sometimes he would do it blindfolded. "When I was about twelve. It barely grazed my toe. I got lucky. I've had guns go off in my house by accident. I've had my friend fire guns in the house by accident" (CMS–8:7). Fourteen of the youths, and in two cases repeatedly, associated guns with this notion of accident.

In this sense, guns are often symbols of danger. Several other youths state that they like guns, but they express concerns about their dangerousness. "They look nice, but they're dangerous," explains a sixteen-year-old Mexican youth (CMS–34:4). "Like, they're, they look nice and everything. They can do powerful stuff, but like, they're dangerous, cuz I have two of my homeboys. One of my homeboys who shot his sister," he goes on. "He was just playing with it. He didn't know that, like, a bullet was there. He didn't have the clip but he didn't know a bullet was in there. He was playing with it and he shot her in the head. He's here with me . . ." (CMS–34:16).

It is worth noting that there are two different senses of danger at play, one an idea of accidents and injuries, the second a more direct notion of "death." I found the second in fewer interviews—about five youths talked about guns in this second sense. One youth, CMS–8, upon being showed the photos, reacted: "they're pretty deadly." (CMS–8:6). Similarly, CMS–23, a sixteen-year-old youth who carried a .22, a .44, a .38, and a .45, first associates guns with "people getting killed," "drive-by shootings" and the fact that guns "take someone's life." (CMS–23:4–6). Under this second meaning, there is a direct connection to death. Guns are *noir*: they smell of death.

Attraction, Dislike, and Respect

The youths expressed strong emotional responses to the pictures of the guns, many of them expressing desire and attraction, some dislike or repulsion, and others a sense of respect for the gun.

"Guns are nice. . . . They just, I don't know, I just, I just like guns a lot" (CMS–46:5). This is a constant refrain, a leitmotif running through the interviews. Many of the youths fixated on the photos and, with expressions of slight laughter or giggling or quiet moaning, manifested a kind of lust for the guns. Many of the youths wanted to go shoot the guns, or touch them. Many were deeply fascinated by and attracted to the picture of guns. Of the thirty youths interviewed, fifteen of them reacted to the pictures with immediate, spontaneous responses of desire, and several others responded with more muted but nevertheless tangible and identifiable desire. Here are some representative excerpts taken verbatim from the interview transcripts.

"I want to go shoot them. . . . Yeah, I want to see how they handle" (CMS–3:8). "I would like to have one of these. . . . I always want, I always like, I always like guns" (CMS–6:6–7). "I'd say they look pretty tight. They look cool" (CMS–7:5). "They look tight. They look nice" (CMS–10:3). "Those are some tight guns. I like the guns on there. I like them. I like the way they look" (CMS–13:5). "Those are some pretty tight guns" (CMS–16:5). "It's just tight right there. I like it. It's just tight like the way it looks. The way you can shoot. Those can shoot like ten rounds, huh? But they get jammed a lot. I had one" (CMS–21:8). "Nice guns" (CMS–25:7). "They look nice" (CMS–34:4). "That's a wicked looking gun . . . (Laughter) I just haven't seen guns in a long time" (CMS–37:8–9). "I kinda like how they look. I just want to go shoot them" (CMS–43:5). "I love guns. Hell ya, I love guns. [I love] everything about a gun" (CMS–62:9). In addition to the fifteen youths who were attracted to guns in a primary, spontaneous way, several others expressed more muted but nevertheless noticeable desire. "I would like to have the .45. . . . I like them, truthfully" (CMS–40:7–8). "They look, as in a term, they look cool to most people. But, not really. . . . Well, they do. I mean, you can look at them mostly and just try to identify them" (CMS–8:6).

Other youths, though, simply dislike guns and respond to guns with a visceral reaction of disgust. Six of the youths expressed primary associations of dislike, and a few others also expressed more muted dislike. CMS–22, a seventeen-year-old Mexican-American youth, is blunt. In response to the first prompt—"What do these pictures make you think?"—he responds: "Pussies" (CMS–22:7). "I don't like that stuff," he explains. "I think that's for punks. . . . I think it's for little girls. If you ain't man enough to scrap somebody, what's the use of you? Why you just gonna take somebody out and then go to prison. What you get out of it? Nothing. Your life's down the drain" (CMS–22:12, 14). He would much rather "scrap" the "old-fashioned" way—with your hands. If someone on the street pulls out a gun on him, he would tell them to put the gun down and fight. "But, most of the time, people, they won't, they're afraid. That's why they use a gun. To me, at least that's what I think. People use guns cuz they're afraid to go out fighting. Afraid of getting beat up" (CMS–22:7). Of course, CMS–22 realizes the risks of not carrying. Once, another guy threw him some gang signs, and he responded by inviting the guy to scrap. The other guy turned around and unloaded a clip on him, shooting him twice. He showed me the wounds (CMS–22:7–9).

A couple of youths expressed both attraction and repulsion. CMS–4, a seventeen-year-old Anglo, first reacted to the pictures of the guns with desire: "They're cool. I want to play with them. . . . I want to go out and shoot them" (CMS–4:3). But later on, in the interview, he expressed contempt for guns. "In my opinion, I don't see people who carry guns as very macho or whatever you say. That's pussy shit. You pull the trigger, the gun does all the work. If you go scrap, you're gonna work, so you can say I beat that guy, but if you shoot him you can't say that" (CMS–4:16).

A third association is a notion of respecting guns. Four of the youths talked at length about firearms requiring "respect." "I like them," CMS–7 explains, "but I respect them. I won't mistreat them or use them in the wrong way" (CMS–7:6). "When I think gun, it's like power," he goes on. "But it's power that you can't neglect, you have to respect it" (CMS–7:31). You have to respect a gun, a seventeen-year-old Hispanic youth explains to me. Respect means "being responsible and knowing that a gun ain't a toy, you know. And like, as easy, it could take away someone's life, you know. Could take away your life, probably, and it's not a toy. I just, that's how I see the gun. A gun [can] potentially kill somebody, I mean" (CMS–46:6). CMS–66 was given a gun by his best friend but also taught by him to respect it. "I remember I shot it a few times till they taught me how to shoot it and how to take care of it, but I never played with it. I was always real instilled with 'don't play with it, it's not a toy, leave it under the seat for in case you need it. Don't play with it, don't show it to people'" (CMS–66:6).

Commodity

To many other youths, handguns have important exchange value. They represent a commodity to be traded or sold for cash or drugs. Seven of the youths interviewed associated guns primarily with their cash value. CMS–14 is a good illustration. He is a seventeen-year-old Mexican-American school dropout and a heavy user of drugs. He said, in the interview, that he didn't really like guns. He admitted that he had fun with guns shooting in the desert and even that guns made him feel "powerful." But his real interest in guns was trading them for drugs. "We used to get in robbing houses that have a lot of guns, and trade 'em for pounds or ounces of cocaine or just sell them. . . . Living close to the border, guns are very valuable to the drug dealers. If you know the right people, you can get good deals for a gun" (CMS–14:7). Guns were simply a commodity to him. The first experience that the photographs of the guns brought to mind:

> when I was fourteen, we broke into a house and a marine happened to live there and we struck gold pretty much, shotguns, handguns, 9s, .22s, .38s, I guess .45s, everything man but we had it. We just thought we should go blast someone, you know, we had our little urges and trigger events when people get us mad when we're drunk, you know. I guess I tried to grow up too quick, you know. I was always hanging around with the older people. And just pretty much we struck gold. We had shotguns, rifles, we had made. Just ended up getting pounds [of marijuana]. (CMS–14:8)

Another youth, a sixteen-year-old high school dropout who spent his time dealing drugs, had a similar reaction to guns. Immediately upon seeing the three guns, CMS–2 states: "This one [9-mm pistol] I would keep. These two [.45-caliber pistols] I would sell. I would keep that one [9-mm pistol] personally" (CMS–2:3). "Forty-fives always sell and that's what I did," he explains (CMS–2:4).

Power

For others youths, guns are power. "When I think gun, it's like power. But it's power that you can't neglect, you have to respect it. . . . [Power is] just something that almost everybody wants. Because to be powerful . . . it's better to be powerful than it is weak and submit. And for certain people a gun gives them the power that they want" (CMS–7:31). Ten out of the thirty youths mentioned power as a primary association with guns. To these youths, "power" means having control of a situation. CMS–6 explains: "if you have a gun you can do whatever you want. Cuz, like, you have it all. Cuz you have a gun. You'll get your way cuz you have a gun. That's the way I feel it sometimes, like if, like when I have a gun. I didn't actually try to use it, in a hard way" (CMS–6:33).

One youth in particular, CMS–16, made a point of emphasizing how guns can intimidate others. He is a seventeen-year-old Mexican gang member youth with an extensive history of gun ownership, possession, and carrying. He likes guns, in part because they make him feel safe but also because they intimidate others: "I like guns. . . . I don't know. It's just a fun thing, I guess. Sometimes they make me feel safe, sometimes it's an intimidation on other people. Like, I can just pull a gun on somebody, if I point a gun at them, they're gonna get scared, stuff like that" (CMS–16:23). CMS–16 explains further: "It's funny, like, you can just be talking to somebody, or like, whatever, you could be doing whatever, and you just point a gun at somebody and they're ready to shit in their pants already. They're like, 'Damn, what the fuck?' Or especially if you look mad, or if you, I don't know, it's weird. Or how easily people will give you something if you have a gun. It's funny" (CMS–16:31).

Jail

"It's too much time to fuck with guns" (CMS–4:4). CMS–4 is one of the few youths who had never possessed a gun—there were only four in all—and the only youth who had never fired a gun. From his interview, it was apparent that he had made the conventional calculation that the costs of carrying outweigh the possible benefits. He wants a gun to protect himself and his family, and he thinks guns are "cool," but he perceives the risk of incarceration—as well as the danger of guns—as simply too great. "It's kind of hard. It's a loser situation to be caught with a gun. You get time" (CMS–4:16).

This sentiment—that guns are likely to land you in jail—was shared by eleven youths, each of which associated guns primarily with getting caught and doing time. Guns, pretty simply, can "put you in jail" (CMS–46:5). To CMS–2, guns are what "got me here now" (CMS–2:9). He doesn't want to have guns in his house when he is older because he wants to have children, and he does not want them to end up like him. A sixteen-year-old African American youth is incarcerated on a gun possession charge, and, for him, the picture of a gun makes him think of "when I got caught with it." "I was about to sell one of them, me and my friend," he explains. "And we met a couple of my friends at the park, and somehow I guess the neighbors seen one of them. And they called the police. And the police came up, we got patted down and everything. Got caught with them" (CMS–31:5). What does he think about guns today? In his words, "You can get a lot of money off of them. You can get in a lot of trouble with them too" (CMS–31:17).

This is not to suggest that all youths are worried about getting caught and serving time. A good number of youths indicated in the interviews that they simply disregard the risk of incarceration. In their universe, the risk of death at the hands of rivals or other peers greatly outweighs the risk of being sent to juvenile detention for carrying a gun. A sixteen-year-old European-American youth who carried a .38 for several months while he was on the run from his family explains the trade-off: "If I get caught and I go to jail, I'll still be alive. If I didn't have a gun, and someone held a gun to me, and say I was going to be a slave or die, it's like, there goes my life. And I had nothing to protect me for it" (CMS–17:47). Another youth, a seventeen-year-old, claims that he had to carry a gun, even though he might have gotten caught. "It's either them shoot me and kill me and my family being all depressed and quiet or just try and protect myself. . . . I'd rather have my life . . ." (CMS–48:27). One youth, in fact, stated that he does not think about getting caught *on purpose.* He tries to avoid thinking about the police when he is carrying a gun "because I just think that's kind of like jinxing myself" (CMS–16:47).

Recreation and, Separately, Fun

A number of youths immediately associate guns with hunting, target practice, shooting in the desert, or other forms of recreational gun use. Youths often reminisce about hunting trips with their fathers and families or about going out to the desert and shooting at cacti or cans. Eleven of the youths associated guns primarily with recreation.

CMS–8, an Anglo youth of Irish descent, saw the pictures of guns and immediately thought of "just going out and shooting sometimes." "When I was like nine years old was the first time I went shooting. We tried almost every gun there was. It was with my mom's boyfriend. Twenty gauges, 12-gauges, 14-gauges, 16-gauges, elephant gun, 9-mm, .45s, .44 Desert Eagles, Barettas, SKSs, tech-9s, tech elevens, .22s, .22 full auto, total .25s. . . . My mom's boyfriend collects them. He collects them all the time" (CMS–8:7). The right way to use a gun, he explains, is for hunting or self-defense. His association with guns is going out and shooting for recreation.

"I just want to go shoot them," explains CMS–43, a seventeen-year-old youth. "I would like to, just, to shoot them at cans and stuff. . . . Like out to the desert" (CMS–43:6). "I just, I just like guns a lot. . . . Just cuz, in New Mexico, ever since I was raised, I used to go hunting a lot with my dad," states another seventeen-year-old (CMS–46:5). "I think they're stupid unless you're hunting," explains another youth (CMS–69:5). For these youths, the guns remind them of hunting, or target practicing, or shooting in the desert: "Just target practicing with my brothers" (CMS–7:5); "shooting out in the desert or whatever" (CMS–14:6); "shooting with grandpa" (CMS–70:6).

Many youths like the way guns handle. They like the feel of shooting a gun. They like the action of the gun. CMS–37, for instance, explained that he likes "the way they look" and "the action that they have" (CMS–37:21). CMS–40 likes their mechanism, the way they are made, how the powder works. He compares them to a plane or a car (CMS–40:11). CMS–46, who has been around guns since he was a small child, likes "just shooting and feeling the gun . . . just feeling it, and shooting it, the sound of it." "It just makes me feel like kind of excited," he explains. "Like in, having fun, having a good time. Shooting at targets. Seeing if, I don't know, just trying to, you know, like get good at it, where you could shoot at targets, and you know, just practice" (CMS–46:8–9).

Action

It's about living in the fast lane, shooting others and getting shot, confronting and fronting, taking risks. CMS–34, a Mexican member of Brown Pride, looks at the pictures and immediately responds: "getting shot at."

> I was like, down Sixth, like, like, the railroad. Some guys were talking stuff to us, to my friend, and I was in the other car. And then he just pulled out a weapon. . . . He pulled out one of those [AK47] and he shot my home boy and killed him. Shot him in the throat. And my other two home boys ran, and then they started shooting at them, and hit my home boy in the arm and then in the leg. And then that's when

we came and then I had my .45. I mean I had my 9, the Glock, and I started shooting at them. And they shot back. . . . We're from the south, they're from the west. So, something happened, but, that guy, he was all messed up, so he shot at my home boys and killed them. . . . We were in a Blazer, we're like five. I only had my 9, my home boy had two .45s, and my other home boy had a .357, I forgot. And we started shooting at them. And I remember two, I heard that two of them died. But, one of us died, too. (CMS–34:5–6)

For eight youths, the pictures of the guns immediately trigger memories of shootouts and street life *with guns.* Later on in the interviews I asked each youth about gun incidents, and I heard many stories like this. But, for these eight youths, the stories came out without any prompting. These are the things that guns immediately make them think of.

Getting shot at. . . . I was coming from a friend's house and he's a gang member. . . . On the North Side. Right there at River and. . . . First, I think it was. . . . We were walking from a friend's house. And he was gonna go to my house. And these kids were like, "Hey, remember me. . . ." And then they just started blasting at me and my friend. . . . My friend just looked back and right when we looked back all of a sudden. BOOM. We just heard shots. . . . Like the whole round, I think. (CMS–37:9–12)

Reminds you of the streets. . . . Just that I had the same type of gun before. I been shot at with the same type of gun. . . . It's just cause my neighborhood, people don't like my neighborhood, cause, you know, they're rivals. They always shoot up my neighborhood. . . . Just that I've a lot of friends that have been shot by guns myself and since. (CMS–39:4–5)

People getting killed. . . . It was an apartment with some friends and another group of guys come on us with guns. . . . My friends pulled out their guns. . . . Cops pulled up. They . . . I don't know where they were. They just—we heard the sirens. . . . And everybody just started running. (CMS–23:4)

Shootings . . . We were cruising down Sixth Avenue and just fool started shooting. There was a big gun fight. . . . They were shooting at each other. Los Betos. You know where Los Betos is at? I just saw little fools shooting at each other. Like four against three other dudes. Just shooting at each other. Bullets flying everywhere. (CMS–62:7–8)

For these youths, guns were about living in the fast lane.

Killing and, Separately, Revenge

Even more raw, for some youths, guns are specifically about killing people they hate or seeking revenge in moments of anger. CMS–25 was an angry youth. The sight of guns made him think of "killing people." "Killing people. I wish I had a gun. . . . Kill the people I hated. . . . People make fun of me because of my sexual orientation. They make fun of me because of who I am. They make fun of me, of other things, and I hate them for that. So I'd rather kill them then put up with their bullshit" (CMS–25:7–8). When asked what it was about guns that he thought was cool, CMS–25 responded, in a flat tone, "You can kill people with them. If you really wanted to" (CMS–25:16).

CMS–65 is a sixteen-year-old Yaqui gang member who lives on the Pascua Yaqui reservation. When he looked at the pictures, they made him think of "murder" and "killing people" (CMS–65:13–14). For him, guns are for killing people, not for protection. He explains: "I don't carry around a gun for protection. Like if I'm going to carry around a gun, I'm going to go do something with it. But I don't carry, like, 'Oh. They're going to shoot me.' Like I should pull out my gun too. If they catch me sleeping, like I'm walking by myself and I don't have my gun, and if they want to kill me, they're going to kill me. But I know when I have my gun, that's when I'm going after people. I'm not doing it to defend myself. I'm doing it because I want to kill somebody else. I want to shoot somebody else" (CMS–65:19).

Belonging

For other youths, guns are associated with being a part of something, with belonging—being a gang member, or having friends, or covering for others. Five youths spoke about guns in this manner. CMS–21 is a good example. He is a fourteen-year-old Mexican-American youth who is a ward of the state. He talked a lot about guns, but he never owned his own. Instead, he held guns for other people, mostly for his home gang members. Once he held a Desert Eagle for a friend for three months. "He gave it to me," he explains. "Just told me to hold it. I never really had a gun of mines. People just told me to hold them. . . . Like they had bodies on it or something. They'll be like, 'Hold this shit. Hide this shit.' Good enough" (CMS–21:9). And so he did; he held guns for three peers. Many times, it was just for a day, or even for just an hour—if they were on the run. "I used to hold probably like, maybe . . . for only three people. Only three different people. But the, I would hold different guns. . . . I would go out in like the desert. . . . And kind of like bury it under some bushes. I would never bring it to my house though, cause of the fact that my mom would probably throw it out or call the cops or something" (CMS–21:22).

CMS–66, an Anglo youth, talks about guns in a similar way. Carrying a gun—and carrying *someone's* gun in particular—means being a part of a group. It means having a bond, being close, sharing something important. CMS–66 was given his gun by a mentor of sorts. "It was given to me by an older friend of mine," he explains. "'Hey, if you need this, have this, in case anything happens,' cause I hung around with really the wrong crowd. They were really heavy hitters in the drug community. 'So if you hang around with us, you just might need this, so take this. But be careful with it, don't play around with it'" (CMS–66:6). The giving of the gun was part of becoming a member of the group.

Showing Off, Suicide, and Tools

For some of the youths, guns are associated primarily with showing off. CMS–6, a seventeen-year-old who likes guns a lot, carried a .25-caliber semiautomatic pistol "just to try to show off with it. You know 'I got a gun,' and stuff" (CMS–6:9). "I just try to show off," he explains, "cuz like a lot of kids, I don't know, had guns, and you know, it's just like, yeah, it's tight, you got a gun, you know" (CMS–6:13). CMS–54 carried a gun simply to look cool. "To look harder, or to look like all the, you know, someone mean and stuff you know" (CMS–54:23). CMS–21, a fourteen-year-old youth, brought a .22 pistol to school just to impress his school friend and to prove to him that he actually had the gun (CMS–21:23). In all, six of the youths admitted that they associate their own gun carrying with trying to impress other people and looking cool; two of the youths immediately spoke about showing guns off.

For others, the pictures of guns immediately trigger memories of friends who may have committed suicide or even of times when they thought of committing suicide themselves. CMS–40 was one of those youths. He had stolen a car and found a 9-mm in the car. He kept it overnight and was contemplating committing suicide. He eventually returned the gun to its owner the next day—he had stolen the car from someone he knew. But he was marked by the experience of almost committing suicide. For him, guns trigger thoughts of suicide (CMS–40:5). Several others, when presented with the pictures of guns, immediately thought of friends who had committed suicide. A seventeen-year-old European-American recalls, "My friend killed himself with a 12-gauge. . . . It was when we were walking in the door, he shot himself. Couldn't stop him" (CMS–8:7).

Finally, for one youth, guns are just a "tool." This youth, CMS–17, spent a lot of time target shooting with his father and had been around guns all his life. For him, guns are "a tool": a tool "for life. For hunting. It's just that you see everyday tools and that's why we have it here with us. . . . It's your protection, it's a tool for you to go out hunting to survive with. . . . I put it in a category with a sledgehammer, crowbar . . . a grinder, and stuff" (CMS–17:9).

Registers in the Language of Guns

To practically all the youths at Catalina, guns have not one but multiple primary associations, and it is precisely the relationship between these associations that helps give them their meaning. Using correspondence analysis, I explored the relations between meanings in order to decipher which ones go together (or not) and to investigate how this changes in different contexts, such as gun carrying or gang membership. What I discovered is that the youths speak in three distinct registers—that there are, in effect, three different clusters of related ways of talking about guns.

In the first register, the Catalina youths associate guns with the need for protection and the desire to live a risky, dangerous, active life. I call this the "action-protection" cluster. In this register, youths talk about the power of having or brandishing a gun, of the risk of dying in a gun fight, of the possibility of going to jail. These associations are tinged with desire and a deep attraction to guns and are linked by the "action" motif. Here guns are perceived as dangerous, yet attractive, necessary for aggressive, confrontational protection, powerful and power giving. Despite the fact that—or perhaps because—guns are perceived as instruments of death, the youths value them for their power, for their ability to control their immediate environment. Guns are attractive because they confer control: "If somebody is doing something I don't like and I point a gun at them, they'll stop," one youth explains (CMS–4:17). Guns mean being able to get what you want, to do as you please. In this sense, the different symbolic associations in the action-protection cluster help give meaning to each other. The very idea of attraction is linked to the danger of guns. It is the action, the danger, the death—the risk of being caught and sent to jail—that makes guns attractive and powerful in this first cluster of meaning.

A second register connects importantly two associations: commodity and dislike. I refer to this as the "commodity-dislike" register. The close relation of the two associations, again, helps to give them context. Viewing guns as a commodity is more often associated with disliking guns than with attraction to guns. This is reflected well in the comments of one seventeen-year-old Mexican-American youth. "I don't like them," he volunteered. "They take a life. Why you gonna be taking a life for? Ain't no good." But he had guns. Why? "I just have guns to sell them. Make some money off them. That's actually what they're for. . . . I sold them, just buy me my clothes or buys some jewelry or something. . . . Just like, Guess clothes, Tommy Hillfiger, and then jewelry . . . hats, glasses, stuff like that" (CMS-48:8). The Catalina interviews reveal a close above-average association between disliking guns and wanting them for their exchange value. This suggests an intriguing feature about how some of these youths think about gun possession—namely in an entrepreneurial, free-market way. It may be, in fact, that it is precisely because they are not enamored of guns that they are willing to part with them and sell them. Or it may be that the commodification renders them less attractive. In either event, the emotion of dislike is closely associated with the political economy of the gun.

A third register connects the idea of guns as recreational devices with the feeling of needing to "respect" guns, as well as conceptions of guns as tools for self-defense or for suicide. This cluster suggests an association between using a gun for hunting, target practice, or personal self-defense and treating guns with respect. I refer to this as the "recreation-respect" register. This association is reflected in individual comments, like that of a seventeen-year-old European-American youth who was brought up with guns and enjoyed target practice with his family: "I respect them," he emphasized, referring to guns. "I might carry one. But I won't go around telling everyone, yeah, I got a gun. Let's go do something. Let's go shoot in the desert. Yeah, I can shoot better than you. Yeah, I'm a sharp shooter, yeah I can do this, I can shoot thirty yards away and still hit dead center. I don't brag about that. I know I could do it, that's the end of it" (CMS–17:28).

These three registers help organize the language of guns among the male youths at Catalina, and they are related in fascinating ways to different youth contexts. One of the more dramatic findings from my research is that the three registers line up neatly along gun-carrying status: youths who carry guns frequently or constantly tend to talk about guns in the action-protection register; youths who carry guns less frequently tend to talk about guns in the recreation-respect register; and youths who do not carry guns, or carry them even less frequently, tend to speak about guns in the commodity-respect register. The fact that youths view guns as dangerous *and* attractive coincides with higher rates of carrying. It suggests that the elements of danger and death may be a positive attraction and an important element in gun carrying. Concerns about danger could hypothetically have been associated with less carrying, but, among these youths at the Catalina Mountain School, the danger of guns is more closely associated with gun possession. They go together. They give meaning to each other. They do not necessarily *cause* each other; it is not that danger and attraction cause gun carrying—or, for that matter, that gun carrying causes youths to claim that guns are dangerous and attractive. Rather, their relation helps us interpret the different associations.

In contrast, the registers line up somewhat differently in the gang context. Although the action-protection cluster is more highly associated with gang membership—with actually being a gang member—the recreation-respect cluster is more closely associated with having no ties to a gang. Here, the commodity-dislike cluster takes the middle ground and is more highly associated with having friends in a gang, though not with personally being a gang member. In other words, whereas commodity-dislike was more highly associated with the lowest gun-carrying status, in the gang context it is associated with a middle position—having friends in gangs. This might reflect the fact that gangs are often a source of guns and a venue for selling guns, which may explain why youths who have friends in gangs may be more involved in gun transactions. Again, the relationship of the primary associations in context helps us interpret their meaning.

The Passions of Guns

Equally important, the Catalina interviews reveal multiple and rich symbolic dimensions to guns and gun carrying—important sensual, moral, and political-economic dimensions. Guns trigger deep emotions and visceral reactions among these youths. To begin with, carrying a gun has a strong sensual dimension for most of the youths. The very sight of the handguns inspires a deep sense of awe and desire in at least half of them and equally visceral negative reactions in many others. As a seventeen-year-old tried to explain, "Everybody likes guns these days, dude. Hell, yeah. They're exciting. I mean, what the hell. You feel powerful when you have a gun. You get respect" (CMS–62:11).

It is difficult for me to express in words the richness of emotions that the pictures of guns evoked in my informants. The moaning and slight laughter, the awe, the lust in so many youths reflect a deep pleasure, almost of the same magnitude and somehow connected to a sexual drive. CMS–10, a seventeen-year-old Mexican-American gang member, recounted his experience with his favorite guns in these subliminal terms: "I had me two baby 9s. I fell in love with those. They look beautiful to me. They were chrome, like perfect size, they had some power to them. I was like damn, I really don't use them because I don't want to get them burned. Somebody's body to it. . . . I don't really use those. Those just like, I'm gonna keep those for a long time. . . . They're like tight. They're just all chrome" (CMS–10:35).

The intensity of the attraction, in some cases, is simply remarkable. As a sixteen-year-old Yaqui youth tried to make me understand, "I like guns. I like 'em. It just gives you a rush. Gives me a rush" (CMS–65:22). Similarly, the intensity and the sexuality of the opposition to guns, for those who are repelled by guns, is striking. To these few, guns are "pussy shit" (CMS–4:16); they're for "pussies" and "wimps" (CMS–2:6). Real men do not need guns, because real men scrap with their hands.

At the same time, carrying a gun has a strong moral dimension for many youths. Most of the youths associate guns with protection, and many of them feel morally self-righteous about carrying a gun—entitled in the much the same way that adults speak of their own right to carry arms in self-defense. A Mexican gang member raised in L.A. explains in indignant terms that when he and his gang peers are carrying guns for protection, they wouldn't even think of not using them. "We don't choose not to [use guns] because it's either our life or their life" (CMS–10:23). In other cases, youths invoke notions of "enemies" and moral conceptions of warfare. Guns, for them, are about getting back, seeking revenge in gang rivalries. Recall the Yaqui youth gang member who explained: "I know when I have my gun, that's when I'm going after people. I'm not doing it to defend myself. I'm doing it because I want to kill somebody else. I want to shoot somebody else" (CMS–65:19).

In addition, guns have a political-economic dimension. To many youths, handguns represent a commodity to be traded or sold for cash or drugs. Guns are their way of participating in our market economy. "Sell those and party and buy things, you know . . . stereos, gold, help my family out, rent hotels, buy all kinds of beer, get all faded, live the fast life. Party hardy, all kinds of drugs, coke, cook all kinds of crack, sell it, too, you know" (CMS–14:7). "That's what I had guns for," another youth explains. "I sold them all the time. I only got caught with one. And that was the one" (CMS–31:14).

From this perspective, there are interesting and provocative parallels between adjudicated youth culture and late-modern capitalist entrepreneurship. Many of the Catalina youths perceived themselves as entrepreneurs—independent, self-motivated, market driven, and street savvy. Like the start-up or venture capitalist, many of these youths had a robust sense of individual responsibility and self-sufficiency. When asked whether they had a role model, many responded that they were their own model. "I am my own role model," one sixteen-year-old youth explained. "I look up to my own self, my own accomplishments" (CMS–3:12). "I look to myself," explained another (CMS–17:29). Or, as yet another explained, "[I'm] making my own way up" (CMS–54:7). CMS–13, a black youth, says: "I'm my own role model. . . . I can't really be nobody's follower. I'm my own person, you know" (CMS–13:9). Many of the Catalina youths want to be fully responsible for themselves and their own success. They have a strong desire for material wealth—for clothes, drugs, and cars. They have a fine sense for making money, for trading and bartering guns for drugs or cash or other pleasures. They, too, want to make it on their own. And guns represent that special commodity that allows them to become self-reliant, to become entrepreneurs.

Guns are, in these multiple ways, deeply fascinating objects of desire to the male youths detained at the Catalina Mountain School. They hold a surprisingly powerful grip over these youths. They generate deep passion. They are seductively dangerous.

NOTES

The quotation in the title of the essay is from an interview of a seventeen-year-old Tucson male incarcerated youth who recounted a conversation about robbing another youth (CMS–16:50). Special thanks to Ronald Breiger, Ted Gerber, and Calvin Morrill for their insights and guidance regarding the research; to two exceptional graduate students at the University of Arizona, Timothy Jafek and Craig LaChance, for their assistance with the research; and to the participants at the University of Arizona Conference on Guns, Crime, and Punishment in America. This essay should be read in conjunction with another essay, "Measured Interpretation: Introducing the Method of Correspondence Analysis to Legal Studies," *University of Illinois Law Review* (forthcoming 2002).

1. Seventeen-year-old Tucson male incarcerated youth recounting a gun incident (CMS–8:29).

2. These rates are consistent with existing research. See Bernard E. Harcourt, Introduction of this volume.

3. For a detailed exposition of the methodology employed in this research, see Harcourt, *Measured Interpretation.*

4. This, too, is highly consistent with other research on juvenile gun possession. In their book *In the Line of Fire: Youths, Guns, and Violence in Urban America* (New York: A. de Gruyter, 1995), Joseph F. Sheley and James D. Wright report that their respondents' desire to arm themselves is motivated primarily by a perceived need for self-protection (64–65, 67, 115). Similarly, in the Ash study conducted in Atlanta, Georgia, forty-seven, or approximately 89 percent, of the fifty-three juvenile offenders who had carried guns responded that the most important reason to carry a gun was "for protection." See Peter Ash et al., "Gun Acquisition and Use by Juvenile Offenders," *Journal of the American Medical Association* 275:22 (1996): 1755, 1757 n. 5 and 14.

B. The Second Amendment

Chapter 5

The Historians' Counterattack

Some Reflections on the Historiography of the Second Amendment

Sanford Levinson

New things are constantly being created in the world. Inevitably, at least if we are historically oriented, we are curious about what combination of individual and social forces accounted for the creation of these respective objects. We may be interested in why they came forth at the time they did and not earlier (or later). To what extent can their creation be imputed to individual creators? What ideas had to be in the air in order to make the conceptions not only thinkable by gifted creators but, just as important, accepted by a complicated network of associates who would translate what could otherwise have been only intellectual daydreams into reality? What material preconditions were necessary for the events to take place? How did initial audiences respond to the objects in question? And so on. Inevitably, a concatenation of answers (and explanations) will be offered.

In this essay, I am concerned with the debates surrounding a very particular cultural object, the Second Amendment to the United States Constitution: "A well regulated Militia, being necessary to the security of a free State, the right of the people to keep and bear Arms shall not be infringed." In 1989, I published an article[1] whose main theme was that "mainstream" constitutional analysts had quite scandalously avoided recognizing the existence in the Constitution of that strange patch of text. The situation is now quite different. Many important articles and books have appeared in the ensuing decade. And Laurence Tribe's "announcement," in the new edition of his magisterial treatise on constitutional law, that he regarded it as "impossible to deny that some right to bear arms is among the rights of American citizens" was treated as a major event justifying a full-scale article in the Sunday *New York Times* "News of the Week in Review."[2]

In *The Embarrassing Second Amendment,* I offered some quite tentative suggestions—perhaps "hypotheses" would be a better word—as to how one might approach the amendment as an historical artifact. On the basis of work of other scholars, I suggested, for example, that one might well place it within the context of so-called Republican ideology, including both its opposition to standing armies and its emphasis on "independent yeomen, armed and embodied in a militia," who are "a popular government's best protection against its enemies, whether they be aggressive foreign monarchs or scheming demagogues within the nation itself."[3] And I suggested, as well, that one should grasp the extent to which American political thought is importantly mistrustful of the organized political state, as opposed to the Germanic insistence by Max Weber that the state must monopolize the use of violence.[4]

In no way was I offering an argument as to how the amendment should be interpreted in our own time.[5] My primary purpose was to encourage a long overdue conversation with those who *did* take the Second Amendment seriously. One reason for doing this was simply that the amendment raised intellectually challenging problems. But another, I must confess, was more politically motivated. I believe that liberal Democrats have unwisely "overinvested" in supporting basically symbolic antigun legislation—"symbolic" because, as suggested by a variety of other articles in this volume, there is no serious reason to believe that most suggested legislation will have significant consequences with regard to reducing the amount of violence connected with the widespread availability of firearms. I fear that this has contributed to the unfortunate alienation from the Democratic Party of many working-class gun owners who are ill served by Republicans on any issue other than protection of gun rights. Given my own politics, I personally lament this alienation, but it is obvious that this is not remotely a "constitutional" argument.

All of this being said, I remain interested in what might be termed the *production* of the Second Amendment in 1789 and the set of associations linked throughout the years following with that particular patch of text. How do we explain its being in the Constitution—or, at least, the Bill of Rights—in the first place? Why did Congress propose it, and what accounted for its ratification? What was the initial understanding of the first audience that gazed upon the new amendment, and how has that understanding—or, more likely, set of understandings, which may or may not have been in tension with one another—changed over time, particularly with regard to the supporters of the Fourteenth Amendment in 1868? Even if one reasonably believes that the answers to these questions carry no normative thrust, they still should interest anyone concerned with American constitutional development.

One set of answers to these questions has been offered by a group of lawyers who have, I believe unwisely, claimed that their views represent a "consensus"[6] or even the legal equivalent to the "standard model" that structures the contemporary understanding of particle physics.[7] One description of the Standard Model is offered by Professor Michael Bellesiles: "The people retain the individual right to bear arms as an implicit threat to revolution. In good times, that threat keeps the government in line; in bad, when the government oversteps its bounds, the people may rise up and overthrow the government."[8] It is clear that nothing has stirred the ire of professional historians more than the suggestion that an important historical controversy has basically been "settled," as is suggested by the term "Standard Model." Bellesiles's essay, for example, appeared in a symposium of four articles recently published by distinguished historians[9] in *Constitutional Commentary*,[10] all of which attack the claims of "consensus" and the existence of a "standard model." A similarly critical symposium was published first in the *Chicago-Kent Law Review* and then, in a shortened version edited by Carl Bogus, as *The Second Amendment in Law and History*.

The Ohio State University historian Saul Cornell suggests that "partisans [of the Standard Model] . . . have not only read constitutional texts in an anachronistic fashion, but have also ignored important historical sources vital to understanding what Federalists and anti-Federalists might have meant by the right to bear arms."[11] The University of Oklahoma professor Robert E. Shalhope, the author of an important article that taught many of us to pay due heed to the civic republican origins of the defense of the right to bear arms,[12] wrote that many of his ostensible admirers have "displayed little if any interest in the political culture that spawned the Second Amendment; those that did displayed an appalling ignorance of this intellectual climate. The result was, of course, an incredibly anachronistic presentation of the Second Amendment."[13] Jack N. Rakove, the leading historian of James Madison and one of the leading historians of the entire early National period, agrees, writing that some of the "campaigners" in behalf of what might be termed a "strong" Second Amendment are "raiders who know what they are looking for, and having found it, they care little about collateral damage to the surrounding countryside that historians better know as context."[14]

It is clear that I have a personal, and not only an intellectual, interest in this recent body of critical literature.[15] What follows is not, however, meant to serve even as a full-scale response, let alone a "refutation" of this recent body of scholarship. Instead, I want to treat it as an invitation to further conversation. The "anti-Standard Modelers" are altogether correct in criticizing moves toward premature closure in what is obviously an extremely complex debate; but this also means that it would be equally mistaken to treat the case as closed in the opposite direction, so that the conclusion is that one should reject, without further ado, the arguments made by Reynolds, Barnett, and others, including myself. What follows, then, is an assessment of the logic of various arguments presented in recent critical literature and suggestions as to questions that future participants in the debates might profitably ask.

I. Can We Resolve the Dialectical Tension between Consensus and Fragmentation?

First, a bit of autobiography. I entered graduate school in the heyday of the so-called consensus approach to American history. By the time I left graduate school, in 1968, "consensus history" was one of the casualties of the Civil Rights movement and the Vietnam War, as increased emphasis was placed on the presence of conflicting traditions of American thought. Moreover, as American historians turned to the often closely textured study of social groups, it became increasingly difficult to credit *any* generalizations about the American past. Not only were farmers different from urban dwellers, but Scotch-Irish farmers in the South were also considerably different from Scandinavian farmers in the North, and, indeed, one would be well advised to distinguish between Swedes and Norwegians or German Catholics and Lutherans. And so on. By the time I embarked on my own scholarly career, I was thoroughly imbued with the view that any seeming "consensus" was the result of a more or less authoritarian social process that covered up (I use these political metaphors advisedly) the presence of strongly conflicting understandings of the American past (and present).

I thus have little hesitation in accepting the attacks of both Cornell and Rakove on the notion that American thought of the eighteenth century was unified in its view of firearms, any more than it was unified, say, in its view of the rightful status of the North American British colonies vis-à-vis the Parliament in London. With regard to the linkage of the right to bear arms and republican politics, Cornell offers John Adams's devastating observation that "[t]here is not a more unintelligible word in the English language than republicanism."[16] To understand any given use of a word, one must place it in a highly particularized context, and different contexts generate quite different meanings. Thus, says Cornell, even within Pennsylvania, there was no ascertainable consensus as to what was meant by the right to bear arms. "[T]he historical evidence suggests that there was considerable conflict over how to understand this right."[17] Indeed, the conflict was not simply between Federalists and anti-Federalists; rather, says Cornell, "[w]hen the views of Pennsylvania Anti-Federalists are examined in historical context,"[18] they gainsay the presence of consensus even within this subset of presumably ideologically mated Pennsylvanians.

Cornell is playing what I am sometimes tempted to describe as the "nominalist card," by which any and all generalizations about the past (or, for that matter, the present) are subjected to refutation by pointing to contrary examples. As should already be clear, I am quite sympathetic to playing this card, insofar as my tendency is to emphasize conflict and even fragmentation as against consensus. The problem with this play, however, is that it tends to make one wary of any generalization at all. At best, one might be able to establish statistical tendencies, but even those arguments are subject to well-known methodological debates.

One of the things we must struggle with, then, is whether Cornell and Rakove are simply challenging the "overreaching" of adherents of "the Standard Model," a challenge that I can readily sympathize with, or instead asserting the presence of a contrary "Standard Model" that establishes "the definitive truth" of the matter. I am quite willing to believe the former; they have not yet convinced me of the latter, and I am not sure they could without violating their own emphasis on the complexities of the American past.

But my point is more than simply philosophical. I doubt that anyone could believe that sufficient scholarly work has been done on the Second Amendment to justify unequivocal statements about its origins. In terms of scholarly treatment, I suspect that we are roughly where the First Amendment was, say, in 1940,[19] when Zechariah Chafee's (now discredited)[20] volume, which of course was written as well to advocate a particular contemporary stance toward the amendment, was the standard treatment of the history and meaning of freedom of speech and the press. Six decades of subsequent scholarship have scarcely left us with a consensus as to either history *or* doctrine, partly, of course, because of the ideological valence attached to one or another position regarding the freedom to be given to spewers of hate speech, pornographers, advocates of political assassination, and the like, not to mention the use of the First Amendment to shield certain processes of campaign finance. Present scholarship about the Second Amendment could not possibly satisfy either the professional historian or anyone who truly cares about the role that firearms should play in contemporary society.

II. What Is the Relationship between Ideas and Material Reality?

Perhaps at the heart of the debate is an understanding of the ideology or set of interpretive constructs that underlay those who viewed the Constitution of 1787 as deficient insofar as it did not adequately protect some kind of right to keep and bear arms. As already suggested, I (and others) have emphasized the importance of civic republicanism traceable to Machiavelli and transmitted to the British colonies in America via theorists like James Harrington. This ideology almost naturally generates an image of sturdy yeomen ever ready (and able) to pick up their guns in defense of their political liberties against tyrants foreign or domestic. Indeed, every well-socialized American does carry this image around in his or her head: It is the statue of the Minuteman in Lexington, Massachusetts, celebrating, in Ralph Waldo

Emerson's words, the "poor farmers who came up that day [in April 1775] to defend their native soil" against the British interlopers.[21] This citizen-militia, obviously organized and operating against the wishes of the (legitimate) British-controlled government of Massachusetts, is viewed by many as the paradigm image of America, and the Revolution is imagined as well as the triumph of citizen-soldiers against the professional military of the British and their hired Hessians.

Garry Wills[22] and, more substantially, Michael Bellesiles have delivered withering attacks on this image.[23] In my own defense, I note that *The Embarrassing Second Amendment* included a footnote pointing out that Edmund Morgan, whom I had cited for the importance of Harringtonian ideology, had argued "that the armed yeomanry was neither effective as a fighting force nor particularly protective of popular liberty," but "that," I added, "is another matter."[24] Rakove quotes my footnote about Morgan's skepticism about the importance of armed yeomen, including a sentence that I did not quote earlier: "For our purposes, the ideological perceptions are surely more important than the 'reality' accompanying them."[25] Rakove responds as follows:

> It may well be true that all our constructions of reality (whose existence I, for one, do not doubt) are shaped by ideology, but what is at issue here is, I believe, a more fundamental problem that has deeper echoes in the historiography of the Revolutionary era more generally. No historian would deny that the legacy of radical Whig ideology was a major element in American political thinking, both in 1776 and in 1787. Yet by the latter date, experience (whose existence Levinson seems to posit as "reality") had called into question many of the propositions that were stock elements of that ideology; and the framers of the Constitution, as well as the Federalist majority who proposed the Second Amendment, represented that portion of American political thinking who were now less beholden to the received wisdom. That is, they were more inclined to test the ideological inheritance against the lessons of recent experience. Far from this being, in Levinson's words, "another matter," it lies at the heart of the question.[26]

In his own contribution to the *William and Mary Quarterly* symposium on Bellesiles's book, Rakove explicitly contrasts two approaches to the understanding of legal events (such as the addition of the Second Amendment to the Constitution's text). One is the focus on "structure[s] of belief, as articulated in legislative in public debate."[27] Those who focus on such structures are inclined to dismiss as irrelevant the evidence about possession of firearms, their likely (in)accuracy, and the general competence of ostensible militias. Instead, says Rakove, "I am partial to the implications of Bellesiles's behaviorism," which gives great emphasis to "what I like to call 'lessons of experience,' or inferences and attitudes that participants might have drawn and derived from their own involvement in events."[28] Rakove notes, altogether accurately, I believe, that most of the legal academics who have written on the Second Amendment tend to focus on the former, in part because it involves the kind of research that most (of us) are more comfortable with.

Rakove's general argument repays close analysis. I certainly agree that there is a complex dialectical relationship between "experience" and the ideological pictures that people carry in their heads, though, of course, it is these pictures that help to define an "experience" in the first place. I doubt that Rakove is a naïve empiricist who believes that facts come to observers unmediated by theories or ideologies that provide a framework by which to identify and assess them. We need only draw on our own political lives to appreciate how complicated is the relationship between "experience"—or a scare-quoted "reality"—and the ideas we posit about our circumstances.

Consider in this context the well-documented decline in crime rates over the past decade.[29] One might first ask how important it is to those who have actually felt the experience of being the victims of criminal violence. Are those of us privileged to have been "experience-free" more inclined to credit the importance of the decline because, as a matter of fact, we were never that concerned about crime in the first place? Or one might ask how many Americans are truly knowledgeable about the actualities of crime rates, given the encouragement by various media practices and opportunistic politicians to believe that reality is more dire than it is. "If it bleeds, it leads," appears to be the motto of all too many television stations and newspapers, whatever the actual decline in the statistical frequency of such events.

And, of course, even those who are aware of these developments may offer strikingly different explanations for their occurrence. Is the cause the deterrence generated by the immense amounts of money that have been poured into building prisons and, concomitantly, confining millions of Americans who would almost certainly not be so confined in other societies? Is one of the major causes, as might be suggested by John Lott, the very ownership of guns by millions of Americans who can therefore more effectively protect themselves against crime (and therefore deter attempts by rational criminals who are aware that a consequence of such attempts might be armed resistance)?[30] Is a cause changes in policing styles, and, if so, *which* styles—aggressive, in-your-face policing or a more community-oriented policing?[31] Is a major cause simply changes in demographics, because there were fewer persons from the youthful age cohorts most likely to commit crime? To some extent, there are "facts" (once again, I use the dreaded "scare quotes") about these matters, but, obviously, there is also present the tendency to process any such "facts" through overarching ideologies that make some suggestions about what explanation is more palatable than others.

In any event, I have no difficulty agreeing with Rakove that significant changes occurred within the minds of many Americans between 1776 and 1789 (the date the Second Amendment was proposed), including, perhaps, the mind of James Madison. Any "full" history of the amendment should certainly be attentive to these changes, and Rakove effectively criticizes many previous writers, including myself, for being less attentive to them than we might have been. That being said, he himself admits that radical Whig thought remained part of the American "legacy," and it would surely be astonishing if many Americans had not interpreted the events of the Revolution and thereafter in congruence with that ideology. I am not confident that we know enough about how a full range of Americans of the time thought about guns to be able to say with confidence what the "dominant" position was.

III. Who "Proposed" the Second Amendment? (And Is James Madison a 'Trickster' Who Gulled an Easily Fooled American Public?)

Rakove emphasizes that it was "the Federalist majority who proposed the Second Amendment."[32] This refers, presumably, to the fact that the proponents of the Constitution dominated the First Congress. We should pay far more attention to their views than to those articulated outside the halls of Congress by anti-Federalists and others, who had, after all, missed the train carrying history forward.

As a literal matter, it is obviously true that "the Federalist majority" proposed the amendment and that, moreover, James Madison played a particularly important role in the proceedings of the First Congress that considered and then proposed what we today know as the Bill of Rights. That being said, one cannot possibly overlook the fact that this majority, including Madison, probably would never have felt any need to propose any such amendments had that not in effect been the price of gaining assent from moderate anti-Federalists and others who did not share the enthusiasm of James Wilson or the authors of the *Federalist* for an unamended Constitution. As Paul Finkelman has demonstrated,[33] Madison's support for a Bill of Rights is explicable far more as the response to the political realities of Virginia, including, of course, the role played by anti-Federalists, than as a fundamental change of position as to the desirability of such amendments.

Consider in this context various proposals issued by state conventions as a result of the debates over ratification:

New Hampshire, June 21, 1788:

> Congress shall never disarm any Citizen unless such as are or have been in Actual Rebellion.[34]

New York, July 26, 1788:

> That the People have a right to keep and bear Arms; that a well regulated Militia, including the body of the People *capable of bearing Arms,* is the proper, natural and safe defence of a free State.
>
> That the Militia should not be subject to Martial Law except in time of War, Rebellion or Insurrection.
>
> That standing Armies in time of Peace are dangerous to Liberty, and ought not to be kept up, except in Cases of necessity; and that at all times, the Military should be under strict Subordination to the civil Power.[35]

North Carolina, August 1, 1788:

17th. That the people have a right to keep and bear arms; that a well regulated militia composed of the body of the people, trained to arms, is the proper, natural and safe defence of a free state. That standing armies in time of peace are dangerous to Liberty, and therefore ought to be avoided, as afar as the circumstances and protection of the community will admit; and that in all cases, the military should be under strict subordination to, and governed by the civil power.

. . .

19th. That any person religiously scrupulous of bearing arms ought to be exempted upon payment of an equivalent to employ another to bear arms in his stead.[36]

Or, from Madison's own state of Virginia, June 27, 1788:

Seventeenth, That the people have a right to keep and bear arms; that a well regulated Militia composed of the body of the people trained to arms is the proper, natural and safe defence of a free State. That standing armies in time of peace are dangerous to liberty, and therefore ought to be avoided, as far as the circumstances and protection of the Community will admit; and that in all cases the military should be under strict subordination to and governed by the Civil power.[37]

There are, of course, also the well-known "minority" resolutions, the most famous, or notorious, probably being that of the Pennsylvania Minority, on December 12, 1787:

7. That the people have a right to bear arms for the defense of themselves and their own state, or the United States, or for the purpose of killing game; and no law shall be passed for disarming the people or any of them, unless for crimes committed, or real danger of public injury from individuals; and as standing armies in the time of peace are dangerous to liberty, they ought not to be kept up; and that the military shall be kept under strict subordination to and governed by the civil power.[38]

It is, admittedly, difficult to extract a single meaning from these various proposals. What seems clearest is that most have something to do with fears of the standing army that is in fact authorized by Article I, § 8, clause 12, of the Constitution and the linked fear that leaders of the new, untried, and somewhat fearsome national government might try to take advantage of the linked power, in clause 16, to "provide for organizing, arming, and disciplining, the Militia. . . ." "Most," of course, does not mean "all," and one sees, especially in the declaration of the Pennsylvania minority, the most vivid articulation of a more individual rights conception, as, arguably, is the case in at least one other state constitution presumably known to Madison.[39]

In any event, Madison and his political allies, including the Federalist majority, believed themselves under political pressures to respond to such concerns, and thus we get the Second Amendment. The universe of interpreters of the amendment can be divided into those who emphasize the "preamble," focusing on the importance of a militia, and those who emphasize instead the more categorically announced right of "the people" to "keep and bear arms." As suggested earlier, one way to defend the latter focus is by placing the amendment within a framework of Anglo-American ideology that emphasized the right of popular revolution, a right, of course, instantiated in the Revolution of 1775.

Rakove, like Garry Wills, rejects the provenance of the populist, revolution-oriented interpretation of the amendment. "[W]hat was under debate," Rakove writes, both at the convention and then in the First Congress with regard to the amendment, "was not the need to protect a right to revolution but a debate about federalism—that is, a debate about the respective competence and authority and the national and state governments."[40] He offers the following summary of his long and complex argument:

> What matters is that the framers, clearly reasoning on the basis of hard-earned experience, saw the militia as an institution that would henceforth be regulated through a combination of national and state legislation firmly anchored in the text of the constitution, rather than some preexisting, preconstitutional understanding. Wherever the exact balance between national and state responsibility would be struck, the militia would always be subject to legislative regulation. When the framers referred to the "states" in these debates, they were always alluding to their governments, not the people at large. The "authority of training the militia according to the discipline prescribed by Congress" that the Constitution reserved to the states was a power and responsibility of the state governments to implement national law.[41]

Even if one accepts this view, *arguendo,* what precisely follows for the interpretation of the amendment? For example, does the national government retain, even after the Second Amendment, a plenary right, arguably granted by clause 16, to exercise effective dominance over state militias, including an all-important limitation of the right to keep and bear arms only to those deemed fit by Congress to do so? As I read Garry Wills's argument, presented initially in an influential essay in the *New York Review of Books,*[42] the answer is basically yes, which means, substantially, that the amendment is without genuine semantic or legal bite. Wills's reading avowedly turns Madison into a kind of "trickster," an illusionist who, seeming to respond to the concerns of those who insisted on the Second Amendment, actually provided them nothing. One thinks of Justice Jackson's suggestion that we should refrain from interpreting "our heritage of constitutional privileges and immunities [as] only a promise to the ear to be broken to the hope, a teasing illusion like a munificent bequest in a pauper's will."[43] I am not certain about Rakove's reading of Madison on this point, though it is clear that Rakove's version of his will presents Madison, even if not as a teasing pauper, then most certainly giving to the Pennsylvania minority far less than they had hoped for.

Still, even if we accept the proposition that the amendment is basically about control of militias, might it not be the case that the initial audience (outside Congress) for the amendment reasonably understood it as assigning to the states the exclusive authority to determine *who* is to be viewed as potentially within the militia and, concomitantly, who is to have a protected right to bear arms, in order, among other things, to make sure that the states could maintain a significant state militia as a potential counterweight to the dreaded standing army? The point is that one might agree with Rakove that the "Framers' intent" was exactly what he says it is. He is surely a more authoritative historian than I am, and I have no particular reason to challenge his reconstruction of the legislative history of the amendment. But one can also speak of "audience understanding," which may, of course, be quite different from "Framers' intent," not least because of the ambiguities contained within the text of the amendment. And, of course, all of the attention in the world on the intricacies of legislative argument is basically irrelevant to trying to understand what the "naïve reader," almost certainly unfamiliar with these arguments, would make (and did make) of the language actually sent to the states for ratification.

In any event, most opponents of "strong" readings of the Second Amendment place great emphasis on the importance of the "preamble" and its stress on "well-regulated" militias, so one might ordinarily expect some embrace of this reading, which places exclusive power in the states over the crucial issues of membership and control of the conditions of access to firearms themselves. The problem, from a contemporary perspective, of course, is that this seemingly acknowledges, at least as a matter of original understanding, far too strong a limit on national power. It would, for example, make questionable attempts by the national government to ban possession of any weapon that is legal in the possessor's state, though, of course, Congress at the very least could, given contemporary understandings of the Commerce Clause, ban the interstate shipment of guns.

IV. Is State History Relevant to Understanding the Second Amendment?

This last point leads us quite naturally into Saul Cornell's important article, which concentrates on the history of arms control in colonial and postrevolutionary Pennsylvania. He picks Pennsylvania in part because it appears, on the surface, to have been one of the more "pro-gun" states, as reflected in the declaration noted earlier from its 1776 constitution, which in fact was substantially carried over, in a somewhat rewritten form, in the 1790 constitution to state "[t]hat the right to citizens to bear arms, in defence of themselves and the state, shall not be questioned."[44] These seem to give strong support to the so-called individual rights reading of the Second Amendment, by which individuals retain a strong right to bear arms, as does the claim, by the "Dissent of the Minority," which "attained a semi-official status as the statement of the Anti-Federalist minority of Pennsylvania's ratification convention,"[45] that "the people have a right to bear arms for the defense of themselves and their own state, or the United States, or for the purpose of killing game."[46] Cornell then scores a telling point by noting that even the dissenting minority affirmed the legitimacy of regulation of firearms with regard to those individuals who present a "real danger of public injury,"[47] and he demonstrates as well that Pennsylvania in fact engaged in significant regulation of the people's right to bear arms.

Cornell concentrates on the Test Acts, passed in 1777 and 1778, which prohibited many prerogatives of citizenship, including the right to vote, to hold public office, to serve on juries, and to bear arms, from "persons disaffected to the liberty and independence of this state."[48] Cornell writes that up to 40 percent of Pennsylvania's population was deprived of any right to bear arms. Lest one believe that these were simply rather extreme wartime measures, he views them as exemplifying precisely "a particular republican ethos" that, quoting another historian, Douglas Arnold, "reduce[d] the political community to the 'faithful.'"[49]

If Cornell is to be refuted, it will be by someone far better trained in historical research than I am. What I *can* ask, as both lawyer and consumer of historical research, is whether the demonstration that states, including the otherwise "progun" Pennsylvania, regulated their citizens shows us anything about likely national powers. It certainly does not logically follow that acceptance of state power implies a similar tolerance of national regulation.[50] Nor am I familiar with scholarship demonstrating that Congress in fact attempted to prevent access to firearms of any of its citizens.

Even with regard to state traditions involving regulation of firearms, one wants far more information than we currently have about the actual legislation (and behavior) in the various states. Surely anyone interested in the "contexts" of overall American culture and the various responses to the experience of the time should find the degree of actual regulation to be significant, especially when American states began to feel secure in the actual achievement of independence from Great Britain and less fearful of the presence of "unAmerican" fellow inhabitants who might not be entirely trustworthy.[51] We are, for example, aware of the great sea change that took place with regard to freedom of speech and of the press between 1776 and 1800.[52] We should be sensitive to the possibility that similar events took place with regard to firearms and, comcomitantly, that the "lessons of experience," at the state level, might have been somewhat different from those attributed to some of the Federalists who met in New York in 1789. Consider the implications, for example, of Ohio's 1802 Constitution: "That the people have a right to bear arms for the defence of themselves and the State; and as standing armies, in time of peace, are dangerous to liberty, they shall not be kept up, and that the military shall be kept under strict subordination to the civil power."[53] Or there are the

Alabama Constitution of 1819—"That every citizen has a right to bear arms in defence of himself and the state"[54]—and the 1820 Missouri Constitution, which included the following: "That the people have the right peaceably to assemble for their common good, and to apply to those vested with the powers of government for redress of grievances by petition or remonstrance; and that their right to bear arms in defence of themselves and of the State cannot be questioned."[55] To be sure, one might be tempted to place these latter two constitutions within the narrative that Carl Bogus has suggested, where the right to bear arms is linked with the suppression of slaves,[56] but this scarcely seems to explain Vermont and Ohio. It is, of course, naïve in the extreme to assume that any of the quoted language, without more, tells us much about the actual practices of any of these states. Still, all of this underscores the complexity of organizing a single narrative of the story of guns in America.

V. How Important Is 1787–91 Anyway? What about 1868?

The historians' critique of the "Standard Model" thus argues, in effect that its adherents (including "fellow travelers" like myself) are deficient in our understanding of the complexities and nuances of eighteenth-century thought and politics and that the actual supporters of the Second Amendment in both Congress and, presumably, the ratifying states saw the text at most as a protection of the ability of the state to operate its own militia, which remained subject, of course, to a certain measure of regulation under Article I, § 8, clause 16. The next challenge facing historians, though, is to take account of the fact that all cultural products take on lives of their own, which may go off in quite surprising paths relative to the intentions and understandings of the creators and the initial audience of the text in question. Quite obviously, historians who emphasize the importance of attentiveness to very specific context when interpreting any given piece of language should appreciate the fact that the Second Amendment is highly unlikely to be any more stable in its meaning(s) across time than is any other significant patch of text.

We must be interested, then, in whether post-1791 legal analysis of the "right to keep and bear arms," much of it based on state constitutional provisions rather than the Second Amendment, emphasized its relationship to the militia. As already suggested, this would be quite surprising indeed in those states that did not include any reference to militias in their own constitutional texts. Don Kates writes that "every one of the twenty-two pre-1906 state cases construing a state constitutional right to arms provision, including some provisions that referred to common defense purposes, recognized an individual right to possess at least militia-type arms."[57] And Kates cites four antebellum state cases that "were based upon the second amendment in addition to the state constitutional provision."[58]

It is also well worth looking at another antebellum case, *Dred Scott*, in which the Supreme Court deprived blacks of the very possibility of being citizens of the United States. In the course of his analysis, Chief Justice Taney sets out among the "privileges and immunities of citizens" the right "to keep and carry arms wherever they went."[59] To put it mildly, Taney makes no linkage of this right with participation in a militia. If that were central, then the "problem" posed by black citizens could be taken care of simply by denying them the right to participate in militias, as indeed was the case.[60] Taney seems to view the right as being a far more personal right, one that attaches to all citizens regardless of their membership in an official militia. The right to bear arms has become a "privilege" of United States citizenship, a fundamental right presumptively protected against governmental infringement.[61] And the unthinkability of blacks enjoying that particular constitutional right, which necessarily attaches to the status of citizen, helps to explain why they *cannot* enjoy that status.

Perhaps the best support for this reading comes from Senator Jacob Howard's well-known speech to the Senate upon introducing the text of the Fourteenth Amendment, of which he was a proud sponsor, and its protection of the "privileges or immunities of citizens of the United States."[62] After quoting Justice Bushrod Washington's famous delineation of privileges and immunities in *Corfield v. Coryell*,[63] Howard goes on to say that

> to these should be added the *personal rights* guaranteed and secured by the first eight amendments of the Constitution; such as the freedom of speech and of the press; the right of the people peaceably to assemble and petition the Government for a redress of grievances, a right appertaining to each and all the people; the right to keep and to bear arms. . . .[64]

Akhil Amar identifies no fewer than twelve additional "Reconstruction Republicans" who offered "odes to arms in speeches in the Thirty-ninth Congress."[65] Indeed, any "originalist" analysis of the Second Amendment, at least with regard to limitations on *state* regulation, must rest on the Reconstruction debates and not at all on the debates of 1789–91, given the fact that whatever "incorporation" of the amendment should occur would be the result of the Fourteenth Amendment and, for an originalist, the vision of that amendment held by the Reconstruction framers and ratifiers.[66] By 1866, that vision was a profoundly individualistic one, not least because the advocates of Reconstruction were rightly aware that state governments could no longer necessarily be trusted to engage in acceptably impartial, non-discriminatory regulation, especially where the rights of newly freed former black slaves and their white sympathizers were concerned. For them, the right to bear arms was no theoretical claim; the actual possession of arms was all too necessary to defend themselves against the nascent Ku Klux Klan and other agents of white terror.

Note as well in this context Section 14 of the Freedmen's Bureau Act of 1866, which listed a variety of rights that "shall be secured to and enjoyed by all the citizens of such state or district without respect to race or color, or previous condition of servitude," explicitly "including the constitutional right to bear arms." It would be quite remarkable to interpret this as referring only to a right to have only such access to arms as might be required by membership in a state militia.

Or consider the brave and inspiring federal prosecutor in South Carolina who vigorously attempted to prosecute members of the Klan for depriving local blacks of their Second Amendment right to keep and bear arms. As described by Lou Faulkner Williams in her invaluable study of the Klan trials of 1871–72,

> [District Attorney David] Corbin insisted specifically that the Fourteenth Amendment guaranteed the Second Amendment right to keep and bear arms. The Fourteenth Amendment, he said, "lays the same restrictions upon the States that before lay upon the Congress of the United States." . . . Corbin argued that the right to bear arms did not exist under the common law but was guaranteed by the United States Constitution for the first time in history. Thus the Second Amendment, according to Corbin, was one of the privileges and immunites which the Fourteenth Amendment secured to the citizens against the

state. Because many of the Klan's outrages had focused on taking the guns that had been issued to black militia members, Corbin considered the Second Amendment right vital to the prosecution. "We will never abandon it," he insisted," until we are obliged to." Without their weapons, these men had no way to protect themselves, their homes, or their families from the marauding night riders.[67]

Most readers well know, of course, that such Reconstructionist appeals to the Second Amendment were unsuccessful, both in South Carolina and in the nation at large. Thus, in 1875, the Court in *United States v. Cruikshank* stated that the Second Amendment, to the extent that it protects any right at all, "means no more than that it shall not be infringed by Congress. This is one of the amendments that has no other effect than to restrict the powers of the national government. . . ."[68] There are, of course, a number of ways of analyzing *Cruikshank*. It is certainly congruent with other cases of the time that ruthlessly rejected the view that the Privileges or Immunities Clause of the Fourteenth Amendment was designed at all to place on the states *any* of the restrictions of "the powers of the national government." This was, after all, the position taken in *Pumpelly v. Green Bay Co.*,[69] in which the Court explicitly rejected the view that the new Fourteenth Amendment imposed a duty upon Wisconsin, derived from the Fifth Amendment, to compensate its citizens for taking their property. "[I]t is well settled," said the Court, in what has to be one of the most astonishingly self-confident assertions in the *United States Reports,* "that this is a limitation on the power of the Federal government, and not on the States." The Court blithely ignored evidence that for many framers of the Fourteenth Amendment a specific purpose of the Privileges or Immunities Clause was to apply the Bill of Rights to the States. As Pamela Brandwein has well argued,[70] the United States Supreme Court almost immediately, following the conclusion of the War, adopted de facto the position of the Northern Democrats and so-called moderate Republicans that the legal consequences of the Fourteenth Amendment were in fact quite minimal, keeping basically in place the division of powers between national and state governments that had been present prior to the great conflict.

There is a more ominous explanation: *All* of American constitutional doctrine has been affected, and often warped, by the indelible stains of chattel slavery and the overarching racism that justified the particular American variant of slavery. Just as Taney used the logic that citizenship brought with it the right to bear arms as an implicit reason to deny blacks that status, so it was tempting, following the (relative) universalization of citizenship[71] in the Fourteenth Amendment, to reduce the rights of citizenship in order to prevent blacks succumbing to any temptation to become too "uppity" merely because they were now co-citizens. (And what can make one feel more "uppity" than the right to keep and bear a firearm?) In any event, anyone interested in an originalist analysis of the Second Amendment must learn the lesson that there are in fact (at least) *two* Second Amendments, one proposed and ratified between 1789 and 1791, the other proposed and ratified (under quite unusual circumstances)[72] between 1866 and 1868, and each may teach its own quite distinct lessons.

Conclusion

One should rejoice at the appearance of serious, professional historical scholarship that is grappling with the many profound issues raised by the presence of the mechanisms of violence within the American political and social order.[73] What it establishes is the prematurity of declaring *any* given view of the history of the Second Amendment to be "standard" and beyond serious dispute. There is much to be learned, and, dare one say, much to be surprised about as we delve further into the mysteries of the American past, whatever may be our answer to the entirely separate question of whether we have any duties to maintain the understandings or traditions of that past.

NOTES

This essay was prepared for presentation at the University of Arizona Law School, January 28, 2001. I am grateful to my University of Texas colleague Scot Powe and to my Internet colleagues Randy Barnett, James Lindgren, and Eugene Volokh for their exceedingly helpful responses to an earlier draft of this essay. Needless to say, none should be held liable for the particular views I put forth.

1. See Sanford Levinson, "The Embarrassing Second Amendment," *Yale Law J. 99* (1989): 637.

2. See William Glaberson, "Right to Bear Arms: A Second Look," *New York*

Times, May 30, 1999, Section 4, at 3. Tribe's new views are spelled out in *American Constitutional Law 1* n. 221 (3d ed. 2000): 901–902.

3. See Levinson, at 647, quoting Edmund Morgan, *Inventing the People,* 156. Morgan is discussing the thought of James Harrington, described by Frank Michelman as a "pivotal figure in the history of the 'Atlantic' branch of republicanism that would find its way to America," "The Supreme Court 1985 Term—Foreword: Traces of Self-Government," *Harv. L. Rev. 100* (1986), 4, 39.

4. See ibid. at 650, citing Max Weber, *The Theory of Social and Economic Organization* (T. Parsons ed. 1947), 156.

5. I did note, however, the irony in the fact that many distinguished law professors blithely seemed to assume that an adequate last word on the amendment had been articulated by the otherwise thoroughly egregious Justice James McReynolds in a 1939 case, *United States v. Miller,* 307 U.S. 174 (1939). As my colleague Scot Powe, among other, has detailed, among the other odd features of this case is that it was neither briefed nor argued by the respondent, who was apparently on the lam. See L. A. Powe Jr., "Guns, Words, and Constitutional Interpretation," *Wm. and Mary L. Rev. 38* (1997): 1311, 1327–32. It is also the case that the opinion itself is far more ambiguous than is often assumed. See, e.g., *Yale L. J. 99* at 654–55.

6. See Randy E. Barnett and Don B. Kates, "Under Fire: The New Consensus on the Second Amendment," *Emory L. J. 45* (1996): 1139. I should note that included in this article is a vigorous (and much appreciated) defense of me against an egregious attack on my intellectual integrity in Andrew Herz, "Gun Crazy: Constitutional False Consciousness and Dereliction of Dialogic Responsibility," *B. U. L. Rev. 75* (1995): 57.

7. See Glenn Harlan Reynolds, "A Critical Guide to the Second Amendment," *Tenn. L. Rev. 62* (1995): 461, 461–71.

8. See Michael Bellesiles, "Suicide Pact: New Readings of the Second Amendment," *Constitutional Commentary 16* (1999): 247–62, 250 (hereafter "Suicide Pact"). Although perhaps I should be flattered to be labeled by Professor Bellesiles as "one of the leading voices in favor of the Standard Model" (ibid. at 259), I must note that I have never once used the term in any of my own scholarship and that I am uncomfortable with the term inasmuch as I find it much too assertive about the present state of our knowledge about what remains one of the more obscure aspects of our constitutional past.

9. Unfortunately, it has become necessary, with regard to describing Professor Bellesiles as "distinguished," to note that there is currently raging a controversy about the integrity of some of the research underlying his famous book *Arming America: The Origins of America's Gun Culture* (New York: Knopf, 2000). See, e.g., "Forum: Historians and Guns," *William and Mary Q. 59,* 3d Series (2002): 203, featuring essays by Jack Rakove, Ira D. Gruber, Gloria Main, and Randolph Roth, with a reply by Bellesiles. Northwestern law professor

James Lindgren, who is currently pursuing a Ph.D. in sociology with a concentration in social statistics at the University of Chicago, has written two devastating reviews of Bellesiles's book. See James Lindgren, "Fall from Grace: *Arming America* and the Bellesiles Scandal," *Yale L. J. 111* (2002): 2195–2249; James Lindgren and Justin L. Heather, "Counting Guns in Early America," *William and Mary L. Rev. 43* (2002): 1777–1842. There can simply be no doubt that Bellesiles is a totally unreliable source with regard to gun ownership in America in the eighteenth century.

10. Saul Cornell, "Commonplace or Anachronism: The Standard Model, the Second Amendment, and the Problem of History in Contemporary Constitutional Theory," *Constitutional Commentary 16* (1999): 221–46 (hereafter "Cornell"); Michael Bellesiles, *Suicide Pact*; Don Higginbotham, "The Second Amendment in Historical Context," *Constitutional Commentary 16* (1999): 263–68; and Robert E. Shalhope, "To Keep and Bear Arms in the Early Republic," *Constitutional Commentary 16* (1999): 269–82.

11. Indeed, pointing to the propensity of these scholars to quote one another rather than engage in truly original historical scholarship, Cornell says, "recent writing on the Second Amendment more closely resembles the intellectual equivalent of a check kiting scheme than it does solidly researched history." "Commonplace or Anachronism" at n. 10.

12. See Robert E. Shalhope, "The Ideological Origins of the Second Amendment," *J. Am. Hist. 69* (1982): 599.

13. Shalhope, *To Keep and Bear Arms,* at 270.

14. Jack N. Rakove, "The Second Amendment: The Highest State of Originalism," *Chi.-Kent L. Rev. 76* (2000): 103.

15. For example, Rakove, a good friend, does not spare me from some of his jibes. See especially ibid., 152 n. 140.

16. Quoted in Cornell at 226.

17. Ibid. at 227.

18. Ibid. at 227–28.

19. With regard to the judicial elaboration of the Second Amendment, William Van Alstyne has famously written that "it is substantially accurate to say that the useful case law of the Second Amendment, even in 1994, is mostly just missing in action. In its place, what we have is roughly of the same scanty and utterly underdeveloped nature as was characteristic of the equally scanty and equally underdeveloped case law (such as it then was) of the First Amendment in 1904, as of which date there was still to issue from the Supreme Court a single decision establishing the First Amendment as an amendment of any genuine importance at all." See William Van Alstyne, "The Second Amendment and the Personal Right to Arms," *Duke L. J. 43* (1994): 1236, 1239.

20. See the withering critique by David Rabban, who labels Chafee "The

Scholar as Advocate." David M. Rabban, *Free Speech in Its Forgotten Years* (1997), 316–35.

21. Quoted in Edward T. Linenthal, *Sacred Ground: Americans and Their Battlefields,* 2d ed. (Urbana: University of Illinois Press, 1993), 11.

22. See Garry Wills, *A Necessary Evil* (New York: Simon and Schuster, 1999).

23. As have other historians of the American military. But, of course, determining that the myth is undoubtedly false to historical reality does not establish the converse, that the militia was of absolutely no importance. See Ira D. Gruber, "Of Arms and Men: Arming America and Military History," *William and Mary Q. 59,* 3d Series (2002): 219—"Bellesiles's treatment of the militia is much like that of guns: he regularly uses evidence in partial or imprecise ways."

24. *Yale L. J. 98,* 648 n. 54.

25. Quoted in Rakove at 152 n. 140.

26. Ibid.

27. Jack N. Rakove, "Words, Deeds, and Guns: Arming America and the Second Amendment," *William and Mary Q. 59,* 3d Series (2002): 205, 208.

28. Ibid.

29. See, e.g., Fig. 3.5, "U.S. Crime Rates from 1960–1996 (from FBI Uniform Crime Reports)," in John Lott, *More Guns, Less Crime: Understanding Crime and Gun Control Laws,* 2d ed. (Chicago: University of Chicago Press, 2000), 44–45, which indicates a significant drop in the crime rate from 1990 to 1996. See also James B. Jacobs, *Can Gun Control Work?* (New York: Oxford University Press, 2002), at 118–19. "In explaining the unprecedented decline in crime, criminologists stress a variety of other factors [besides the consequences of the Brady law in arguably making it harder to purchase guns], including a drop in alcohol consumption, economic prosperity, improved and innovative police tactics, and a massive increase in the prison population. Many criminologists have pointed to the decline of crack use." Ibid. at 199. A June 24, 2002, press release from the FBI stated, however, "that preliminary 2001 data indicate a 2.0-percent increase in the Nation's Crime Index from the 2000 figure." Even if the rate seems to have fallen off from its highs around 1990 or so, it remains far higher, for all crimes, than it was in 1960.

30. See John Lott, *More Guns, Less Crime.*

31. See Bernard E. Harcourt, *Illusion of Order: The False Promise of Broken Windows Policing* (Cambridge, Mass.: Harvard University Press, 2001).

32. A similar point is made in Paul Finkelman's contribution to the Chicago-Kent symposium, "'A Regulated Militia': The Second Amendment in Historical Perspective," *Chi.-Kent L. Rev. 76* (2000): 195.

33. Paul Finkelman, "James Madison and the Bill of Rights: A Reluctant Paternity," *1990 Supreme Court Review* (1991): 301.

34. Neil H. Cogan, ed., *The Complete Bill of Rights: The Drafts, Debates, Sources, and Origins* (New York: Oxford University Press, 1997), at 181.

35. Ibid. at 181–82 (Cogan's underlining). I am not certain about the importance of the fact that the given passage is underlined in Cogan's text.

36. Ibid. at 182.

37. Ibid. at 182–83.

38. Ibid. at 182. The Pennsylvanians might well have drawn their views from Article XIII of the first Chapter of the Declaration of Rights in the radical Constitution of 1776: "That the people people have a right to bear arms for the defence of themselves and the state. . . ." Ibid. at 184.

39. Vermont, 1777: "That the people have a right to bear arms for the defence of themselves and the State—and as standing armies in time of peace are dangerous to liberty, they ought not to be kept up; and that the military should be kept under strict subordination to and governed by the civil power." Chapter I, Article 15. The Kentucky constitution of 1792 would adopt even more categorical language: "That the right of the citizens to bear arms in defense of themselves and the State shall not be questioned." Article XII.

40. Rakove, "The Second Amendment," at 141.

41. Ibid. at 132.

42. Garry Wills, "To Keep and Bear Arms," *New York Review of Books*, Sept. 21, 1995, at 62–73.

43. *Edwards v. California*, 314 U.S. 160, 186 (1941) (Jackson, J., concurring).

44. Pennsylvania Constitution of 1790, Article IX, § 21, quoted in ibid.

45. Cornell, at 233.

46. Ibid.

47. Ibid.

48. Ibid. at 228.

49. Ibid., quoting Douglas Arnold, *A Republican Revolution: Ideology and Politics in Pennsylvania 1776–1790* (New York: Garland Publishing, 1989), 109.

50. This point is demonstrated most clearly in the controversy over the Sedition Act of 1798, in which the heated critique of federal power was joined with an acceptance of the legitimacy of *state* limitations on speech should such be deemed necessary. See, e.g., Leonard W. Levy, *Emergence of a Free Press* (New York: Oxford University Press, 1985), at 306. For example, the Kentucky Resolutions of 1798, which were drafted by Jefferson himself, both denounced the Sedition Law as beyond the constitutional power of the national government and explicitly affirmed the power of states "to retain to themselves the right of judging how far the licentiousness of speech, and of the press, may be abridged without lessening their useful freedom." Id. As Scot Powe writes, "A consequence . . . of the Sedition Act controversy is that subsequently the Supreme Court, historians, and lawyers would ask of the First Amendment a question it was not intended to answer: what did the First Amendment say

about the *scope* of freedom of the press? The First Amendment was not intended to answer that question because that was left entirely to the states," which were thought, at least initially, to maintain wide discretion unless limited by their own state bill of rights. See Lucas A. Powe Jr., *The Fourth Estate* (Berkeley: University of California Press, 1991), 48.

51. One notes, for example, the surprising use of such language in James Madison's essay "Foreign Influence," where he refers to ostensible Americans "who are truly British in one or all their characteristics," and this "merits very serious attention, in the present estimate. The influence from this class of persons is the greater, as they are in no small degree scattered over the whole face of the country. . . ." Madison takes the gloves off on the next page: "[O]ur country is penetrated to its remotest corners with a foreign poison vitiating the American sentiment, recolonizing the American character, and duping us into the politics of a foreign nation." See Jack Rakove, *Madison: Writings* (1999), 597–98 (January 23, 1799).

52. See, e.g., Leonard Levy, *Legacy of Suppression: Freedom of Speech and Press in Early American History* (Cambridge, Mass.: Belknap Press of Harvard University Press, 1960). I fully realize that Levy's thesis has been subjected to well-merited criticisms in terms of overstatement, but he seems correct, nonetheless, in his basic point that a fully articulated theory of freedom of speech appeared to await the events of 1798–99, particularly the passage of the Sedition Act.

53. Article VIII, § 20.

54. Article I, § 26.

55. Article XIII, § 3.

56. See Carl Bogus, "Race, Riots, and Guns," *Southern California L. Rev. 66* (1993): 1366; "The Hidden History of the Second Amendment," *U. Cal. Davis L. Rev. 31* (1998): 309.

57. Don Kates, "Handgun Prohibition and the Original Meaning of the Second Amendment," *Mich. L. Rev. 82* (1983): 204, 244.

58. Ibid. at 245, citing *State v. Buzzard*, 4 Ark. 18 (1842); *Nunn v. State*, 1 Ga. 243 (1846); *State v. Chandler*, 5 La. Ann. 489 (1850); *Cockrum v. State*, 24 Tex. 394 (1859).

59. *Dred Scott v. Sanford*, 60 U.S. (19 How.) 393, 417 (1857). It is also worth noting that "[t]he first party to protest infringement of the 'right of the people of keep and bear arms' was the Republicans in 1856, at a time when, as the Whig party platform of 1856 expressed it, 'a portion of the country [was] being ravaged by civil war.'" Mark E. Neely Jr., *The Union Divided: Party Conflict in the Civil War North* (Cambridge, Mass.: Harvard University Press, 2002), 160. As it happens, the Democratic platform of 1864 also invoked the Second Amendment as it expressed concern over "interference with and denial of the right of the people to bear arms in their defense." Ibid.

60. After all, Taney makes effective use of the fact that the Congress, when passing the first militia law in 1792, required that only "free able-bodied white male citizen[s]" enroll in the militia.

61. I have benefited greatly from reading an unpublished paper by Professor Lewis H. Larue, "Liberty, Equality, and the Privileges and Immunities Clauses: Lost Knowledge."

62. United States Constitution, Amendment XIV, § 1.

63. 6 F.Cas. 546, 551–52 (C.C.E.D. Pa., 1823).

64. Cong. Globe, 39th Cong., 1st Sess. 2765–66 (1866) (emphasis added).

65. Akhil Reed Amar, *The Bill of Rights* (New Haven: Yale University Press, 1998), at 258.

66. After discussing the Reconstruction history, which offers no support for the view that an incorporated Second Amendment would relate specifically to state militias, Powe observes that "[a] right that the Fourteenth Amendment protects is individual and states may not abridge it." Powe at 1375.

67. Lou Falkner Williams, *The Great South Carolina Ku Klux Klan Trials 1871–1872* (Athens: University of Georgia Press, 1996), 75. Corbin attempted other such prosecutions. See, e.g., ibid. at 107–8.

68. 92 U.S. 542, 553 (1875)

69. 13 Wall. 166 (1871).

70. Pamela Brandwein, *Reconstructing Reconstruction: The Supreme Court and the Production of Historical Truth* (Durham: Duke University Press, 1999).

71. The parenthetical is designed to recognize that American Indians were not viewed as grantees of citizenship under the Fourteenth Amendment. See *Elk v. Wilkins,* 112 U.S. 94 (1884).

72. See Bruce Ackerman, *We the People: Transformations* (1998), 99–252 (setting out the remarkable circumstances by which the Fourteenth Amendment was added to the Constitution).

73. Only limitation of space prevents me from discussing the remarkable contribution to the Chicago-Kent symposium by H. Richard Uviller and William G. Merkel, "The Second Amendment in Context: The Case of the Vanishing Predicate," *Chi.-Kent L. Rev.* 76 (2000): 403, an almost two-hundred-page article that, on my reading at least, supports the "republican" background of the amendment as an historical proposition, while going on to argue that the predicate assumptions that underlie republicanism have vanished from our polity, thus rendering the amendment nugatory as a limitation on government. What is especially valuable about their article is the recognition that the historical background of the amendment is of questionable relevance to deciding what it means today unless one is an originalist of a certain type.

Chapter 6

What Does the Second Amendment Restrict?
A Collective-Rights Analysis

Carl T. Bogus

I. Introduction

The collective-rights model asserts that the Second Amendment grants people the right to keep and bear arms only within the militia organized by Congress, which today is the National Guard.[1] Some say this seems to give the amendment very little bite. What kind of right gives individuals the right to keep and bear arms only within an entity organized and controlled by the government itself?

This question has enormous significance in the debate between advocates of the collective-rights model and those who believe the amendment grants individuals a right to keep and bear weapons for their own purposes.[2] Advocates of the individual rights model can argue that an interpretation that renders the amendment meaningless should be disfavored.[3] While it is possible that the Second Amendment had meaning in 1791 but has since become an anachronism, or that the right is presently dormant but may someday reawaken,[4] a canon of constitutional construction mandates that when two possible interpretations of a provision are available, the one that renders the provision purposeless should generally be avoided.[5]

I do not believe that this is the case, however. Although the Second Amendment grants only a collective right, it had genuine meaning with potential real-world consequences in 1791 and still has. I submit that the proper reading of the amendment is not the one it is generally given.

The Second Amendment reads: "A well regulated Militia, being necessary to the security of a free State, the right of the people to keep and
bear Arms, shall not be infringed."[6] While all serious commentators acknowledge that the Second Amendment is in some fashion tied to the
militia, individual-rights advocates downplay that connection. Some
suggest the prefatory phrase merely explains why the right is granted
but does not define it; they believe the amendment essentially has the
same meaning as it would if the first thirteen words did not exist. Some
argue the Founders believed in a universal militia. While the eighteenth-century America militia included only white males, they argue
that a contemporary interpretation would include all adults. Both arguments drive to the same conclusion: Every adult American has a
right to keep and bear arms, regardless of whether one serves in the
militia.

These arguments have problems, however. First and foremost, not
all of the Founders believed in a universal militia. Notwithstanding
popular myth and Fourth of July rhetoric, the militia was a flop in the
war against the British. General Nathanael Greene explained why:

> People coming from home with all the tender feelings of domestic life
> are not sufficiently fortified with natural courage to stand the shock-
> ing scenes of war. To march over dead men, to hear without concern
> the groans of the wounded, I say few men can stand such scenes un-
> less steeled by habit and fortified by military pride.[7]

So often did the militia turn and run in the face of the enemy that it
became Continental Army doctrine to position militia forces in front of
and between Continental Army regulars, who were ordered to shoot
the first militiamen to bolt.

By the end of the war, therefore, many Founders no longer believed in a universal militia, and at the Constitutional Convention the
Founders decided the Constitution should not permanently mandate
how the militia should be organized. Rather, Congress was given the
authority to organize the militia as it deems best, with the ability to
change it as the passage of time and circumstances might demand.[8]

Why provide that Congress can organize the militia as it sees fit—
deciding who serves in the militia and regulating possession and use
of weapons in militia service—but also provide that the people have a

right to keep and bear arms within the militia? A little background is necessary to answer that question.

As I have explained in more detail elsewhere,[9] I believe Madison wrote the Second Amendment to assure the South that Congress, which had just been given the lion's share of authority over the state militia in the recently ratified Constitution, would not use that power to undermine the slave system. In part, this was an amendment to the slave compromise in the Constitution. While scrupulously avoiding the words "slave" and "slavery," the Constitution prohibited Congress from abolishing the African slave trade until 1808 or imposing an import tax of more than ten dollars per slave. It also required that runaway slaves who escaped across state lines (and into free territory) be returned to their owners. And it provided for counting slaves as three-fifths of free persons for the purposes of apportioning congressional representation and direct taxation.

The southern delegates told their constituents that, most important of all, the Constitution did not grant Congress any authority to abolish slavery. But, during the ratification debates, southern anti-Federalists argued that, by giving Congress the power to organize and arm the militia[10] and to call them into federal service,[11] the Constitution provided a means to undermine the slave system indirectly. Congress might either disarm the militia or physically remove them from a state, thus leaving the white population vulnerable to slave revolt. It was a frightening prospect.

Madison sought to correct part of this problem by writing the Second Amendment. His objective was to strengthen the slave compromise by adding another provision to the militia clauses of the Constitution. Madison wanted to make it clear that, although Congress had the authority to arm the militia, it could not disarm the militia, at least not entirely. Put somewhat more succinctly, the states were to have a right to armed militia. This makes sense once one understands that, from Madison's and the South's point of view, the principal function of the militia was slave control.

If the states were to have the means to provide for their own security, they needed an armed militia. This did not mean that the states had a right to a fully armed populace; nor did it mean the states, rather than the federal government, were to have the right to regulate arms within the militia. Congress continued to have the authority to discipline—that is, to regulate—the militia, with the new qualification that Congress could not entirely deprive a state of an armed militia and thus the means to provide for its own security.

Over the second half of the twentieth century, we became accustomed to thinking about whether the amendment prohibits gun control legislation that affects the general population. But a correct interpretation of the amendment focuses instead on the militia. The operative question is whether the Second Amendment restricts federal control of the militia, and, if so, how. This is not a new view. One history of the National Guard, for example, states simply that the Second Amendment "was intended to prevent the federal government from disarming the militia."[12]

II. Three Case Histories

What, then, are some of the circumstances that would raise genuine Second Amendment issues? This section presents three historical episodes for consideration, which I offer as real-world case histories of the kind of federal action to which the Second Amendment is germane. In Section III, I offer some observations about whether, if faced with cases arising out of these incidents, the courts should have found that the federal action did, in fact, violate the Second Amendment.

A. Prohibiting Militia in the Former Confederate States (1867)

After the Civil War, former Confederate Army regiments in the southern states began to reconstitute themselves as state militia units. They often wore Confederate Army uniforms, carried the Confederate battle flag, and intimidated emancipated slaves. This alarmed Republicans in Congress, and, on February 26, 1867, Senator Henry Wilson, of Massachusetts, introduced an amendment to the army appropriations bill then pending in Congress. Wilson's amendment read in its entirety:

> And be it further enacted, That all militia forces now organized or in service in either of the States of Virginia, North Carolina, South Carolina, Georgia, Florida, Alabama, Louisiana, Mississippi and Texas, further organization, arming, or calling into service of the said militia

forces, or any part thereof, is hereby prohibited under any circumstances whatever until the same shall be authorized by Congress.[13]

A debate ensued, focused in part on whether depriving the states of their militias would violate the Second Amendment. Senator Waitman T. Willey, of West Virginia, said:

> [T]his is a very sweeping provision . . . to deprive these States of the use of their militia for the purpose of maintaining their police regulations in many places. The disability, as I understand the amendment, is total; the whole of the militia organizations of these States is to be entirely destroyed; the militia of the States are not to bear arms in any event or under any condition. . . . [T]here may be instances when it would be necessary, for the best of purposes, to keep the peace of the State, to maintain proper police regulations, that the militia should at least carry arms to a limited extent. It strikes me also that there may be some constitutional objection against depriving men of the right to bear arms and the total disarming of men in time of peace.[14]

Senator Wilson defended his proposal by arguing that it would prohibit the formation of militia units but not the enforcement of police regulations by other officials and that the militia ban was to be temporary. It passed twenty-three to eleven.

President Andrew Johnson wanted to veto the measure but could not do so without vetoing the entire army appropriations act and depriving Union soldiers of their salaries.[15] He signed it under protest and sent Congress a message protesting the portion of the Act that, in his words, "denies to ten States of the Union their constitutional right to protect themselves, in any emergency, by means of their own militia."[16]

B. Federalizing the Arkansas National Guard (1957)

Two years before the Supreme Court handed down its opinion in *Brown v. Board of Education,* the city of Little Rock, Arkansas, had already designed a seven-year school integration plan.[17] The plan had been crafted under the leadership of the city's mayor, Woodrow W. Mann, and approved by the school board. The plan was to begin in 1957 with the admission of twenty-five black students to the city's two-thousand-student Central High School.

Everything was expected to proceed smoothly until Governor Marvin Griffin, of Georgia, came to town and gave a fiery speech about how he would not tolerate school integration. Griffin's speech found an enthusiastic response in certain quarters, stimulating the governor of Arkansas, Orval Faubus, to seize upon the issue as a means of salvaging his declining political fortunes. Faubus, a colorless individual with declining popularity, was in his second two-year term and confronting an Arkansas tradition that governors should serve no more than two terms.

Faubus's opening gambit was to call Deputy Attorney General William Rogers to ask what the federal government could do to prevent violence when the integration plan went into effect in September. Rogers told Faubus that local disorders were generally the province of the local police, but he dispatched the head of the Civil Rights Division to Little Rock to find out what was going on. When asked why he expected violence, Faubus was so strange and elusive that federal officials began to suspect that Faubus, himself, might stir up trouble.[18]

In August, a white woman asked the state court to enjoin the integration plan because it would lead to violence. Faubus is assumed to have been the moving force behind the lawsuit; he personally testified in the proceeding, stating that revolvers had been found in the possession of both black and white students. The state court granted the injunction. However, the federal district court promptly dissolved the injunction and prohibited the state court from interfering with the desegregation plan.

There were, in fact, no genuine omens of violence. Nevertheless, Mayor Mann and the city police force worked out contingency plans to control demonstrations, should that be necessary. If trouble came, they were confident the 175-member city police force could handle it.

On the evening before the new school term, Faubus appeared on television to announce that Little Rock was plunging into violence. Local stores were selling out their supply of knives, "most to Negro youths," he said. "[T]he evidence of discord, anger, and resentment has come to me from so many sources as to become a deluge," so he had called out the Arkansas National Guard to "to maintain or restore the peace and good order of this community."[19] He had directed the Guard to prevent black students from entering the school because, he said, if they did, "Blood will run in the streets."[20] An hour before

Faubus spoke, National Guard troops, bearing M-1 rifles with fixed bayonets, had already surrounded Central High School.

The FBI checked one hundred stores and found that knife sales were below normal levels. Mayor Mann said there had been no indication whatsoever of possible violence, and three other Arkansas towns peacefully integrated on that same day.

But, when school opened on September 4, Faubus finally generated his mob. Parents of only nine of the twenty-five black students who were scheduled to be enrolled permitted their children to attempt to go to school. As they approached the school, the black students were jostled by angry segregationists screaming racial epithets. Nevertheless, accompanied by white and black ministers, the students made their way to the National Guard perimeter, where they were confronted by a solid wall of Guardsmen and told, "Governor Faubus has placed this school off limits to Negroes."[21]

The federal judge ordered Faubus to appear in court on September 20 to show cause why he should not be enjoined from obstructing the enrollment of black students at the high school. Federal marshals proceeded to the governor's mansion, where they passed easily through a perimeter of National Guardsmen to serve the governor a subpoena to appear in court.

At this juncture, Faubus sought presidential help. In response to a question at a press conference two months earlier, President Eisenhower had said, "I can't imagine any set of circumstances that would ever induce me to send federal troops . . . into any area to enforce the orders of a federal court, because I believe that [the] common sense of America will never require it."[22] Perhaps this led Faubus to believe the president would commit to not using troops to enforce federal court orders. Faubus flew to Rhode Island for a personal meeting with President Eisenhower at the summer White House in Newport. He did not get want he wanted. Eisenhower reiterated what he had told Faubus by telegram several days earlier, namely that "[t]he only assurance I can give you is that the federal constitution will be upheld by me by every legal means at my command."[23]

On September 20, the federal court enjoined Faubus and the Arkansas National Guard from obstructing black students from attending the high school. The order explicitly stated that the governor retained his authority to use the National Guard to maintain peace and order. Peace and order were not what Faubus had in mind, however, and he withdrew the Guard entirely.

When the Little Rock police arrived at Central High School at 6:00 A.M. on September 23 to secure the area for the enrollment of black students that morning, they found themselves confronting an ugly mob. They cleared vital areas with swinging nightsticks and erected sawhorse barricades. At 8:45 A.M., someone in the crowd screamed, "Here come the niggers,"[24] and the crowd overran the police to chase and beat four blacks who, as it happened, were not students but reporters.

During this spectacle, the nine black students slipped unnoticed into the school. Once inside, they had a relatively easy time of it. No white students displayed hostility; some made friendly advances. Meanwhile, matters outside continued to deteriorate. Attracted by news broadcasts, the mob of troublemakers swelled to nearly a thousand. In late morning, the crowd surged forward, overrunning the police and demolishing their barracks. As the mob reached the doors of the school, a now very worried Mayor Mann removed the black students from the school. The next morning, he sent President Eisenhower a telegram in Newport. "The immediate need for federal troops is urgent," it began.[25] The mob was even larger than the day before, armed, and violent. "Situation is out of control and police cannot disperse the mob," it continued. "I am pleading to you as President of the United States . . . to provide the necessary federal troops" to restore peace and order.

Eisenhower was already aware of the situation. The day before, his staff had prepared a presidential proclamation titled "Obstruction of Justice in the State of Arkansas" and providing for the use of federal troops, but the president had not yet signed it. He did so now. That night, he went on national television to explain his action to the American people. "The very basis of our individual rights and freedoms rests upon the certainty that the president and the executive branch of government will support and ensure the carrying out of the decisions of the federal courts, even, when necessary, with all the means at the president's command," he said.[26]

The next day President Eisenhower signed a second proclamation authorizing the Secretary of Defense to call the entire ten-thousand-member Arkansas National Guard into active federal service. Eisenhower was careful not to transmit this order through the normal channels, that is, through the governor of the state. The President placed Major General Edwin A. Walker in command and instructed him to ensure that the order was communicated directly to the Guardsmen.

Eisenhower did not nationalize the Arkansas National Guard in order to use it to restore order. The main objective was to deprive Faubus of the Guard. The main federal force was a thousand paratroopers from the elite 101st Airborne Division, who were flown to Arkansas from Fort Campbell, Kentucky. Nevertheless, as John C. Mahon writes, federalizing the Arkansas National Guard "created a situation without precedent: it directed the Guardsmen to disregard their state commander-in-chief and obey the commands of the president at a time when they were on active state duty."[27]

Southern politicians fiercely denounced Eisenhower's actions. Senator Richard Russell, of Georgia, said Eisenhower was employing Nazi tactics. Senator Olin Johnson, of South Carolina, suggested that Faubus challenge Eisenhower's authority over the Guard. "If I were Governor Faubus, I'd proclaim an insurrection down there, and I'd call out the National Guard, and I'd then find out who's going to run things in my state," he said.[28] Faubus did not do so, however. He referred to the military units as "occupation forces"[29] and claimed they were guilty of all manner of outrages, including bludgeoning innocent bystanders and poking bayoneting into the backs of schoolgirls with "the warm, red blood of patriotic Americans staining the cold, naked, unsheathed knives."[30] The accusations were, of course, hokum. There were confrontations between troops and the mob, during which one man who tried to seize a paratrooper's rifle was hit with a steel butt of an M-1. The students were enrolled and protected.

After the initial period, General Walker discharged all of the Arkansas National Guard (who, for the most part, had been required to spend the days in their armories), except for a special task force of 1,800 Guardsmen. In November, finances required sending the 101st Airborne detachment back to Fort Campbell, and the Guardsmen became the main presence on the scene. The black students continued to be protected by a small contingent of Guardsmen for the balance of the school year.

A similar episode occurred on June 11, 1963, when Governor George C. Wallace, of Alabama, made his famous stand in the schoolhouse door to prevent two black students from enrolling at the University of Alabama.[31] The event ended when President Kennedy federalized the

Alabama National Guard, and National Guard General Henry V. Graham marched up to Wallace, saluted him, and said, "Sir, it is my sad duty to ask you to step aside under orders from the president of the United States."[32]

C. The Montgomery Amendment (1987)

1985, the federal government ordered more than 12,000 National Guardsmen to active duty training in Central America, principally Honduras. President Reagan wanted to use these exercises to intimidate the Sandinista government and to help develop a staging area for a Contra rebel invasion of Nicaragua.[33] At that time, federal statutes permitted the secretary of defense to order members of the National Guard to active duty outside the United States only with the consent of the state's governor. A survey revealed that only twenty-three governors would approve training exercises in Honduras. When the Reagan administration proceeded with the program nonetheless, more than a dozen governors (and the Iowa legislature) balked, and the governors of California and Maine successfully refused directives to send units.[34]

In response, Congress enacted the Montgomery Amendment, a statute authorizing the secretary of defense to order National Guard members to active federal duty for training for up to fifteen days a year notwithstanding a gubernatorial objection on the grounds of "location, purpose, type, or schedule" of the duty.[35] The governor of Minnesota challenged the constitutionality of this legislation.[36] He argued that the Constitution permits the federal government to call forth the militia for only three specific purposes—to execute the laws of the United States, to suppress insurrections, and to repel invasions—and for no other purpose, including training.

The Supreme Court declared the act to be constitutional. The Court's decision was grounded in the dual enlistment program established by Congress, under which members of the National Guard simultaneously enroll in both their state's National Guard and the National Guard of the United States (NGUS), a reserve component of the U.S. armed forces.[37] Federal statutes expressly provides that when members of the National Guard are ordered to active duty, they serve in their capacity as army or air force reserves.[38] The Supreme Court held that, because members of the Minnesota National Guard had voluntarily enrolled in NGUS, they could be ordered to Honduras in that capacity and that during such time they would be "temporarily disassociated" from the state militia.[39] The Supreme Court found this plan constitutionally sound because, it said, the militia clauses of the Constitution gave Congress additional military powers without in any fashion limiting its authority to maintain an army and a navy, under which Congress can draft citizens into the armed forces.

The governor of Minnesota argued that this interpretation of the militia clauses nullified the state's authority over its militia. The Court rejected this argument, stating that its interpretation "merely recognizes the supremacy of federal power in the area of military affairs."[40] Most significant for our purposes, the Court noted that, because the Montgomery Amendment prohibited the governors from objecting to active duty assignments only on the grounds of "location, purpose, type, or schedule," the governor of Minnesota could object to sending his state's National Guard to Honduras if that interfered with the state's ability to respond to local emergencies.

III. Analyzing the Case Histories

Did the federal government violate the Second Amendment in any of these incidents? We can begin by observing that the Constitution appears to guarantee states the right to a militia. While it does not do so expressly, four constitutional provisions[41] refer to the militia and thus presuppose their existence, and one of the provisions gives the states certain powers over the militia. Taken together, these four sections, including the Second Amendment, provide that the states have a right not only to militias but to armed militias.[42]

No right is absolute, however, whether belonging to an individual or to a state. A state may have no right to a militia if Congress calls the entire militia into federal service to repel an invasion. It is less clear whether the federal government can deprive a state of its militia in less dire circumstances, or, if so, under what circumstances or for how long.

From its text, we know the Second Amendment guarantees the states the right to armed militias so that they can provide for their own security. When the amendment was written, the South was not confident it could count on Congress to quell slave insurrections.

Indeed, the South was afraid Congress might encourage slave revolts by disarming or otherwise compromising the militia. By writing the Second Amendment, Madison sought to provide that if Congress failed to furnish the militia with arms, the state governments or the people themselves could do so.

The federal action that most directly infringed on the states' right to an armed militia occurred when the southern states were deprived of their militia during the Reconstruction period. The very purpose of the federal action was to abridge the states' rights to militia, especially armed militia. But that does not necessary mean the action was unconstitutional.

In one sense, the federal government violated the letter of the Second Amendment in order to effectuate its spirit. Ten states had gone to war against the Union. The terms of surrender at Appomattox Court House allowed Confederate officers to keep their guns.[43] Two days later, President Lincoln gave a speech in which he told the nation that, though the war's end was cause for joy, the task of reconstruction was "fraught with great difficulty."[44] "No man has authority to give up the rebellion for any other man," he observed.[45] Three days later, Lincoln was assassinated.

Andrew Johnson and Congress did not see eye to eye about Reconstruction. Congress took the position that the southern states had forfeited their constitutional rights and that it was Congress's prerogative to decide when those rights would be restored.[46] Johnson's desire to take a more lenient approach ultimately led to his impeachment. Prohibiting militia in the former Confederacy was part of Congress's program of withholding the rights of the southern states until Congress believed it prudent to restore them. While Johnson disagreed with both Congress's general policy and this specific measure, he could not afford to veto the militia ban. The measure was included in legislation providing for the payment of Union soldiers, and an unelected president from the South could not afford to stand in the way of paying Union soldiers.

These were unique and extraordinarily difficult times.[47] A civil war had just ended. Many southerners remained hostile to the national government, as well as to freedmen. In June 1866, a congressional committee reported that the South was "in anarchy" and under the control of "unrepentant . . . rebels."[48] No court could properly have substituted its own evaluation for that of Congress. The question is whether, accepting the congressional findings on their face, suspending the states' right to militia was unconstitutional.

The answer depends upon whether the government may exercise extraordinary powers during war or other crises. At least twice, the Supreme Court has held that it may. During World War I, the Court upheld convictions for making speeches and circulating flyers that questioned the government's war policies because they allegedly obstructed military recruiting efforts.[49] In the World War II Japanese internment cases,[50] the Supreme Court more directly held that, during war, the government's power expands as necessity requires. Writing for the Supreme Court in *Korematsu,* Hugo Black declared that the government's "power to protect must be commensurate with the threatened danger."[51] Concurring, Felix Frankfurter declared that "the validity of action under the war power must be judged wholly in the context of war" and that an action should not "be stigmatized as lawless because like action in times of peace would be lawless."[52] In *Hirabayashi,* the Supreme Court invoked Charles Evans Hughes's famous phrase that the "war power of the national government is 'the power to wage successfully.'"[53]

The principle that the government's powers expand during war or other emergencies is, however, controversial. The confinement of Japanese-Americans during the Second World War is considered a national disgrace. In 1988, Congress enacted legislation apologizing for the internment and providing restitution to those who were interned,[54] and the Supreme Court's decisions in the internment cases are generally considered among the worst in American jurisprudential history.[55]

However, when, during the Vietnam War, the government asked the Supreme Court to enjoin publication of the Pentagon Papers (classified documents relating to the origins of the war), the Supreme Court refused. While it is possible that this was the result of a durable change in attitudes about suppressing civil liberties during wartime, it is more likely that the nation could simply afford a more liberal attitude because the Vietnam War never threatened American nationhood. When the nation's existence is in peril, the people expect their leaders to take extraordinary and, if necessary, extralegal measures. Even those who reject the principle that the government's powers should be deemed to expand during war acknowledge these realities. Laurence H. Tribe, for example, writes that "the Supreme Court's tolerance of wartime excesses of Congress and the Executive seems wrong, but in retrospect it is also clear that the Court saw no reasonable alternative to deference."[56]

Yet, there is danger in legitimizing the principle that power expands during national emergencies. To sanction such a principle would give putative autocrats a tool for unraveling the Constitution and seizing power. McCarthyesque figures can create paranoia without the threat of open warfare. Crises can be unscrupulously feigned, manufactured, or sustained—or, indeed, might legitimately last for very long periods of time. And, at this writing, it appears that the threat of terrorism that has griped America since September 11, 2001, will persist indefinitely.

Surprisingly little has been written about whether the power of the national government as a whole—that is, Congress and the president acting together—expands during wartime or periods of dire emergency. Most of the focus has been on presidential power, specifically on whether the president can take military action without congressional approval.[57] Indeed, the phrase "war power" generally refers to the scope of the president's power as commander-in-chief of the army and navy—and, as useful to mention for our purposes, "of the Militia of the several States, when called into the actual Service of the United States"[58]—to send American forces into combat without a congressional declaration of war.

Often the problem is whether the president may act without congressional approval. Nearly the reverse situation occurred when Congress deprived the southern states of their militia during Reconstruction. President Johnson signed the legislation despite his misgivings about its constitutionality because the legislation also provided for paying Union soldiers. Notwithstanding Johnson's reluctance, Congress and the President did act together. The question, then, is not whether one branch of government infringed upon powers that belonged to another but rather whether the federal government—at the maximum extent of its power, based on the combined action of Congress and the president and a situation of warlike exigency—justified temporarily abrogating the states' right to have militias.

One might argue that the federal action was justified regardless of whether the government's powers were enlarged by crisis. The argument is that the spirit of Second Amendment should trump its letter. The amendment's purpose is to allow the states to provide for their own security, and the amendment therefore should be read as guaranteeing a state a right to a militia only when a militia is, in fact, necessary for the security of the state and its citizens. The preamble of the amendment lends special force to this argument. Because the drafters expressly told us why they granted the right, we need not worry about our failing to recognize the founders' objectives and can feel confident about knowing when the right no longer serves its intended purpose. It may also be reasonably argued that the Second Amendment right may be suspended when both Congress (which has the constitutional authority to organize the militia) and the President (who is commander-in-chief of the militia when it is called into national service) agree that state control of a militia jeopardizes the security of the state or its citizens—who, after all, are also United States citizens.[59]

Congress prohibited militia in the ten former Confederate states because it found them to endanger security. It conducted an investigation. It found the southern states to be in anarchy and that the southern militias were being reconstituted from former Confederate Army units. Although the militia normally serves as a counterweight to anarchy, Congress found that, under these circumstances, the militias would endanger the stability of state government during Reconstruction.

Moreover, it does not appear that Congress had an alternative that would allow the southern states to have militias without creating grave risks. Because states select the officers of their militias, Congress may not have been able to ensure that the militias were loyal to the United States. Restricting militia eligibility to those who had not served in the Confederate Army may have excluded nearly everyone fit for military service. Restricting the militia to freed blacks was not a viable option; white citizens, fearing retribution, would have been terrified of a black militia.[60] I conclude, therefore, that Congress did not violate the Second Amendment by prohibiting militia in the ten Confederate States during the early Reconstruction period.

Much of what has been said about the propriety of suspending a state's right to an armed militia during crisis applies to the Little Rock episode, as well. The President called up the state militia pursuant to a specific constitutional warrant, that is, to execute the laws of the United States, as decreed by federal courts. There was a crisis that required federal military intervention. Although the events did not rise to the level of wartime-like emergencies, they were serious and presented challenges to the rule of law. President Eisenhower federalized the Arkansas militia—the entire state militia—not because he intended to use it as his instrument for directly executing the laws (he relied on 101st Airborne units and U.S. marshals for that) but to deprive the state's governor of its use. That was legitimate; once the president decided to dispatch federal personnel, it was only proper that he try to reduce the risks of hostile actions that might threaten federal personnel or interfere with their mission. By calling the Arkansas National Guard into federal service, President Eisenhower was seeking to preserve peace and security in Arkansas, not threatening it.

Governor George Wallace's famous 1963 stand in the schoolhouse door presents another interesting feature. In this case, federalizing the Alabama National Guard had little military significance but potent political significance. Wallace's doorway stand was purely symbolic. The federal government would have had little difficulty protecting the two students without calling up the Guard. Yet somehow federalizing the Guard ended the crisis (or perhaps, in this case, faux crisis). Why was this the case? It was not because this dissolved the possibility that U.S. armed forces and the Alabama National Guard would go to war with each other; that was not even a remote possibility. Perhaps nationalizing the Guard somehow tangibly demonstrated the supremacy of federal authority. The national government's ability to federalize— or the state's ability to retain—the militia has political as well as military significance. In considering when the federal government may properly deprive a state of its militia, it may be relevant to consider the political ramifications, as well as purely military issues.

What if, in time of crisis, a benevolent governor needed her state's militia to preserve peace and order and a malevolent president, desiring uncontrolled rioting, federalized the militia and confined them to their armories?[61] Then we might regret precedents that approve the federalization of state militias to deprive governors of their use. The courts provide the only institutional check on this kind of misuse of power, although it is necessarily a far from perfect check. During crisis, courts must generally defer to the judgment of the political branches; often the best courts can do is condemn actions after the fact.[62] During an emergency, the president must have the ability to call the militia into federal service, against the governor's wishes if need be. It is clearly unacceptable for state forces to clash militarily with federal forces. It would be inappropriate, therefore, to read the Second Amendment as providing an impediment to a president who sought to avoid such conflicts.

The battle between the governors and the Reagan administration over sending National Guard units to Central America and the Montgomery Amendment raise other issues. As a practical matter, the federal government can deprive a state of its armed militia by sending it away. The anti-Federalists raised this specific concern when they objected to giving the federal government authority over the militia.[63] Federal statutes now give the president and the secretary of state considerable powers to call the militia into federal service. The secretary may call up the militia during a war or national emergency declared by Congress, and the militia forces may remain in federal service for the duration of the war or emergency plus six months.[64] The secretary may call up the militia during a national emergency declared by the president, but in this case the militia forces may be retained in federal service for no more than twenty-four consecutive months.[65] Finally, and most broad, the secretary of defense may call up the militia whenever "the President determines that it is necessary to augment the active forces for any operational mission."[66]

The militia may be called into federal service "to execute the Laws of the Union, suppress Insurrections and repel Invasions."[67] Once called into federal service for such a purpose, the president, as commander-in-chief, can send militia forces where she sees fit. If, for example, hostile forces were to invade the western United States, the president could send the entire Massachusetts National Guard to California to repel the invasion, even if this reduced security in Massachusetts. The security of the nation transcends that of individual states. And, although the language of the Constitution seems to contemplate the militia being used only domestically to "suppress Insurrections and repel Invasions," a reasonable interpretation of the president's war power would allow him to send militia abroad if that were required for effective military operations associated with national defense. Nor, at least under Supreme Court precedents, would there be a problem with the president sending some portion of the Massachusetts National Guard to some distant locale for training purposes.

However, if the Second Amendment is properly read as guaranteeing states some minimum right to an armed militia, the president, even with Congress's consent, would not be authorized to send the entire Massachusetts Guard to some distant locale for training or some other nonemergency purpose, especially if this left Massachusetts vulnerable to an internal threat. This does not mean that Congress cannot organize the militia as it has, in which every member of the Massachusetts National Guard is also a member of the reserve forces of the United States. But Congress should not be able to use this as a rationale for depriving a state of its right to an armed militia.

IV. Conclusion

The Second Amendment provides the states with some minimum right to an armed militia, but what are the parameters of that right? How large a militia—in absolute numbers or in proportion to population—is a state entitled to? What types and numbers of arms does a state militia have a right to possess? Those questions cannot be answered in the abstract. The Second Amendment set forth a principle, not a formula. The parameters of the right can sensibly be mapped only on a case-by-case basis. Of course, although in the eighteenth century the militia constituted the state's exclusive instrument of armed force (police forces did not then exist), today states have police to help provide security, and it would be appropriate to take the availability of police into account in such analyses.

Perhaps the need to map the contours of the Second Amendment will never arise. No clash between federal and state governments currently appears on the horizon. But we do not have a crystal ball. When the Constitution was written, the southern states genuinely feared the prospect that the federal government would deliberately attempt to deny them armed militias. It is perhaps no coincidence that concerns that the federal government would undermine the slave system led to the Second Amendment and that the first of the case histories is part of slavery's legacy. Issues that create distrust and dissension between the federal and state governments may be different in the future. No one can foresee what those issues may be. Under a collective-rights interpretation, however, the Second Amendment remains a vital constitutional provision. It is a discrete but important element of federalism, guaranteeing the states not only a right but the capacity to provide for their own security.

NOTES

1. A longer version of this chapter appears at *Constitutional Commentary* 18 (2001): 485.

2. See Carl T. Bogus, "The History and Politics of Second Amendment Scholarship: A Primer," *Chi.-Kent L. Rev.* 76 (2000): 3.

3. See, e.g., *Marbury v. Madison,* 5 U.S. 137, 174 (1803) ("It cannot be presumed that any clause in the constitution is intended to be without effect.")

4. E.g., H. Richard Uviller and William G. Merkel, "The Second Amendment in Context: The Case of the Vanishing Predicate," *Chi.-Kent L. Rev.* 76 (2000): 403.

5. See, e.g., *Massachusetts Assn. of Health Maintenance Orgs. v. Ruthardt*, 194 F.3d 176, 181 (1st Cir. 1999) ("All words and provisions of statutes are intended to have meaning and are to be given effect, and no construction should be adopted which would render statutory words or phrases meaningless, redundant or superfluous.")

6. Const. Art. I Sec. 8.

7. See John K. Mahon, *History of the Militia and the National Guard* (New York: Macmillan, 1983), 43.

8. The belief in a universal militia did not last long, however. Indeed, the belief in the militia as an effective military force—whether universal or select—also did not last long. In his first presidential address, Jefferson said that "a well-disciplined militia [is] our best reliance in peace, and for the first moments of war, till regulars relieve them." But the state militias were so ridiculous at annual musters—often drunk and disorderly, and abysmal shots—that states made it unlawful to mock them during musters. By his second term, Jefferson had given up, declaring that the nation "would have to settle for a standing army."

9. Carl T. Bogus, "The Hidden History of the Second Amendment," *U.C. Davis L. Rev.* 31 (1998): 309.

10. The Constitution gives Congress the power

To provide for organizing, arming, and disciplining the Militia, and for governing such Part of them as may be employed in Service of the United States, reserving to the States respectively, the Appointment of Officers, and the Authority of training the Militia according to the discipline prescribed by Congress. (Const. Art. I Sec. 8)

11. The Constitution gives Congress the power "To provide for calling forth the Militia to execute the Laws of the Union, suppress Insurrections, and repel Invasions" (Const. Art. I Sec. 8).

12. U.S. Advisory Comm'n on Intergovernmental Relations, *The National*

Guard: Defending the Nation and the States 8 (1993) [hereinafter *Defending the Nation*].

13. Cong. Globe, 39ᵗʰ Cong., 2ⁿᵈ Sess. 1848 (1867).

14. Ibid. Some may seize upon Willey's phrase "depriving *men* of the right to bear arms," rather than depriving the state of an armed militia, as evidence that Willey envisioned the Constitution as protecting an individual right to bear arms rather than the collective right of the states to have armed militias (emphasis added). In my judgment, however, it would be a mistake to attach too much significance to Willey's imprecise use of language. After all, the amendment did not disarm individuals; it prohibited militias forces.

15. See Mahon, supra note 7 at 108; Albert Castel, *The Presidency of Andrew Johnson* (Lawrence: Regents Press of Kansas, 1979), 113.

16. Message from the President of the United States to the House of Representatives, 40ᵗʰ Congress, 1ˢᵗ Session, March 2, 1867.

17. For the description of the Little Rock episode, I draw heavily on two works: Jack Greenberg, *Crusaders in the Courts* (New York: Basic Books, 1994), 228–43; and William Manchester, *The Glory and the Dream* (Boston: Little, Brown, 1973), 978–90. I also consulted Taylor Branch, *Parting the Waters* (New York: Simon and Schuster, 1988), 222–25; Mahon, supra note 7 at 224–25; Geoffrey Perret, *Eisenhower* (New York: Random House, 1999), 550–54; Elmo Richardson, *The Presidency of Dwight D. Eisenhower* (Lawrence: Regents Press of Kansas, 1979), 116–23. Where sources have differed, as they have in a number of details, I relied on Jack Greenberg's account generally and John K. Mahon's account of military matters.

18. See Manchester, supra note 17 at 979.

19. Ibid. at 989.

20. Greenberg, supra note 17 at 229.

21. Manchester, supra note 17 at 980.

22. Perret, supra note 17 at 508.

23. Manchester, supra note 17 at 981.

24. Ibid. at 983.

25. Perret, supra note 17 at 511. For stylistic purposes, I have rendered the telegram in capital and small letters, although, as telegrams are, the original was entirely capitalized.

26. Manchester, supra note 17 at 985.

27. Mahon, supra note 17 at 225.

28. Manchester, supra note 17 at 989.

29. Ibid. at 226.

30. Manchester, supra note 17 at 988.

31. For the description of the incident, see Dan T. Carter, *The Politics of Rage* (New York: Simon and Schuster, 1995), 133–55; Stephan Lesher, *George Wallace:*

American Populist (Reading, Mass: Addison-Wesley, 1994), 201–35; E. Culpepper Clark, *The Schoolhouse Door* (New York: Oxford University Press, 1993).

32. See Lesher, supra note 31 at 233.

33. See *Defending the Nation,* supra note 12 at 24.

34. Ibid.

35. 10 U.S.C. Sec. 12301(f). Members of the reserve components, including the National Guard, may be ordered to active duty without gubernatorial consent in times of war or national emergency declared by Congress or a national emergency declared by the president. 10 U.S.C. Secs. 12301(a), 12302(a).

36. *Perpich v. Department of Defense,* 496 U.S. 344 (1990).

37. 10 U.S.C. Sec. 10101.

38. 10 U.S.C. Sec. 12403.

39. *Perpich,* supra note 36 at 348.

40. Ibid. at 351.

41. I refer to the provisions (1) giving Congress the authority to call forth the militia for certain purposes (Art. I Sec. 8); (2) dividing authority over the militia between the federal and state governments (Art. I Sec. 8); (3) making the president the commander-in-chief "of the militia of the several states" when called into federal service (Art. II Sec. 2); and (4) the Second Amendment.

42. Don Higginbotham, an authority on the eighteenth-century militia, agrees. He writes that "the amendment seems to imply that the concurrent power of the state and federal governments over the militia will not threaten the states or obstruct their use of the militia when not in federal service." Don Higginbotham, "The Federalized Militia Debate: A Neglected Aspect of Second Amendment Scholarship," *Wm. and Mary Q.* 55 (1998): 39, 50.

43. See Paul Johnson, *A History of the American People* (New York: HarperCollins, 1998), 494.

44. See Stephen B. Oates, *With Malice toward None: The Life of Abraham Lincoln* (New York: Harper and Row, 1977), 423 (quoting Lincoln's speech).

45. Ibid.

46. Johnson, supra note 43 at 500.

47. As Henry P. Monaghan observed, "A bloody Civil War, an event wholly unforeseen by the founding generation, may not be a fruitful source for deriving constitutional lessons." Henry P. Monaghan, "The Protective Power of the Presidency," *Colum. L. Rev.* 93 (1993): 1, 27.

48. See Johnson, supra note 43 at 502.

49. *Schenck v. U.S.,* 249 U.S. 47 (1919); *Debs v. U.S.,* 249 U.S. 211 (1919); *Frohwerk v. U.S.,* 249 U.S. 204 (1919). While the Supreme Court purported to apply the same test used in peacetime (the clear and present danger test), Justice Holmes, writing for the Court, added: "When a nation is at war many things that might be said in time of peace are such a hindrance to its effort that

their utterance will not be endured so long as might fight and that no Court no regard them as protected by any constitutional right." *Schenck* at 52.

50. *Korematsu v. U.S.*, 324 U.S. 885 (1944); *Hirabayashi v. U.S., Hirabayashi v. U.S.*, 320 U.S. 81 (1934).

51. 324 U.S. at 220.

52. 324 U.S. at 224.

53. 320 U.S. at 92.

54. Civil Liberties Act of 1988, 50 U.S.C. App. Sec. 1989 et seq.

55. See, e.g., Bernard Schwartz, *A Book of Legal Lists* (New York: Oxford University Press, 1997), 69, 76–78 (placing *Korematsu* among the ten worst Supreme Court decisions of all time). See also J. M. Balkin and Sanford Levinson, "The Canons of Constitutional Law," *Harv. L. Rev.* 111 (1998): 963, 1018; William N. Eskridge Jr. and Philip P. Frickey, "Forward: Law as Equilibrium," *Harv. L. Rev.* 108 (1993) 26, 94b. But see William H. Rehnquist, *All the Laws but One: Civil Liberties in Wartime* (New York: Knopf, 1998) (defending the Court's decisions in the internment cases).

56. Laurence H. Tribe, *American Constitutional Law,* 3d ed. (New York: Foundation Press, 2000), 966.

57. See, e.g., Carl T. Bogus, "The Invasion of Panama and the Rule of Law," *Int'l Law* 26 (1992): 781; Jules Lobel, "Emergency Power and the Decline of Liberalism," *Yale L. J.* 98 (1989): 1385; William Van Alstyne, "The President's Powers as Commander-in-Chief versus Congress' War Power and Appropriations Power," *Miami L. Rev.* 43 (1988): 17.

58. Const. Art. II Sec. 2.

59. While I generally leave aside the question of how much deference the Supreme Court ought to give the political branches, I concur generally with the view that the Court must not abdicate its responsibilities to uphold the Constitution and that, as Thomas M. Franck has put it, "in our system a law that is not enforceable by adjudicatory process is no law at all." Thomas M. Franck, *Political Questions/Judicial Answers: Does the Rule of Law Apply to Foreign Affairs?* (Princeton: Princeton University Press, 1992), 8.

60. I am not suggesting that Madison and the founders' concern about slave control should forever shape how we interpret the Second Amendment. They wrote the amendment in general terms, and the amendment therefore did not expire with the end of slavery. It will continue to have viability as long as there are threats to the security of states and their citizens from any source. Nor I am suggesting that a black militia was a greater threat to white citizens than a white militia was to black citizens. However, the formation of black militias probably would have caused the formation of white paramilitary organizations (which, of course, eventually occurred with the Ku Klux Klan and similar groups), frustrating reconstruction efforts.

61. As Garry Wills observes, however, history has shown that abuse of in-

dividual rights and peccancy tend to thrive more at the local level, and the federal government has often been the rescuer of the weak abused by the powerful. See Garry Wills, *A Necessary Evil: A History of Distrust of Government* (New York: Simon and Schuster, 1999), 110.

62. By invoking the political question doctrine, as first articulated in *Luther v. Borden*, 48 U.S. (7 How. 1) (1849), courts may escape condemning improper action after the fact as well.

63. See Bogus, *The Hidden History of the Second Amendment*, supra note 9 at 344–54.

64. 10 U.S.C. Sec. 12301(a).

65. 10 U.S.C. Sec. 12302(a).

66. 10 U.S.C. Sec. 12304(a).

67. Const. Art. I Sec. 8.

Chapter 7

Moral Principle and the Second Amendment

Christopher L. Eisgruber

In the political battle over gun control and the Second Amendment, both sides claim history for their cause. Proponents of gun control invoke history to argue that the Second Amendment guarantees only rights related to militia service. Their adversaries use history to argue that the Second Amendment protects the right of private individuals to own guns for self-defense, recreation, and other purposes.

In this essay, I argue that both sides are wrong. I contend that the Second Amendment states an abstract moral principle, which we might translate roughly as follows: "The American people shall enjoy those rights to gun ownership and military service which ought to belong to citizens of all free governments." Like any abstract moral principle, this one is susceptible of multiple interpretations. Proponents and opponents of gun control will undoubtedly disagree sharply about the meaning and application of the principle, just as they now disagree about what lessons to draw from history. Yet, if I am correct about the Second Amendment, debates about it should take a new form. They should be cast in the language of political theory, rather than in the language of history; in other words, they should focus upon what American gun policy *ought to be*, rather than upon what it *was* long ago. Those who favor gun control will no longer be able to resist expansive interpretations of the Second Amendment by claiming that the framers were interested principally in preserving the power of state governments to organize militias. Nor, conversely, will gun control opponents be able to justify a right to gun ownership by saying that the framers believed that an armed citizenry would effectively check domestic tyranny.

The Second Amendment's Moral Language

What reason is there to suppose that the Second Amendment states an abstract moral principle? First and foremost is the text of the amendment, which reads, "A well regulated milita, being necessary to the security of a free State, the right of the people to keep and bear arms, shall not be infringed." "The right of the people to keep and bear arms" is an abstraction, much like "the freedom of speech" or "the free exercise of religion." Matters would be different if the Second Amendment said, for example, that "every American citizen of voting age shall have the right to keep one musket in his home." This hypothetical Musket Amendment does not state an abstract principle. Instead, like many other constitutional provisions, the Musket Amendment stipulates a bright-line rule. If the Second Amendment took that form, we would not have much trouble interpreting it. Nor would we much care about it–the Musket Amendment would be self-evidently irrelevant to any modern debate about gun policy.

On its face, however, the Second Amendment is very different from the Musket Amendment. If the words of the Second Amendment are construed according to their ordinary meaning in twenty-first century American English, they state a moral principle. Moreover, the principle they state seems to be a very broad one. "The people" is sufficiently abstract that it might be interpreted to refer either to a community of citizens acting collectively or to all individual persons. "Keep and bear arms" is sufficiently abstract that it might refer either to organized military service or to individual gun ownership and use, or to both.

Of course, the Second Amendment, unlike the other provisions of the Bill of Rights, has its own preamble: "A well regulated militia, being necessary to the security of a free state . . ."[1] Does the Second Amendment's preamble also give us any reason to revise our conclusion that the Second Amendment states a moral principle or that the principle is a very broad one? I do not believe so. The preamble tells us something about why the framing generation thought that the "right to keep and bear arms" was sufficiently important to deserve explicit mention in the Constitution. The right that the Second Amendment guarantees should serve the purposes expressed in the preamble. Reading the Second Amendment as an abstract moral principle clearly satisfies that requirement: providing Americans with whatever "rights to gun ownership and military service ought to belong to citizens of all free governments" guarantees them the rights (if any there be!) useful to the maintenance of a "well regulated militia" capable of defending "the security of a free state." Of course, reading the Second Amendment as an abstract principle may also provide Americans with additional rights not useful to military service, such as the right to own guns for self-protection. But that possibility does not contradict the amendment's preamble. The preamble states one (presumably sufficient) justification for the right guaranteed in the Second Amendment; it says nothing about whether that right might also serve other, additional purposes.

Is the Plain Text Misleading?

My analysis thus far belabors the obvious: If the Second Amendment is read according to the ordinary rules of current American usage, the amendment states a very abstract moral principle. So perhaps the right question to ask is, "Why would anybody suppose that the Second Amendment does *not* state an abstract moral principle?" There are, I think, several possible answers to that question, and I take them up in the order of their importance.

1. Ordinary Usage in the Eighteenth Century (the Framers' "Linguistic Intentions")

I have thus far supposed that it is possible to read the Second Amendment on the basis of the ordinary meaning its words would carry had they been written today. Perhaps that is a mistake. Many people suppose that when the Second Amendment was ratified, it carried a different (and more specific) meaning than the same words would express today.

Claims of this kind, of course, get us into "originalism," a topic that is fraught with difficulties. In my view, any satisfactory account of originalism must begin by recognizing an important distinction that has been elaborated by Ronald Dworkin, among others. Dworkin distinguishes between the *linguistic intentions* and the *legal intentions* of the Constitution's framers.[2] The framers' linguistic intentions pertained to what propositions they wanted to include in the Constitution. The framers' legal intentions pertained to what would happen by virtue of those statements. According to Dworkin, "We make constant assumptions about the framers' linguistic intentions, and we never contradict these in our views about what the Constitution says."[3] Originalism becomes controversial and problematic only insofar as it insists that interpreters abide by the framers' *legal* intentions, as well as their *linguistic* intentions.

I have elsewhere illustrated Dworkin's distinction with a nonconstitutional example.[4] Imagine that when Grandpa is on his deathbed, he whispers to his beloved grandson, "Sonny, promise me this: You'll eat only healthy foods." Sonny makes the promise. How should Sonny interpret the word "healthy"? He is obviously bound by Grandpa's *linguistic* intentions: when Grandpa said "healthy," he invoked a word that meant, roughly speaking, "nutritious" or "medically beneficial." If "healthy" later evolves into a synonym for "cool" or "awesome," Sonny cannot capitalize on this linguistic accident to evade his original promise to Grandpa. But it is not so obvious that Sonny is bound by Grandpa's *legal* intentions—that is, by Grandpa's particular expectations about what foods are or are not healthy. So, for example, if Grandpa believed that it was unhealthy to drink even moderate amounts of alcohol, Sonny might be free to ignore Grandpa's judgment on the basis of scientific studies showing that red wine has medically beneficial effects. Sonny's freedom in this regard is itself a consequence of Grandpa's *linguistic* intentions: Grandpa intended to use an abstract concept, "healthy," which was open to multiple different interpretations. Matters would be different if Grandpa had made Sonny promise never to drink alcohol or never to eat any foods that Grandpa regarded as unhealthy.

I will later have something to say about the framers' *legal* expectations regarding the Second Amendment. For the moment, however, I want to focus attention upon the framers' *linguistic* intentions. In some constitutional disputes, those intentions alter interpretive conclusions that we might otherwise draw. For example, the Constitution specifies, in Article II, Section IV, that the president may be impeached for "high crimes and misdemeanors." In ordinary language today, "misdemeanors" refers to a class of relatively minor crimes. It is most often used in distinction to "felonies." There is, accordingly, some temptation to translate "high crimes and misdemeanors" as "high crimes and minor crimes" or as "felonies and misdemeanors"—in effect, "all crimes but only crimes." From what we know about usage of the term "misdemeanor" in 1787, that would be a mistake. "Misdemeanor" was used as a synonym for "maladministration." It therefore made sense to speak of "high misdemeanors"; the phrase "high crimes and misdemeanors," accordingly, may encompass some non-criminal behavior, and it does not necessarily extend to all crimes.[5]

The ordinary meaning in 1787 of the words in the "high crimes and misdemeanors" clause thus differs from their meaning now. Is the same thing true about the Second Amendment? Perhaps. The meaning of the phrase "keep and bear arms" may have been transformed by its usage in contemporary debates about gun control. Suppose, for example, that the state of Arizona held a constitutional convention yesterday and wrote an entirely new state constitution, which included a provision providing that "the right of the people to keep and bear arms shall not be infringed." Suppose, now, that somebody were to claim that these words in the Arizona constitution specifically addressed militias and had no possible application to individual rights of gun ownership. Most of us would consider that assertion silly. And rightly so. The idea that Arizona's brand-new constitution had anything to do with the regulation of a nonexistent militia is absurd, and we could confidently assume that the battle over Arizona's "right to keep and bear arms" had been fought between the National Rifle Association on the one hand and gun control advocates on the other.

It is at least possible that in 1791 (when the Bill of Rights was ratified), "the right to keep and bear arms" had a different meaning. More specifically, it is possible that in 1791 "the right to keep and bear arms" was a widely understood term of art. Perhaps the phrase was understood to refer only to a collective right of state peoples to form militias—and not to any individual right to own guns. Or perhaps the right was understood to guarantee private citizens the right to own the weapons (but only the weapons) that they would have to use proficiently if called to service in the militia. If the Second Amendment invoked a term of art of this kind, then it would be a mistake to interpret it on the basis of the abstract moral principle its words seem to express today, just as it would be wrong for Sonny to take advantage of linguistic transformations that made "healthy" into a synonym for "cool."

We now come upon one of the polarized debates so characteristic of Second Amendment scholarship.[6] Remarkably enough, both proponents and opponents of gun control have claimed that the plain language of the Second Amendment, interpreted as per its ordinary meaning in 1791, entitles their side to victory. For example, Don Kates Jr. is an opponent of gun control legislation; he insists that the word "bear" means "to carry" and that only individual persons, not communities, can carry weapons.[7] Kates also contends that "'keep' was commonly used in colonial and early state statutes to describe arms possession by individuals in all contexts, not just in relation to militia service."[8] On the basis of the latter observation, Kates concludes that "the amendment's phrase 'right of the people to keep' imports not a right of the states or one limited to military service, but a personal right to possess arms in the home for any lawful purpose."[9]

Garry Wills, who favors gun control legislation, takes precisely the opposite position about both "keep" and "bear." According to Wills, "'bear arms' refers to military service, which is why the plural is used . . . one does not bear arm, or bear an arm." He continues on to say that "[a] whole series of uses shows that 'arms' means military service in general—to be under arms (*sub armis*), to call to arms (*ad arma vocare*), to take up arms (*arma capere*), to lay down one's arms (*arma ponere*)."[10] About "keep," Wills maintains that "[i]t was a point of militia doctrine that it must keep its arms in readiness, while a king's army must 'depone' its arms after a specific campaign, so as not to be standing in readiness." Wills maintains that it is "outlandish" to suppose that the "plural 'arms' means nothing but a singular gun for each individual" so that "keep arms" would entail the right "to stor[e] that gun at home." That interpretation would be a mistake because the "militias had common stores of arms—not only guns but bayonets, artillery, ammunition, flags, drums, and all the *arma* (equipage) of war."[11]

These competing interpretations get repeated, in various forms, throughout the burgeoning literature on the Second Amendment, often accompanied by vigorous denunciations of the intellect or honesty of anybody so benighted as to endorse the opposing view. Scholars duel over particular pieces of evidence, such as an amendment to the Constitution proposed (unsuccessfully) by Robert Whitehill at the Pennsylvania ratifying convention. The amendment reads as follows:

> 7. That the people have a right to bear arms for the defense of themselves and their own state, or the United States, or for the purpose of killing game; and no law shall be passed for disarming the people or any of them, unless for crimes committed, or real danger of injury from individuals; and as standing armies in time of peace are dangerous to liberty, they ought not to be kept up; and that the military shall be kept under strict subordination to and be governed by the civil power.[12]

Whitehill's amendment is cast in terms of the "right" of "the people" "to bear arms," and it clearly extends to hunting and to individual gun possession ("no law shall be passed for disarming the people or any of them"). It appears to refer to individual self-defense ("for the defense of themselves"), although that is not obvious ("themselves" might refer to the people collectively—"the people" might, for example, have to protect "themselves" against a despotic state government). Kates and others claim that Whitehill's amendment is evidence that the word "bear," as used in the Second Amendment, implies an individual right to own guns. Wills, however, has an answer. He says that Whitehill's use of the word "bear" is an instance of the "rhetorical figure called zeugma." Zeugma is the use of a "word to modify or govern two or more words when it is appropriate to only one of them . . . as in *to wage war and peace*."[13] According to Wills, Whitehill was able to use "bear arms for the defense of" in connection with "themselves" only because he also applied it to "their own state or the United States."[14]

Kates mounts a convincing argument that "keep" and "bear" can support the interpretation he prefers. So does Wills. Precisely because both arguments are convincing about the meanings the words *might* support, neither Kates nor Wills is able to demonstrate that the Second Amendment's words can support *only* his preferred interpretation (which is the conclusion each wants!). On the basis of the evidence cited on both sides of the issue, it seems likely that "the right of the people to keep and bear arms" was ambiguous in 1791 in exactly the way that it is ambiguous now: that is, it might refer either to an individual right or to a collective right, and, in either the collective or the individual case, the right described is a very abstract one.

2. Intratextualism

Some scholars have proposed that we interpret the Second Amendment by reference to a different kind of context: They have suggested that we should determine the meaning of the Second Amendment by cross-referencing its terms with other constitutional provisions. Akhil Reed Amar has offered the most elaborate account of this interpretive practice, which he calls "intratextualism."[15] "Intratextualist" interpreters of the Second Amendment point out that the Bill of Rights makes reference to "the people" not only in the Second Amendment but also in many other amendments, including, for example, the Fourth Amendment.[16] They maintain that these multiple references to "the people" should be interpreted consistently with one another. Hence, if we conclude that the Fourth Amendment "right of the people to be secure . . . against unreasonable searches and seizures" protects the right of individual persons to be free from such searches and seizures, then we should likewise conclude that the Second Amendment "right of the people to keep and bear arms" protects the right of individual persons (not state-run militias) to "keep and bear arms."

In my view, this kind of intratextualist argument rests on mistaken premises. The Constitution is a practical document, written by committees to accommodate diverse and conflicting interests. Like all political compositions, the Constitution occasionally uses language in ways that are obscure, imprecise, or redundant.[17] It is consequently a mistake to suppose, as Amar occasionally does, that the Constitution can be compared to "[a] great play [which] may contain a richness of meaning beyond what was clearly in the playwright's mind when the muse came."[18] One might, perhaps, find traces of subconscious literary genius in the works of individual members of the founding generation, such as James Madison or Thomas Jefferson. But it is distinctly odd to believe that any similar "muse" descended upon the political negotiations in the Constitutional Convention's Committee on Style.

When interpreting constitutions, it is entirely possible that identical (but ambiguous) words in different provisions should be interpreted differently. Of course, I do not mean to deny that intratextualism can sometimes provide useful interpretive insights. Amar himself correctly notes that "[t]he lighter the load a given [intratextualist] argument seeks to bear, the easier it is to defend."[19] Intratextualism is particularly effective when it is used to *expand* the range of meanings that a constitutional term might bear. For example, Amar nicely describes how John Marshall used intratextualism in *McCulloch v. Maryland*[20] to show that the word "necessary" in the Necessary and Proper Clause of Article I *might* mean "convenient and useful" or "practically desirable," rather than "strictly indispensable."[21] Marshall pointed out that in the Duty and Tonnage Clause of Article I, Section 10, the Constitution itself uses the phrase "absolutely necessary."[22] If "necessary" always meant "strictly indispensable," then it would be bizarre to preface "necessary" with "absolutely." Hence, Marshall's intratextualist observation strongly suggests that "necessary" might sometimes mean something other than "strictly indispensable." It does not follow from Marshall's intratextual comparison, however, that "necessary" can never mean "strictly indispensable" or that it never bears that meaning in any constitutional provision. As Amar himself notes, "it is difficult to prove a universal linguistic negative with a less-than-universal linguistic database."[23] Yet, if used to expand the range of meanings the Second Amendment might bear, intratextualism once again puts us right back where we started—that is to say, confronting a very abstract moral principle. It is entirely possible that "the people" might mean "all persons" when used in the Fourth Amendment but "the self-governing collective" when used in the Second Amendment.

There is another reason why intratextualism cannot tell us much about the meaning of the Second Amendment. Intratextualist arguments about the meaning of "the people" are relevant to one traditional form of argument about the Second Amendment, in which parties divide between "the collective-rights view" and "the individual-rights view."[24] The collective-rights view maintains that the Second Amendment is a kind of federalism provision, which protects the right of state and local communities to form "well-regulated militias" but does not confer any rights upon individuals. The individual-rights view contends that the Second Amendment confers rights upon individual persons. If intratextualist references to "the people" were to accomplish anything at all, they would vindicate the individual-rights view on the basis that the Fourth Amendment's reference to "the people" is uniformly regarded as creating individual rights. But that conclusion (even if we were to embrace it on intratextualist grounds) gets us virtually nowhere, for we must then ask *what* individual rights the Second Amendment confers. And it turns out that it is possible to recapture the moral substance of the collective-rights view within the individual-rights view. For example, the Second Amendment might confer upon individual persons only the right to participate on fair terms in collective military enterprises—the right, more or less, to join the National Guard.

Thus, for intratextualism to take the Second Amendment out of the domain of moral argument, the intratextualist arguments would have to be very ambitious indeed. They would have to do more than select between the collective-rights view and the individual-rights view; they would also have to select among possible versions of the individual-rights view. Perhaps clever lawyers can construct elaborate intratextualist arguments of that kind.[25] Yet, to borrow again from Amar's own analysis (slightly paraphrased), the heavier the burden that intratextualist argument must bear, the more strained the technique becomes. If it is questionable whether political committees used the same word in identical ways in neighboring amendments, it is still more doubtful that they encoded complex principles in subtle cross-references among sections.

3. Originalism More Generally (the Framers' "Legal" Intentions)

Of course, most of the historical arguments about the Second Amendment have little (if anything) to do with either intratextualism or the framers' linguistic intentions. Instead, they dwell on the framers' political theories, their general views about militias, the actual operation of the militias during the American Revolution, patterns of gun ownership, and so on.[26] These factors are taken (in differing degrees by different commentators) to be relevant to what Dworkin calls the framers' "legal intentions"—that is, their expectations about how the Second Amendment should be applied. These wide-ranging (and highly polemical) historical debates matter to the meaning of the Second Amendment only if originalism is a legitimate strategy for interpreting the Constitution.

The debate about originalism is long running and complex. My own view, which I elaborate at length elsewhere,[27] is that originalism is an indefensible approach to constitutional interpretation insofar as it is concerned with the framing generation's *legal* intentions. (I believe, along with Dworkin, that originalism is a perfectly acceptable and indeed correct theory if it is concerned exclusively with the framers' *linguistic* intentions.) I do not propose to renew the debate over originalism here.[28] I accordingly cannot rule out the possibility that a thorough-going originalist could find historical grounds for reading the Second Amendment one way or another.

Nevertheless, it seems to me that even those who find originalism appealing should be cautious about relying upon history to decide how the Second Amendment should affect modern gun control policy. In some constitutional domains, the choices that face Americans today are comparable in character to problems confronted by the framing generation. So, for example, when the framers enacted laws about taxation or military service or courtroom procedure, they had to decide whether justice required them to carve out exemptions for the benefit of persons whose religious exercise might be burdened by those laws.[29] The framers accordingly had to think about how to reconcile the claims of individual conscience with the public good. We can disagree about how to interpret the framers' ideas, or what weight to give them when reading the Constitution, but at least the framers *had* ideas about the relevant issue. One might say the same thing about some other familiar constitutional problems, such as the conflict between free speech and national security, or the tension between the right against self-incrimination and the need to convict criminals, or the opposition between the right of private property and the government's need to take property for public purposes. In all of these cases, of course, the range and detail of policies in play has changed enormously, as have the political stakes and the social and moral context of the policies. But the bare-bones moral structure of the issues facing us today would have been familiar to thoughtful members of the framing generation.

In this regard, the Second Amendment is different. Although the historical context of the amendment is vigorously (even acrimoniously) contested, three points seem incontrovertible. First, the founding generation's debate over the Second Amendment focused upon the militia, an institution that no longer exists (at least in anything like its eighteenth-century form). Second, the founding generation did not have, and did not envision, a major societal problem involving the use of guns by criminals. Third, the "arms" extant today are radically different from anything that existed in the eighteenth century. In light of these three facts, it seems batty, even by the standards of originalism, to suppose that the framers had any intention about how the Second Amendment should be applied under circumstances where citizen militias no longer exist, automatic weapons do exist, and gun violence has become a serious social problem.

Should Free Citizens Have a Right to Own Guns?

We can now summarize the argument in favor of interpreting the Second Amendment by reference to moral principle, rather than historical detail. As a matter of ordinary, twenty-first century American English, the Second Amendment states an abstract principle akin to "the American people shall enjoy those rights to gun ownership and military service which ought to belong to citizens of all free governments." History provides no ground to believe that the amendment should be interpreted differently. More specifically, interpreting the Second Amendment as a broad, abstract moral principle appears to be consistent with the *linguistic* intentions of the Constitution's framers. Even if we were to accept the (badly mistaken, in my view) methodological premises of intratextualism or originalism, there is no reason to suppose that either of those approaches can usefully narrow the scope of the Second Amendment.

So where does that leave us? Judges confronted with a Second Amendment claim must ask a question of moral and political theory. More specifically, they must ask what judicially enforceable rights of gun ownership and military service citizens of a free republic ought, in principle, to enjoy. My principal purpose in this essay is not to resolve this question but to insist that it is the appropriate one to ask. We can, however, make a preliminary assessment of the relevant arguments.[30] Two different moral justifications have been advanced to justify a constitutionally protected, judicially enforceable right to gun ownership. The first asserts that private gun ownership is necessary for reasons related to the democratic authority of citizens: Private gun ownership secures the right of citizens to resist a tyrannical government. The second asserts that private gun ownership is necessary for reasons related to individual autonomy: Private gun ownership secures the right of citizens to defend their own persons against violent attack.[31] In my view, both of these arguments fail, although the first fails more spectacularly than the second.

The argument from democracy presupposes that private arms enable "the people" to resist illegitimate government action. But there is

152 CHRISTOPHER L. EISGRUBER

no reason to suppose that armed, politically motivated violence by private citizens advances democracy rather than undermines it. Weapons enable an individual (or a small group of individuals) to exert power over others without showing any respect whatsoever for anybody else's opinions. For that reason, politically motivated violence is, in general though not always, profoundly undemocratic. Core principles of democracy require that disagreements be mediated through fair and impartial procedures and that the use of violence be controlled by deliberative public judgment. The democratic accountability of public officials must therefore depend upon the freedom of speech and the right to vote, rather than upon any private right of gun ownership. To exercise power through words, one must persuade others. To exercise power through votes, one must combine one's vote with numerous others. But, to exercise power with weapons, one need neither persuade anybody nor have numerous allies. A lone gunman is accountable to nobody. A small posse of terrorists can make its idiosyncratic political grievances the basis for cold-blooded murder of innocent democratic citizens. And matters only get worse if the armed insurgents are more numerous; they may be able to destabilize or destroy the political system, even if that system has widespread popular support.

But suppose that words and votes fail. Suppose that the government does fall into the hands of tyrannical officials who take over the military and use it to govern at the people's expense. That is possible, is it not? And, if that nightmare scenario occurs, would not the people have a better chance to resist if they were well armed? Maybe. Let's concede, at least for purposes of argument, that if the United States fell into the hands of an undemocratic despot, the people would be *more* able to resist if they owned private weapons (*how much* more able is another question). Still, it does not follow that private gun ownership helps democracy. The most significant bulwarks of democracy are free speech and the right to vote. The fact that these bulwarks might fail does not require us to embrace a right (private gun ownership) that might itself be used to undermine those bulwarks (through antidemocratic violence) and that is likely to be only marginally useful if a despot arises.[32]

Concerns with democratic political accountability do not, in my view, plausibly support a private right of gun ownership. They might perhaps be used to guarantee that every citizen has a right to participate on fair terms in the military. If the national army "looks like America," then it is less likely to turn its arms upon its fellow Americans. So one might suppose that the Second Amendment prohibits the military from excluding gays or from limiting the combat roles of women.[33]

The second argument for private gun ownership, derived from concerns about self-defense and individual autonomy, has more to be said in its favor. Gun ownership bears a more direct relationship to individual autonomy than to democratic accountability, since, as we have just seen, guns enable individuals to exercise power without explaining themselves to anybody or getting anybody's consent. There is no reason to suppose that individual citizens are good judges of everybody else's interests (that is, of "the people's" interests); hence, there is no reason to believe that private gun ownership enhances democratic accountability. On the other hand, we typically assume that people are sound judges of what is in their own interests. So it is plausible that people who own guns will use them to protect their own lives, families, and property.

Of course, that by itself is not a sufficient ground for defending a private right of gun ownership. Widespread private ownership of powerful weapons might impair, rather than enhance, the autonomy of most citizens. If you own a gun, you may be able to shoot, scare off, or deter would-be assailants, but if the assailants own guns, they may be able to shoot you first. That is why some people favor gun control (and why some free countries, such as Great Britain, have banned guns). Whether or not gun control increases the security of law-abiding citizens seems to be a complex and purely empirical question; people disagree not about the baseline moral principle (individuals should be able to protect themselves against crime and violence) but about whether widespread gun ownership makes people more or less secure.

We ordinarily entrust such complex and purely empirical judgments to the legislature, rather than entrench them in a judicially enforced constitutional rule.[34] Consider, for example, how we treat medicine. Drugs are important to life, just as guns are important to security. People may need drugs to save their lives or their health. Yet, people may misuse or abuse drugs in ways that damage their health. We trust legislatures to strike the appropriate balance between freedom and restraint. We do not recognize a constitutional right guaranteeing people the freedom to take whatever medicines they think they need; instead, we allow legislatures discretion to regulate drugs in (almost) whatever way they think will best serve the interests of public health. We assume that if free access to experimental drugs really promoted public health, legislators would facilitate it—since they and their constituents presumably agree that it is good for people to have the capacity to improve their own health.

The case in favor of legislative discretion seems even stronger when we deal with rights like gun ownership that raise obvious risks of harm and injury to innocent persons. For example, we value the right to travel but leave legislatures vast freedom to regulate the ownership and use of cars and other dangerous vehicles. We value the freedom of contract but allow legislatures to regulate all manner of commercial relationships. Likewise, we value personal security, but we might nevertheless trust legislatures to regulate weapons. If private gun ownership really improves the security of all (or even most) law-abiding citizens, then we should expect democratically elected legislatures to favor private gun ownership.

Perhaps, though, there is some reason to believe that, in the domain of gun policy, legislatures are especially prone to neglect the public interest. What might that reason be? If the point of the Second Amendment were to enable people to resist corrupt legislation, then we might have good reason to distrust the legislature: gun control policies, like gerrymanders, would entrench the power of incumbent officials and diminish their accountability. I have already argued, however, that there is no good reason to suppose that private gun ownership is a useful check upon government power. We are now considering the more plausible suggestion that gun ownership might, under some circumstances, enhance the ability of people to defend themselves. With regard to this concern, the legislature seems to have exactly the right incentives. The vast majority of voters will prefer policies that decrease the risk of crime and violence, and, hence, legislators, if they want to keep their seats, will have an incentive to enact such policies.

Of course, legislators may err. They may wrongly believe that gun control reduces crime when the opposite is true, or vice versa. Yet, in that respect gun control is no different from a vast range of policy issues—such as medical care, communications technology, labor law, environmental protection, education, welfare rights, and national security—over which legislatures exercise enormous discretion. The fact that legislators might make mistakes about gun control is not sufficient reason to enshrine individual rights of gun ownership in the Constitution.

As I said earlier, I offer these arguments only to provide a preliminary sketch of the considerations relevant to interpretation of the Second Amendment. It is possible that someone else will identify compelling reasons why we should distrust legislatures to regulate guns, even though we trust them to regulate all sorts of other devices that are equally important to the security of basic freedoms. We should notice, however, one response that is *not* available to those who favor rights of gun ownership. They cannot say that gun control is different from medicine or education or welfare rights simply because the framers of the Constitution specifically mentioned the "right to keep and bear arms" but said nothing about those other topics. That is precisely the sort of argument we ruled out earlier, when we determined that the Second Amendment states a broad moral principle. If the Amendment states a broad principle, claims about its interpretation must stand or fall on the basis of political theory, not blunt references to textual or historical facts. And, if political theory leads us to conclude that citizens of free governments ought to have only those rights of gun ownership granted by the legislature after due consideration of the relevant empirical issues, then the plain text of the Second Amendment poses no obstacle to that result.

Conclusion

The argument about gun violence is complex. Reasonable people may disagree about the merits of gun control policies and about what institutions should have the final say in the debate. Yet, whatever one's position about gun control, it is nutty to suppose that we should determine America's gun control policies today on the basis of arguments about, for example, how many Americans owned muskets in the late eighteenth century. People sometimes suppose, however, that the Constitution requires us to argue in that way. I have tried to show that is not so. The Second Amendment invites us to have an argument predicated upon moral principle and institutional strategy, not historical arcana. That is the right debate to have, and we should get on with it.

NOTES

1. On the significance (or insignificance) of the Second Amendment's preamble, see Eugene Volokh, "The Commonplace Second Amendment," *New York University Law Review* 73 (1998): 773, and David C. Williams, "Response: The Unitary Second Amendment," *New York University Law Review* 73 (1998): 822.

2. Ronald M. Dworkin, *Freedom's Law: The Moral Reading of the Constitution* (Cambridge, Mass.: Harvard University Press, 1996), 291. See also the distinction between "meaning" and "application" in Mark D. Greenberg and Harry Litman, "The Meaning of Original Meaning," *Georgetown Law Journal* 86 (1998): 569, 586–591, and between "rich" and "spare" semantic intentions in Michael Moore, *Southern California Law Review* 58 (1985): 279, 340.

3. Dworkin, *Freedom's Law*, 291.

4. Christopher L. Eisgruber, *Constitutional Self-Government* (Cambridge, Mass.: Harvard University Press, 2001), 29–32.

5. See, e.g., Laurence H. Tribe, "Defining High Crimes and Misdemeanors: Basic Principles," *George Washington Law Review* 67 (1999): 712, 717.

6. For descriptions of the polemical character of historical argument about the Second Amendment, see William Glaberson, "Dueling Scholars Join Fray over a Constitutional Challenge to Gun Control Laws," *New York Times*, 21 September 2000, p. A26, and Jack N. Rakove, "The Second Amendment: The Highest Stage of Originalism," *Chicago-Kent Law Review* 76 (2000): 103, 103–108.

7. Don B. Kates Jr., "Handgun Prohibition and the Original Meaning of the Second Amendment," *Michigan Law Review* 82 (1983): 204, 261.

8. Ibid., 219.

9. Ibid., 220. For arguments to similar effect, see Stephen Halbrook, "What the Framers Intended: A Linguistic Analysis of the Right to 'Bear Arms,'" *Law and Contemporary Problems* 49 (1986): 151.

10. Garry Wills, *A Necessary Evil: A History of American Distrust of Government* (New York: Simon and Schuster, 1999), 257.

11. Ibid., 259.

12. Merrill Jensen, ed., *The Documentary History of the Ratification of the Constitution* (Madison: State Historical Society of Wisconsin, 1976), 2:623–624.

13. *Webster's New Universal Unabridged Dictionary*, s. v. "zeugma."

14. Wills, *A Necessary Evil*, 257.

15. Akhil Reed Amar, "Intratextualism," 112 *Harvard Law Review* 747 (1999).

16. The point is common in the Second Amendment literature. An elaborate version is Akhil Reed Amar, *The Bill of Rights: Creation and Reconstruction* (New Haven: Yale University Press, 1998), 47–49, 51, 64–67; see also Akhil

Reed Amar, "The Bill of Rights as a Constitution," *Yale Law Journal* 100 (1991): 1131, 1162–1167. See also Kates, "Handgun Prohibition," 218.

17. I have elaborated this point in Eisgruber, *Constitutional Self-Government,* 113–115.

18. Amar, "Intratextualism," 793.

19. Ibid., 792.

20. *McCulloch v. Maryland,* 17 U.S. (4 Wheat.) 316 (1819).

21. Amar, "Intratextualism," 756–757.

22. *McCulloch,* 414–415.

23. Amar, "Intratextualism," 792.

24. The literature on these two views is voluminous; for review essays, written from competing points of view, see Randy E. Barnett and Don B. Kates, "Under Fire: The New Consensus on the Second Amendment," *Emory Law Journal* 45 (1996): 1139, and Carl T. Bogus, "The History and Politics of Second Amendment Scholarship: A Primer," *Chicago-Kent Law Review* 76 (2000): 3.

25. Amar's own, very elaborate intratextualist theory produces the surprising suggestion that the Second Amendment may prohibit the national government from conscripting soldiers. Amar, *Bill of Rights: Creation and Reconstruction,* 58–59.

26. For guides to some of the extensive, and tendentious, literature, see Barnett and Kates, "Under Fire," and Bogus, "History and Politics."

27. Eisgruber, *Constitutional Self-Government,* 25–44.

28. A trenchant application of general arguments against originalism to the Second Amendment is Daniel A. Farber, "Disarmed by Time: The Second Amendment and the Failure of Originalism," *Chicago-Kent Law Review* 76 (2000): 167.

29. For competing accounts of the framers' views about the topic, see Philip A. Hamburger, "A Constitutional Right of Religious Exemption: An Historical Perspective," *George Washington Law Review* 60 (1992): 915, and Michael W. McConnell, "The Origins and Historical Understanding of Free Exercise of Religion," *Harvard Law Review* 103 (1990): 1409.

30. My analysis and conclusions share much in common with Michael C. Dorf, "What Does the Second Amendment Mean Today?" *Chicago-Kent Law Review* 76 (2000): 291, 328–338.

31. Both the political (prodemocratic) and individualist (self-defense) justifications are well articulated by Nelson Lund, "The Second Amendment, Political Liberty, and the Right to Self-Preservation," *Alabama Law Review* 39 (1987): 103, 111–121. See also Sanford Levinson, "The Embarrassing Second Amendment," *Yale Law Journal* 99 (1989): 637, 645–646. Don Kates identifies three, rather than two, purposes for the Amendment: "(1) crime prevention, or what we would today describe as individual self-defense; (2) national defense;

and (3) preservation of individual liberty and popular institutions against domestic despotism." Kates, "Handgun Prohibition," 267–268. I do not treat the "national defense" argument separately from the "domestic despotism" argument; in my view, all the objections applicable to the latter are equally applicable to the former. Nor do I see any good reason to suppose that citizens' interest in "national self-defense" must be protected against invasion by the government—which has nearly perfect incentives to guard that interest vigorously.

32. In an effort to prove that private gun ownership can be an effective mechanism for political resistance to oppressive governments, both Kates and Levinson recite various instances in which armed citizens have used small weapons to repel or stymie powerful national armies. They claim that it does not matter that some of their examples involve undemocratic or terroristic behavior; what matters, they say, is that the examples prove that the right of insurrection has practical value today. Referring to Northern Ireland and to Israel's occupied territories, Levinson remarks, "The fact that these may not be pleasant examples does not affect the principal point, that a state facing a totally disarmed population is in a far better position, for good or ill, to suppress popular demonstrations and uprisings." Levinson, "Embarrassing Amendment," 657; see also Kates, "Handgun Prohibition," 270. But the fact that the examples are "unpleasant," in the sense of involving threats to justice and democracy, does matter. There is no good reason to recognize a right of insurrection that empowers minority radicals to destroy democratic government. And it is no accident that gun ownership is conducive to minority exercises of power; that is how weapons work, and that is why words and votes are better guarantors of democracy.

33. Carl Riehl, "Uncle Sam Has to Want You: The Right of Gay Men and Lesbians (and All Other Americans) to Serve in the Military," *Rutgers Law Journal* 26 (1995): 343.

34. I have elsewhere argued that courts should in general refrain from resolving issues in which strategic and empirical considerations predominate over moral ones. Eisgruber, *Constitutional Self-Government,* at 139–140, 169–175.

Part II

Policy Interventions in the Gun Arena

A. Gun Tracing

Chapter 8

New Law Enforcement Uses for Comprehensive Firearms Trace Data

Philip J. Cook and Anthony A. Braga

A. Introduction

In 1999, more than 150,000 firearms were submitted by law enforcement agencies for tracing by the Bureau of Alcohol, Tobacco, and Firearms (ATF), three times as many as in 1993.[1] This growth in trace requests indicates the success of ATF's program to persuade state and local agencies of the strategic value of comprehensive firearms tracing. About four dozen cities now submit all firearms confiscated by the police for tracing. The growing database of trace results has great potential for aiding local law enforcement agencies in identifying the dealers and traffickers who are supplying guns to youths and criminals.

Firearms tracing is nothing new. The Gun Control Act of 1968 established the regulations that make it possible, at least in principle, to determine the chain of commerce for a firearm from the point of import or manufacture to the first retail sale. Best practice in a police investigation of a gun homicide or assault often includes submitting the gun (if available) for tracing, in the hope of identifying a suspect or developing the case against a suspect. But law enforcement agencies obtain hundreds of thousands of firearms every year that are not linked to a particular violent crime but were confiscated for some other reason—most often because they were being carried or possessed illegally. While tracing such guns is unlikely to provide information useful in solving a particular homicide or assault, the data from such traces, when brought together and analyzed, can provide guidance to the regulatory and criminal enforcement activities of ATF

164 PHILIP J. COOK AND ANTHONY A. BRAGA

and, more generally, provide a statistical basis for attacking the supply side of the gun-violence problem.

The Treasury Department's success in expanding and improving ATF's tracing capacity, persuading more jurisdictions to submit all recovered guns for tracing if they are linked to a crime, and developing methods for analyzing the results, has created a new tool for combating gun violence. The promising uses for these data can be placed in three categories: (1) informing strategic planning efforts to interdict the transactions by which criminals tend to acquire their guns; (2) identifying specific firearm dealers and traffickers as targets for enforcement actions; and (3) providing a basis for evaluating the effects of changes in gun control laws.

The next section provides some background on the tracing process and the development of comprehensive tracing. The following section provides an analysis of what the trace data tell us about trafficking patterns: that newer guns are overrepresented in crime even though criminal users are rarely among the first purchasers and that the percentage of crime guns imported from out of state tends to be closely linked to the stringency of local controls. Taken together, these findings suggest that licensed dealers are playing a significant role in "supplying the suppliers" of guns to criminals and that firearms trafficking may be one of the important channels by which guns reach criminals, especially in the tight-control states. Subsequent sections review the prospects and problems of using trace data to guide enforcement efforts against specific dealers and traffickers and illustrate the use of trace data in the evaluation of gun control laws. The final section offers conclusions concerning the promise and pitfalls of wholesale tracing.

B. Procedures

The rather cumbersome procedure used by ATF to trace firearms reflects the fact that most of the relevant commercial transactions records are not centralized but rather are kept piecemeal by the dealers, distributors, and manufacturers. This arrangement reflects the intention of Congress to create a mechanism for tracing guns used in crime without establishing a national registry of firearms owners.

1. The Legal Framework

The Gun Control Act of 1968 (GCA) established the legal framework for regulating firearms transactions and the associated recordkeeping. The act was intended to limit interstate commerce in guns so that states with strict regulations were insulated from states with looser regulations. To that end, the GCA established a system of federal licensing for gun dealers, requiring that all individuals engaged in the business of selling guns must be a Federal Firearms Licensee (FFL). The FFLs serve as the gatekeepers for interstate shipments; only they may legally receive mail-order shipments of guns, and they may not sell handguns to residents of other states. FFLs are explicitly required to obey state and local regulations in transacting their business.

The Gun Control Act also set forth conditions on the transfer of firearms. FFLs may not sell handguns to anyone under the age of twenty-one, or long guns to anyone under the age of eighteen, nor may they sell any gun to someone who is proscribed from possessing one. The list of those proscribed by federal law includes individuals with a felony conviction or under indictment, fugitives from justice, illegal aliens, and those who have been committed to a mental institution. FFLs must require customers to show identification and fill out a form swearing that they do not have any of the disqualifying conditions specified in the Gun Control Act. Beginning in 1994, the Brady Violence Prevention Act required that FFLs initiate a background check on all handgun purchasers through law enforcement records; as specified in the act, the background-check requirement was expanded to include the sale of long guns beginning in 1998.

Most important for our purposes, the Gun Control Act established a set of requirements designed to allow the chain of commerce for any given firearm to be traced from its manufacture or import through its first sale by a retail dealer. Each new firearm, whether manufactured in the United States or imported, must be stamped with a unique serial number. Manufacturers, importers, distributors, and FFLs are required to maintain records of all firearms transactions, including sales and shipments received. FFLs must also report multiple handgun sales and stolen firearms to ATF and provide transaction records to ATF in response to firearms trace requests. When FFLs go out of business, they are to transfer their transaction records to ATF, which then stores them for use in tracing. Thus, the GCA created a paper trail for gun transactions that, at least in principle, can be followed by ATF agents.

2. The Tracing Process

The tracing process begins with a law enforcement agency submitting a trace request form to ATF's National Tracing Center (NTC).[2] The form requests information regarding the firearm type (e.g., pistol, revolver, shotgun, rifle); the manufacturer, caliber, and serial number; the location of the recovery; the criminal offense associated with the recovery; and the name and date of birth of the firearm possessor. This information is entered into ATF's Firearms Tracing System at the NTC, where it is first checked against two partially computerized databases kept by ATF: records of out-of-business FFLs that are stored by ATF and records of multiple handgun purchases reported on an ongoing basis by FFLs.

If there is no "hit" from these two databases, NTC contacts the firearm manufacturer (for domestic guns) or the importer (for foreign guns) and requests information on which distributor first handled the gun. ATF then follows the chain of subsequent transfers until it identifies the first retail seller. That FFL is then contacted with a request to search his or her records and provide information on when the gun was sold and to whom. Under current law, FFLs are compelled to comply with such requests and usually do.

In 1999, there were 154,000 firearms submitted for tracing.[3] Of these, just 54 percent were successfully traced, usually through the FFL who first sold the gun at retail. About one gun in ten was traced through the out-of-business records or multiple-sales reports from FFLs. The 46 percent of trace requests that failed did so for a variety of reasons. About 10 percent of the traces failed because the gun was too old.[4] Similar proportions failed because of problems with the serial number, errors in the submission form, or problems in obtaining the necessary information from the FFL that first sold the gun at retail.

It should be clear that, even when a trace is "successful," it provides rather limited information about the history of the gun. Most successful traces access only the data on the dealer's record for the first retail sale of the gun. Generally, subsequent transactions cannot be traced from the sorts of records required by federal law.

Most transactions involving used guns are either off-the-books transfers by private individuals, which cannot be traced because no recordkeeping is required, or are documented transactions by FFLs that are not reported to ATF and hence are not included in one of their computerized databases.[5] In exceptional instances where a firearm is involved in a particularly important crime, ATF may launch an "end to end" or "investigative" trace in an attempt to document the chain of possession beginning with an interview of either the first or the most recent known owner.[6] Needless to say, this type of trace is expensive and far from routine.

Someone learning about tracing for the first time may find it a remarkably cumbersome process in this age of computers and telecommunications. Modest changes in the current system could make a big difference.[7] For example, if FFLs were required to report serial numbers for all sales to NTC, then the tracing process would be greatly facilitated without creating a central registry of gun owners. The states could also develop reporting or registration systems. Currently, just eleven states have such a system, and only three (California, Maryland, and Massachusetts) have systems that are useful for tracing purposes.

C. The Implementation of Comprehensive Tracing

Until recently, most law enforcement agencies did not trace firearms unless they needed the information to solve a particular crime. In 1993, about 55,000 trace requests were submitted to ATF.[8] A concerted effort by ATF and the Clinton administration generated a considerable increase in the volume of trace requests. This effort entailed enhancements in the capacity and efficiency of the National Tracing Center and an outreach effort that persuaded a number of jurisdictions to submit all guns for tracing and provided local officials with training in how to do so.

The expansion in firearms tracing was part of the Clinton administration's campaign to strengthen ATF's licensing and regulatory enforcement efforts while attacking illicit gun trafficking. Previously, obtaining a federal dealer's license from ATF had been just a matter of paying a small fee and filling out a form. By 1993, there were more than 280,000 people who had done so, most of whom were not actually in the business of selling guns to the public. ATF at that time lacked the authority and resources to screen applicants effectively or to inspect their operations after issuing the license.[9] Thus, the federal licensing system, which had been intended to regulate retail commerce in guns, was itself unregulated. Beginning in 1993, ATF stiffened license application requirements and worked with state and local agencies to ensure that FFLs were complying with applicable state and local laws governing firearms retailing.[10] Further, the Crime Control Act of 1994 increased the fee for a three-year license from $30 to $200. The cumulative effect has been to reduce the number of federal licensees to about 100,000, thereby enhancing ATF's ability to serve its regulatory function.

ATF's push to expand firearms tracing was in part grounded in the development of new applications for trace data. In the early 1990s, methods for utilizing firearms-trace data to detect gun traffickers were developed by several ATF field divisions and by ATF's National Tracing Center. ATF's Boston Field Division was among the pioneers of a comprehensive approach, tracing all guns recovered by the Boston Police Department beginning in January 1991.[11] In partnership with academic researchers, ATF and the Boston Police Department analyzed the resulting data to describe the nature of the local gun market and to provide tactical guidance to investigators.[12]

The results of these trace studies, paired with convincing anecdotal evidence on the successful application of trace data in detecting gun traffickers, generated interest in the value of firearms trace data. In July 1996, President Clinton announced the Youth Crime Gun Interdiction Initiative (YCGII), with commitments from a number of cities to trace all recovered crime guns.[13] The program expanded from seventeen cities in 1996 to about four dozen cities by 2002. Other jurisdictions have also expanded their use of gun tracing. Six states, for example, have recently adopted comprehensive tracing as a matter of state policy, either by law (California, Connecticut, North Carolina, and Illinois), by executive order (Maryland), or by law enforcement initiative (New Jersey).[14]

One result of this comprehensive approach is that a large percentage of the "crime guns" submitted for tracing are not directly tied to a violent crime or a known criminal. Of the handguns submitted for tracing from YCGII cities in 1999, only 13 percent were connected to specific violent crimes; most were confiscated in connection with firearms offenses such as illegal carrying or possession (65 percent) or with drug offenses (20 percent).[15] Nonetheless, given these circumstances, it is a reasonable presumption that many of these guns were used to threaten or shoot someone or were quite likely to be used that way in the near future. In any event, in the aggregate, guns confiscated in connection with firearms and drug offenses have proven to be quite similar to guns connected to violent crimes with respect to source, age, and other characteristics.

D. Trafficking Indicators

Perhaps the most important use of the data generated from comprehensive tracing has been to make the case that FFLs play an important role in the diversion of guns to the hands of youths and criminals. This use has also been the most controversial, since it contradicts the conventional wisdom that criminals, for the most part, obtain their guns from the huge inventory already in private hands.[16]

That inventory exceeds 200 million, with 35 to 40 percent of households owning at least one gun.[17] Since guns are highly durable commodities, used guns appear to be a close substitute for new ones. More than 500,000 guns are stolen each year from private homes and vehicles, a number apparently sufficient to satisfy the "needs" of robbers and drug dealers.[18] These stolen guns merge with informal voluntary sales to supply a vast secondary market that is largely unregulated.[19]

1. Survey Evidence

Prior to the advent of comprehensive tracing, the sources of guns available to youths and criminals were documented by three surveys: Wright and Rossi's survey of prisoners,[20] the survey of state prisoners reported by Beck et al.,[21] and Sheley and Wright's survey of youths in juvenile correctional institutions. These surveys document the variety of channels by which guns are diverted to illegal use, including theft, family members, and the black market.

The survey data actually complement the trace data in suggesting a fairly substantial role, either direct or indirect, for the FFLs. About one-quarter of the respondents in the survey of state prisoners said that they had acquired their most recent gun from a retail outlet.

While this percentage is much lower for the juvenile respondents, Sheley and Wright note that "[t]hirty-two percent of the [juvenile] inmates . . . had . . . asked someone to purchase a gun for them in a gun shop, pawnshop, or other retail outlet.[22] In most cases these straw purchase arrangements involved family or friends as the purchaser. All three survey studies find that "street" and "black market sources" are important, sources that may well include traffickers who are buying from retail outlets and selling on the street.[23]

The comprehensive trace data serve to focus greater attention on that part of the market that links sales by FFLs to criminal use. The evidence is indirect but quite compelling. FFLs either unwittingly or corruptly sell to straw purchasers or to purchasers with false identification or sell guns off the books.[24] The YCGII reports note, for example, that while "crime" guns are rarely recovered from the person who is listed as the first retail buyer on the dealer's record, a relatively high percentage of these guns were first sold less than three years before they are recovered by police.[25] In states that have the most stringent regulations, a majority of crime guns (including those that are quite new) are first sold out of state. And a disproportionate number of traced handguns are part of a multiple sale when new. The suggestion, then, is that a substantial portion (albeit a minority) of the guns that end up in crime are first purchased from an FFL by a "straw purchaser"—someone who intended to resell them to a trafficker (illicit dealer) or to a proscribed individual. Alternatively, the first purchaser may in fact have been the same person as the possessor but presented false identification at the time of purchase. The FFL in such illicit transactions may be negligent, or a knowing confederate. In any case, these findings suggest that FFLs, straw purchasers, and traffickers play important roles in diverting guns to crime. If this is true, then the ATF's efforts to regulate FFLs and investigate trafficking may have the potential for effecting a reduction in gun violence.

2. The Importance of Newer Guns

Newer guns are greatly overrepresented among the crime guns submitted for tracing, despite the fact that it appears quite rare for the purchaser and the possessor to be the same person. Table 8.1 reports evidence in support of this view, based on the data on handguns submitted by the YCGII cities in 1999. Overall, 54 percent of these were

TABLE 8.1
Time from Retail Sale to Recovery by Police by Circumstance of the Recovery
(YCGII Handguns Submitted for Tracing, 1999)

	Homicide	Assault and Robbery	Vice and Narcotics	Firearms Offenses	Total
# submitted for tracing	1,427	5,682	10,621	35,064	54,433
# traced	818	3,357	5,962	18,233	29,302
(percentage)	(57%)	(59%)	(56%)	(52%)	(54%)
1 year old or less	14.9%	15.0%	14.0%	15.8%	15.3%
3 years old or less	32.4%	33.5%	30.6%	32.7%	32.4%

SOURCE: Original computations from ATF's 1999 firearm trace requests database for YCGII cities.

successfully traced so that the first retail sale could be dated. Of these, about 15 percent of the guns were less than one year old, and 32 percent were less than three years old. The results in this regard are remarkably uniform across the different recovery-circumstance categories, from homicide to vice to firearms offenses. But, in one way, these statistics overstate the percentage of guns submitted for tracing that are "new," since one of the important reasons that a gun cannot be traced is that it is too old. Adjusting for that consideration reduces the percentages to 13 for those less than one year and 27 for those less than three years.[26] These percentages are still very high in comparison with the corresponding statistics for all guns in private hands; the annual sale of new handguns represents less than 3 percent of the number of handguns in circulation.

It should be noted that some of the untraceable guns are also likely to be quite new. In some cases, FFLs may sell guns off the books, either in their state or in another. Guns from such sales can be traced to the dealer but the trace is generally recorded as incomplete when there is no record of the sale. About 10 percent of all traces are unsuccessful due to problems with dealer records.

Crime guns are rarely in the hands of the original buyer; only 18 percent of the handguns that are identified as less than three years old (and in which the name of the final owner was recorded in the trace request) were in the possession of the original buyer at the time they were recovered by police.[27] There are two caveats. First, in only 68 percent of these successfully traced "new" guns is a possessor identified. Second, in some fraction of the cases in which the purchaser and the possessor are identified as having different names, they may in fact be the same person, if false identification was used in the purchase. However, in making the case for regulatory enforcement, the distinction between false identification and straw purchaser actually does not matter much; whether the first purchase was by a criminal with false identification, or a straw purchaser, it remains true that the FFL is implicated in a transaction that resulted in diversion of the gun to criminal hands.

From one perspective, the disproportionate representation of new guns among those recovered by the police provides a basis for optimism about the potential crime-reducing effects of gun control measures. Franklin Zimring was the first to document this pattern and to interpret it.[28] He suggested that "new" guns and "old" guns were not perfect substitutes for criminal use, so an intervention that was successful in reducing the rate of introduction of new guns into a jurisdiction might have greater leverage on criminal gun use than would be expected, given the large inventory of guns in private hands.

A still more optimistic interpretation is that the "new guns" pattern is simply a reflection of a broader pattern. This view posits that people who use guns in crime usually acquire them shortly before the criminal use. Hence, the time since first retail sale is less important in determining the likelihood of criminal use than the time since the most recent transaction.[29] The population of active street criminals is characterized by brief careers and a high turnover rate.[30] Further, there is considerable evidence that gun-using criminals go through a number of guns during the course of their brief "careers."[31] Therefore, we expect that gun use by gang members, robbers, and drug dealers occurs shortly after the gun is acquired, if at all. The trace data tell us not about the time from the most recent transaction but rather (in most cases) about the time from the first retail sale. Many of the older guns had a short time to crime measured from the (unobserved) most recent transaction. Thus, the new guns may show up disproportionately because new guns tend to be in more active circulation.[32]

But this interpretation, with the focus on the transaction, does not detract from the strategic importance of the "new guns" finding. Some types of transactions are easier for authorities to interdict than others, and the transactions that divert guns from the licit to the illicit market may be particularly vulnerable to enforcement efforts.[33] Those transactions include off-the-books sales of new guns by FFLs and sales to straw purchasers. The importance of the "new guns" finding, then, is

TABLE 8.2
Trafficking Indicators in Three Tight-Control Cities
(YCGII Handguns Submitted for Tracing, 1999)

	Washington, D.C.	New York	Boston	YCGII Cities Total
A. # traced[a]/# submitted (percentage)	1,312/3,809 (34%)	2,736/6,080 (45%)	188/447 (42%)	29,302/54,433 (54%)
B. % out-of-state	100%	89%	69%	38%
C. % "new"[b]	19%	21.5%	21%	32%

SOURCE: Original computations from ATF's 1999 firearm trace requests database for YCGII cities.
[a] The number successfully traced that include both a "date of first sale" and a "date of recovery."
[b] Three years or less from time of first sale to time of recovery.

to identify transactions involving FFLs as being among those that lead more or less directly to criminal use.

Cities in tight-control, low-density jurisdictions tend to have a different "new guns" pattern than other cities. Table 8.2 breaks out the relevant data for Washington, D.C., New York, and Boston, all tight-control cities. For each of these cities, new handguns form a relatively small percentage of their 1999 crime guns. One explanation is that, since there are few legal sales of handguns to residents by FFLs in these cities, most handguns that end up being used in crime have been imported. New handguns are relatively expensive in these cities, since the transactions by which the gun moved from the retail dealer to the criminal were conducted under legal threat.

Also shown in Table 8.2 are the results of matching names of the first purchaser and the possessor. For new handguns in the three cities, the possessor is less likely to be the retail purchaser than is the case in other cities, again bespeaking the importance of informal (and mostly illegal) transactions in supplying these cities.

3. Interstate Movements

Firearms trace data allow law enforcement agencies to determine where recovered firearms were first sold at retail. A key result is that the percentage of crime guns imported from out of state is closely linked to the stringency of local firearm controls. In 1999, 62 percent of traced YCGII firearms were first purchased from FFLs in the state in which the guns were recovered. However, this fraction was far lower in the tight-control northeastern cities such as Boston, New York City, and Jersey City, where less than half of the traceable firearms were first sold at retail within state. In contrast, Birmingham, Gary, Houston, Miami, New Orleans, and San Antonio had at least 80 percent of their traceable firearms first sold at retail in the state in which the city was located.[34]

Table 8.2 provides specific results for Washington, D.C., New York, and Boston. The most extreme case is Washington, which has banned the acquisition of handguns by residents since 1975. Boston and especially New York also import most of their crime handguns. The corresponding percentages for "new" handguns (less than three years old) are just as high, suggesting that the process by which handguns reach criminals in these cities is not one of gradual diffusion; rather, the handguns that make it into these cities are imported directly after the out-of-state retail sale.

4. Other Indicators of Trafficking

The recovery of firearms with obliterated serial numbers is viewed by ATF as a key indicator of firearms trafficking. Guns with thoroughly obliterated serial numbers are untraceable, thus protecting a criminal who is concerned about being tied to an illegal use of the gun. But the prevalence of obliterated serial numbers among crime guns is not great.[35] In the eleven YCGII cities that reliably submitted information on guns with obliterated serial numbers in 1999, the prevalence was 9 percent for semiautomatic pistols and 5 percent for revolvers. The percentages for cities where most crime guns are imported appear to be higher—13 percent of recovered handguns had obliterated serial numbers in New York, and 16 percent in Boston. Obliterated serial numbers are more common among guns recovered from youths than among guns recovered from adults. In a study of Boston data, firearms with obliterated serial numbers were found to closely resemble newer crime guns in that they were mostly semiautomatic pistols, concentrated among particular brands and calibers, and recovered in neighborhoods that suffer from youth gun violence.

Another possible indicator of trafficking is multiple sales by FFLs. Trace results suggest that handguns that were first sold as part of a reportable multiple sale are much more likely than others to move quickly into criminal use.

5. Implications

A successful supply-side strategy for reducing gun crime does not require that today's street criminals have guns taken away from them. It is sufficient to block the transactions that supply guns for criminal use. Given the high turnover among the ranks of the criminally active, that strategy could be effective in short order. The transactions that put guns in the hands of criminals take a variety of forms, some of which appear more vulnerable to law enforcement efforts than others. In particular, the illicit, consensual transactions by which guns make the transition from the legal to the illegal market constitute a target that is vulnerable to ATF's capacities for regulation and enforcement. The trace data suggest that these transactions, including the sale of guns by FFLs to straw purchasers and traffickers, figure to a surprising extent as a direct source of crime guns. The importance of FFLs in such transactions is in fact understated by the trace data, since illicit, off-the-book sales by FFLs are not traceable.

But what will be the ultimate effect of an enforcement strategy that is effective in reducing the importance of FFLs and traffickers as a direct source of crime guns? In jurisdictions with a high density of gun ownership and lax regulations on sales, other sources, such as theft and informal sales, may provide a ready substitute for straw purchasing and scofflaw FFLs. It may be more feasible to make a difference with a supply-side strategy in cities with tight controls. The stakes are high enough to warrant a direct test.

E. Trace Data as an Investigative Tool

Comprehensive trace data provide a lens, however clouded, for viewing the big picture of how guns are diverted into criminal use. They also provide more focused information on the identity of FFLs and others who are most active in this illicit trade. These data have become an increasingly important tool in the enforcement effort.

The use of trace data as an investigative tool has been enhanced by the development of Project LEAD beginning in 1993. Project LEAD is a computer software application that contains information on all traced firearms from the NTC's Firearms Tracing System. The system provides ATF agents with data useful in identifying gun traffickers, straw purchasers, and scofflaw FFLs.

One of the more interesting applications of comprehensive trace data has been as a guide to licensing and regulatory enforcement. As it turns out, relatively few FFLs account for the bulk of all first retail sales identified through tracing of crime guns. To be specific, in 1998, 1.2 percent (1,020) of FFLs accounted for 57 percent of all successful traces.[36] It makes sense for ATF to focus its investigations on this small group. Indeed, in 2000, ATF began requiring certain FFLs with ten or more crime-gun traces with a time-to-crime of less than three years to report certain firearms transaction information to the NTC,[37] presumably as a prelude for closer scrutiny of their business practices.

It has also been suggested that information of this sort could be used by manufacturers and distributors as the basis for self-policing the industry.[38] The 2000 settlement of the law suits brought against Smith and Wesson by the U.S. Department of Housing and Urban Development and several cities includes some language concerning this possibility.[39]

The concerns about using trace data to implicate FFLs begin with the possibility that the concentration of trace data may simply reflect the concentration of sales. If the FFL's sales volume tends to be proportional to the number of traces, then it would be unfair or at least inefficient to use trace data as a basis for singling out certain FFLs. Unfortunately, it has been difficult to determine the distribution of sales among FFLs in most states using available data.[40] One exception is California, where handgun sales by dealers are tabulated by a state agency. One analysis of these data found that sales of handguns are highly concentrated: the 13.1 percent of FFLs with more than one hundred sales during 1996–1998 accounted for 88.1 percent of all sales.[41] Handgun trace volume from 1998 was strongly correlated with handgun sales volume and is highly concentrated among the high-volume dealers, yet "trace volume varied substantially among dealers with similar sales volumes." The study did not determine whether this variation was greater than could be explained by chance alone, however.[42]

One would expect that guns sold by some FFLs would be more likely to be traced than others, even if all dealers were equally scrupulous in their dealings, for two reasons that do not imply wrongdoing by the high-trace FFLs. First, tracing policies are still highly uneven. FFLs that operate in areas that have not adopted comprehensive tracing are going to be largely invisible to trace results unless their guns end up in other cities that do trace. Second, FFLs that operate in high-crime urban neighborhoods are more likely to inadvertently supply criminals than those whose clientele are primarily sportsmen. All of this is to say that the guidance provided by the number of traces to a particular FFL is only a rough indicator of the likelihood that the FFL is engaging in negligent or criminal sales practices. The continuing expansion of comprehensive tracing will help, as will continuing efforts to refine the indicators from trace data used to identify bad actors among the FFLs.

Finally, ATF has been working with academic researchers to develop a decision-support system for law enforcement agencies to assess the investigative potential of particular crime gun traces beyond the current database-querying capacities of Project LEAD.[43] The goal of the decision-support system research was to identify potential behavioral predictors of quick time-to-crime guns so that law enforcement agencies can focus their limited resources on the parts of the illegal gun market composed of direct supply lines of guns from retail sources to criminals and youth. The research revealed that nearly a third of all 1999 traced crime guns had two or more indicators of gun trafficking: ATF had had to send the dealer multiple record-request letters, the buyer had at one time or another purchased two or more guns recovered in crime, or the purchaser was a known associate of a crime-gun possessor. The decision-support system, when implemented, will provide investigators with routine reports of suspicious purchase and sales patterns. Investigators will also be able to easily customize these intelligence reports to be sensitive to the nature and volume of the local illegal gun markets they seek to disrupt.

Another developing frontier is the effort to combine trace data with ballistics data contained in the National Integrated Ballistics Information Network (NIBIN).[44] The NIBIN database contains the unique images of casings and bullets recovered at crime scenes, as well as casings or bullets from test fires of recovered guns. By matching images, investigators can determine that a gun was used in one or more assaults and then determine from the trace something about the transactions history of the gun.

F. Using Trace Data in Policy Evaluation

In addition to the uses described, trace data have increasingly been used in policy evaluation. Of the early uses of this sort, the analysis by Weil and Knox is the most prominent.[45] They studied the effects of Virginia's law limiting handgun purchases by any individual to no more than one during a thirty-day period. Prior to the implementation of this law, in July 1993, Virginia had been one of the leading source states for guns recovered in the Northeast.[46] The study showed that during the first eighteen months the law was in effect, Virginia's role in supplying guns to New York and Massachusetts was greatly reduced. In particular, guns recovered in the Northeast corridor that were first sold in the Southeast were much less likely to have originated in Virginia if they were sold after its one-gun-a-month law went into effect than before.[47] Subsequent studies have made use of the fact that the gun-trace database includes detailed characteristics of these guns.[48]

To further illustrate the use of trace data for evaluation purposes, we use such data to assess the effects of the Brady Handgun Violence Prevention Act (Brady Act) on interstate trafficking. Implemented in February 1994, it requires FFLs to conduct a background check on all handgun buyers and mandates a one-week waiting period before the gun is transferred to the purchaser. FFLs operating in eighteen states were not affected because state law already required a background check; FFLs in the remaining states were required to institute the change. Thus, the Brady Act created a sort of experiment with a natural control group—the "no-change" states. A recent evaluation of this act found that there was no discernible difference in homicide trends in the affected ("Brady") states as compared with the eighteen "non-Brady" states,[49] concluding that the Brady Act had no direct effect on homicide rates. That result leaves open the possibility that the Brady Act had an *indirect* effect on homicide rates by reducing interstate gun trafficking and hence gun violence in the "no-change" states.

Here we limit our illustrative analysis to Chicago, where, as noted, the police recover an exceptionally large number of guns every year. It was one of the first cities to adopt comprehensive tracing, in 1996.[50] In what follows we utilize the database on traces conducted on guns recovered in Chicago during the period 1996–1999.

Handguns used in crime in Chicago are imported either from the

TABLE 8.3
The Effect of the Brady Law on Chicago: Comprehensive Trace Data of
Handguns Recovered during 1996–1999

Location of First Sale	First Sold before 1994	First Sold in 1994 or After
In-State (Illinois)	54.0%	68.3%
Out-State, Brady State	32.5%	16.0%
Out-State, Other State	13.5%	15.7%
Total	100%	100%
(Count)	(14,862)	(11,571)

SOURCE: Original computations from ATF's YCGII firearm trace requests from Chicago, 1996–1999.

rest of Illinois or from other states. Illinois was one of the states that required a background check even before the Brady Act was implemented, and so it did not make any changes in 1994. Hence if *Brady* requirements affected the flow of guns into Chicago, it must have been due to reductions in interstate trafficking. And that, according to the trace data, is just what happened.

In the years prior to the Brady Act's implementation in 1994, about half of the handguns recovered in Chicago were first sold in Illinois, and half were sold in other states (Table 8.3). Thereafter, the percentage of such handguns first sold in Illinois jumped to about 68 percent. Handgun imports from other states fell correspondingly, but the fall was confined to those source states (designated "Brady" states) that were required by the Brady Act to institute a waiting period for handgun sales and to begin conducting background checks (Figure 8.1). Figure 8.2 provides more detail on how interstate flows into Chicago were affected. As can be seen, the South-Central states, and Mississippi in particular, accounted for most of the out-of-state handguns in Chicago; all of these were *Brady* states. The effect of the Brady Act's implementation appears to have been immediate and large. A natural interpretation of these results is that the Brady Act made interstate gun running from lax-control states to Chicago less profitable by making it more difficult for traffickers to buy handguns from FFLs in those states. The result was a large reduction in imports from those states, replaced (as a portion of the total) by an increase in the use of in-state sources.

The next question, of course, is whether these changes made it more difficult for Chicago residents to obtain handguns in Chicago and, in particular, whether gun violence was curtailed. It is certainly

FIGURE 8.1
Source States of Traceable Handguns Recovered in Chicago, 1996–1999

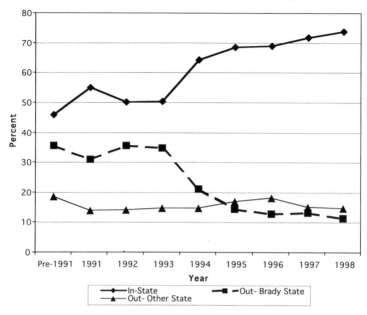

FIGURE 8.2
Traceable Firearms Recovered in Chicago Imported from Brady States, 1996–1999

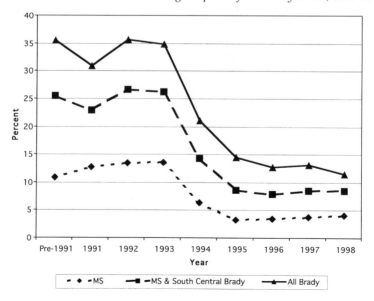

plausible that the Brady Act increased the cost of supplying new handguns to Chicago criminals, since new sources had to be found to replace those that were no longer convenient because of the new requirements. But that speculation cannot be tested directly, since there are no data available on the street prices of handguns in Chicago. The ultimate question, whether gun use in violent crime was reduced, requires an analysis of data on gun use in violent crime.[51] Thus, the trace data are helpful in suggesting whether the intervention may have been effective in reducing gun availability, but they do not provide a bottom line on violence.

Trace data provide a direct basis for assessing the effects of a policy on gun movements or the use of particular types of guns in crime. Of course, any results must be qualified, since the trace data are not necessarily a representative sample of guns used in crime. Nevertheless, these data provide an accurate basis for tracking changes over time if the "sample" bears a consistent, albeit imperfect, relationship to the population from one period to the next. It would be surprising indeed if the intertemporal patterns we found in the Chicago trace data were simply some sort of sampling artifact.

Another limitation is that gun control policies' ultimate purpose is the reduction of gun use in crime, and trace data do not provide direct evidence on that outcome. Rather, trace data provide a basis for tracking the proximate effects of a policy intended to work through the supply side of the gun market. If the intervention is effective in affecting trafficking patterns, then it becomes at least plausible that it also curtails criminal use of guns.

G. Concluding Thoughts

The case for comprehensive tracing rests on a belief that enforcement efforts directed at the supply of guns to criminals have the potential of reducing the use of guns in violence. That potential can be most efficiently realized if enforcement efforts are guided by data.

The case against comprehensive tracing follows from the belief that guns in America are so readily available, and from such a variety of sources, that efforts to restrict supply are futile. For example, if we view every one of the 35 million or so handgun owners[52] as a potential source of a crime gun, then the enforcement task does indeed appear overwhelming. It is conceivable that regulatory measures such as requiring guns to be locked or personalized and stored safely could help restrict criminal access to such diffuse sources. But current enforcement efforts are more tailored to identifying and shutting down what could, in the parlance of environmental regulation, be called "point" sources—scofflaw dealers or trafficking rings that are diverting guns to criminals on an ongoing basis.

The trace data provide evidence that these point sources are quite important in supplying criminals, thus strengthening the case for a supply-side strategy. The distribution channels connecting FFLs to criminal uses are often short and well traveled. About one-quarter of crime guns in the YCGII cities are less than three years old and have changed hands at least once since the initial purchase, suggesting that the initial purchase was made with the intent of diverting the gun into the black market. In addition, there are an unknown but possibly large number of crime guns that are untraceable because corrupt FFLs sold them off the books, presumably to criminals.

These patterns stand side by side with data indicating that more than half a million guns are stolen each year and that most youths and criminals report obtaining their guns from casual, informal sources. A reasonable conclusion is that, as in the case of pollution, both point sources and diffuse sources are important. Quite possibly, the actual mix depends on the stringency of state-level controls and the prevalence of gun ownership—systematic gun trafficking may well be more important in strict-control jurisdictions such as Boston and New York than in looser-control jurisdictions such as Atlanta and Dallas.

Given that there is a mix of concentrated and diffuse sources, the question is whether a successful regulatory or enforcement action against the former will reduce gun availability and hence gun use in crime. On that question we have little direct evidence. Given the high stakes in this area, systematic experimentation with different tactics appears warranted.

We have sought to document in this essay the potential uses of trace data in guiding a supply-side strategy. Trace data have improved rapidly during the past seven years as more and more jurisdictions have adopted comprehensive tracing and as ATF has expanded its capacity to handle trace requests.

The growing database of trace data, together with the LEAD software, is an increasingly important tool in identifying particular FFLs and nonlicensed individuals as being important in trafficking. This seems like the least controversial basis for demonstrating the usefulness of the data.

Trace data are also establishing a unique niche in policy evaluation, providing a basis for exploring the effects of supply-oriented interventions on the types and sources of guns used in crime. The example offered demonstrates both the usefulness of these data and their limits. We learn that the implementation of the Brady Act was associated with a dramatic change in sources of crime guns in Chicago but do not learn what effect the act might have had on gun violence.

Comprehensive tracing of firearms is one of the important legacies of the Clinton years. The hope for the future is that this new resource will be utilized with due awareness of its limitations.

N O T E S

Reprinted by permission of the *Arizona Law Review*.

1. We would like to thank Terry Austin, of the Bureau of Alcohol, Tobacco, and Firearms, for providing us with the 1999 ATF firearms trace data as part of ATF's efforts to enhance the development of the Youth Crime Gun Interdiction Initiative. We would also like to thank Glenn Pierce and Alan Saiz, of Northeastern University, for their assistance in acquiring the data utilized in this study, and Jens Ludwig, Susan Ginsburg and John Freeman for their helpful comments.

2. Bureau of Alcohol, Tobacco, and Firearms (ATF), *Commerce in Firearms in the United States* (Washington, D.C.: Bureau of Alcohol, Tobacco, and Firearms, 2000), 19.

3. This total omits the 11,000 requests from foreign agencies.

4. Firearms manufactured or imported before 1968 cannot be traced in most cases because they were not subject to the serial number and recordkeeping requirements of the Gun Control Act. Bureau of Alcohol, Tobacco, and Firearms (ATF), *Crime Gun Trace Analysis Reports: The Illegal Youth Firearms Market in 17 Communities* (Washington, D.C.: Bureau of Alcohol, Tobacco, and Firearms, 1997).

5. Between 30 and 40 percent of firearms are acquired used from someone who is not an FFL. Philip J. Cook and Jens Ludwig, *Guns in America: Results of a Comprehensive Survey of Gun Ownership and Use* (Washington, D.C.: Police Foundation, 1996).

6. See Bureau of Alcohol, Tobacco, and Firearms (ATF), *Crime Gun Trace*

Reports (1999): National Report (Washington, D.C.: Bureau of Alcohol, Tobacco, and Firearms, 2000), 54.

7. Jeremy Travis and William Smarrito, "A Modest Proposal to End Gun Running in America," *Fordham Urban Law Journal* 19 (1992): 795.

8. ATF, *Commerce in Firearms*, 21.

9. Josh Sugarmann and Kristen Rand, *More Gun Dealers Than Gas Stations: A Study of Federally Licensed Firearms Dealers in America* (Washington, D.C.: Violence Policy Center, 1992).

10. Garen J. Wintemute, "Guns and Gun Violence," in Alfred Blumstein and Joel Wallman, eds., *The Crime Drop in America* (New York: Cambridge University Press, 2000), 45.

11. David M. Kennedy, Anne M. Piehl, and Anthony A. Braga, "Youth Violence in Boston: Gun Markets, Serious Youth Offenders, and a Use-Reduction Strategy," *Law and Contemporary Problems* 59 (Winter 1996): 170.

12. Kennedy et al., "Youth Violence in Boston," 147.

13. Fox Butterfield, "Federal Program Will Track Sales of Guns to Youth," *New York Times*, July 8, 1996, 1. The name of this initiative is a bit misleading, since it was not limited to youths.

14. ATF, *Crime Gun Trace Reports (1999)*, 51.

15. Philip J. Cook and Anthony A. Braga, "Comprehensive Firearms Tracing: Strategic and Investigative Uses of New Data on Firearms Markets," *Arizona Law Review* 43 (summer 2001): 296.

16. As summarized by Gary Kleck, "BATF Gun Trace Data and the Role of Organized Gun Trafficking in Supplying Guns to Criminals," *St. Louis University Public Law Review* 18 (1999): 23.

17. Philip J. Cook and Jens Ludwig, *Gun Violence: The Real Costs* (New York: Oxford University Press, 2000).

18. Cook and Ludwig, *Guns in America*; Kleck, "BATF Gun Trace Data."

19. Philip J. Cook, Stephanie Molliconi, and Thomas Cole, "Regulating Gun Markets," *Journal of Criminal Law and Criminology* 86 (1995): 59–92.

20. James D. Wright and Peter H. Rossi, *Armed and Considered Dangerous: A Survey of Felons and Their Firearms* (expanded edition) (New York: Aldine de Gruyter, 1994).

21. U.S. Bureau of Justice Statistics, *Survey of State Prison Inmates 1991* (Washington, D.C.: U.S. Department of Justice, 1993).

22. Joseph Sheley and James Wright, *In the Line of Fire: Youth, Guns and Violence in Urban America* (New York: Aldine de Gruyter, 1995), 48.

23. Julius Wachtel, "Sources of Crime Guns in Los Angeles, California," *Policing: An International Journal of Police Strategies and Management* 21 (1998): 220–239; Kennedy et al., "Youth Violence in Boston."

24. By themselves, trace data do not demonstrate that FFLs sell either unwittingly or corruptly to straw purchasers or to purchasers with false identifi-

cation. See Bureau of Alcohol, Tobacco, and Firearms (ATF), *Following the Gun: Enforcing Federal Laws against Firearms Traffickers* (Washington, D.C.: Bureau of Alcohol, Tobacco, and Firearms, 2000).

25. ATF, *Crime Gun Trace Reports, 1999.*

26. This adjustment assumes that about 10 percent of all trace attempts fail because the gun is too old and that the other guns that are not successfully traced have the same age distribution as those that are.

27. Cook and Braga, "Comprehensive Firearms Tracing."

28. Zimring, "Firearms and Federal Law: The Gun Control Act of 1968," *Journal of Legal Studies* 4 (1975): 133–198; Zimring, "Street Crime and New Guns: Some Implications for Firearms Control," *Journal of Criminal Justice* 4 (1976): 95–107.

29. Philip J. Cook, "The Technology of Personal Violence," in Michael Tonry, ed., *Crime and Justice: An Annual Review of Research* (Chicago: University of Chicago Press, 1991). We are not arguing that the age of the gun is irrelevant to criminals. For example, the preferences of criminal consumers for certain types of guns may partially explain why semiautomatic pistols have quicker time-to-crime distributions; Kennedy et al. "Youth Violence in Boston."

30. See Alfred Blumstein, Jacqueline Cohen, Jeffrey A. Roth, and Christy Visher, eds., *Criminal Careers and "Career Criminals,"* vol. 1 (Washington, D.C.: National Academy Press, 1986), 4.

31. Cook et al., "Regulating Gun Markets."

32. We are unaware of any documentation on this pattern but are confident that it is true. Older guns may be war souvenirs or family heirlooms kept in deep storage. A new gun is more likely to be in good working order and to be put to whatever use the current owner intended at the time that he acquired it.

33. Christopher S. Koper and Peter Reuter, "Suppressing Illegal Gun Markets: Lessons from Drug Enforcement," *Law and Contemporary Problems* 59 (winter 1996): 119.

34. ATF, *Crime Gun Trace Reports, 1999.*

35. Kleck, "BATF Gun Trace Data."

36. ATF, *Commerce in Firearms in the United States.*

37. ATF, *Crime Gun Trace Reports, 1999.*

38. See National Economic Research Associates (NERA), "Expert Report of Lucy Allen and Jonathan Portes," 95-CV-0049 (JBW); *Hamilton v. Accu-Tek*, 935 F. Supp. 1307, 1330 (E.D.N.Y. 1996).

39. Agreement between Smith and Wesson and the Departments of the Treasury and Housing and Urban Development, Local Governments and States, March 17, 2000.

40. Since all FFLs are required to initiate a background check before transferring a gun to a buyer, the number of such checks that originate from a dealer should provide a good proxy for his volume of sales. But data on the

number and distribution of background checks are not generally available from centralized sources. Currently, only Brady-denial information is centrally compiled by the National Instant Check System (NICS). See U.S. Department of Justice and U.S. Department of Treasury, *National Integrated Firearms Violence Reduction Strategy* (Washington, D.C.: U.S. Department of Justice and U.S. Department of the Treasury, 2000).

41. Garen J. Wintemute, "Relationship between Illegal Use of Handguns and Handgun Sales Volume," *Journal of the American Medical Association* 284 (2000): 556.

42. One approach would be to compare the distribution of traces with the distribution that would result from a circumstance in which every gun sold, regardless of by which FFL, had the same probability of being traced. The latter hypothetical distribution would have the same qualitative characteristic as that found by Wintemute; FFLs with the same level of sales would have widely differing numbers of traces, just by chance alone.

43. Glenn L. Pierce, Anthony A. Braga, Christopher Koper, and Raymond Hyatt, *The Characteristics and Dynamics of Illegal Firearms Markets: Implications for a Supply Side Strategy* (Boston: Center for Criminal Justice Policy Research, Northeastern University, 2002).

44. U.S. Bureau of Alcohol, Tobacco, and Firearms, *The Missing Link: Ballistics Technology That Helps Solve Crimes* (Washington, D.C.: Bureau of Alcohol, Tobacco, and Firearms, 2001).

45. Douglas S. Weil and Rebecca C. Knox, "Effects of Limiting Handgun Purchases on Interstate Transfer of Firearms," *Journal of the American Medical Association* 275 (1996): 1759.

46. Weil and Knox reference a series of unpublished ATF memorandums reporting that 41 percent of a sample of guns seized in New York City in 1991 had been traced to Virginia. The reports also identified Virginia as a primary source state for guns recovered in Boston and Washington, D.C. Weil and Knox, "Effects of Limiting Handgun Purchases on Interstate Transfer of Firearms," 1760–1761.

47. Weil and Knox, "Effects of Limiting Handgun Purchases," 1760–1761.

48. A recent study used trace data to analyze the effect of the national assault weapons law implemented in 1994. See Jeffrey A. Roth and Christopher S. Koper, *Impacts of the 1994 Assault Weapons Ban: 1994–96* (Washington, D.C.: National Institute of Justice, 1999). A study of the Maryland law that banned "Saturday-night special" handguns found that these guns were less likely to be recovered by the police in Baltimore than in fifteen cities outside Maryland where no such ban was in effect. See Jon S. Vernick and Stephen P. Teret, "New Courtroom Strategies Regarding Firearms: Tort Litigation against Firearm Manufacturers and Constitutional Challenges to Gun Laws," *Houston Law Review* 36 (1999): 1713.

49. Jens Ludwig and Philip J. Cook, "Homicide and Suicide Rates Associated with Implementation of the Brady Handgun Violence Prevention Act," *Journal of the American Medical Association* 284 (2000): 585–591.

50. Personal communication with ATF National Tracing Center Chief Terry Austin. See also Kennedy et al., "Youth Violence in Boston," 170.

51. In fact, there was little change in the percentage of homicides committed with guns in Chicago during the three years following implementation of the Brady Act, which suggests that access to guns by violent people was not much affected.

52. Tom W. Smith, *1999 National Gun Policy Survey of the National Opinion Research Center: Research Findings* (Chicago: National Opinion Research Center, University of Chicago, 2000), 49. This report provides a survey-based estimate that 17.1 percent of adults owned at least one handgun in 1999. In 1999, there were about 201 million people in the United States age eighteen and over; see U.S. Bureau of the Census, *Statistical Abstract of the United States, 1999* (Washington, D.C.: U.S. Bureau of the Census, 1999), 17.

B. Gun-Oriented Policing and Community Interventions

Chapter 9

Policing Guns
Order Maintenance and Crime Control in New York

Jeffrey A. Fagan and Garth Davies

I. Introduction

Beginning in 1985 and continuing for more than a decade, the United States experienced an unprecedented epidemic of gun violence.[1] The spiking rates of gun violence triggered a crisis of social and political consequences that mobilized legal institutions, especially the police, to develop effective programs to reduce gun deaths and injuries. Even before this most recent homicide crisis, however, numerous experiments and innovations in policing were taking place in cities across the United States, and some of these were quickly adapted to meet the crisis of gun violence.[2] Under the flag of "community policing," "problem-oriented policing," and "order-maintenance policing," police departments launched a variety of reforms and experiments aimed at chronic problems of crime and gun violence.

As gun violence began its decline in American cities in the early 1990s, "Do police matter?" became a hotly contested question. On one side of this debate are researchers who suggest that police strategies directly and exclusively contribute to crime declines.[3] These scholars claim that "but for" new police strategies, crime rates would not have fallen as sharply or as persistently as recent trends show. On the other side are researchers who claim that crime declined steeply across cities that applied quite different police strategies, inviting explanations other than policing to account for the crime decline.[4] Researchers looking across cities describe policing as one of many interacting social and economic forces that together produced downward pressures on crime.[5] Unfortunately, there is little hard evidence to back up any of these claims.

Despite controversies about research that compares cities, studies *within* cities have shown that police practices can make a difference through small-scale, carefully targeted interventions. Many of these practices have targeted guns, at times with impressive results. In Boston, police and other law enforcement agencies parsimoniously selected individuals for police surveillance and interdiction.[6] In Indianapolis and in Pittsburgh, police used directed patrols and proactive stops of citizens to reduce gun carrying and gun crimes in specific areas where gun violence rates were highest.[7] Chicago[8] and San Diego[9] used recurring data analysis processes to strategically focus on situations and locations where crime rates were highest. Police in Jersey City targeted specific violence reduction strategies at specific problems within public housing projects to reduce violence.[10]

Many of these efforts were based on the notion that expanding the toolkit of police to include solving aggravating social problems through interaction and collaboration with citizens would involve citizens in the coproduction of security.[11] Police focused their efforts on the issues that concerned residents the most, while at the same time motivating citizen cooperation in the everyday policing of crime. These efforts created new forms of neighborhood-police partnerships, often called "community policing."[12] Research on these innovations shows that directed patrol practices and other targeted strategies have produced declines in gun crimes that exceed the general regression in crime in most cities.

Each of these local developments expresses its own vision about the role of police in ensuring both short-term and residual security. They vary on critical dimensions including the amount of discretion accorded to police both tactically and in setting priorities, their role in addressing noncrime problems, the role of data in the management and deployment of police resources, the nature and degree of interaction with different segments of their communities, the regulation of police performance and mechanisms of police accountability, and the priority accorded to citizen perceptions of the legitimacy of police actions.

No experiment has received as much popular attention or political acclaim as the policing innovation in New York City: intensive and aggressive street-level interdiction of low-level social and physical disorder.[13] The strategy was informed by the influential essay by James Q. Wilson and George Kelling titled "Broken Windows," describing the contagious effects of disorder on crime commission.[14] Police officials in New York translated "Broken Windows" into a policing strategy known as "order-maintenance policing" (OMP). As crime rates fell in New York, OMP captured popular and political imagination in the 1990s. OMP has been the subject of numerous books[15] and has influenced police theory and practice in cities both in the United States and abroad.[16]

Despite its popularity, OMP not been studied systematically, and political claims of its comparative advantage fall short of social science rules of inference.[17] Only one study thus far has examined the specific effects of OMP, and problems in methods and measurement undermine its claims for the superiority of OMP compared to other crime control and violence reduction strategies.[18] In this chapter, we assess the theoretical principles and origins of the New York city policing innovation and then estimate its effects on gun violence and crime more generally.

II. Order Maintenance and Gun-Oriented Policing in New York City

A. Broken Windows, Order Maintenance, and Racial Policing

Beginning in 1994, New York City police officials reordered crime control strategies to focus on two related problems: social and physical disorder and gun violence. Both the strategic and the tactical innovations were inspired by Broken Windows theory. This theory has had an extraordinary influence on American policing in the past two decades. Its creators, James Q. Wilson and George Kelling, argued that police should address minor disorders to strengthen police-citizen interactions and, in turn, informal social control.[19] For Wilson and Kelling, signs of physical and social disorder invite criminal activity.[20] Disorder indicates to law-abiding citizens that their neighborhoods are dangerous places, scaring citizens into withdrawal from everyday acts of informal social control and regulation. At some tipping point, the theory suggests that disorder trumps order by defeating the willingness of citizens to interact with the police to coproduce security. Accordingly, disorder invites more disorder in a contagious process that progressively breaks down community standards and encourages would-be criminals. Disorder ultimately invites criminal invasion.

In New York City, Broken Windows theory was translated into a police strategy known as "order-maintenance policing," or OMP.[21] Under OMP, police aggressively enforced laws against social disorder with "zero tolerance" that required arrest for any law infraction.[22] The NYPD adopted a tactical policy of aggressive stop-and-frisk practices to implement the new crime-fighting strategy. Policing disorder required intervention and arrest for low-level disorder problems that might invite more serious crime problems.

Many observers have noted that OMP in New York City has eschewed (what are for police) the more esoteric dimensions of community policing targeted at physical disorder in favor of an aggressive policy of arrest and other traditional law enforcement tactics aimed squarely at social disorder. While OMP promotes active engagement with and arrest of law violators, more traditional community policing emphasizes ameliorative measures that also are consistent with Broken Windows theory but that avoid coercive encounters with citizens on the street.[23] These ameliorative measures are consistent with the Broken Windows tenet that police should focus equally on protecting communities and on protecting individuals.

While remaining true to the theoretical origins of Broken Windows, strategy documents issued by the NYPD in 1994[24] unveiled two policies that cemented the marriage of OMP and "gun-oriented policing."[25] First, Police Strategy No. 5, *Reclaiming the Public Spaces of New York,* directed police to "reclaim the streets" by aggressively enforcing laws against low-level *social* disorder: graffiti painting, aggressive panhandling, fare beating, public drunkenness, unlicensed vending, public drinking, public urination, and other low-level misdemeanor offenses. "By working systematically and assertively to reduce the level of disorder in the city, the NYPD will act to undercut the ground on which more serious crimes seem possible and even permissible."[26]

Second, Police Strategy No. 1, *Getting Guns Off the Streets of New York,*[27] focused police strategies on guns. Homicide trends in New York City since 1985 provided strong empirical support for emphasizing gun violence in enforcement policy. Nearly all the increases in homicides, robberies, and assaults during this period were attributable to gun violence.[28] The political fallout of the homicide crisis lasted for several years more. The homicide crisis was a critical theme in the mayoral election campaign of 1993 and focused the attention of the incoming Giuliani administration's crime-control policy on gun violence.[29] These tactical shifts were intended to make it riskier for criminals to carry guns in public, since they would be more likely to be stopped for minor crimes or infractions. In other words, the rhetoric of disorder served as a fig leaf for intensive street-level enforcement focused on the removal of illicit guns.[30]

Two realities about crime and disorder nudged OMP in New York City toward a practice of racial policing. First, the signs of physical disorder often are more prevalent in urban neighborhoods with elevated rates of poverty and social fragmentation.[31] Accordingly, the implementation of Broken Windows policies was disproportionately concentrated in minority neighborhoods and was conflated with poverty and other signs of socioeconomic disadvantage. Thus, what was constructed as "order-maintenance policing" was widely perceived among minority citizens as racial policing, or racial profiling.[32] The fact that the principle tactic was an aggressive form of stop-and-frisk policing involving intrusive *Terry* searches further intensified perceptions of racial animus.[33] The reality of the racial imbalance in the application of OMP was confirmed by studies by the New York State Attorney General[34] and also by researchers who decomposed its effects into racial groups and specific precincts.[35]

Second, by explicitly linking disorder to violence, order-maintenance policing (as informed by Broken Windows theory) further focused police resources and efforts on the neighborhoods with the highest crime and violence rates. That these were predominantly minority neighborhoods further reinforced the disproportionate exposure of New York's minority citizens to policing. Thus, this construction of disorder broadened the concept to include *places* where violent and other serious crimes were most likely to occur. Those places tended to be ones with the highest concentrations of socially disadvantaged minority populations.[36]

In the end, OMP strategies and stop-and-frisk tactics produced a style of racial policing with stigmatizing effects on minority communities and widened an already troubling racial breach in the city. While the precise contribution of OMP to lower crime rates is contested, the social costs from the crackdown on crime threatened to compromise its original intent to redirect and rebuild social norms.[37] OMP was a Solomonesque split between traditional police goals focusing on major crimes (e.g., murder and armed robbery) and the goals of community residents concerned with chronic low-level crimes and disorder problems. But this strategic shift did not necessarily imply a tactical change toward aggressive policing. Moreover, this tactical shift departed sharply from the pristine Wilson and Kelling version and even the Kelling and Cole models of Broken Windows, as well as most contemporary models of community policing. As conceptualized by Kelling and Coles, OMP involved the enforcement of these standards "through non-arrest approaches—education, persuasion, counseling, and ordering—so that arrest would only be resorted to when other approaches failed."[38] OMP, instead, emphasized arrest for any law violation. As Harcourt observed, these efforts "have little to do with fixing broken windows and much more to do with arresting window breakers—or persons who look like they might break windows, or . . . strangers . . . or outsiders."[39]

B. Empirical Perspectives on Aggressive Enforcement and Gun Violence

Aggressive enforcement strategies, crackdowns, and other intensive applications of police surveillance and enforcement have long been a staple of crime control policy. OMP, or "zero tolerance," is a recent and influential development in this area. Crackdowns on prostitution, drug selling, public (social) disorder and incivilities, panhandling, even traffic enforcement, are old police stories that have been reconstructed through the lens of Broken Windows as efforts to influence more serious crime. Some studies suggest that such efforts can reduce crime generally, but the designs leave open the causal connection between enforcement and crime; the effects on gun violence are ambiguous. In cross-city research, Robert Sampson and Jacqueline Cohen report that cities with higher arrest rates for drunk driving and disorderly conduct have lower rates of robbery.[40] Experiments within cities on mandatory arrest for domestic assault show significant reductions in repeat (violent) victimization following arrest, but the effects are small relative to the general regression in domestic assault within six months of arrest.[41] A 1990 review of eighteen studies of police crackdowns showed that crime declines often were followed by decay in deterrence over time.[42]

When guns and violence are the targets of "directed patrol," sometimes including aggressive interdiction of citizens who meet *Terry* standards for reasonable suspicion, recent experiments show that selective enforcement can produce short-term reductions. Studies of selective enforcement targeted at guns in San Diego,[43] Boston,[44] Kansas City,[45] Indianapolis,[46] Jersey City, and Pittsburgh[47] all show that gun violence declined in targeted areas compared to areas that received "standard" police services. These efforts share the common ground of targeting firearms violence in the places where the risks are highest and among specific populations whose base rates exceed the base rates for the general population. Enforcement varied in intensity in each of these experiments. In the Kansas City experiment, police in directed patrols issued 1,090 traffic citations, made 616 nontraffic arrests, and seized twenty-nine guns. In Indianapolis, police made more than 5,000 vehicle stops in less than five months, made 992 nontraffic arrests, and seized twenty-five illegal guns. Police in Boston made only twelve arrests among the individuals targeted for intensive surveillance. Police in Pittsburgh used intermittent patrols on peak crime days and at peak crime hours. In a fourteen-week period, they stopped 175 citizens, stopped thirty-nine vehicles, seized ten guns and made eighteen arrests. Although differences in measures and methods complicate comparisons, all these experiments report significant reductions either in violence arrests, gun homicides or homicides generally, gun shots fired, hospital admissions for gun injuries, or gun arrests.

New York's policing experiment has received less research attention. Many writers claim that OMP produced broad crime declines, including in gun violence, greater than declines in other cities with differing policing models.[48] These claims about New York generally wave off concerns about the social costs of the strategy—racial animus and citizen complaints—as either irrelevant or well worth the lower crime rates.[49] The implementation of OMP in New York—though sharing a focus on guns, surveillance, and proactive stops of citizens—couldn't be more different from the directed patrols in other cities. The New York State Attorney General documented 189,000 stops of citizens in fifteen months in 1998–1999, a conservative estimate given underreporting of stops by officers and other citizen encounters.[50] Police averaged 3,034 misdemeanor arrests in New York's seventy-five precincts in 1998.[51] Even adjusting for New York City's population of nearly 8 million people, this level of stop, search, and misdemeanor arrest is quite high compared to the surgical tactics in cities that experimented with directed patrol.

Only one study to date has tested the effects of OMP on crime. George Kelling and William Souza used hierarchical linear models to estimate the effects of misdemeanor arrests from 1989 through 1998 on violent crimes, controlling for exogenous factors such as drug consumption (a proxy for drug markets), demography (the population of young males), and economic factors.[52] They report that twenty-eight misdemeanor arrests produce one less violent crime per police precinct. Among competing social explanations, only employment is significantly associated with violent crime: Rising unemployment increases the risks of violent crime. Kelling and Souza conclude that, "contrary to 'root cause' advocates, overall declines in violent crime cannot be attributed to our measure of the economy, changes in drug use patterns, or demographics. Instead, . . . 'broken windows' policing achieved significant gains . . . in reducing violent crime. . . ."[53] But these claims go well beyond the limits of the study and in fact are based on a shaky empirical and analytic foundation. First, measurement error is pervasive, and the weak influence of "social factors" reflects the handicap of the poor expressions of poverty, demography, and drug use in the design.[54] Second, the statistical model is misspecified. The analysis is cross-sectional, meaning that arrests and crimes are analyzed within the same year. Causal claims are not possible under these conditions.[55] In addition to the citywide statistical analysis, Kelling and Souza conducted six case studies of precincts from each of the boroughs to illustrate how OMP can reduce crime. The authors are silent on how or why these precincts were selected and do not discuss whether practices in these six were representative of the larger set of OMP practices and effects.

The OMP strategy in New York differs sharply from the strategies used in several other cities. While there is robust evidence of positive effects on gun violence from cities that use targeted and directed patrol, more empirical evidence is needed to assess New York's experiment. We describe a modest empirical test in the next section that will contribute to the policy debate about the acclaimed New York policing strategy.

III. Crime Control Returns of Gun-Oriented Policing: Empirical Results

To what extent did OMP contribute to reductions in gun violence and violence generally in New York? To address this question, we analyzed whether precinct crime rates in 1999 are predicted by the level of stop-and-frisk activity in the preceding year, controlling both for the level of crime in that precinct in the preceding year and for the precinct's social and economic makeup.

As in many other cities, gun violence and homicides in New York were concentrated in neighborhoods characterized by physical disorder and concentrated socioeconomic disadvantage, and these neighborhoods were the focal points of OMP strategies of aggressive stops and frisks. Accordingly, the twin emphasis on guns and disorder was, in fact, a strategy focused on policing poor people in poor and disordered places.[56] Since race interacts with other neighborhood factors that also correlate with social and physical disorder,[57] the burdens and benefits of gun-oriented policing in New York City fell most heavily on the city's minority citizens.

This raises two questions for understanding the effects of OMP strategies and the search for guns in the city's poorest neighborhoods. First, how effective were stop-and-frisk actions in reducing gun violence? We take advantage of the variation in stop-and-frisk activity across police precincts to see whether the intensity and focus of enforcement produced declines in gun violence. Since both enforcement and gun violence were concentrated in poor and heavily minority neighborhoods, we control for social and economic factors in police precincts. This serves as an additional control for differential allocation of police enforcement across precincts.

Second, do stop-and-frisk actions produce general declines in crime, not just declines in gun violence? OMP focused not only on guns and violence but also on social disorder generally, including drug selling, property crimes, and "quality-of-life" crimes. Stops for minor offenses were seen as chances to leverage police surveillance to catch a wide range of offenders committing an equally wide range of offenses. Since social disorder—the starting point for citizen stops—is correlated with poverty and race, we again control for socioeconomic characteristics of precincts, including race.

We also control for the level of crime in each precinct, for both substantive and measurement reasons. NYPD officials explained the disproportionate number of stops of minority citizens as a reflection of the racial distribution of crime suspects, on the basis of reports to the police from crime victims or witnesses.[58] However, suspect descriptions provide an incomplete picture of criminal activity, since many crimes—such as auto theft or larceny—occur without a suspect identification.[59] Stops by police occur both because suspects match a description provided by a witness or victim and because police observe a suspect involved either in an actual crime or in behavior that rises to the constitutional standard of "reasonable suspicion" that justifies an interdiction by police. Since data for each of these dimensions—for example, estimating how many people are engaged in "suspicious" behavior or understanding the subjective process of how police officers form "suspicion"—are very difficult to obtain, we chose instead to measure actual crime, as reflected in police arrests in each precinct.

A. Data and Methods

We included measures of social and economic factors that reflect contemporary theory regarding "place" and violence, theories that incorporate not just the structural deficits of social areas but also their dynamic processes of social control.[60] We selected nineteen tract-level variables from the 1990 census files and sorted them into seven separate dimensions that reflect theoretical domains. We then aggregated them to construct measures for each police precinct. The means and standard deviations for each measure are shown in Appendix Table 9.A1. To avoid redundancy among the measures in each domain, we computed a composite score for each dimension using principle components factor analysis; the results also are shown in Appendix Table 9.A2.

Counts and rates of stops and arrests within precincts were compiled from data published in the 1999 study of NYPD stop-and-frisk practices by the New York State Office of the Attorney General.[61] In addition to stop counts, the ratio of stops to arrests was computed for each precinct and for each of four types of alleged crimes that motivated the stops. Cases involving stops that occurred during calendar year 1998 were included. The data tables were compiled by the OAG from files created by the NYPD from UF-250 forms that are completed by officers following each stop event.[62] We included only stops where a UF-250 form was mandated.

Measures of crime and gun violence were constructed from two sources. Race- and crime-specific arrest data for each precinct were obtained for each year from 1997 to 2000 from New York State. Arrests were aggregated into four types of crime: drugs, violence, weapons, and property crimes. A race-specific rate per 10,000 population for each precinct for each year was computed. Measures of gun violence were obtained from the Injury Surveillance System of the New York City Department of Health. These included data on homicides caused by guns versus other means. Public health measures such as Vital Statistics have the advantage of being immune to the subjectivity that is endogenous to official crime statistics—endogeneity that reflects both the decision by police to make an arrest and also the decision of what charge to file. Vital Statistics data were reported by census tract and then aggregated to the precinct. Race-specific rates of gun and nongun homicides were computed for each precinct for each year.

We used a two-stage least squares regression procedure to estimate the effects of stops in 1998 on crime rates in 1999, controlling for crime and precinct social and economic characteristics. In the first stage, we estimated the effects of 1997 race- and crime-specific precinct crime (arrest) rates on 1998 race- and crime-specific ratios of stops to arrests. We chose 1997 crime rates to avoid the confounding effects of using data on stops and crimes from the same year (1998). By using 1997 arrests as the measure of crime and 1998 stop-to-arrest ratios as the measure of enforcement, we include both the magnitude of crime (arrests) and the intensity of enforcement (ratios) relative to crime.[63] We then used the standardized residuals from those models in a second-stage regression model to predict the effects of 1998 race- and crime-specific stops on 1999 race- and crime-specific arrest rates. We included the socioeconomic measures as controls in this model, to estimate the effects of neighborhood characteristics that might influence crime rates as well as enforcement intensity and, therefore, 1999–2000 arrest rates.

B. Results

1. STOPS AND ARRESTS

Table 9.1 shows two dimensions of police stops of citizens by race and type of crime, averaged across precincts. Violent crimes included robbery, assault, homicide, kidnapping, and sex crimes. Weapons

TABLE 9.1
Arrest Rates per 100,000 Persons and Stop to Arrest Ratios,
New York City, 1997–1999

Crime Type	Arrest Rates*		Stop: Arrest Ratio
	Mean	Std. Dev.	
White			
Violent	75.6	124.3	5.94
Property	33.3	57.9	7.61
Drugs	278.7	581.0	5.22
Weapons	59.5	102.7	15.89
Black			
Violent	288.6	285.6	7.03
Property	101.8	89.5	7.04
Drugs	531.9	956.1	6.94
Weapons	318.0	675.3	20.08
Hispanic			
Violent	119.4	70.1	7.20
Property	45.7	24.9	8.47
Drugs	215.2	194.8	6.14
Weapons	104.2	218.8	16.74

* Rates per 10,000 precinct population
SOURCE: New York State Office of the Attorney General, Report on the Stop and Frisk Practices of the New York City Police Department, December 1999.

crimes included arrests for both gun and other illegal weapons possession. Property crimes included larceny and burglary. Drug crimes included both possession and sale offenses. Means and standard deviations for arrest rates are shown for three years (1997–1999). The stop-
to-arrest ratio is based on 1998 data. Both measures are citywide rates,
the average of rates across the City's seventy-five police precincts.

Arrest rates for African Americans are highest of the three race and
ethnic groups for all four offense categories. The African American
arrest rate for drugs, for example, is more than twice as high as the
Hispanic drug arrest rate, and nearly twice as high as the rate for
whites. The African American arrest rate for violent crimes is nearly
four times the rate for whites and about 2.5 times the Hispanic rate.
For weapons, the arrest rates for African Americans is five times
higher than the rate for whites and three times higher than the rate for
Hispanics.

Of course, these differences beg the question of differential offending rates, and the true offending rate may be unknowable. Higher arrest rates for African Americans for weapons and violent offenses par-

allel their elevated homicide victimization rates.[64] Table 9.2 shows gun homicide and gun assault injury rates by race. Among African Americans in New York City, 12.0 per 100,000 were murdered with firearms, and 22.5 per 100,000 were hospitalized due to firearm injuries, rates that are more than twice the rate for Hispanics and nearly ten times the rate for whites.

At the same time, higher surveillance in minority neighborhoods means that both minor and major law violations are more likely to be observed by police and evoke a reaction. During 1998–1999, for example, enforcement was far more active in neighborhoods with high percentages of African American residents, well above what would be predicted by the crime rates in those neighborhoods.[65] It seems that both disorder and crime invite more intensive police surveillance in minority neighborhoods, leading to more arrests, which in turn intensifies surveillance, leading to higher detection and arrest rates. The systemic nature of the relationship among crime, arrests, and police stops suggests that higher arrest rates and stop rates may be endogenous processes within neighborhoods with elevated homicide risk.[66]

A manifestation of this can be seen in the higher stop-to-arrest ratio of for violence, drugs, and weapons charges among nonwhites compared to whites and among African Americans compared to all other racial or ethnic groups. Once police officers decide to stop a citizen,

TABLE 9.2
Race-Specific Homicide and Gun Assault Rates, New York City, 1999

	Total	White	African American	Hispanic
Population	7,304,287	3,175,354	1,865,895	1,732,369
Homicide				
N	638	104	339	165
Rate*	8.73	3.28	18.17	9.52
Gun Homicide				
N	367	40	224	92
Rate*	5.02	1.26	12.01	5.31
Gun Assaults**				
N	963	33	420	115
Rate*	13.18	1.04	22.51	6.64

SOURCE: New York City Department of Health, Injury Prevention Program.
* Rate per 100,000
** Race is missing in 38.2% of cases.

the outcomes of those stops—including whether a frisk or search is conducted and whether an arrest is made—should not differ by race. Presumably, the "reasonable suspicion" articulated in *Terry v. Ohio* and incorporated into both the formal training and professional judgment of police officers should lead to stops with race-neutral outcome probabilities.[67] In other words, there is no rationale for police to exercise discretion differently by race, leading to a higher rate of "false positives" for any racial group. Accordingly, stop rates should reflect a similar efficiency and strategic allocation of police efforts across races.

But Table 9.1 shows there are more stops per arrest for African Americans than for whites for three types of crime; there are more stops of Hispanics for every arrest made compared to whites for all four crime types. A higher ratio indicates less efficiency in stops or an excessive rate of stops needed to effect an arrest. A high stop rate may also indicate more indiscriminate stop practices, or simply broadened suspicion of individuals on the basis of their race alone.[68] In our previous article on OMP, we concluded that factors other than crime rates in the precincts drove these imbalances—after controlling for crimes, stop rates were higher for all offense categories in places with high concentrations of poverty, poor housing, and racial isolation. Whether the result of racial profiling or just inefficiency, the effects were most pronounced in stops of African Americans where weapons offenses were alleged, a reflection of aggressive enforcement focused on guns and violence. We take these factors into account in the next section when we model the effects of stops on crimes one year later.

2. OMP, STOP-AND-FRISK, AND CRIME CONTROL

To estimate the effects of OMP on crime one year later, we included the four stop categories in models predicting race-specific crime rates. The models in Table 9.3 focus on both official crime (arrests for violence and homicide) and homicide fatalities (both deaths caused by guns and deaths caused by any means). Table 9.3 shows the effects of stops in 1998 for four different crime categories on 1999 crimes, adjusted for violence arrest rates in 1997. Table 9.4 focuses exclusively on homicide victimization, including both gun homicides and total homicides. Like Table 9.3, it shows the effects of 1998 enforcement on 1999 crimes, adjusted for 1997 gun homicides or overall homicide fatalities. Both models include controls for precinct social and economic characteristics. For ease of presentation, we report only the regression coeffi-

TABLE 9.3

*Ordinary Least Squares Regression of 1998 Race- and Crime-Specific Stops on 1999
Race-Specific Violence and Homicide Rates by Police Precinct, Controlling for
1997 Violence Arrest Rates and Precinct Social Structural Characteristics
(Unstandardized Coefficients, p (t))*

1998 Race-Specific Stop Rate	White	African American	Latinos
1999 Violence Arrests			
Violence	1.78	0.86	0.14
Weapon	−1.11	0.23	−0.78
Drugs	−0.07	1.77	−0.20
Property	0.04	0.73	1.23
1999 Homicide Arrests			
Violence	0.46	0.12	−0.43
Weapon	−0.96	−0.95	−1.23
Drugs	−0.66	1.55	0.79
Property	0.42	−0.67	−0.72
1999 Gun Homicide Deaths			
Violence	2.07*	−1.08	−2.43**
Weapon	−1.15	−1.00	−0.36
Drugs	0.58	−0.22	−2.24*
Property	0.08	0.04	0.13
1999 All Homicide Deaths			
Violence	2.49*	−0.81	−2.34*
Weapon	−1.68	−1.08	−0.10
Drugs	0.14	0.70	−2.37*
Property	0.29	0.12	0.22

Significance: * $p < .05$, ** $p < .01$, *** $p < .001$

cient for each stop category on each crime outcome. Full model results
are available from the authors.

Table 9.3 shows that none of the 1998 enforcement measures are
significant predictors of 1999 arrest rates. For both violence arrests
broadly and homicide arrests specifically, there is no single category of
citizen stops by police that predicts whether crime will increase or decrease in the following year. When we measured fatalities, a measure
independent of police subjectivity and organizational influences on reporting, we see crime control returns that vary by type of stop and the
victim's race. Stops for violence are significant predictors of reductions
in both gun homicide deaths and overall homicide deaths, but only
among Hispanics. For whites, the data suggest that stops for violence
may increase homicide risks. However, these results are most likely
anomalous because of the low white homicide victimization rate of 3.3
per 100,000 persons in 1999. Stops for drug offenses also predict lower

TABLE 9.4

Ordinary Least Squares Regression of 1998 Race- and Crime-Specific Stops on 1999–2000 Race-Specific Violence and Homicide Rates by Police Precinct, Controlling for 1997 Homicide Fatality Rate and Social Structural Characteristics (Unstandardized Coefficient)

1997 Base Rate	1998 Race-Specific Stop Rate	Whites	African Americans	Latinos
All Homicide			*1999 All Homicide Deaths*	
	Violence	2.52*	−1.55	−1.99*
	Weapon	−1.58	−0.95	−0.15
	Drugs	−0.01	0.79	−2.26*
	Property	−0.12	0.26	0.30
All Homicide			*1999 Gun Homicide Deaths*	
	Violence	2.16*	−1.95	−2.05*
	Weapon	−1.01	−0.88	−0.40
	Drugs	0.37	−0.12	−2.11*
	Property	−0.41	0.16	−0.22
Gun Homicide			*1999 All Homicide Deaths*	
	Violence	2.55*	−1.43	−2.02*
	Weapon	−1.63	−0.97	−0.20
	Drugs	0.11	0.86	−2.22*
	Property	0.02	0.21	0.36
Gun Homicide			*1999 Gun Homicide Deaths*	
	Violence	2.19*	−1.86	−2.07*
	Weapon	−1.04	−0.86	−0.46
	Drugs	0.42	−0.07	−2.06*
	Property	−0.32	0.11	0.27

Significance: * $p < .05$, ** $p < .01$, *** $p < .001$

homicide rates for Hispanics but, again, for no other ethnic group. The effects on crime reduction among Hispanics occur for both total homicides and gun homicides, suggesting a more general crime reduction from enforcement that may not be specific to gun violence.

Table 9.4 also shows the effects of stop activity, but here we use homicide victimization in the previous year as the control. Regardless of the homicide victimization measure, stop activity for violence and drugs predicts lower homicide victimization rates, but only for Hispanics. As in Table 9.3, stop activity seems to have an iatrogenic effect on white homicide victimization, but this again may reflect the low rates of white homicide victimization in these years. For African Americans, no type of stop activity seems to predict homicide victimization. Also, as in Table 9.3, there are no differences in the predictions of gun homicides versus any homicides.

IV. Race, Context, and Diminishing Returns from Aggressive Policing

These results tell several stories about citizen responses to aggressive enforcement. First, the intensity of stop activity seems unrelated to race-specific violence or homicide *arrest* rates, but stops do lead to reductions in the homicide *victimization* rates one year later. The contrast between findings based on different crime measures raises a recurring controversy in criminology—the validity of official records as indicators of criminal activity. Some argue that, for more serious crimes such as robbery and assault, official records are an accurate picture of the prevalence and frequency of actual crimes.[69] Others argue that discretion in charging for crimes with subjective standards, such as assault, weakens the validity of crime records as they become susceptible to external pressures to rate specific crimes more seriously.[70] Such disagreements are evident in the contradictory results. Since most homicides are intraracial, we can dismiss a challenge based on differences between offender race and victim race. And, since the NYPD records of homicide victimization parallel the NYCDOH Vital Statistics records, we can also dismiss a challenge based on the Medical Examiner's classification of deaths as homicides or accidents.

Accordingly, we lean toward assigning greater validity to the homicide victimization data from public health records. We see significant reductions in homicides of Hispanics controlling for stop rates for Hispanics, but not for African Americans. This leads then to the second question: Why are the effects of stop activity on homicide victimization limited to Hispanics? Why are there no effects on African American homicide victimization rates? And, despite the focus on guns in OMP policy and strategy, why did *weapons* stops fail to produce reductions in homicide victimization or violence arrests? This is especially surprising in light of the absence of effects for African Americans, whose weapons arrest rates were two to five times higher than those for other groups. Why did such an enormous and widespread police effort fail to produce reductions in crime for the racial group whose homicide arrest and gun homicide victimization rates were so much higher than those of the others?

One clue can be found in the different rates of exposure of Hispanics and African Americans to OMP policing generally, and specifically to aggressive stop-and-frisk tactics aimed at guns. During 1998, for example, the OAG report shows that the stop rate for African Americans was 36.5 per 1,000 persons, 50 percent higher than the rate of 24.1 for Hispanics and nearly nine times higher than rate of 4.2 for whites. These stops were more inefficient for African Americans (7.3 stops per arrest) compared to Hispanics (6.4) and whites (4.1). Not only were African Americans more often the targets of OMP tactics; the interaction quality between citizens and police was quite different across races. The city's Civilian Complaint Review Board reported African American citizens filed 63 percent of all complaints over a twenty-seven-month period in 1997–1999, although they accounted for 51 percent of the stops in a comparable period.[71] Hispanics filed 24 percent of civilian complaints, but they accounted for 33 percent of all stops.[72] The same report showed that African Americans alleged that officers used physical force more often than Hispanics and that police officers were more than twice as likely to use a gun during stops of African Americans (29 percent of all complaints) compared to Hispanics (13 percent) or whites (6 percent). Of the ninety-nine civilians who reported that police used a gun, police found a gun on only one of them. Several accounts of "roughhouse" tactics by the police showed that OMP tactics exacted social costs that were disproportionately borne by New York City's African American citizens.[73]

This differential exposure to, and differential treatment of, African Americans to harsh policing has vicarious effects that may adversely shape citizens' reactions to the law and to the legal actors who enforce it. Disproportionate surveillance and harsh treatment of African Americans by the police may desensitize respect for the law, if not engender active defiance of the law.[74] Broad surveillance of African Americans is stigmatizing, undermining respect for authorities and commitment to law and discouraging the everyday interactions (or collective efficacy) that expresses social control and conveys respect to other members of the group. Together with their higher arrest and incarceration rates, harsher policing of African Americans in New York threatened to foster a perception of unfairness and illegitimacy of policing law among members of the stigmatized minority group.[75]

In this context, when African Americans are stopped more often, when the process—physical force, pulling guns—is more toxic, when the stops appear unjustified (more inefficiency, more pretextual or unujustified stops), the outcomes are skewed (higher arrest and incarceration rates), the fairness of the law and its legitimacy, including its social meaning of obligations to comply with it, are undermined. For African Americans, unfair and harsh treatment by the police is an important "race-making" factor,[76] contributing to their sense of racial disenfranchisement more generally in public life.[77] African Americans in New York more often live in racially segregated neighborhoods[78] and public housing,[79] contributing to their perception of *linked fate* in evaluating their life chances.[80] It is not surprising then, that the salience of poor treatment is higher for African Americans, and spreading easily and deeply through close communities.

When harsh treatment by the police and the law generally becomes simply an expectation of everyday life, regardless of whether one complies with the law or defies its, policing loses its contingent value that lends credibility to its claims of fairness and proportionality. Daniel Nagin, in a review of evidence on deterrence, terms this "stigma saturation."[81] When the stigma is applied harshly and unfairly, it may also have iatrogenic effects.[82] That is, sanctions that are applied unfairly may actually increase the likelihood of reoffending, rather than reduce it. If the social and cultural distance between police and African American communities remains wide and deep, respect for the legitimacy of policing and punishment will suffer. This is one source of the absence of effects of harsh policing.

V. Conclusions

In New York, aggressive stop-and-frisk strategies produced a style of racial policing that had stigmatizing effects on minority communities, generally, and socially toxic effects on African Americans. Police in New York explained that the high rate of stops of African Americans simply reflected both their involvement in crime and descriptions of suspects provided by crime victims or witnesses. Neither claim passes an empirical test. The disproportionate stops by police of minorities (African Americans, in particular) stigmatizes those persons, whether they are categorized as lawbreakers or law abiders, and reduces incentives for compliance with law and participation in informal social control.

Criminologists generally agree that social control within communities functions well when there is a strong interaction of informal and formal (legal) social control.[83] When legal control engenders resistance, opposition, or defiance, the opportunity to leverage formal social control into informal social control is lost. The absence of crime control returns from OMP policing may reflect just such a dynamic among African Americans, who shouldered much of the burden of OMP.

OMP creates a Hobbesian choice for "law abiders" in African American communities, who disproportionately shoulder the burden of crime victimization. African Americans are divided on this issue, with some willing to tolerate aggressive law enforcement in order to remove lawbreakers from their communities;[84] others see lawbreakers as victims of a racist state and prefer responses to crime that avoid vengeance and offer solutions to recurring conditions that cause crime.[85] This portrayal suggests a zero-sum choice between the interests of lawbreakers and law-abiding citizens in African American communities. Between these two choices is a more complex analysis that calls for legal policies that recognize the social links among "community," law abiders, lawbreakers, and democratization of crime policies to take into account sentiments of communities most affected by crime.[86]

In the original expression of Broken Windows theory, Wilson and Kelling imagined that the cues of crime would be removed and replaced with alternative cues that signaled order and social regulation. This is a far cry from the removal of "window breakers," or blanketing some communities with police surveillance and interdiction of citizens. Indeed, there is ambiguity surrounding the terms "lawbreaker" and "law abider" in communities with high crime rates; this sometimes blurry distinction confounds the goals of aggressive policing. When lines cannot be easily drawn between law abiders and lawbreakers, a policy that maximizes deterrence cannot differentiate between the two groups. Instead, the challenge to police in designing tactics for neighborhoods beset with crime problems is to create enduring forms of social interaction by citizens—working with police —to prevent and control crime.[87] Interactions between citizens and police in analyzing crime problems and forming solutions can launch a democratic process that rearranges the dynamics of policing and community.[88] In this case, a little transparency in policing can go a long way.

NOTES

1. Philip J. Cook and John H. Laub, "The Unprecedented Epidemic of Youth Violence," in *Youth Violence* (Michael Tonry and Mark H. Moore, eds.) (Chicago: University of Chicago Press, 1998), 27; Philip J. Cook and John H. Laub, "After the Epidemic: Recent Trends in Youth Violence in the United States," in *Crime and Justice: A Review of Research* (Michael Tonry, ed.) (Chicago: University of Chicago Press, 2002), 1.

2. Herman Goldstein, *Problem-Oriented Policing* (Philadelphia: Temple University Press, 1990); Jack Greene and Stephen D. Mastrofski, eds., *Community Policing: Rhetoric or Reality* (New York: Praeger, 1988).

3. See, for example, George Kelling and William Souza Jr., "Do Police Matter? An Analysis of the Impact of New York City's Police Reforms." New York: Manhattan Institute, December 2001.

4. See, for example, John Eck and Edward Maguire, "Have Changes in Policing Reduced Violent Crime?" in *The Crime Drop in America* (Alfred Blumstein and Joel Wallman, eds.) (New York: Cambridge University Press, 2000), 207.

5. Andrew Karmen, *New York Murder Mystery* (New York: New York University Press, 2000); Jeffrey Fagan, Franklin E. Zimring, and June Kim, "Declining Homicide in New York: A Tale of Two Epidemics," *Journal of Criminal Law and Criminology* 88 (1998): 1277.

6. David M. Kennedy, "Guns and Violence: Pulling Levers: Chronic Offenders, High-Crime Settings, and a Theory of Prevention," *Valparaiso Law Review* 31 (1997): 449.

7. Edmund F. McGarrell, Steven Chermak, Alexander Weiss, and Jeremy Wilson, "Reducing Firearms Violence through Directed Police Patrol," *Criminology and Public Policy* 1 (2001): 119; Jacqueline Cohen and Jens Ludwig, "Policing Gun Crimes," in *Evaluating Gun Violence: Effects on Crime and Violence* (Jens Ludwig and Philip J.Cook, eds.) (Washington, D.C.: Brookings Institution Press, 2003), 217.

8. Wesley Skogan and Susan M. Hartnett, *Community Policing, Chicago Style* (Boulder, Colo.: Westview Press, 1997).

9. Judith Greene, "Zero Tolerance: A Case Study of Police Policies and Practices in New York City," *Crime and Delinquency* 45 (1999): 171.

10. Anthony Braga et al., "Problem-Oriented Policing in Violent Crime Places: A Randomized Controlled Experiment," *Criminology* 37 (1999): 541.

11. Jack R. Greene and Ralph B. Taylor, "Community-Based Policing and Foot Patrol: Issues of Theory and Evaluation," in *Community Policing: Rhetoric or Reality* (Jack R. Greene and Stephen D. Mastrofski eds.) (New York: Praeger Press, 1988), 195.

12. For a detailed and thorough analysis of the conceptual bases of these

innovations and a description of them in practice, see Debra Livingston, "Police Discretion and the Quality of Life in Public Places: Courts, Communities, and the New Policing," *Columbia Law Review* 97 (1997): 551.

13. See, for example, William Bratton and Peter Knobler, *Turnaround: How America's Top Cop Reversed the Crime Epidemic* (New York: Random House, 1998); Eli Silverman, *The NYPD Battles Crime* (Boston: Northeastern University Press, 1999).

14. James Q. Wilson and George L. Kelling, "The Police and Neighborhood Safety: Broken Windows," *Atlantic Monthly,* March 1982.

15. See, for example, George L. Kelling and Catherine M. Coles, *Fixing Broken Windows: Restoring Order and Reducing Crime in Our Communities* (New York: Free Press, 1996); Bernard E. Harcourt, *Illusion of Order: The False Promise of Broken Windows Policing* (Cambridge, Mass.: Harvard University Press, 2001); Eli Silverman, *The NYPD Battles Crime: Innovative Strategies in Policing,* supra n. 13; William Bratton and Peter Knobler, *Turnaround,* supra n. 13; Andrew Karmen, *New York Murder Mystery,* supra n. 5; Regina Lawrence, *The Politics of Force: Media and Construction of Police Brutality* (Berkeley: University of California Press, 2000); Malcolm Gladwell, *The Tipping Point* (Boston: Little Brown, 2000); Alfred Blumstein and Joel Wallman (eds.), *The Crime Drop in America,* supra n. 4.

16. See, for example, Benjamin Bowling, "The Rise and Fall of New York Murder," *British Journal of Criminology* 39 (1999): 531, describing the enthusiasm of then Prime Minister–elect Tony Blair for the New York "style" of policing.

17. Lee Epstein and Gary King, "The Rules of Inference," *University of Chicago Law Review* 69 (2002): 1. See also John Monahan and Laurens Walker, *Social Science in Law* (5th ed.) (Westbury, N.Y.: Foundation Press, 2001), and David Faigman, *Legal Alchemy: The Use and Misuse of Science in the Law* (New York: W. H. Freeman, 1999).

18. Kelling and Souza, "Do Police Matter?" supra n. 3.

19. Sarah E. Waldeck, "Cops, Community Policing, and the Social Norms Approach to Crime Control: Should One Make Us More Comfortable with the Others?" *Georgia Law Review* 34 (2000): 1273.

20. Wilson and Kelling, in "Broken Windows," define "minor" disorder to include such problems and crimes as littering, loitering, public drinking, panhandling, teenage fighting on street corners, and prostitution. They also mention signs of physical disorder, including abandoned cars—with broken windows, naturally—and dilapidated buildings, also with broken windows.

21. Bernard E. Harcourt, *Illusion of Order,* supra n. 15.

22. Kelling and Cole list the crimes that constitute disorder to generally include unlicensed peddling and vending, public drunkenness and open drinking, vandalism (including graffiti), public urination, loitering, littering,

panhandling, prostitution, and menacing misbehavior. The latter was symbolized by "squeegee" men who solicit money in return for unsolicited cleaning of motorists' windshields at stop lights, the type of OMP enforcement that most closely expressed popular conceptions of the policy. More recently, OMP was extended to include jaywalking and unleashed dogs. Waldeck, supra n. 19.

23. These include, for example, cleaning up trash-strewn lots, painting over graffiti, and assisting housing inspectors to address code violations. See, for example, George L. Kelling and Mark H. Moore, "From Political to Reform to Community: The Evolving Strategy of Police," in Greene and Mastrofski, eds., *Community Policing,* supra n. 2.

24. Civil Rights Bureau, Office of the Attorney General of the State of New York, Report on the New York City Police Department's "Stop and Frisk Practices" (1999) (hereafter, OAG Report).

25. Fagan et al., "Declining Homicide in New York," supra n. 5.

26. Ibid.

27. Ibid.

28. Ibid.

29. Silverman, *NYPD Battles Crime,* supra n. 13; Bratton and Knobler, *Turnaround,* supra n. 13.

30. Waldeck, "Cops, Community Policing, and Social Norms," supra n. 19; Harcourt, *Illusion of Order,* supra n. 15.

31. Wesley G. Skogan, *Disorder and Decline: Crime and the Spiral of Decay in American Neighborhoods* (New York: Free Press, 1990); Robert J. Sampson and Stephen W. Raudenbush, "Systematic Social Observation of Public Spaces: A New Look at Disorder in Urban Neighborhoods," *American Journal of Sociology* 105 (1999): 603.

32. OAG Report, supra n. 24; David Kocieniewski, "Success of Elite Police Unit Exacts a Toll on the Streets," *New York Times,* February 15, 1999, at A1; Kit R. Roane, "Minority Private-School Students Claim Police Harassment," *New York Times,* March 26, 1999, at B5.

33. Citizens who are stopped and frisked on the basis of a profiling or racial policing strategy understand that they have been singled out because of their race. These encounters have been termed "race-making situations." David R. James, "The Racial Ghetto as a Race-Making Situation: The Effects of Residential Segregation on Racial Inequalities and Racial Identity," *Law and Social Inquiry* 19 (1994): 407. The shared danger of profiling encounters reflects the concept of "linked fate" among residents of minority neighborhoods. See Michael C. Dawson, *Behind the Mule: Race and Class in African-American Politics* (Princeton: Princeton University Press, 1994), 77. "Linked fate" refers to the empathy that people have with family and friends. It can also exist among strangers. Dawson explains that in the African American community, linked

fate has its foundation in the fact that the life chances of African Americans historically have been shaped by race.

34. OAG Report, supra n. 24.

35. Jeffrey Fagan and Garth Davies, "Street Stops and Broken Windows: Race, *Terry,* and Disorder in New York City," *Fordham Urban Law Journal* 28 (2000): 457.

36. Ibid.

37. Tom R. Tyler, "Public Trust and Confidence in Legal Authorities: What Do People Want from the Law and Legal Institutions?" *Behavioral Science and the Law* (forthcoming).

38. Kelling and Coles, supra n. 15.

39. Bernard E. Harcourt, "Reflecting on the Subject: A Critique of the Social Influence Conception of Deterrence, the Broken Windows Theory, and Order-Maintenance Policing New York Style," *Michigan Law Review* 97 (1998): 291.

40. Robert J. Sampson and Jacqueline Cohen, "Deterrent Effects of the Police on Crime: A Replication and Theoretical Extension," *Law and Society Review* 22 (1988): 163.

41. Christopher Maxwell, Joel H. Garner, and Jeffrey Fagan, "The Preventive Effects of Arrest on Intimate Partner Violence: Research, Policy, and Theory," *Criminology and Public Policy* 2 (2002): 51.

42. Lawrence W. Sherman. "Police Crackdowns: Initial and Residual Deterrence," in *Crime and Justice: An Annual Review of Research* 12 (1990): 1.

43. John Boydstun, *San Diego Field Interrogation: Final Report* (Washington, D.C.: Police Foundation, 1975).

44. Kennedy, "Guns and Violence," supra n. 6.

45. Lawrence Sherman and Dennis Rogan, "Effects of Gun Seizures on Gun Violence: 'Hot Spots' Patrol in Kansas City," *Justice Quarterly* 12 (1995): 673.

46. Edmund F. McGarrell, Steven Chermak, Alexander Weiss, and Jeremy Wilson, "Reducing Firearms Violence through Directed Police Patrol," *Criminology and Public Policy* 1 (2001): 119.

47. Cohen and Ludwig, "Policing Gun Crimes," supra n. 7.

48. Silverman, *The NYPD Battles Crime,* supra n. 13. Among those claiming credit were the city's mayor, three police commissioners who served under him, the governor of New York State, and the U.S. attorney general.

49. Heather MacDonald, "The Myth of Racial Profiling," *City Journal* 11 (2001): 14.

50. OAG Report, supra n. 24.

51. Kelling and Souza, "Do Police Matter?" supra n. 3

52. Ibid.

53. Ibid.

54. For example, employment and drugs are measured at the borough

level, yet boroughs are broad heterogeneous places encompassing several police precincts. Assuming that what is true in the borough is invariant across all
its police precincts is risky. Kelling and Souza assume, incredibly, that unemployment and drug use are the same on the Upper East Side and on the Lower
East Side, or on the Upper West Side and in Central Harlem. Kelling and
Souza operate under similar assumptions about drug use. Their measure of
drug use—drug overdose discharges from local hospitals—is a weak proxy
for the influence of drugs on violence. Drug markets are the culprits in street
violence, not drug use. The measure of drug use itself is weak—hospital admissions and discharges represent an unknown fraction of drug use events
and capture complications from a wide range of drugs—opiates, cannibis, bar-
biturates, psychedelics, cocaine products—with different marketing patterns
and different associations with violence. Both Richard Curtis and Bruce Johnson have shown the complexity of street-level drug marketing and how
changes in drug marketing have accompanied the decline in violence in New
York City. See Bruce Johnson et al., "The Rise and Decline of Hard Drugs,
Drug Markets, and Violence in Inner City New York," in Blumstein and Wallman, eds., *The Crime Drop in America,* supra n. 4. See also Richard Curtis, "The
Improbable Transformation of Inner-City Neighborhoods: Crime, Violence,
Drugs and Youth in the 1990s," *Journal of Criminal Law and Criminology* 88
(1998): 1223.

The measure of population is similarly weak. Kelling and Souza estimate
the young male population from school enrollment records. These records ex-
clude private school students and school dropouts, biasing this measure in a
nontrivial way: school dropouts are at high risk for assaults and robberies.
More puzzling is their use of the school-age (below-18) population to represent the supply of potential arrestees, whose average age exceeds twenty-
three years. See New York City Criminal Justice Agency, Annual Report, 2001.

55. See, for example, the classic text by Thomas Cook and Donald T.
Campbell, *Quasi-Experimentation* (New York: Houghton-Miflin, 1979), for a
discussion of the limitations on causal inference from cross-sectional research
designs. There are several other limitations. First, the design ignores the effects of time, ruling out the consideration of regression to the mean—or natural cycles of recurring crime increases and declines—as a competing explanation. Also, time is important because of the possibility that the predictors may
interact with time and may be more salient at one interval during the study
period. Also, panel data are serially correlated, meaning that the strongest pre-
dictor of each data point is its preceding data point. These effects also require
statistical controls, such as adjustments for an autoregressive covariance structure. See Peter Kennedy, *A Guide to Econometrics* (3rd ed.) (Cambridge, Mass.:
MIT Press, 1997). Finally, the analytic model is silent on the distributions of
the predictors or the crime variables. They fail to include quadratic terms

to test whether the effects of arrests are linear or nonlinear. Also, skewed or nonlinear data may violate the assumptions of the statistical procedure and hide the influence of a few outliers or extreme cases on the overall results. See John Fox, *Regression Diagnostics* (Beverly Hills: Sage, 1991).

56. Fagan and Davies, "Street Stops and Broken Windows," supra n. 35.

57. Sampson and Raudenbush, "Systematic Social Observation," supra n. 31; Skogan, *Disorder and Decline*, supra n. 31; Robert J. Bursik Jr. and Harold Grasmick, *Neighborhoods and Crime: The Dimensions of Effective Community Control* (New York: Lexington Books, 1993).

58. OAG Report, supra n. 24.

59. Arrest counts are preferable to crime complaint data, since many types of crime, such as drug crimes or minor property crimes, are not reported in citizen complaints to the police. In addition, complaints often include crimes with no suspect information, while arrests include information on the demographic characteristics of the suspect. In the OAG report, fewer than one in four stops was based on a suspect description provided to the police.

60. Lauren J. Krivo and Ruth D. Peterson, "The Structural Context of Homicide: Accounting for Racial Differences in Process," *American Sociological Review* 65 (2000): 547.

61. See OAG Report, ch. 5, Tables I.A.1, I.B.1, and I.B.2, and Appendix Tables I.A.1, I.B.1, and I.B.2.

62. Although the UF-250 was initially designed as a tool for investigation, completion of this form has been required by the NYPD Patrol Guide since 1986. In 1997, the police commissioner assigned a high priority to filing UF-250s. NYPD policy mandates that officers complete a UF-250 under four specific circumstances: when (i) force is used in the course of the stop, (ii) the suspect is frisked and/or searched during the course of the stop, (iii) the suspect is arrested; or (iv) the suspect refuses to identify him or herself. See NYPD, Patrol Guide. See OAG Report, ch. 3.II.c, for a description of the UF-250 form and the NYPD policies regulating the filing of these reports.

63. We do not report the results of this first stage analysis, but the results are available upon request from the authors.

64. These rates were computed from New York City Department of Health Vital Statistics records for homicide victimizations and from New York State Department of Health records on hospitalizations.

65. Fagan and Davies, "Street Stops and Broken Windows," supra n. 35.

66. These race-specific differences are similar to results from a study by Professor Douglas Smith of citizen-police encounters in three cities, conducted nearly two decades ago. Using data from the Police Services Study, Smith studied five measures of police behavior and eleven neighborhood characteristics to test the neighborhood context hypothesis. He found that suspects confronted in lower-status (SES) neighborhoods incurred a higher risk of being

arrested, while those encountered in nonwhite or racially mixed communities were more apt to be handled coercively by police. In subsequent analyses, Smith observed a significant interaction between the suspect's race and the racial composition of the neighborhood in which coercive confrontations occurred; police were more likely to exercise coercive authority toward black offenders in primarily black neighborhoods. In fact, black suspects in white neighborhoods were handled less coercively by police than were black suspects in black neighborhoods. In sum, Smith concluded that police responded differently depending on the type of neighborhood in which encounters occurred and that police respond to both "places and people." See Douglas A. Smith, "The Neighborhood Contexts of Police Behavior," in *Communities and Crime* (Albert J. Reiss Jr. and Michael Tonry, eds.) (Chicago: University of Chicago Press, 1986), 12.

67. Anthony C. Thompson, "Stopping the Usual Suspects: Race and the Fourth Amendment," *New York University Law Review* 74 (1999): 956.

68. One could also argue that a higher stop rate for one group may indicate "understops" of other groups, or a reluctance to stop more often persons of one race or another. That is an unlikely explanation, however, since the OAG Report shows that the racial distribution of stops was consistent across precincts and stable over the fifteen months. It is unlikely that the pattern of underdocumentation or depressed stop rates for whites would remain so consistent across the NYPD's many precincts and neighborhoods.

69. Alfred Blumstein, Jacqueline Cohen, and Richard Rosenfeld, "Trend and Deviation in Crime Rates: A Comparison of UCR and NCS Data for Burglary and Robbery," *Criminology* 29 (1991): 237; Michael J. Hindelang, Travis Hirschi, and Joseph G. Weis, "Correlates of Delinquency: The Illusion of Discrepancy between Self-Report and Official Measures," *American Sociological Review* 44 (1979): 995; D. Wayne Osgood, Patrick M. O'Malley, Jerald G. Bachman, and Lloyd D. Johnston, "Time Trends and Age Trends in Arrests and Self-Reported Illegal Behavior," *Criminology* 27 (1989): 389.

70. See, for example, Franklin E. Zimring and Gordon Hawkins, *Crime Is Not the Problem: Lethal Violence in America* (New York: Oxford University Press, 1997).

71. Civilian Complaint Review Board, "Street Stop Encounters Report: An Analysis of CCRB Complaints Resulting from the New York City Police Department's 'Stop and Frisk' Practices" (June 2001).

72. The CCRB report has methodological limitations that suggest caution in interpretation, especially self-selection in filing complaints. Having said that, the consistency in the pattern of dispositions of civilian complaints suggests that their internal validity may be consistent across races. See CCRB Report, Table 3-2.

73. David Kocieniewski, "Success of Elite Police Unit Exacts a Toll on the

Streets," *New York Times,* February 15, 1999, at A1 (discussing reactions of citizens to aggressive policing in New York City); Kit R. Roane, "Minority Private-School Students Claim Police Harassment," *New York Times,* March 26, 1999, at B5 (citing complaints by minority students of indiscriminate and frequent police harassment).

74. Jeffrey Fagan and Tracey Meares, "Punishment, Deterrence and Social Control: The Paradox of Punishment in Minority Communities," *Punishment and Society* (2003, forthcoming); Elijah Anderson, *Code of the Street: Decency, Violence, and the Moral Life of the Inner City* (New York: W. W. Norton, 1999); Sudhir A. Venkatesh, *American Project* (Cambridge, Mass.: Harvard University Press, 2001).

75. Jason Sunshine and Tom R. Tyler, "The Role of Procedural Justice and Legitimacy in Shaping Public Support for Policing," *Law and Society Review* (in review); Sara E. Stoutland, "The Multiple Dimensions of Trust in the Police," *Journal of Research in Crime and Delinquency* 38 (2001): 226.

76. James, "The Ghetto as a Race-Making Situation," supra n. 33.

77. Kendall Thomas, "Racial Justice: Moral or Political?" in *Looking Back at Law's Century* (Austin Sarat, Bryant Garth, and Robert A. Kagan, eds.) (Ithaca, N.Y.: Cornell University Press, 2002).

78. According to 1990 census data for New York, African Americans are far more likely than Hispanics to live in racially segregated areas. We computed an index of racial fragmentation for New York, using methods developed by Charles Lewis Taylor and Michael C. Hudson, *World Handbook of Political and Social Indicators* (2nd ed.) (New Haven: Yale University Press, 1972), 216. Racial fragmentation is a measure of the racial heterogeneity within an area and is computed as:

$$1 - ((P)^2)$$
where P = proportion of each race within the spatial unit.

We divided census tracts into quintiles of this index. African Americans are more likely to reside in the most homogeneous tracts, while Hispanics are far more likely to live in racially heterogeneous areas.

TABLE. 9.5
*Degree of Residential Segregation for African Americans and Hispanics**

Quintile	% African Americans	% Hispanic
1 (Most segregated)	33.74	5.63
2	23.25	13.01
3	25.32	27.68
4	27.34	36.32
5 (Least segregated)	20.26	32.09

* Based on 1990 U.S. Census data.

79. Based on 1990 U.S. Census estimates, 12.0 per 100,000 African Americans in New York City lived in public housing, compared to 8.3 Hispanics and 0.8 whites.

80. Dawson, *Behind the Mule,* supra n. 33.

81. Daniel Nagin, "Criminal Deterrence Research at the Outset of the Twenty-First Century," *Crime and Justice* 23 (1998): 51.

82. Lawrence W. Sherman, "Defiance, Deterrence, and Irrelevance: A Theory of the Criminal Sanction," *Journal of Research in Crime and Delinquency* 30 (1993): 110; Paternoster et al., "Do Fair Procedures Matter? The Effect of Procedural Justice on Spouse Assault," *Law and Society Review* 31 (1997): 163; Jeffrey Fagan and Tracey Meares, "Punishment, Deterrence and Social Control: The Paradox of Punishment in Minority Communities," *Punishment and Society* (forthcoming).

83. Robert J. Bursik Jr. and Harold G. Grasmick, *Neighborhoods and Crime,* supra n. 57; Robert J. Sampson, Stephen Raudenbush, and Felton Earls, "Neighborhoods and Violent Crime: A Multilevel Study of Collective Efficacy," *Science,* Aug. 15, 1997, at 918.

84. Tracey L. Meares and Dan M. Kahan, "Law and (Norms of) Order in the Inner City," *Law and Society Review* 32 (1998): 805.

85. Regina Austin, "The Black 'Community,' Its Lawbreakers, and a Politics of Identification," *Southern California Law Review* 65 (1989): 1769; Angela P. Harris, "Criminal Justice as Environmental Justice," *Gender, Race and Justice* 1 (1997): 1.

86. David Cole, "The Paradox of Race and Crime: A Comment on Randall Kennedy's 'Politics of Distinction,'" *Georgetown Law Review* 83 (1995): 2547. For example, in Boston, the interaction between police and the faith community had reciprocal effects on the way that each approached youth violence problems, creating an "umbrella of legitimacy" for fair and effective policing. Christopher Winship and Jenny Berrien, "Boston Cops and Black Churches," *Public Interest* 136 (1999): 52.

87. The original Broken Windows theory recognized that a disorder-focused policing strategy would "only be effective if applied in conjunction with a wide variety of other police tactics" and "pursued in partnership with . . . other social agencies. See Wilson and Kelling (1982), "The Police and Neighborhood Safety," supra n. 14.

88. Archon Fung, "Accountable Autonomy: Toward Empowered Deliberation in Chicago Schools and Policing," *Politics and Society* 29 (2001): 73. See also Mark H. Moore, *The Bottom Line of Policing: What Citizens Should Value (and Measure!) in Police Performance* (Washington, D.C.: Police Executive Research Forum, 2002).

APPENDIX

TABLE 9.A1

Demographic and Social Structural Characteristics of N = 75
New York City Police Precincts*

Variables	Mean	Standard Deviation
% households under poverty level	20.6	12.8
% households with public assistance income	15.5	11.7
Gini for total household income	0.40	0.07
% high school graduates (total—25+)	66.3	14.4
Labor force participation rate	60.9	8.0
Employment skills—managerial, professional, or technical jobs	32.2	14.7
Employment rate	89.9	4.5
Racial fragmentation index	0.48	0.15
% nonwhite	58.5	30.6
% youth population (5–15)	14.6	5.5
% female-headed households with children under 18	10.9	8.4
Supervision ratio (25–64 by 5–24)	2.32	1.17
Population—1990	97,390	11,757
Residential mobility—same house as 1985	62.7	5.1
Linguistic isolation	12.0	8.5
Foreign born	26.5	12.7
% occupied units that are rentals	74.1	18.5
Density (mean persons per occupied room)	0.66	0.11
Vacancy rate	6.0	3.3

* The Central Park precinct was excluded.

TABLE 9.A2
Factor Structure for New York City Police Precincts, 1990 Census Data

Factor	Factor Load	Eigenvalue	% Variance Explained
Poverty/Inequality		2.86	95.4
% households under poverty level	.993		
% households with public assistance income	.979		
Gini for total household income	.958		
Labor Market/Human Capital		3.37	84.2
% high school graduates (total—25+)	.966		
Labor force participation rate	.915		
% in managerial, professional, or technical jobs	.896		
Employment rate	.892		
Segregation		1.17	58.3
Racial fragmentation index	.763		
% nonwhite	.763		
Supervision		2.60	86.6
% youth population (5–15)	.981		
% female headed households with children < 18	.905		
Supervision ratio (population 25–64/population)	.904		
Anonymity		1.22	60.8
Population—1990	.780		
Residential mobility—same house as 1985	.780		
Immigration		1.62	81.0
Linguistic isolation	.900		
Foreign born	.900		
Housing Structure		1.73	57.6
% occupied units that are rentals	.936		
Density—mean persons per occupied room	.919		
Vacancy rate	.093		

Chapter 10

Should We Have Faith in the Churches?
The Ten-Point Coalition's Effect on Boston's Youth Violence

Jenny Berrien and Christopher Winship

Introduction

During the 1990s, the number of homicides in Boston plummeted from 152 in 1990 to 31 in 1999. Perhaps even more impressive, for the twenty-nine-month period ending in January 1998, Boston had no teenage homicide victims. Homicide rates fell in other cities as well during the 1990s. For example, New York's homicide rate dropped from 30.7 per 100,000 to 8.7, a decline of 71.7 percent; Houston's rate dropped from 34.8 to 12.0, a decline of 65.5 percent; and Los Angeles's dropped from 28.2 to 14.8, a decline of 47.5 percent. Some cities, however, saw only minimal declines. For example, Phoenix's homicide rate fell from 13.0 to 11.7, a decline of 10.0 percent, and Baltimore's fell from 41.4 to 40.3, a drop of only 2.7 percent.[1] In most, if not all, of these cities, the reduction in homicide rates has been accompanied by even sharper declines in youth violence. Why has youth violence fallen so significantly in some cities but not in others?

Most likely, part of the decline in youth violence is due to the U.S. economy's strong performance in the mid- to late-1990s, as well as to a drop nationwide in the number of youths ages fifteen to twenty-four, the most crime-prone age group. But these factors are present in almost all cities and thus cannot explain the discrepancy. Additionally, similar declines in homicide rates did not occur in the mid- and late 1980s, when the U.S. economy was also strong. Further-

more, the drop in the number of youths ages fifteen to twenty-four—
7.7 percent from 1986 to 1996—is simply too small to account for
much of the improvement.[2]

The story of Boston's downward trend in violence is similar to that
of other cities but is unusual in an important respect. Boston's distinction is that a group of ministers, the Ten-Point Coalition, is credited with
playing a key role in reducing the city's homicide rate.[3] As far as we are
aware, ministers have not been credited with major contributions to
any other city's achievements in reducing the level of violence.

This essay addresses the question of whether the Ten-Point Coalition has in fact played an important role in the reduction of youth violence in Boston. At first glance, the answer appears to be no. Crime
rates have dropped dramatically in other cities without significant involvement from clergy. Moreover, only three ministers with substantial additional commitments were centrally involved during the period when crime dropped most precipitously, suggesting that the total
number of man-hours that the ministers have devoted to the cause is
actually quite modest and not enough to account for the substantial
observed changes. Finally, David Kennedy and his colleagues at the
John F. Kennedy School of Government[4] at Harvard have documented
how new police and probation policies and practices have led to more
effective procedures for dealing with youth violence. The assertion
that the Ten-Point Coalition has been fundamental to Boston's effort
would seem at best to be good politics and public relations.[5]

Our analysis has several goals. First and most important, we show
that, despite these observations, the Ten-Point Coalition has played an
important role in reducing youth violence in Boston.

Second, we analyze why it has been difficult for police departments
to effectively reduce violence. Racial conflict is a problem that must be
considered when assessing violence reduction tactics in many cities.
We argue, more generally, that any police action in the inner city is inherently problematic. The decision of whether to imprison a destructive youth is a tough choice: Either the community is left vulnerable to
the youth's potentially violent tendencies or one of the community's
own children loses his freedom. The lack of any intermediary institution in the inner city to ensure that such decisions are made in a fair
and just way is enormously problematic. Reaching a consensus as to
what constitutes legitimate and constructive police activity has been
extremely challenging for many cities.

Our third goal is to suggest what types of policies are likely to be effective in reducing youth violence in the inner city *over the long run.* Although many cities have reduced youth violence successfully, the strategies utilized are often very aggressive, involving frisking and intimidating minority males. Our conjecture is that such strategies are not sustainable over the long term as inner-city residents conclude that the resulting sacrifice of civil liberties is simply too great.

Our argument has multiple parts. Our key assertion is that a principal barrier to reducing youth violence in the inner city over the long run is the hostile and highly confrontational relationship that exists in many cities between the police (and other agents of the judicial system) and the inner-city community. That relationship has made it nearly impossible to devise legitimate and effective long-term solutions to youth violence.

The second component of our argument is that many cities (including Boston in the past) pursue an approach that is likely to succeed in the short run but not over the long term. In some cases, inner-city residents become so frustrated by the high levels of violence in their neighborhood that they come to accept quite aggressive police tactics. Although such tactics may produce immediate results, eventually there is likely to be a community backlash. We examine the recent history of New York in this regard.

The third component of our argument is that the key contribution of the Ten-Point Coalition lies not so much in their work with at-risk youth as in how they have changed the ways in which Boston's law enforcement and inner-city communities relate to each other.[6] The coalition has done so by becoming an intermediary between the two parties. Ten-Point has achieved a balance between the community's desire for safe streets and its reluctance to see its children put in jail. In so doing, the coalition has created what we call an umbrella of legitimacy for police efforts to prevent and control crime. The coalition legitimizes police activities, first through a process of informal oversight and second by demonstrating its willingness to go to the press when police actions exceed the limits of tolerance. To avoid painting an overly rosy picture, we acknowledge that in Boston the relationship between the police and the community, especially its youth, is far from completely harmonious. Much of the transformation that has taken place has involved special units of the police department that are particularly sensitive to community needs and sentiments. The typical

beat cop, for the most part, appears not to have been part of this refor-
mation. In some cases, street-level patrol officers continue to pursue
the aggressive stop-and-frisk policies of the past. Only time will tell
whether their behavior will change or whether it will instead undermine the legitimacy of the partnership that has been built between the
police and the Ten-Point Coalition.[7]

The Boston Story

Although Boston has never been considered a violence-plagued city to
the extent that Los Angeles or New York has, in 1990 a record-breaking 152 homicides stunned Boston into realizing that it had a serious
violence problem.[8] The roots of the problem took hold in the late 1980s
when crack cocaine was introduced in Boston's inner city. As the crack
market developed, so did turf-based gangs and gang violence. To protect their financial stakes in the booming crack-cocaine market, as
well as to maintain "respect," gang members increasingly turned to
firearms. A vicious cycle developed, in which individuals joined one
gang to protect themselves from another gang. With firearms serving
as the primary means of aggression, the level of violence grew to a
rate and severity never before seen in the Boston area.

Because Boston law enforcement agencies had little experience with
turf-based violence and criminal gang activity, their initial response to
the situation in the late 1980s and early 1990s was disorganized. Until
1990, police department policy directed officers and administrators to
publicly deny the existence of a gang problem. Many current Boston
police officers have vouched for the fact that the department had no
policy for combating gang violence in the late 1980s. Without an in-
depth understanding of the problem or a plan of attack, police officers
engaged in a fall-back to the aggressive, riot-oriented tactics of the
1960s. In addition, because homicide cases traditionally were handled
on a case-by-case basis, the police department focused primarily on
making the "big hit" and arresting the "big player," rather than addressing the uniquely group-based quality of gang violence.

In 1988, the City Wide Anti-Crime Unit (CWACU), traditionally responsible for providing support across district boundaries, was permanently assigned to the most violent neighborhoods of Boston's
inner city. In 1989, the police department issued a statement that any

individual involved in a gang would be prosecuted to the full extent of the law. Thus, the department finally acknowledged the existence of a gang problem. But to what effect is another matter. According to one police captain, the CWACU was expected to "go in, kick butts, and crack heads" and adopted a mentality that "they could do anything to these kids" in order to put an end to their violence. This attitude resulted in highly aggressive and reportedly indiscriminate policing tactics.

Community Backlash

Two events in 1989, the murder of Carol Stuart and the stop-and-frisk scandal, focused community attention on the police department's initial approach to the violence crisis. Carol Stuart, a pregnant white woman, was murdered in the primarily African American neighborhood of Mission Hill. Her husband, Charles Stuart, who was with her at the time of her death, reported that a black male committed the crime. Relying on Stuart's account, the Boston police department "blanketed" the neighborhood searching for suspects. There were widespread reports of police abuse, as well as coerced statements that implicated a black male suspect, William Bennet. Stuart himself was later alleged to be the perpetrator of the crime, but he committed suicide before an investigation could be completed. The department's reliance on Stuart's dishonest claim and the overall mishandling of the murder investigation created an atmosphere, especially within the African American community, of extreme distrust of and disillusionment with the Boston police department.

The stop-and-frisk scandal intensified these sentiments. A precinct commander's description to the media of the department's approach to preventing gang-related violence as a "stop-and-frisk" campaign shocked the community and solidified the Boston public's suspicion of the police.[9] There is some dissension within the police department about the extent to which its policy was to indiscriminately stop and frisk all black males within high-crime areas, a practice known as "tipping kids upside down." According to several officers, they targeted individuals who either had been spotted previously performing some illegal activity or were known gang members. However, officers also acknowledged that, because it often was difficult to "distinguish the good guys from the bad guys," the approach was critically flawed. In addition, current members of the police force agree that there were "bad seeds" in the police force who acted far too aggressively in certain cases. Accusations of stop-and-frisk tactics led to a court case in the fall of 1989 in which a judge threw out evidence acquired in what he considered an instance of unconstitutional search and seizure.[10]

The bad press surrounding the Stuart case and the stop-and-frisk scandal led to the disbandment of the CWACU in 1990. It should be noted, however, that Boston police had begun to see some rewards from their aggressive street policies as Boston's homicide counts fell from 103 in 1991 to 73 in 1992.[11] Despite the apparent short-term efficacy of these heavyhanded tactics, most officers acknowledged that the department's aggressive actions during this time brought community mistrust to an extreme level.

The Boston press began to question the police department's ability to manage even routine policing activity. In 1991, the *Boston Globe* published a harshly critical four-part series called "Bungling the Basics,"[12] which detailed a succession of police foul-ups during the previous few years. The series highlighted serious failings in the department's Internal Affairs Division. Misguided investigations, problematic policing, and bad press eventually led to the appointment of the St. Clair Commission to conduct a thorough review of the Boston police department and its policies.[13]

At this point, the Boston police department began a desperately needed image and structural overhaul to deal with the negative publicity. "Bad-seed" cops were weeded out. The disbanded CWACU was reorganized into a new unit, the Anti-Gang Violence Unit (AGVU), which embraced a "softer" approach. The aggressive and indiscriminate—though admittedly effective—street tactics of the past were sharply curtailed. Perhaps as a result, the decrease in homicides during 1991 and 1992 was followed by a sharp increase in murders to ninety-eight in 1993.[14]

The release of the St. Clair Commission's report in 1992 spurred further structural changes at the highest level. The report cited extensive corruption within the department and recommended major changes.[15] In 1993, Boston's Mayor Raymond Flynn resigned, and the New York Transit Police Department's Bill Bratton stepped in to replace the departing police commissioner, Mickey Roache.

Innovation in Police Practices

Bratton instilled a new philosophy and commitment to innovation to the Boston police department. Fundamental shifts occurred in overall operations. According to current police officers, the neighborhood policing tactics that formerly "just existed on paper" and had never been implemented under Roache were actively pursued under Bratton. Many officers also agreed that the new administration was simply more open-minded and willing to break away from embedded policing practices.

The newly organized AGVU looked for innovative ways to manage gang activity. The unit targeted areas where it had failed during the past few years. It realized that community support was vital and therefore strove to employ "squeaky-clean" policing strategies in order to win back the public's trust. Its appreciation of the need for collaboration inspired the AGVU to pursue an increasingly multi-agency approach to combat youth violence. In 1993, the AGVU underwent an administrative change, becoming the Youth Violence Strike Force but retaining the same key members.[16]

Other agencies within Boston's law enforcement network were also being revamped. Officers in the probation department became disillusioned by the "paper-shuffling" nature of their jobs. The dangerous levels of violence within certain Boston districts had driven probation officers to all but abandon their presence in the streets and visits to probationer homes. Consequently, the enforcement of curfew, area, and activity restrictions was entirely absent. Lacking enforcement, probation came to be regarded by the law enforcement community as a "slap on the wrist" that had little effect in the battle against youth violence.

In response to these frustrations, a few key individuals within Boston's probation and police departments collaborated to develop an experimental effort called "Operation Night Light." This effort began when three probation officers and two police officers ventured out in a patrol car on the night of November 12, 1992. During this first night, they encountered several youths who were violating the terms of their probation. As the Night Light team continued these "after-dark" enforcement tactics, youths quickly realized that they no longer could disregard the terms of their probation because their PO might, for example, show up at their house after curfew to check on them. Operation Night Light has since become an institutionalized practice of Boston law enforcement agencies and has been widely praised by policy experts and the media across the country.

Interagency collaboration to address the issue of youth violence has become standard practice in Boston. The participation of researchers (primarily David Kennedy and his associates at the Kennedy School of Government) also served a vital role in bringing about a fundamental overhaul of Boston's policing strategies. The Boston Gun Project, which began in 1995, was a three-year effort to address youth violence that brought together a wide range of agencies, including the police department; the Bureau of Alcohol, Tobacco, and Firearms; the probation department; the Boston school police; the Suffolk County district attorney; and many others. The Boston Gun Project was innovative, not only because it involved collaboration but also because it used research-based information to address the problem of youth violence from a new angle. The Gun Project was able to attack the problem on the supply side by cracking down on dealers in illicit firearms and on the demand side by targeting 1,300 individuals who, although they represented less than 1 percent of their age group citywide, were identified by project research as responsible for at least 60 percent of the city's homicides.

In 1994, another collaborative effort to reduce gun violence, Operation Scrap Iron, was initiated to stem the illegal transport of firearms into Boston. Through targeted efforts, gun trafficking was essentially shut down within certain areas of the city. Other tactics, such as "area warrant sweeps," utilized an interagency team to target dangerous areas of the city with intense pressure. In some cases, police arrested all residents with outstanding warrants within particular housing projects. Multiagency teams of youth and street workers provided follow-up support to the remaining residents once the police presence subsided. As one police officer noted, these strategies made sure that "everyone was involved and brought something to the table. Everyone had a piece of the pie and, therefore, would get the benefits."[17] Even more impressive is that, according to this same police officer, not one civilian complaint was filed in response to the sweep tactic.

By mid-May 1996, the culmination of this collaborative work emerged with the implementation of Operation Cease-Fire. Cease-Fire fully institutionalized interagency collaboration among Boston's crime-fighting agencies. Additionally, Cease-Fire extended its collaboration to involve key community members, primarily from faith-based organizations. Together, these groups worked to identify the gangs responsible for violence in specific hot spots around the city. Subsequently, the group executed a forceful intervention by implementing "zero-tolerance" enforcement within the specific targeted area and sending an explicit message to gang members themselves that violence would no longer be tolerated.

Community-Based Change

Members of Boston's religious community were among the most vocal and publicized critics of the police department's earlier aggressive tactics. The Reverend Eugene Rivers, in particular, became a controversial media figure during those years because of his harsh criticism of both local law enforcement agencies and the city's black leaders. It is therefore quite remarkable that these religious leaders later emerged as active participants in such law enforcement initiatives as Operation Cease-Fire.

Boston's African American faith-based organizations did not begin working together until 1992. Until then, they had been following separate agendas, and their activities generally did not involve much street-oriented action to address youth violence within their community. Rivers did establish street outreach efforts to gang members and other community youth, but his repeated criticism of other clergy leaders made his effort a lone endeavor. A single tragic event, in May 1992, finally spurred collaborative action among Boston's African American clergy.[18] Violence broke out among gang members attending a funeral for a youth murdered in a drive-by shooting. The shootout and multiple stabbings in the Morning Star Baptist Church threw the service and the congregation into chaos.

The brazenness of the attack—within the sanctuary of a church—captured the attention of Boston's African American church community and incited it to action. Clergy realized that they could no longer hope to serve their community by remaining within the four walls of their church and ignoring the situation on the street. Instead, they needed to extend their concept of congregation to include youth and others in the surrounding troubled neighborhoods. The incident inspired the founding of the Ten-Point Coalition, a group of some forty churches, with the Reverends Ray Hammond, Jeffrey Brown, and Eugene Rivers III as key leaders.[19] The coalition drew up and published the Ten-Point Proposal for Citywide Mobilization to Combat the Material and Spiritual Sources of Black-on-Black Violence as a call to churches to participate in the effort to address the violence crisis in their communities.[20]

The creation of the Ten-Point Coalition marked the official beginning of Boston's African American religious community's organized involvement in the youth-violence epidemic. This move represented a dramatic shift in the extent of local faith-based collaboration. In contrast, as late as 1992, relations between the African American community leaders and Boston's law enforcement agencies remained contentious. Rivers was constantly "in the face" of Boston law enforcement officials and had gained a reputation as a "cop basher" in police circles. In carrying out his mission to be a support for local youth, Rivers maintained a constant presence in the streets of Dorchester and interacted with the same kids that the AGVU kept an eye on. As an aggressive advocate for local youth, both in and out of the courts, Rivers had many confrontations with members of the police force. But this initial antagonism eventually subsided and was replaced with effective collaboration.[21] The combined effect of a few important events and the revamped police approach spurred this turnaround.

In 1991, Rivers's house in Four Corners, one of the most violent areas of Dorchester, was shot at in the first of two attacks. Though he and his family were not harmed, the incident made him painfully aware of the dangers of carrying out a solitary campaign against youth violence. From this point forward, Rivers increasingly sought allies in the religious and law enforcement communities.

In the past, the Ten-Point Coalition, and especially Rivers, had habitually and severely criticized the Boston police department. When the Ten-Point Coalition was formed in 1992, the public stature and the media influence of Reverend Rivers and other key clergy members such as Ray Hammond and Jeffrey Brown increased. Wielding its power effectively, Ten-Point partnered with another community-based organization, the Police Practices Coalition, to establish a community-based police-monitoring group. The number of positive interactions with law enforcement increased, convincing the clergy that the department was indeed interested in reform. To acknowledge the department's progress, the ministers instituted a Youth Community Award to publicly honor "good cops." These improved interactions between the African American clergy and law enforcement led to important collaborative efforts, such as the previously described Operation Cease-Fire.

Current Relations

The later part of the 1990s was a period of intensive cooperation between the police and the clergy involving a variety of joint efforts. A primary venue for this collaboration has been weekly meetings held at the Ella J. Baker House (the social-service arm of Rivers's Azusa Church.) These meetings bring together a wide array of agencies and community groups to share information and to brainstorm ways to address troubling developments within the community. Beyond these scheduled meetings, informal cooperation plays an important role in ensuring quick responses to tense situations and effective distribution of resources to problematic "hot spots" in the city. Some of the key issues that have been addressed are the burgeoning membership among Boston youth in national gangs such as the Bloods, Crips, and Folk; sexual harassment among youth traveling on the MBTA subway trains; and the eruption of violence among the city's Cape Verdean communities. Presentations in Boston's schools, home visits by police/clergy teams, and community meetings are just some of the tactics that have been developed and carried out by this collaborative team to address community concerns.

This type of collaboration has continued into the new century; however, the accompanying reduction in Boston's violence has not continued as expected. In 2000, the number of homicides in Boston rose to thirty-eight and in 2001 it exploded to sixty-eight, an increase of more than 100 percent since 1999. Although good evidence is not available, many of these homicides appear to be "hits" involving individuals recently released from prison. Whereas the shootings of the early and mid-1990s involved "hot-blooded" turf wars, with youth shooting at each other across streets, many of the homicides in 2001 involved "cold-blooded" executions, with many more occurring indoors and clearly involving individual targets.[22]

As one might expect, Boston is working hard to deal with its new violence problem. The clergy have called for a reinvigoration of their past collaboration with the police department.[23] The police department has launched what it calls Boston Strategy II.[24] The department states that the key component of the new effort is "the collaboration and partnerships between the police, community, and clergy."[25] The new effort has three components: focused efforts on enforcement, intervention, and prevention. The enforcement effort involves warrant apprehension efforts, efforts to disrupt firearm trafficking, and gang and drug investigations. Intervention comprises prison reentry programs run jointly by police, clergy, and individuals from other agencies; revitalization of an earlier police/probation program, Operation Night Light; Operation Homefront, which involves visits to the home of high-risk individuals by teams of police and clergy; and revitalization of Operation Cease-Fire. As in the past, the current effort has involved forums where police and clergy meet with gang members and demand that they end their conflicts. In addition, it has involved major sweeps where members of one particular gang are arrested for drugs and guns, often on federal charges. Prevention efforts involve a host of new and existing programs, including youth service officers, summer jobs, a junior police academy, and summer camps.[26]

The Judicial System and the Inner City

We now turn to the question of why police departments and judicial systems have been unable to deal with past or current youth violence in so many cities. Observers have pointed out that inner-city communities in America's major cities often consider themselves to be at war with the local police and local government, and they frequently compare the police to an occupying military force. The reasons for this perception are well known. While the Rodney King beating in Los Angeles is the most publicized incident of the past decade, almost every major city has its own stories of police brutality. In Boston, the most recent case occurred in January 1995. Michael Cox, a black undercover policeman, was brutally beaten by four uniformed policemen who mistook him for a suspect. In the previous year, police mistakenly broke into the home of Accelynne Williams, a retired black minister, during a drug bust. Williams died of a heart attack brought on by the forced entry. We have already discussed the Stuart case and the stop-and-frisk scandal, additional instances of allegations of racially biased and overly aggressive policing tactics.

As disturbing as such incidents are, the response of inner-city residents has at times been nearly as troubling. Although in most cities inner-city residents are disproportionately the victims of crime (crimes often committed by their fellow residents), they have become increasingly unwilling to cooperate with police or to support police activities. In *Race, Crime, and the Law,* Randall Kennedy describes the growing alienation of black inner-city residents from the criminal justice system. He describes how the black criminal has been glorified in the movies and through gangster rap and records such as "Cop Killer." His point is that excesses of the criminal justice system, both past and present, have led inner-city minorities to see the system as totally lacking legitimacy and, at the extreme, to treat criminals as political dissidents and martyrs.[27]

If Randall Kennedy's portrayal of minority attitudes toward police and the judicial system is even moderately accurate, as we believe it is, it should not be surprising that police have found it difficult to deal with youth violence in our inner cities. When police expect no cooperation from residents, they tend to choose aggressive broad-based tactics that only further alienate community residents. Moreover, the negative publicity they receive undermines their political support. By alienating inner-city residents, the police also lose their best potential source of community surveillance.

Randall Kennedy contends that, although considerable improvements are needed in our justice system, much progress has been made. Certainly, the tense and often dangerous conditions that the police have to work in make it difficult for them to handle potentially explosive situations in a sensitive manner. We would like to suggest an additional reason. Inner-city residents have conflicting goals. On the one hand, they, like all Americans, want safe neighborhoods. On the other hand, they do not like seeing young men from their communities put in jail. As Glenn Loury has noted, "the young black men wreaking havoc in the ghetto are still 'our youngsters' in the eyes of many of the decent poor and working-class black people who are often their victims."[28] Given those conflicting desires, making decisions about whether a particular youth should be arrested or jailed is difficult. Allow him to remain in the community and perhaps endanger other neighborhood residents? Or send him to jail, depriving him of his freedom and removing yet another young man from the community? Neither option is appealing. Parents, neighbors, and other residents are likely to disagree sharply, and a decision-making process that would be widely perceived as fair may be unattainable.

Most inner cities simply do not have institutions that are capable of dealing with these questions in a way that would be perceived as just by both residents and society at large. The police, in addition to their history of racism, are biased in favor of safe streets by any means necessary. Social workers, street workers, and community organizers typically are sympathetic to the kids. Residents themselves are likely to differ depending on who is in trouble and their relationship to the suspect.

We argue that, in Boston, the ministers of the Ten-Point Coalition have become an intermediary institution through which decisions can be made that are perceived as fair. Through their advocacy of at-risk youth and their interventions in potentially inflammatory situations, the Ten-Point ministers have gained the legitimacy needed to convince residents that they will protect the interests of the community. They have created what we term an umbrella of legitimacy for police to work under. The police are sheltered from broad public criticism while engaged in certain activities that are deemed by the ministers to be in the interest of the community and its youth. However, indiscriminate or abusive police tactics that are deemed outside the umbrella are publicly attacked.

The "Heavy-Handed Approach": New York

New York City has perhaps received more media attention than any other city for its accomplishments in reducing violent crime. Like Boston, New York has substantially reduced its annual number of homicides (from 2,245 in 1990 to 664 in 1999, a decline of more than 70 percent). Unlike Boston, however, clergy have not played a central role in New York's violence reduction efforts. How, then, can we explain New York's success? A fully adequate answer to this question would require a study at least as extensive as the one that we have completed of Boston. However, from newspaper accounts and other secondary sources, it is possible to construct a plausible, though not a tested, answer.

As the history of Boston in the early 1990s has shown, aggressive police tactics can lead to substantial reductions in crime. But, in Boston, community criticism eventually caused the department to abandon these tactics. We believe that the recent New York story in important ways parallels the earlier Boston history.[29] Using aggressive tactics, New York is seeing great reductions in its level of violence. The question is whether these policies are sustainable over the long run.

Crime reduction emerged as a central issue on the agenda of New York's former mayor, Rudy Giuliani. His campaign to crack down on "quality-of-life" violations, coupled with sustained attacks on violence and the drug market, gained national attention. Significant increases in money and manpower facilitated the implementation of various labor-intensive strategies to reduce violence. Some notable examples of such approaches have been the successful and innovative uses of computers to target and attack hot crime spots, as well as a "model block" program that focuses intense attention on a particular city block until crime is shut down in the defined area.

In the model block program, the police first implement an "all-out drug sweep," then create "checkpoints at both ends of the street, post officers there around the clock, paint over graffiti and help residents organize tenant groups and a block association."[30] Between two and eight police officers patrol the block twenty-four hours a day, seven days a week for the two months following the initial occupation of the block. Once it is determined by police officials that drug activity is sufficiently suppressed and formal community organizations are solidified, "model block" status is achieved, meaning that crime has been sufficiently shut down in that particular block.[31]

For some people, the extreme nature of this type of strategy is justified by its demonstrated success. A New York Times article reported the achievements of the model block strategy in Washington Heights, a 250-block area that became the "nation's largest wholesale drug market" with the introduction of crack cocaine in the mid-1980s.

> Four "model blocks" have been created within this neighborhood. And slowly, the fear has begun to lift on 163rd Street. People who for years would only leave their apartments in a hurry have begun to step outside merely to be outside—first by peering out of a doorway, then by taking a seat on a stoop, then finally taking the plunge by striking up a conversation with a stranger next door.[32]

For some community residents, the relief of escaping self-imprison-ment and fear justifies any means necessary to achieve it. This form of community response, as well as the positive shift in homicide statis-tics, speaks well for New York's tough strategy.

These aggressive policing strategies are often credited with bring-ing about the dramatic drop exhibited in New York's homicide statis-tics. "New York has enjoyed a significant drop in crime that can't be easily explained by sociological factors," said Mark H. Moore, a crimi-nologist at Harvard University. "Therefore, the claim that this might be the result of police activity looks pretty good."[33] However, the tac-tics are often controversial: "The frisking of low-level offenders has been sharply criticized by some civil libertarians and is one reason for a two-year jump in abuse complaints."[34]

Public gratitude for the city's crackdown on crime appears to be counterbalanced by anxiety about the high level of police presence in their neighborhoods. The familiar, routine presence of drugs and gangs is sometimes viewed as the lesser of two evils when compared to the oppressive and aggressive actions of the police. "Many more (African American individuals) would associate themselves with de-mands for law and order if they did not fear racially prejudiced mis-conduct by law enforcement officials."[35]

New York's crime rate successes do not appear to have led to im-proved relations between the inner-city community and the police. According to the *New York Times* report on model blocks in Washing-ton Heights cited earlier,

> Wary of one another, people hardly put their faith in the police. Ten-sions between the two have been worse in Washington Heights than anywhere else in the city, from the full fledged riots that followed a po-lice officer's fatal shooting of an unarmed man in 1992, to the April 1997 death of Kevin Cedeno, shot in the back by an officer who was named "cop of the month" by his colleagues soon after. "At least the drug deal-ers are not here to hurt you—they're here to make a profit," said Yvonne Stennett, who heads the Community League of West 159th Street . . . in-creasingly aggressive police tactics have convinced many law-abiding residents that officers see them as criminal suspects first.[36]

African American community leaders throughout the city have echoed these complaints.

In May 1998, the Reverend Calvin O. Butts III, a prominent Baptist minister from Harlem, went so far as to call Mayor Giuliani a "racist who is on the verge of creating a fascist state in New York City.[37] Butt's harsh criticism was reportedly "something bubbling up" for a long time but was triggered by the city's layoff of six hundred workers from Harlem Hospital.[38] Leaders in the black community viewed this move as just another action reflecting the city government's unfair targeting of poor minority communities. Although some of the city's black leaders did not condone Butts's labeling of the mayor as a racist, they often echoed his complaints regarding Giuliani's treatment of the black community. Several prominent blacks have used confrontational language to criticize policies they asserted were harmful to their community; both Al Sharpton and David N. Dinkins, the former mayor, said that they have been leveling essentially the same charges against the Giuliani administration for years.[39] Community outcry against tactics has been fueled by well-publicized cases of alleged and in many cases proven police brutality and corruption.

In 1997, a now infamous group of police officers in the New York Thirtieth Precinct, in Harlem, known as "Nannery's Raiders" in honor of their sergeant, was indicted for an extreme example of corruption: breaking into apartments to steal cash and drugs, which they either used or sold.[40] Also in 1997, four New York police officers were accused of beating and abusing Abner Louima, a Haitian immigrant, because he was black; they reportedly used racial epithets during the incident.[41] September 1998's "Million Youth March" also brought claims of discriminatory and abusive policing tactics:

> Reacting to the violent end to the otherwise peaceful Million Youth March, community leaders, Harlem residents and other New Yorkers yesterday blamed Mayor Rudolph Giuliani for the melee, some accusing him of creating a military siege that might have caused a bloodbath except for the attendees restraint. "The heroes were the people of Harlem. If they hadn't been as restrained and acted with such courage and dignity, there would have been a carnage," said author Cornell West. "They were dealing with a whole process of contempt and disrespect from the Giuliani administration, mediated through the police. . . ." Panelists agreed that it was the police, not march organizer Khallid Abdul Muhammad, who touched off the fracas that broke out around 4 P.M., when the rally was scheduled to end. Police in heli-

copters buzzed the crowd and officers in riot gear mounted the stage at precisely 4 P.M., the hour which a court order had set for the rally to end.[42]

The response to these incidents indicates great skepticism by some regarding current policing tactics in New York City. Former Mayor Giuliani remains a staunch supporter of his police department. However, the increasingly expressed sentiment that the city's impressive crime drop does not justify the accompanying loss in civil liberties may eventually force the city's administration to reevaluate its position. The maintenance of current NYPD strategies over the long term may well become impossible.[43]

An Umbrella of Legitimacy

The relationship between the Boston police and the Ten-Point Coalition has progressed from hostility to stable cooperation.[44] The thesis of this essay is that the cooperative relationship established between the Boston police and the coalition has been instrumental in reducing the level of youth violence in two significant ways. Most important, Ten-Point has given increased legitimacy to appropriate police activities within the inner city. Second, the coalition's community surveillance may have increased police effectiveness.

If one were in search of legitimacy, there could perhaps be no better source than through partnership with clergy representatives. Throughout society, ministers have unique moral standing. They are expected to be fair and to protect the interests of the less fortunate; because of that, they often are asked to be problem solvers and to adjudicate between conflicting parties. In the inner city, the churches are among the last formal institutions committed to the welfare of their neighborhoods, and, within the black community, ministers often have been looked to for leadership. In the case of the Ten-Point Coalition, two of the three core ministers live in Boston's inner city, and all three are well known for their extensive work with inner-city youth, factors that give the coalition considerable credibility in speaking for Boston's inner-city community. That is not to say that Ten-Point is universally viewed as the legitimate representative of the black community in Boston. There have been many conflicts between Ten-Point, particularly Reverend Rivers.

Nevertheless, the *Boston Globe* has printed numerous stories praising the coalition, which also has received considerable symbolic and financial support from Cardinal Bernard Law, head of the archdiocese of Boston, and from the Jewish Community Relations Council, the agency principally concerned with social justice issues within Boston's Jewish Federation. All of this has contributed significantly to Ten-Point's perceived legitimacy within Greater Boston.

The new relationship between the police and Ten-Point is built on a number of assumptions, each of which can support legitimate police activity. We discuss five: youth violence needs to be dealt with as a criminal problem; some kids need to be jailed for both their own good and for the good of the community; a small number of youth constitute most of the problem, and the ministers will work with the police in identifying them; the ministers will participate in the decisions about what happens to specific individuals; and, if the police use indiscriminate and abusive methods in dealing with youths, the ministers will take the story to the media.

The first assumption is that, although poverty, single-parent households, poor schools, and other conditions may be factors in youth violence, any effort to reduce violence in the short run must treat it as a criminal problem. In the talks that ministers routinely give in schools and other locations, they make it clear to the kids that they have two choices. If they go straight, the ministers will help them succeed in school, find jobs, and deal with those kids who are trying to pressure them to stay with the gang. However, if they decide to participate in gang activities, the ministers will do their utmost to see them put in jail. The ministers emphasize that the last thing they want to do is to preside over a kid's funeral—that if a kid is going to be involved in a gang, it is safer for him to be in jail than on the street.

Implicit in the "choice" that the ministers offer is a second assumption—that some kids are so out of control that they should be put in jail. It is not apparent that the ministers held that belief initially, and the police doubted the ministers' willingness to support the incarceration of some individuals. Interview after interview with both police and ministers indicates that cooperation became possible only after the ministers publicly acknowledged (Reverend Rivers most vocally) that some kids needed to be put in jail. There was no explicit agreement about what constituted a sufficiently "out-of-control" kid. Cooperation between law enforcement officers and the ministers emerged through negotiations over the particular circumstances under which certain kids should be committed. With improved communication and the acknowledgment of a common objective, both parties began working with the same definition of the problem. The primary issue that remained was what should be done in particular circumstances.

A third assumption is that only a small number of youths are responsible for most of the violence. As noted, David Kennedy placed the estimate at 1 percent of the youths' age group—1,300 youths.[45] That is why standard stop-and-frisk procedures can be so oppressive: for every hundred kids stopped, only one is truly part of the problem. It takes only a few kids shooting off guns to terrorize a whole neighborhood. A part of the agreement is that the ministers will work with the police to identify those kids who truly are problems, thereby informally providing remote surveillance for the police.[46] The information they provide makes police efforts more effective; targeting also increases police legitimacy by ensuring that the police focus on the right youth, employing appropriate measures.

The fourth assumption is that the ministers will work with the police in identifying problem youth. This is not a matter of ascertaining who are the most dangerous individuals. Generally, these individuals are known to the police, the ministers, and the community at large. Rather, it is a process of ongoing assessment as to which youths have the potential to get into serious trouble in the future. This work is done in both formal meetings and informal conversations, as each party attempts to understand and evaluate the youth it is working with. Through these conversations, the police and the ministers come to a shared understanding of the youth that then forms a basis for deciding on when and for whom interventions will occur.

A fifth assumption is that the ministers will participate in determining how particular individuals are treated by the legal system. In some circumstances, that means that the ministers will contact the police and ask to have certain kids arrested; the ministers may also help the police locate them. In some cases, the ministers will encourage judges to sentence troubled youths to alternative programs or to regular "check-ins" at their churches, rather than to time in jail; in others, the ministers will appear in court to argue for a stiff sentence.

These understandings between police and the ministers constitute what we term an umbrella of legitimacy for police activity. However, it is an umbrella that provides coverage only under specific conditions:

when police focus on truly problematic youth; when they deal with these youth in what is perceived as a fair and just way; and when these steps are taken in cooperation with the community through the ministers.

Activities that fall outside these boundaries will be publicly criticized in the media, which is the fifth assumption. The ministers' past criticism of the police in the *Globe* is well remembered. Furthermore, Reverend Rivers, the most outspoken of the ministers, is known for his willingness to criticize anyone, whether the police, the Urban League, or Harvard's Department of Afro-American Studies. The ministers are able to provide informal oversight of police actions in part because they are ministers, in part because they are community members and leaders, and in part because they have exhibited a willingness in the past to be highly critical of the police.

How are we to understand the Ten-Point Coalition's role within the inner city? Operating on the basis of these five assumptions, the coalition has created an umbrella of legitimacy for appropriate police activity. Activities carried out and decisions made under this umbrella are broadly seen by the community as being fair and just; those falling outside are brought to the attention of the media. Some youth have been sent to prison; others have been given second chances; and the vast majority are no longer being harassed on the street, or at least not as much as in the past. Because of the Ten-Point Coalition's involvement, the differential treatment of individual youth is more likely to be seen by the community as legitimate. Hard decisions are being made, but they are being made in a manner that is commonly viewed as fair and just.[47]

Conclusion

In this chapter we have argued that over the long run it is difficult if not impossible for police activity in the inner city to be successful unless it is viewed as legitimate and supported by local residents. Our argument goes further. Vigorous law enforcement initiatives and preventive tactics all play important roles in preventing and reducing youth violence.[48] We have argued also that police work dealing with youth violence is inherently problematic. Communities want safe streets, but they also want their kids to stay out of jail. Difficult choices need to be made that are likely to be seen as unjust by some residents. In this environment, it is difficult to establish legitimacy for police actions, no matter what those actions are.

We claim that, in Boston, the Ten-Point Coalition has evolved into an institution that has at least partially ameliorated this dilemma. By supporting police activity that it believes to be beneficial to the community and criticizing activities that are not, it has created an umbrella of legitimacy for the police to work under. That in turn has allowed the police to effectively deal with youth violence by pursuing a strategy that targets the truly dangerous youth. We contend that this situation, which is far different from that in most major cities, has contributed significantly to the spectacular drop in homicide rates observed in Boston.

If our analysis is correct, it suggests that police need to create a strong community of partners who engage in a cooperative effort to deal with youth violence; there also must be a delineation of what constitutes legitimate police behavior. Police strategies can acquire true legitimacy within the inner city only if the community partner supports police tactics when they are appropriate, as well as publicly criticizes activities that are not. In this role, churches and ministers are ideal partners.

The goal of our research was to establish the plausibility of the claim that the Ten-Point Coalition made a critical contribution to the dramatic reduction in homicides exhibited in Boston during the 1990s. We have argued that the coalition's primary contribution to Boston's success most likely has not been a result of its street ministry, that is, its attempt to turn kids around through one-on-one counseling, but rather stems from its role in both controlling and legitimizing police activity.

While we believe that our research has established the plausibility of the Ten-Point Coalition's importance, interesting questions remain. More research is needed to uncover what facets of the ministers' work have been most important. Furthermore, we do not know exactly how the three core ministers have come to obtain the power and standing they enjoy in the Boston community. If their charisma has been the critical factor, it may be difficult to replicate the Ten-Point program in other cities. More generally, there is the question of why homicide rates and rate declines have varied among cities. Until we have a good understanding of what initiatives and factors have been important overall in reducing homicide rates in Boston and elsewhere, it will be impossible to determine precisely the full extent of the coalition's contribution in Boston.

As the Ten-Point Coalition reaches its first decade, it does so against the backdrop of a rise in the number of adult homicides and juvenile homicides in Boston in 2001—to sixty-four and four, respectively—although the numbers are still below the 1992 levels.[49] The coalition remains a vigorous presence in Boston. As Reverends Hammond and Roberts have observed, "in the past year alone member churches and staff of the Boston Ten Point Coalition have made more than 200 visits to the homes of high-risk youths, made presentations to more than 3,000 young people in the Boston public schools . . . worked with more than 500 high-risk youths in Department of Youth Services facilities, walked the streets (especially after several homicides), participated in crisis response teams at the funerals of several victims, and begun the mentoring and reintegration of some 20 recently released ex-offenders."[50] On behalf of a maturing coalition looking to the future, Reverend Rivers has warned of the need for a retooled grassroots effort with greater police involvement.[51] The coalition has also cautioned that the present decade poses challenges different from those of the 1990s and that there will be a need for new initiatives that target an older, ex-offender population, as well as continuing interventions for high-risk youths.

The possibility that Boston has found an effective strategy for reducing youth violence without severely and broadly compromising the civil liberties of its inner-city residents is exciting. But only the future can tell whether our interpretation of the Boston story is correct. Proof or disproof of our assertions will emerge as Boston's partnership-based strategy is put to the test across the nation and produces or fails to produce substantial long-term reductions in youth homicide rates.

NOTES

Portions of this essay are adapted, with permission, from Jenny Berrien and Christopher Winship, "An Umbrella of Legitimacy: Boston's Police Department—Ten-Point Coalition," in Gary S. Katzmann, ed., *Securing Our Children's Future: New Approaches to Juvenile Justice and Youth Violence*, ch. 7 (Washington,

D.C.: Brookings/Governance, 2002). The research in this essay was supported by a grant from the Smith Richardson Foundation. Kathy Newman provided us with extensive comments. Mary Jo Bane, Jim Quane, Gwen Dordick, John DiIulio, and David Kennedy made many useful suggestions, as did anonymous reviewers. Participants in colloquia at University of Illinois-Chicago, Northwestern University, and the Center for the Study of Public Values at Harvard University, as well as at the May 1998 Public-Private Ventures' Philadelphia-Boston conference provided constructive criticisms. Lynne Farnum and Suzanne Washington provided valuable editorial assistance. Of course, any mistakes are solely our responsibility.

1. Federal Bureau of Investigation, *Uniform Crime Reports,* 1990–1999.

2. Many cities in which there have been declines have implemented community policing programs. These efforts typically try to be proactive rather than reactive in dealing with crime. Future research is needed to determine how important these new efforts might be in explaining differences across cities in the drop of homicide rates.

3. Charles Radin, "Reaching Up against Crime," *Boston Globe,* February 19, 1997, at A1.

4. David Kennedy, "Pulling Levers: Chronic Offenders, High-Crime Settings, and a Theory of Prevention," *Valaparaiso University Law Review* 31 (spring 1997): 449; David Kennedy, Anne M. Piehl, and Anthony A. Braga, "Kids, Guns, and Public Policy," *Law and Contemporary Problems* 59 (winter 1996): 147; David Kennedy, "The (Un)known Universe: Mapping Gangs and Gang Violence in Boston," working paper, Program in Criminal Justice Policy and Management, John F. Kennedy School of Government, 1996. Anthony A. Braga, David M. Kennedy, Elin J. Waring, and Anne M. Piehl, "Problem-Oriented Policing, Deterrence, and Youth Violence: An Evaluation of Boston's Operation Ceasefire," *Journal of Research in Crime and Delinquency* 38:3 (2001): 195–225; and Boston Police Department, *Strategic Plan for Neighborhood Policing: Citywide Strategic Plan,* July 1996.

5. The most significant publicity that the Ten-Point Coalition has received was in *Newsweek.* In the June 1998 issue, the Coalition's work is the feature story and the Reverend Eugene Rivers's picture is on the front cover. The Ten-Point Coalition has also been the focus of a PBS documentary and of articles in *Time* (July 21, 1997 v. 150 n. 3), *Sojourners Magazine, Impact,* the *Weekly Standard,* and several national newspapers such as the *Atlanta Journal-Constitution,* the *New York Times,* and, frequently, the *Boston Globe.*

6. Other Boston ministers, such as the Reverends Bruce Wall and Michael Haynes, fellow members of the Boston Ten-Point Coalition, also have engaged in intensive street ministry during the past decade. However, as we discuss later, Reverends Rivers, Hammond, and Brown have been the key actors in

establishing a partnership with the police and in publicly establishing the legitimacy of their activities. As in other cities, there are many other groups in Boston involved in working with at-risk youth. Prominent examples are the Dorchester Youth Collaborative and the Boston Violence Prevention Program. Although these programs have almost certainly contributed to the dramatic reductions in crime we have seen in Boston, we believe that their direct impact on the overall homicide rate through one-on-one counseling of street youth, like that of the three Ten-Point ministers, has been modest.

7. Interview with public defender.

8. The information in this section is derived primarily from interviews conducted by the authors during the fall of 1997 with members of the Boston Police Department, Boston Probation Department, employees of the city's street worker program, and David Kennedy. The Federal Bureau of Investigation's *Uniform Crime Reports* state that 143 homicides were committed in Boston in 1990; however, current Boston police statistics and current police officers report 152 homicides for that record-breaking year.

9. Interview with public defender.

10. "Events Leading to St. Clair Report," *Boston Globe,* January 15, 1992, at 23.

11. Federal Bureau of Investigation, *Uniform Crime Reports,* 1991–1992.

12. "Events Leading to St. Clair Report," 23.

13. Ibid.

14. The question of timing and causality here is complex. The most aggressive period of stop-and-frisk tactics ended in 1990; yet the homicide rate continued to fall in 1991 and 1992. If one believes that the causal connection is contemporaneous, then this is evidence of lack of a causal effect. However, if the causal effect of police enforcement is lagged, then this is evidence for a causal effect.

15. James D. St. Clair, *Report of the Boston Police Department Review Committee,* January 14, 1992.

16. David Kennedy, conversation, October 1997.

17. Kennedy, "Pulling Levers," 449.

18. Jenny Berrien, "The Boston Miracle: The Emergence of New Institutional Structures in the Absence of Rational Planning," senior thesis, Department of Sociology, Harvard University, March 20, 1998.

19. Robert A. Jordan and *Globe* staff, "Clergy's Anger Can Bring Hope," *Boston Globe,* May 16, 1992.

20. These pastors serve different types of congregations and have very personal styles. Reverend Rivers is the pastor of the Azusa Christian Community, which has a congregation of around forty members who live mostly within the Four Corners neighborhood of Dorchester. He is sometimes accused of running a storefront church because of the surprisingly small congregation.

Rivers also tends to be the most politically outspoken and controversial of the three ministers. Reverend Hammond oversees the Bethel AME church in Dorchester, a much more populous church that attracts people from a variety of neighborhoods. He is described as less controversial than Rivers but equally strong in his convictions and drive for social change. Jeffrey Brown is the pastor at the Union Baptist Church in Cambridge. Brown's congregation has several hundred congregants, but, like Rivers, he remains very active in street-based outreach.

21. Jordan, "Clergy's Anger Can Bring Hope," 13. See Berrien and Winship, "An Umbrella of Legitimacy," for a complete description of The Ten-Point Plan to Mobilize the Churches.

22. See Berrien, "The Boston Miracle," and Berrien and Winship, "An Umbrella of Legitimacy," for more detail.

23. Ray Hammond and Wesley Roberts, "Renewing Efforts against Violence," *Boston Globe*, February 19, 2002, at A11.

24. Ibid.

25. Ibid.

26. Ibid.

27. Randall Kennedy, *Race, Crime, and the Law* (Pantheon, 1997), 24–25.

28. Ibid, 19.

29. Currently, Giuliani continues to have tremendous citywide support. We, therefore, may need to temper our argument to recognize his continued political popularity.

30. David Halbfinger, "Where Fear Lingers: A Special Report; A Neighborhood Gives Peace a Wary Look," *New York Times,* May 18, 1998, A1.

31. A much more in-depth discussion of New York City's Model Block program is available in "Community Policing without Communities: The New York Police Department's Citywide Model Block Program," a thesis by Katherine Anne Wagner-McCoy for the Committee on Degrees in Social Studies, Harvard College, March 1999. Christopher Winship was the adviser.

32. Halbfinger, "Where Fear Lingers."

33. Clifford Krauss, "New York's Violent Crime Rate Drops to Lows of Early 1970s," *New York Times,* December 31, 1995, section 1, at 1.

34. Ibid.

35. Kennedy, *Race, Crime, and the Law.*

36. Halbfinger, "Where Fear Lingers."

37. Dan Barry, "Butts, Harlem's Prominent Pastor, Calls Giuliani a Racist," *New York Times,* May 21, 1998, at B1.

38. Ibid.

39. Ibid.

40. Barbara Ross, "Dirty 30 Sergeant Gives Prison Term," (New York) *Daily News,* June 17, 1997, at 10.

41. Associated Press, "Protesters Rage/Demand Feds Probe Police Brutality," (New York) *Newsday,* September 13, 1997.

42. Merle English, "Leaders Fault Mayor for Melee," (New York) *Newsday,* September 7, 1998, at A3.

43. After this essay was completed, the Amadou Diallo killing occurred in New York. Diallo, a black immigrant street vendor, was shot forty-one times in the entryway to his apartment building by four policeman. He was unarmed at the time. His shooting resulted in months of public protests over the aggressiveness of New York Police Department's tactics.

44. See Berrien, "The Boston Miracle," for a detailed exposition.

45. David Kennedy, conversation, October 1997.

46. Some have been concerned that the ministers' role in identifying troublesome youth may allot them too much power, which is a legitimate fear. However, the Ten-Point Coalition's own standing in Boston is quite fragile; it has its enemies and vocal critics. As a result, it would be difficult for the ministers to abuse their power without consequences. Moreover, the remote surveillance function, while important in terms of utilizing the coalition's presence in the community and providing a channel of communication to law enforcement, is also limited. The coalition does not have prior review power over the routine arrest and enforcement activities of the Boston Police Department.

47. An important piece of research that has not been carried out is to interview a broad section of community residents to see whether the activities and decisions that are made collaboratively by the police and the coalition are seen as just and fair. At this point, our claim is based only on the fact that there has not been any public outcry over these activities in the *Boston Globe* or *Boston Herald* or in the local African American newspaper, the *Bay State Banner.* Jenny Berrien and Christopher Winship, "Lessons Learned from Boston's Police-Community Collaboration," *Federal Probation* 63 (1999): 25–32.

48. Boston Police Department Statistics. See Corbett, chapter 6.

49. Hammond and Roberts, "Renewing Efforts against Violence." Reverend Roberts is the president of the Black Ministerial Alliance.

50. Douglas Belkin, "Rivers Seeks New Vigor for Coalition," *Boston Globe,* January 11, 2002, at B2.

51. See Berrien and Winship, "Lessons Learned."

Chapter 11

Guns, Drugs, and Profiling
Ways to Target Guns and Minimize Racial Profiling

Jerome H. Skolnick and Abigail Caplovitz

Introduction

After September 11, 2001, the world of racial profiling shifted in two fundamental ways: the attacks on the World Trade Center and the Pentagon energized the expansion of profiling to new targets, and the New Jersey Supreme Court cited its state constitution in a ruling to minimize "driving while black."

Following 9/11, Muslims, Arabs, and those who resembled them were violently attacked by private citizens[1] and were singled out for additional scrutiny by the Federal Bureau of Investigation.[2] The FBI itself is being reshaped to avoid past errors in failing to identify Muslim terrorists and to prevent future attacks.[3] Immigrants and immigration generally have become the focus of increased scrutiny, and police forces have been asked to enforce immigration laws to aid the war on terror.[4] Like the drug war, the war on terrorism invites profiling. How should a police officer on the street identify a potential terrorist? What are the tell-tale signs that terrorism is afoot? Police have become sensitive to charges of racial profiling and have resisted recent calls to search for terrorists within illegal immigrant communities.[5] We cannot predict the war on terrorism's long-term impact on racial profiling by police; nonetheless, terrorism-related pressure is being exerted to expand the practice by police and other officials.

On June 23, 2000, in view of the retroactivity of the New Jersey Supreme Court's decision,[6] New Jersey fundamentally changed its car-stopping practices. We discuss this decision at length later in this essay. The key holding, however, is this: Under the New Jersey Constitution, police cannot seek consent to search a car legitimately stopped for a traffic violation without reasonable suspicion that some other crime is, or is about to be, committed. New Jersey officers now have little incentive use the vehicle code to target black or Latino drivers in the hope that they will turn out to be drug dealers.

I. Race and Crime

Minorities—people of color—are the main victims of crime in New York and other cities. Murder rates in New York City have declined precipitously since 1994, when the police first started their vigorous gun detection efforts. Had homicides instead continued at the 1993 rate, the dead would have included 2,229 additional African Americans, 64 more Asians, and 1,842 more Hispanics (a total of 4,205 people of color), compared to 308 whites.[7] Thus, nonwhites have been the major beneficiaries of these decreases. And crime has plunged in all categories, not just murder.[8]

The police and Mayor Rudolph Giuliani claimed credit for the crime decline across the city, but especially in minority neighborhoods, pointing to innovative strategies such as COMPSTAT and a renewed emphasis on "quality-of-life crimes."[9] COMPSTAT, an abbreviation for computer statistics, provides real-time computer mapping of crime to reveal crime "hotspots," which enables the police to better allocate resources. COMPSTAT was introduced by former Police Commissioner William Bratton and has been imitated by many police departments.[10] Bratton also began the targeting of quality-of-life crimes, embracing Wilson and Kelling's Broken Windows theory.[11]

Police claims that they caused the crime decline are, however, controversial.[12] One critic, Professor Bernard Harcourt analyzed New York crime data and questioned the police role in crime reduction. He pointed to a dip in crack popularity and use, a booming economy, the aging of baby boomers, and the rise in the prison population as alternative explanations.[13] He also argued that, if police actions had any significant impact, it was through increased surveillance, not because of Broken Windows theory.[14] No one has been able to pinpoint how much variance is accounted for by any correlative factors; nor does this essay. The researchers John Eck and Edward Maguire have care-

fully examined the literature and the explanations that link police tactics to crime reduction and have concluded that, historically, each
crime surge and decline may be attributable to different causes at different times.[15]

There is no question, however, that the reduction, especially in New
York City, correlates with the introduction of new policing tactics.
And, in the area of gun crime, the correlation may be causal. Professors Jeffrey Fagan, Frank Zimring, and June Kim, who generally question the police role in reducing crime, nonetheless found that police efforts to get guns off the street seemed to decrease gun homicide.[16]

Whatever factors caused the overall crime decline, three conclusions
seem incontrovertible. First, the NYPD carried out an aggressive "stop-
and-frisk" policy in communities of color, focused on, but by no means
limited to, collecting guns.[17] Police confiscated guns and drugs using
their authority to stop and frisk and to search incident to arrests for
minor misconduct, such as riding a bicycle on the sidewalk or drinking
beer in public. Second, blacks and Hispanics, especially blacks, as State
Attorney General Elliott Spitzer found, were disproportionately the target of these stops.[18] Third, the residents of these now safer neighborhoods are those who appeared most fearful and critical of the New York
City police.[19] Their discontent manifested itself in complaints about the
NYPD,[20] rising jury awards and settlements in police brutality cases,[21]
low police approval ratings,[22] and antipolice protests.[23] Civilian anger
with the police may have influenced jury verdicts in the Bronx, a heavily policed (and high crime) borough.[24]

The policing tactic generating this discontent has a name: racial
profiling. Police often overidentify people of color as "symbolic assailants," that is, "as persons who use gesture, language, and attire
that police have come to recognize as a prelude to violence."[25] Racial
profiling—police targeting people solely or primarily because of their
skin color—is nothing new in American history, nor has it been confined to the states of the Confederacy.[26]

Racial profiling is particularly difficult to combat because of the
unique character of the policing enterprise: Although it is authorized by
law, its operational strategies are powerfully influenced by sociopolitical factors. Extralegal, idiosyncratic influences such as the personalities
of elected officials, their political commitments, the values conveyed by
police managers and prosecutors, and the culture of the police organization shape officer behavior more than judicial decisions. This is

notably true in the gun and drug context, where police may choose to ignore the Fourth Amendment search requirements and focus on confiscation rather than conviction.[27] The effectiveness of the recent New Jersey Supreme Court decision, despite its explicit targeting of profiling on the highway, rests on how that decision functions in the sociopolitical context of policing. Indeed, the decision itself was likely a product of that very context.

New Jersey authorities released 91,000 documents late in November 2000 showing that prosecutors and police officials knew and approved of racial profiling for many years.[28] The documents reveal that the popular "war on drugs" provided an acceptable justification for New Jersey state troopers to pull over and search blacks and Hispanics on the state's roadways.[29] On New Jersey roadways, black and Hispanic drivers were unjustifiably stopped and searched so often that they complained of an unwritten violation in the state's traffic code, "driving while black."[30] To conceal their targeting of blacks, some New Jersey Troopers engaged in "ghosting."[31] Troopers would stop a black motorist and record the facts of the stop on a form. But, instead of recording the black motorist's license plate number, the officers would record the plate number of a passing car driven by a white.

On February 2, 2001, the *New York Times* front-page lead story reported that New Jersey's Attorney General, John J. Farmer Jr., had settled the state's most notorious racial profiling incident. Four young black and Hispanic men were driving a van to a college basketball game when they were stopped by New Jersey state troopers. Three of the men were shot and wounded when the van (accidentally, according to the driver) backed up toward the trooper. The case, which was settled for $13 million, cast a nationwide spotlight on racial profiling as a civil rights issue.[32]

In an effort to dampen the aftershocks of the case, the attorney general dismissed criminal charges against 128 other defendants, some of whom were actually in possession of guns and drugs. In a statement that reflected the frustration of a public official whose cases are tainted by unlawful police conduct, Mr. Farmer wrote: "The defendants in these cases may have prevailed in their motions to suppress, but they are criminals nevertheless." Nor did the state, in the civil case settlement agreement, admit guilt in the shooting of the three men. But the attorney Peter Neufeld, one of the lawyers representing the men, said that the size of the settlement "speaks volumes about what happened that night."[33] New Jersey continues to face civil cases from motorists who were stopped and not charged.[34]

This history is the context within which the New Jersey Supreme Court's March 4, 2002, decision in *State of New Jersey v. Carty*[35] must be understood. The case was decided 4-0, with a fifth justice concurring in the result but rejecting the constitutionality of the standard. Two justices abstained, including Peter Verniero, whose role in the New Jersey profiling scandal as the state's attorney general generated great controversy during the process of his appointment and confirmation to the court. The history is also apparent when the court references the real world of stops and consents in explaining its reasoning.[36]

The court recognizes that the "consent" to be searched of a motorist who has been pulled over and ticketed is scarcely any consent at all. "In the context of motor vehicle stops, where the individual is at the side of the road and confronted by a uniformed officer seeking to search his or her vehicle," the court wrote, "it is not a stretch of the imagination to assume that the individual feels compelled to consent." Analogizing the stopped motorist search to a *Terry* stop, the Court requires troopers to have a "reasonable and articulable suspicion of criminal wrongdoing" before asking for consent to search a lawfully stopped motor vehicle. This is to prevent "the police from turning routine traffic stops into a fishing expedition for criminal activity unrelated to the lawful stop."[37]

But a stopped motorist is no less likely to be intimidated by an officer's authority when the officer is able to articulate grounds for reasonable suspicion than when he or she does not. In either case, the motorist is likely to feel "compelled to consent." How we evaluate this decision depends on our focus. If we consider it as limiting the discretion of *officers* to search stopped motorists, by imposing a *Terry* standard for a roadside search, it seems to protect motorists' rights. But, if we focus on the authenticity of the motorist's *consent,* it is troubling. Like *Terry* itself, it seems avoids the Constitution's probable cause requirement for a search.

Whatever the doctrinal justification for the New Jersey decision, its consequences will not be known for some time. If effectively enforced, the decision and its progeny could dramatically reduce racial profiling on New Jersey highways and streets. The effective enforcement caveat is important because police officers may try to evade the standard by falsifying grounds for "reasonable suspicion," or judges may lower the "reasonable and articulable suspicion" bar. If the latter occurs, the protection afforded people of all colors will be reduced.

New Jersey is, at the moment, sui generis. What about "profiling" elsewhere? Defenders of profiling, as part II of this essay discusses, argue that profiling is an effective police tactic soundly grounded in empirical data, as New Jersey's Attorney General Farmer seemed to argue in justifying illegal searches. Part II examines and questions that claim using data from several police departments and contexts. Part III takes on the more difficult question of how, given the unique socio-political context of policing, racial profiling can be minimized.

II. Racial Profiling and the Myth of Empiricism

Few, if any, public or law enforcement officials endorse racial profil-ing. Former President Clinton called profiling "morally indefensible," charging that "racial profiling is in fact the opposite of good police work where actions are based on hard facts, not stereotypes."[38]

And yet, "profiling" (without the discrediting adjective "racial")[39] has been justified as good policing, on the basis of descriptions of sus-pects and crime patterns.[40] Profiling has achieved such legitimacy within police forces that officers have been trained to do it.[41] In fact, most officers may believe in good faith that they are "playing the per-centages" when they profile.[42] But if police reject racial profiling as wrong, what cues do they typically attend to when they profile? In practice, is there any significant kind of profiling other than racial?

It is worth considering the meaning of the term "profile." A *profile* differs fundamentally from a *description*. A *description* is witness gener-ated and is used to guide police to an individual who committed a re-ported crime. A *profile* is a police conceptualization of a type of crimi-nal person and is used as a screening device to sift through the public for persons who commit unreported, victimless crimes.[43] Like a socio-logical model, the accuracy of a profile is contingent on the quality of the data supporting it.

In defense of profiling, Los Angeles Police Chief Bernard Parks of-fered the following illustration:

We have an issue of violent crime against jewelry salespeople . . . the predominant suspects are Colombians. We don't find Mexican-Americans, or blacks, or other immigrants. It's a collection of several hundred Colombians who commit this crime. If you see six in a car in front of the Jewelry Mart, and they're waiting and watching people with briefcases, should we play the percentages and follow them? It's common sense.[44]

Indeed, this profile makes a good deal of sense since its specificity increases its accuracy. In this example, the profile:

1. Focuses on a limited type of criminality, presumably theft or robbery, against a single type of victim, jewelry salespeople
2. Targets a distinctive pattern of ethnic offenders, Colombians
3. Places the targeted offenders in a specific location, the Jewelry Mart, where victims can be found
4. Describes actions that perpetrators of the crime, seeking a victim, could be expected to take—waiting and watching for people with briefcases.

Although such behavior could be innocent, the information suffices to meet a "reasonable and articulable suspicion" standard. Targeting men who fit the profile properly plays the percentages. Stopping and questioning them should detect a significantly higher proportion of violent jewelry thieves than would random stops on the street.[45] The actor James Woods reasonably "profiled" some of the Al-Queda terrorists before 9/11 on a cross-country flight to Los Angeles. Four of his fellow first-class passengers were well-dressed men who appeared to be Middle Eastern and who were traveling together. Woods told the story of his reaction to Seymour M. Hersh. "I thought these guys were either terrorists or F.B.I. guys." Woods focused on their behavior, rather than their ethnicity. They simply did not behave like normal first-class passengers. "The guys were in sync—dressed alike. They didn't have a drink and were not talking to the stewardess. None of them had a carry-on or a newspaper. Nothing." Woods reported his suspicions to a flight attendant and to the pilot. Presumably, a report was filed, but nothing came of it.[46]

Such *empirically based* profiles can legitimately include race and ethnicity. If factual support for such inclusion exists, listing race or ethnicity, along with other identifying factors, especially behavior, is and should be lawful.[47] By contrast, a *racial profile* generally identifies one prominent characteristic: black or brown skin, although "young" and "male" may also be included, and assumes criminality.[48] Unlike the Jewelry Mart example, the profile "young black male" is not sufficiently detailed to serve as a screening device. Empirically grounded profiles should "work." They should "lower the cost of obtaining and processing information"[49] and make policing more efficient. Police using profiles should find the same number of offenders while stopping and searching fewer people—the ratio of false to true positives should decrease.

Rather than "work," racial profiles *increase* the rate of false positives, disproportionately raising the social cost of policing to innocent nonwhites.[50] The inefficiency of racial profiles results from the basis of their information: overbroad or false assumptions, rather than Jewelry Mart–style data analysis.

Racial profiling in the drug context is based on the belief that nonwhites are more likely to be involved in the drug trade. But several sets of data challenge this assumption. First, rates of reported marijuana use (and thus possession) are higher for whites than nonwhites.[51] Similarly, whites use more cocaine than blacks, and, until recently, Hispanics used more than either whites or blacks.[52] Hispanic usage rates in 1997 and 1998 were virtually equal to those of whites, though still higher than those of blacks.[53] Second, the famed disproportionate rates of offending, at least in the area of drug crimes, are likely an artifact of police tactics, not underlying offending rates.[54] Third, the U.S. Customs Service's seizure data demonstrate that blacks and Hispanics are less likely than whites to be possessing drugs.[55] Finally, data from the Maryland State Police show that black and white motorists driving through Maryland on Interstate 95 are discovered with drugs at statistically indistinguishable rates, despite vastly greater numbers of searches of black motorists.[56] Unfortunately, such data are difficult to obtain, since police do not routinely publicize their search success rates, much less break down search results by crime or race.

The Maryland State Police likely learned to profile racially from the DEA, which disseminated videotapes through Operation Pipeline that told the police what to be suspicious of.[57] David Cole reviewed profiles relied upon by DEA officers in identifying drug couriers.[58] Examining the testimony of the officers in various cases, Cole found that contradictory factors were part of the DEA drug courier profile. Some of these were:

[A]rrived late at night; arrived early in the morning; arrived in the afternoon; one of the first to deplane; one of the last to deplane; deplaned in the middle; purchased ticket at the airport; made reservation on short notice; bought coach ticket; bought first-class ticket; used one-way ticket; used round-trip ticket; paid for ticket with cash; paid for ticket with small-denomination currency; paid for ticket with large-denomination currency.[59]

The self-contradictory nature of such profile "factors" defeats any claim that they were empirically based. Rational drug carriers will try not to bring attention to themselves, and so police may come to rely on racial stereotypes.

The reliance on an allegedly *empirical*, but actually *racial*, profile is easiest to prove in the area of pretextual car stops, since drivers often violate some traffic law, such as exceeding the posted speed limit.[60]

Though more difficult to prove, racial profiling also affects pedestrian stops and enforcement. Street policing affords officers two very different classes of opportunities to search large numbers of people: *Terry*[61] stops-and-frisks and searches incident to pretextual misdemeanor arrests.[62] These two search opportunities have important differences, and this essay discusses them separately. However, both facilitate race-centered policing.

To legitimate a *Terry* frisk, an officer needs "reasonable suspicion" to believe that "crime is afoot" and that the suspect is dangerous, because armed.[63] Theoretically, if "reasonable suspicion" is a strictly enforced, high standard, *Terry* frisks should be infrequent. Nevertheless, working cops may choose to discount the judicial standard even if it is strictly enforced.[64] If the New York City of the 1990s is an appropriate example, *Terry* stops-and-frisks were common, concentrated in minority urban neighborhoods, and effected with slight regard for the legal standards.[65]

A comprehensive study by the New York Office of Attorney General Elliot Spitzer, in conjunction with Columbia University's Center for Violence Research and Prevention, showed that racial disparities in the NYPD's stops-and-frisks could not be fully accounted for by demographics and crime rates.[66] It could be argued, as it was by Police Commissioner Howard Safir, that the stops were made in high-crime areas, which was true.[67] The highest rate of stop-and-frisk activity took place in precincts with high crime and with majority black and

Hispanic residents.[68] Nevertheless, in precincts where blacks and Hispanics constituted less than 10 percent of the population, they accounted for more than half the persons "stopped."[69]

Race was not the only factor to correlate with the efficiency of stops. The constitutionality of the stops[70] strongly correlated with the success of the attendant searches. Citywide, when police officers (SCU and non-SCU) lacked constitutional justification, they stopped 29.3 people in order to make an arrest; when they did have constitutional justification, they stopped 7.3 persons per arrest.[71] Such a correlation makes sense since the constitutional standard—reasonable suspicion—is designed to ensure that suspects are more likely to be guilty of a crime. Thus, we might infer that where reasonable suspicion was lacking, the decision to frisk was influenced by some other factor, likely the race of the suspect.[72] However, we don't know whether constitutional grounds were lacking or just not reported. Before racial profiling became an issue, cops tended to report fully on the circumstances underlying a frisk only when the frisk resulted in an arrest. If an arrest resulted, the frisk form would come into evidence, and officers knew it would be challenged if not complete. When they did not make an arrest, many saw no purpose in defining grounds for the stop. Thus, many officers just documented that they made the stop without saying why. Accordingly, the ratio of 29.3 frisks to one arrest may be more related to the arrest incentive to document than to the constitutionality of the stop. Nonetheless, the low ratio of 7.3 frisks for each arrest when the stop was definitely constitutional strongly suggests that the reasonable-suspicion standard correlates with search success.

The potential for race-based enforcement in the context of a *Terry* stop is obvious, given that the stop may be triggered solely by an officer's suspicions that cannot be reasonably articulated. We usually call that a "hunch" (which is what Officer McFadden had when he first spotted Terry and his associates—two of whom who were, in fact, black teenagers.) Misdemeanor enforcement would seem, at first glance, to be insulated from race-based enforcement because the arresting officer can point to the misdemeanor as the motive for his action. However, the wide violation of minor misdemeanors like jaywalking or riding a bicycle on the sidewalk means that these crimes offer police discretionary authority not unlike earlier statutes that have been voided for vagueness.[73] The NYPD explicitly embraced pretextual misdemeanor arrests as a strategy to search for guns.[74] Given a tendency toward racially influenced behavior in *Terry* stops, it is likely that misdemeanor enforcement stops would be similarly slanted.

However, no statistic, such as a false-to-true positive ratio, can be calculated to demonstrate the influence of race in pretextual enforcement decisions. The baseline data problem is compounded by the nature of some of the offenses targeted, such as drinking in public. Summertime heat can turn the sidewalks of poor neighborhoods into dens of "criminality." Residents escape from their overheated apartments to socialize over beers the way more affluent people gather in air-conditioned taverns or living rooms. Because poverty still correlates with race in America,[75] more of these urban "offenders" are likely to be nonwhite.

In sum, countless millions of police searches and frisks are influenced by race, and the overwhelming majority of those searches target innocents. This is not to deny that lawless searches may prevent crime by searching at random, or by race, and finding some who are in possession of guns, drugs, or other contraband. Rather than admit to a lawless search, however, police who understand the legal requirements for a search are likely to claim they had "reasonable suspicion," a term of considerable elasticity.

When it is stretched too far—and experienced police know well how to stretch it—it may turn out that, as a practice, young males are stopped for a category of crime that might be called "walking while black." Professor William Stuntz describes the fourfold harm that flows from a false positive search as follows:

> The first is a harm to the victim's privacy—the injury suffered if some agent of the state rummages around in the victim's briefcase, or examines the contents of his jacket pockets. The second is . . . "targeting harm," the injury suffered by one who is singled out by the police and publicly treated like a criminal suspect. Third is the injury that flows from discrimination, the harm a black suspect feels when he believes he is treated the way he is treated because he is black. Fourth is the harm that flows from police violence, the physical injury and associated fear of physical injury that attends the improper police use of force.[76]

Professor David Harris details several harms in addition to the impact on the innocent: the criminalization of blackness; the tolerance of "rational" discrimination; the distortion of the legal system; the distortion of the social world; and the undermining of community-based policing.[77] More concretely, such interactions generate tensions between nonwhite communities and police, which can lead to incendiary violence.[78] However, such important costs are hard to trace directly and are difficult to quantify.

Racial profiling might be defined more usefully as the distortion of the distribution of false positives that results from race- (or otherwise unconstitutionally) based decisions to stop, frisk, or search. Two types of distortion result. One (the *Terry* problem exemplified by the SCU data) is an increase in the rate of false positives suffered by nonwhites relative to whites. When the false positive rate is high, it seems reasonable to assume that the police are stretching "reasonable suspicion" to a point that qualifies as "racial profiling." The other type of distortion, resulting from pretextual enforcement of quality-of-life crimes or of highway speed limits, as exemplified by the Maryland data, is a vastly disproportionate and larger absolute number of false positives.

Our preceding discussion may suggest that the problem of "profiling" on the sidewalks, streets, and highways can be solved; simply making profiling "empirical" will eliminate harms we have described. But that is not the case. Is the Colombian jewelry thief scenario described by Chief Parks, or the terrorist identification by James Woods, truly "profiling"? We called it empirical profiling, but what, in fact, distinguishes those two scenarios from standard, good police work? In both cases, the observers involved could articulate objective factors that, taken together, conferred reasonable suspicion. In neither case were the observers looking at a checklist and then sifting the crowd for people who matched it. In both cases, the observers looked at behavior as a primary source of suspiciousness. In both cases, context was critical (as it was in *Terry*).

The critical role of context may explain why the Street Crimes Unit, a few hundred officers who patrolled a city of several million, instead of a precinct of tens of thousands, was more likely to frisk nonwhites than the rest of the NYPD was. The SCU engaged only in proactive stops and did not respond to calls reporting, for example, that "a suspicious twenty-year-old black male with a red shirt had a gun." A stop-and-frisk resulting from the latter kind of report is more likely than a purely proactive stop to result in the discovery of contraband

and an arrest and to lead to fewer false positives. It is also more likely to be done by precinct cops than by the SCU.

When police search for guns, drugs, terrorists, for criminals of any sort, what should they do? If they are being reactive, they should be searching for someone who fits a description. If they are being proactive, they should be making specific observations of deviance from the local norm—a fixation with the briefcases of jewelry store employees, an eschewing of food and drink, of even movement, in the first-class cabin—as factors leading to the reasonable suspicion that is legally necessary to stop and frisk or to pretextually use misdemeanor law or the vehicle code to search. The question then, is: How do we get police to rely on their observational skills, not on a "profile"? One answer, as we discuss in the next section, is to employ data-centered management tools like Compstat, which can produce the necessary combination of empirical evidence and observational skills.

III. Searching for Tomorrow

In his influential 1994 article on gun searching, James Q. Wilson hoped for a device that would enable police "to detect the presence of a large lump of metal in someone's pocket from a distance of 10 to 15 feet."[79] However, even if such a device were to be developed, it would have to distinguish a gun from a cell phone or a pager.[80]

How to assess such surveillance devices is a complex issue. Like us, most of the public seems inclined, with some reservations, to support such measures in high-crime public settings, and certainly in places of limited access, such as subways, apartment and office buildings, banks and ATMs. Nevertheless, the level of privacy invasion by a such a gun detector would be unprecedented. Not confined to an airport gate entrance or other building checkpoint, a barrier voluntarily crossed, such a detector could be aimed across oblivious, nonconsenting crowds. Such a detector would give new meaning to a "sweep" for criminals.[81]

Privacy issues aside, such a sophisticated technological fix is unlikely in the near future, despite Wilson's confidence that "underemployed nuclear physicists and electronic engineers in the post-coldwar era surely have the talents for designing a better gun detector."[82]

By 2002, there is no such fix. What, then, should be done to minimize racial profiling and the false positive distortion that results?

The short, unhelpfully simple answer is—improve police accuracy, which can be improved in three basic ways: sophisticated data collection, analysis, and management; management-driven training and cultural shifts; and civilian efforts to raise profiling costs. None of these is a panacea, nor are they mutually exclusive. Rather, they are an attempt to identify how police organizations can use, and outsiders can generate, incentives for police action. Since racial profiling usually occurs on the beat, away from direct supervision, no one strategy will work everywhere. Change will require the dedication of police managers and, where possible, the cooperation of police unions.

A. Collecting and Managing Data

By tracking false-positive rates, police departments or outside monitors can quantify the profiling problem. An ideal data set would contain, for each officer: (1) stops, frisks, and the "reasonable suspicion" triggering them; (2) arrests, and the crime triggering the arrest (or at least whether or not it was a street misdemeanor); (3) the results of all frisks and searches (incident to arrest or otherwise); and (4) the race, age, and gender of the person stopped/frisked/arrested. Such a data set should assist in identifying "problem" officers or clusters of officers and should facilitate tracking problems over time. In the era of COMPSTAT and its copies, police departments are developing the technical resources to track officer behavior. Whether they have the institutional inclination to do so is another question.[83]

To acquire such data, every officer should complete paperwork accurately. Given that most frisks and searches occur far from the purview of police management, the task of ensuring compliance will be formidable[84] and will demand the cooperation of midlevel supervisors, such as sergeants and lieutenants.

B. Police Management

The potential of police managers to affect police behavior cannot be overstated. Two recent studies make the point clear. The Vera Institute of Justice completed a study of two South Bronx high crime precincts and found an unusually high level of community satisfaction with the police.[85] Vera found that both precincts targeted crime just as aggressively as other New York precincts, and with similar success. But strong leadership in each precinct made reducing civilian complaints a priority, and their officers behaved accordingly.

The U.S. Customs Service (Customs), formerly headed by Raymond Kelly, was the focus of a comprehensive General Accounting Office (GAO) report titled, "Better Targeting of Airline Passengers for Personal Searches Could Produce Better Results."[86] This remarkable report summarized the search training, policies, standards, and success rates of airport searches for contraband and analyzed the results by race and gender. On the basis of its findings, which showed that the correlation of race and gender with search selection was different from its correlation with search success, Customs overhauled its practices.[87] While airport searches and street policing may seem so dissimilar that the lessons from the Customs report can be disregarded, the Customs experience powerfully illustrates the depth of change that committed management can achieve.

Responding to the documented racial disparities in its search targeting, Customs changed the way it taught inspectors to identify suspicious people. The 1999 Personal Search Handbook eliminated the forty-three-item factor list—the notoriously contradictory profile list—and replaced it with six categories of information that could generate reasonable suspicion for an intrusive search.[88] The categories are: (1) behavioral analysis, which means looking for physiological signs of nervousness, such as cold sweats, flushed face, and eye contact avoidance; (2) observational techniques, which focus on physical discrepancies in appearance, such as an unnatural gait; (3) inconsistencies identified in the interview or documentation; (4) intelligence developed by another officer; (5) signals from K-9 units; and (6) evidence gathered incident to a seizure or arrest.

These factors are racially neutral and must be generated and articulated by an officer each time. In addition, the conceptual groupings encourage officers to notice unlisted but similarly significant behaviors. Thus, the categories encourage inspectors to really *look* at each person's behavior, not just his race. Moreover, the categories are not static, while the forty-three-factor list had been in existence for more than ten years.[89]

Customs also standardized search procedures throughout airports, modified training practices, and increased supervision of searches.[90]

Further, passenger complaints are being addressed systematically through a new Customer Satisfaction Unit.[91]

Last, Customs has made its practices data driven and uses a classical experimental design to measure its success. Since Customs officers can search without articulated reasonable suspicion, Customs management can experiment by comparing profiled passengers against a control group of those randomly searched.[92] Although police departments cannot implement such experiments, one lesson is transferable: Strong management can improve the accuracy of officers' searches.[93]

C. Raising the Cost

What would be an acceptable false-positive rate? Although there is no answer to the question, we can assume that raising the costs of racial profiling can energize management's commitment to fair police practices. Prosecutors can fulfill their quasi-magisterial oversight obligations by refusing to accept cases or by seeking to vacate convictions based on racial profiling stops, as has happened in New Jersey.[94] Judicial oversight, through vacating convictions, excluding evidence,[95] and ordering discovery,[96] can provide a significant positive incentive to change police behavior. As the New Jersey Supreme Court recently demonstrated, judges can also change the constitutional standards, which, coupled with the exclusionary rule, can provide strong disincentives.

Financial penalties or incentives offer a second path to reform. These can be imposed by lawsuits that seek damages or by city councils or legislatures, relying on profiling data. However difficult they are to bring and to win, lawsuits do open police practices to public scrutiny, as they have in New Jersey and in Maryland. Pattern and practice/Monell-type suits, whether brought privately as damage awards or brought by the federal government through consent decrees, could strongly influence departments to comprehensively revise how searches are conducted.[97]

Conclusion

Racial profiling is a policy choice. It is made by elected officials, judges, prosecutors, police managers, and police rank-and-file. Consequently, it is difficult to reshape racially influenced frisk-and-search practices without the engaged commitment of those who, at every level of politics and management, control the reins of police policies and practices.

Community leaders may influence police strategies through community give-and-take with governors, mayors, city managers, and police managers, who could reduce or eliminate pretextual searching.

Accountability could surely be heightened through collection and analysis of stop, frisk, and arrest data. Prosecutors, who are supposed to perform a quasi-magisterial role in the system of criminal justice, could teach and insist upon a meaningful reasonable suspicion standard, as well as a standard of truthfulness in describing and offering evidence.

Taking guns off the streets necessarily involves stopping and frisking citizens, but officers do not need to abuse their authority to accomplish crime control. When the burden of stop-and-frisk searches is borne equitably by citizens of whatever color or ethnicity, the privacy-security tradeoff can be set to a socially acceptable level. When race motivates police stop, frisk, and search decisions, more innocent non-whites will be searched than innocent whites.

On May 13, 2002, Raymond Kelly, who was appointed Commissioner of the NYPD by Mayor Michael Bloomberg, issued an order banning racial profiling, which he defined as "the use of race, color, ethnicity or national origin as the determinative factor for initiating police action."

Citing the Fourth Amendment, Kelly's order requires officers to "be able to articulate the factors which led them to take enforcement action, in particular those factors leading to reasonable suspicion for a stop and question, or probable cause for an arrest." Officers are not precluded from using race, color, ethnicity, national origin, religion, gender, gender identity, or sexual orientation, but only as "pedigree information" comparable to height, weight, and age. The order further promises that compliance with the order will be part of the protocol for command inspections and Compstat review.

Kelly's order is a model for how police managers should confront the issue of targeting illegal gun and drug possessors without myopically focusing on race. In the process, such policies can—and should— guide police in achieving a constitutionally sanctioned set of norms for stopping, questioning, and frisking—and a safer community.

NOTES

Reprinted by permission of the *Arizona Law Review*. We thank Commissioner James J. Fyfe of the NYPD for his incisive comments. He, however, is not responsible for any errors of fact or analysis.

1. Ann Zimmerman, "Convenience Stores Are Taking Steps to Protect Employees," *Wall Street Journal*, September 25, 2001, p. B5; "U.S. Islamic Groups Threatened, Harassed as Some Lash Out at Scapegoats," *Wall Street Journal*, September 13, 2001, p. A6; "A Nation Challenged: Immigrants: More Insulted and Attacked," *New York Times*, March 11, 2002, p. A12.

2. Maureen Tkacik and Rick Wartzman, "Muslim Lawyer Terms FBI Probe Discriminatory," *Wall Street Journal*, October 15, 2001, p. B1.

3. Neil A. Lewis, "F.B.I. Chief Admits 9/11 Might Have Been Detectable," *New York Times*, May 30, 2002, p. 1.

4. Susan Sachs, "A Nation Challenged: Immigrants: Long Resistant, Police Start Embracing Immigration Duties," *New York Times*, March 15, 2002, p. A11; Eric Schmitt, "Ruling Clears Way to Use State Police in Immigration Duty," *New York Times*, April 4, 2002, p. A19;

5. Eric Schmitt, "Administration Split on Local Role in Terror Fight," *New York Times*, April 29, 2002, p. A1; Eric Schmitt, "Two Conservatives Tell Bush They Oppose Plan for Police," *New York Times*, June 2, 2002, Section 1, p. 24.

6. *State of New Jersey v. Carty*, 2002 N.J. LEXIS 58 (March 4, 2002).

7. Editorial, "The Crime Drop: A Boon to Minorities," *New York Post*, February 17, 1999, p. 22.

8. Michael Cooper, "Homicides Decline below 1964 Level in New York City," *New York Times*, December 24, 1998, p. A1. Other, similar statistics are available at Michael Grunwald, "Coursework in New York: Surviving the Police," *Washington Post*, March 16, 1999, p. A3. John Marzulli, "Apple's a Safer Place," *New York Daily News*, December 4, 1998,; K. C. Baker and Corky Siemeszo, "Violent Crime Dips 7% in Apple and the U.S.," *New York Daily News*, May 17, 1999, p. 20. Early in 2000, crime in New York City rose slightly. Newspaper stories cited "sources" who suggested the rise is related to decreased police vigilance in the wake of the Diallo crisis. Larry Celona and Andy Geller, "Rudy and Bronx Brass to Hold Powwow on Jump in Crime Stats," *New York Post*, March 16, 2000, p. 7; Larry Celona, "City Homicide Rate Jumps 13%," *New York Post*, April 4, 2000, p. 2.

9. See Jim Newton, "The NYPD: Bigger Bolder—Is It Better?" *Los Angeles Times*, December 24, 1995, p. 1. The use of data to target police efforts has received empirical and academic support. See David M. Kennedy, "Pulling Levers: Chronic Offenders, High-Crime Settings, and a Theory of Prevention," 31 *Val. U. L. Rev.* 449, 479 (1997) (discusses Boston's experience), and Dan M.

Kahan, "Privatizing Criminal Law: Strategies for Norm Enforcement in the Inner City," 46 *UCLA L. Rev.* 1859, 1864–65 (1999).

10. William Bratton, *Turnaround: How America's Top Cop Reversed the Crime Epidemic* (New York: Random House, 1998). The LAPD version is FASTRAC; Boston began Operation Ceasefire; San Diego uses SARA.

11. See George L. Kelling and William J. Bratton, "Declining Crime Rates: Insiders' Views of the New York City Story," 88 *J. Crim. L. and Criminology* 1217 (1998); Peter A. Barta, Note, "Giuliani, Broken Windows, and the Right to Beg," 6 *Geo. J. on Poverty L. and Pol'y* 165, 167 (1999). (Both articles claim the NYPD embraced Broken Windows. Targeted crime included drinking in public and riding a bicycle on the sidewalk.) But see fn. 50 infra.

12. See, e.g., Bernard E. Harcourt, "Reflecting on the Subject: A Critique of the Social Influence Conception of Deterrence, the Broken Windows Theory, and Order-Maintenance Policing New York Style," 97 *Mich. L. Rev.* 291, 308–43 (1998); see also Bernard E. Harcourt, *Illusion of Order: The False Promise of Broken Windows Policing* (Cambridge, Mass.: Harvard University Press, 2001).

13. See Harcourt, "Reflecting on the Subject," pp. 331–39

14. Ibid., pp. 339–43.

15. John E. Eck and Edward R. Maguire, "Have Changes in Policing Reduced Violent Crime? An Assessment of the Evidence," in Alfred Blumstein and Joel Wallman, eds., *The Crime Drop in America* (New York: Cambridge University Press, 2000).

16. Jeffrey Fagan, Franklin E. Zimring, and June Kim, "Declining Homicide in New York: A Tale of Two Trends," 88 *J. Crim. L. and Criminology* 1277 (1998) (analyzes homicide data and concludes that policing caused/helped cause the drop in gun-related homicides). See also Alfred Blumstein and Richard Rosenfeld, "Explaining Recent Trends in U.S. Homicide Rates," 88 *J. Crim. L. and Criminology* 1175, 1196 (1998) (increased gun possession correlated with increased gun violence); David Garland, "Criminology, Crime Control, and 'The American Difference,'" 69 *U. Colo. L. Rev.* 1137, 1150 (stops and searches drive up costs of gun possession, discouraging it, lowering violent potential of incidents).

17. Whether or not enacted in response to James Q. Wilson's arguments, this policy mirrors Wilson's suggestions in James Q. Wilson, "Just Take Away Their Guns," *New York Times Magazine,* March 20, 1994, Section 6, p. 47. Wilson predicted that such a policy would result in minorities being disproportionately targeted, and he accepted the disparate impact as a cost of reducing crime.

18. See Eliott Spitzer, "The New York City Police Department's 'Stop and Frisk' Practices: A Report to the People of the State of New York from the Office of the Attorney General," Civil Rights Bureau, December 1, 1999, New York, N.Y.

19. Polls of New Yorkers have consistently revealed that minorities are less happy with police than are whites, with their discontent spiking around high-profile incidents such as the brutalization of Abner Louima and the killing of Amadou Diallo. In the past year, the NYPD has gained a new commissioner who has made the improvement of race relations a priority. A recent poll shows he is having some success; as of January 15, 2001, 59 percent of blacks disapproved of the job the NYPD was doing (down from 75 percent in April 2000), and 31 percent approved of the job the NYPD was doing (up from 17 percent in April 2000). Hispanics attitudes toward the job the NYPD was doing underwent a similar change; 46 percent disapproved, down from 61 percent, and approval rose to 39 percent from 33 percent. Kevin Flynn, "Poll Reveals Higher Marks for Police," *New York Times*, February 3, 2001, p. B1.

20. Civilian complaints increased 46 percent in the first six months of 1994. See Peter Mancuso, "Currents," *New York Newsday*, November 20, 1994, p. A43. In just the first six months of 1995, complaints against NYPD officers rose by 31.8 percent. More than 75 percent of the complainants were black or Latino. Ruben Castenada, "As D.C. Police Struggle On, Change Pays Off in New York," *Washington Post,* March 30, 1996, p. A1. Officers were accused of improper force, abuse of authority, discourtesy, and use of racial slurs. A total of 1,778 use-of-force allegations alone were filed in six months of 1995. Jim Newton, "The NYPD: Bigger, Bolder—Is It Better?" *Los Angeles Times,* December 24, 1995, p. 1. The meaning of the spike in complaints is unclear because the NYPD merged with the housing and transit police around that time, significantly increasing the pool of officers to be complained about. However, the increases certainly also reflect the increased contact the police were having with civilians as a result of the emphasis on quality-of-life crimes.

21. Payouts by the city in brutality cases totaled $7 million in 1990 and $32 million in 1996. From 1991–1996, victims received more than $100 million. David A. Love, "What's Going On? Rising Tide of Police Brutality," *New York Amsterdam News,* April 26, 1997, p. 13. Court settlements alone went from $20.6 million in 1995 to $28.3 million in 1998. See "Currents and Books," *Newsday,* August 29, 1999, p. B1.

22. According to the Polling Institute at Quinnipiac College in Hamden, Connecticut, the degree of trust citizens had in the New York City police declined in 1997, even as crime rates were falling. In a report released October 2, 1997, only 48 percent of New York City voters approved of the way in which NYPD officers were doing their jobs—down from 61 percent in February 1996. In the survey, which was conducted shortly after the Abner Louima case, 80 percent of respondents described police brutality as a "very serious" or "somewhat serious" problem.

A later Quinnipiac poll, reported in the *New York Times* on February 3, 2001, by Kevin Flynn (Metro Section, p. B1) suggests that "the bitterness many black and Hispanic New Yorkers feel toward the police has softened." Flynn attributed the change in attitude partly to the efforts of a new police commissioner, Bernard Kerik, who made a point of reaching out to minority neighborhoods and partly to the fact that nearly a year had elapsed since the last high-profile episode of police brutality.

Across the United States, a national poll has revealed that blacks are twice as unhappy with the police as whites are, and, although the rates varied across cities, the two-to-one ratio was fairly constant. The national rate of discontent was 24 percent for blacks, 10 percent for whites, and 15 percent overall. See Stephen K. Smith et al., "Criminal Victimization and Perceptions of Community Safety in 12 Cities, 1998," Bureau of Justice Statistics, May 1999, NJC 173940. A poll taken of Los Angeles County residents in the wake of the O. J. Simpson acquittal revealed other distrust: 75 percent of blacks and 56 percent of Latinos believed that the police planted evidence against Simpson. Only 21 percent of whites believed so. Cathleen Decker, "Trial and Error Focus Shifts to a Justice System and Its Flaws," *Los Angeles Times,* October 8, 1995.

23. One major recent protest against the police was triggered by the killing of Amadou Diallo. See Laura Italiano et al., "1,175 Busted in Protests Hoping DA Will OK Deal," *New York Post,* March 30, 1999, p. 16.

24. Tara George, "Bronx Justice a Coin Toss," *Daily News,* July 11, 2000, p. 22.

25. Jerome H. Skolnick, *Justice without Trial, Law Enforcement in Democratic Society,* 3rd ed. (New York: Macmillian, 1993), pp. 44–47; See also Anthony C. Thompson, "Stopping the Usual Suspects: Race and the Fourth Amendment," 74 *NYU L. Rev.* 956, 983–91 (discussing how social science research of categorizing, schemas, and stereotyping explains police behavior).

26. See Gunner Myrdal, *An American Dilemma: The Negro Problem in Modern Democracy* (New York: Harper and Brothers, 1941) (southern police participation in lynchings); James Richardson, *New York Police: Colonial Times to 1901* (New York: Oxford University Press, 1970) (description of police participation in riots against blacks); David S. Cohen, "Official Oppression: A Historical Analysis of Low-Level Police Abuse and a Modern Attempt at Reform," 28 *Colum. Hum. Rts. L. Rev.* 165, 180–81 (1986); Randall Kennedy, "Race, Law and Suspicion: Using Color as a Proxy for Dangerousness," *Race, Crime and the Law* (New York: Random House, 1997), pp. 136–63; Tracey Maclin, "*Terry v. Ohio*'s Fourth Amendment Legacy: Black Men and Police Discretion," 72 *St. John's L. Rev.* 1271, 1271–75 (1998); Albert Alschuler and Stephen Schulhofer, "Antiquated Procedures or Bedrock Rights? A Response to Professors Meares and Kahan," 1998 *U. Chi. Legal F.* 215, 234 (1998) (deconstructing the enforcement of Chicago's antiloitering statute); Dorothy Roberts, "Foreword: Race, Vagueness, and the Social Meaning of Order-Maintenance Policing," 89 *J. Crim. L. and Criminology* 775 (1999).

27. This phenomenon was described by Jerome H. Skolnick in Jerome H. Skolnick, *Justice without Trial*, 3rd ed. (New York: Macmillan, 1993), p. 214. More recently, the point was made by Arlene Schulman, *23rd Precinct: The Job* (New York: Soho Press, 2001), p. 195.

28. David Koceniewski and Robert Hanley, "An Inside Story of Racial Bias and Denial," *New York Times,* Metro Section, December 3, 2000, p. 53.

29. Ibid. New Jersey's practices were heavily influenced by the Drug Enforcement Administration (DEA), which enlisted local police in the federal War on Drugs. DEA officials praised New Jersey troopers for their contribution to "Operation Pipeline" and hailed the troopers as exemplary models for other states.

30. Kocieniewski and Hanley, "Inside Story." See also http://www.aclu .org/profiling/tales/index.html for anecdotes from fifteen states, and Katheryn K. Russell, "'Driving While Black': Corollary Phenomena and Collateral Consequences," 40 *B.C. L. Rev.* 717 (1999) (citing cases to describe such corollary phenomena as walking, idling, standing, and shopping while black).

31. David Kocieniewski, "Trenton Charges 2 Troopers with Falsifying Drivers' Race," *New York Times,* April 20, 1999, p. B1.

32. Iver Peterson and David M. Halbfinger, "New Jersey Agree to Pay $13 Million in Profiling Suit," *New York Times,* Late Edition, February 3, 2001, p. 1.

33. Ibid.

34. Iver Peterson, "Profiling Disclosure May Prompt Dismissal of Cases and Review of Judge," *New York Times,* November 29, 2000, Section B, p. 6.

35. *State of New Jersey v. Carty,* 2002 N.J. LEXIS 58 (March 4, 2002).

36. Ibid. at *26-30.

37. Ibid. at *9-10 (emphasis added). The *Terry* decision is reported at *Terry v. Ohio,* 392 U.S. 1 (1968).

38. Clinton ordered federal law enforcement agencies to compile race data on those they question, search, or arrest to facilitate the detection of profiling. Steven A. Holmes, "Clinton Orders Investigation on Possible Racial Profiling," *New York Times,* June 10, 1999. Even Congress is concerned; in recent years, it has considered legislation to quantify the "driving while black" phenomenon. H.R.1443, Traffic Stops Statistics Study Act of 2000; S. 821 Traffic Stops Statistics Study Act of 1999.

39. Racial profiles have always been condemned, even from the first newspaper usage, although profiles not specifically so labeled have been consistently defended. A search of the "Newsgroup File-All" on LEXIS of "Racial w/1 profil! and police" uncovered the first usage in 1987, where highway troopers were denying they used "racial" profiles to effect pretextual stops. Nonetheless, the troopers looked for Hispanics and cars with out-of-state plates. See "Utah Troopers Seize Couriers in 'Cocaine Lane' Crackdown," *San Diego Union-Tribune,* October 8, 1987, p. A32. Only one other use of racial pro-

filing showed up before 1990; between 1990 and the start of 1994, there were eight uses; from 1994 to 1996, there were thrity-one hits; from 1996 to 1998 there were sixty-three, from 1998 to 1999 there were 187, and then there was an enormous spike—in 1999–2000, more than 1,000 hits and from January to October 2000 another 1,000 hits.

40. New York Mayor Rudolph Giuliani asserted that the NYPD stopped and frisked people on the basis of suspect descriptions. Guiliani argued that 71 percent of crime victims in specific precincts had said their attackers were black and that 63 percent of the stops in those precincts were of blacks. Giuliani's defense seems to equate "black" with a suspect description. See Kevin Flynn, "Two Polar Views of Police and Race at U.S. Hearing," *New York Times,* May 27, 1999. William J. Stuntz has defended police reliance on profiles this way: "The problem is not, as some would have it, that the police are too quick to use 'profiles' when identifying drug suspects. Given the nature of both street-level policing and downscale drug markets, they could hardly do otherwise: *How else is one to identify* plausible candidates for street stops than by *a set of readily observable visual cues* (emphasis added)?" See William J. Stuntz, "Race, Class and Drugs," 98 *Colum. L. Rev.* 1795, 1824 (1998). Even critics of racial profiling, like Professor Randall Kennedy, concede the "empiricism" of profiling. See Randall Kennedy, "Suspect Policy," *New Republic,* September 13–20, 1999, p. 32. However, the evidence he offers of disproportionate criminality to support the empiricism—that blacks commit 25 percent of the violent crime despite being 12 percent of the nation's population—is simply not support. First, the statistic means that 75 percent of the violent crime is done by nonblacks; thus, 75 percent of violent criminals will be missed if police rely on a black profile. Second, national statistics cannot have any relevance in any individual's case.

41. The New Jersey documents revealed that officers, including minority officers, were trained to use racial profiling. Koceniewski and Hanley, "An Inside Story," p. 53. Police elsewhere received similar training. A police organization, Black Cops against Police Brutality, revealed that a police training manual offered this advice for car stops: "Jamaicans/Rastafarians have been known to operate and transport narcotics in the following types of vehicles . . . Toyota Corollas and Celicas, a Datsun B210, BMWs and Volvos . . . [drug trafficking cars] may display the Ethiopian flag or the colors of the flag . . . red, yellow and green, Jamaican paraphernalia, bumper stickers or slogans." "Police Training Manual Is Criticized," *New York Times,* March 17, 1999, p. B5. In 1993, a former New Hampshire state police officer, as part of a motion to dismiss charges against twenty-six blacks, reported that he had been instructed to use racial profiles. See Alabama Opelika, "Across the USA: News from Every State," *USA Today,* July 20, 1993, p. 8A. On paper at least, the NYPD stands in sharp contrast, counseling its officers: "Do not be a victim of the

'SYMBOLIC OPPONENT SYNDROME,' . . . [the] preconceived notion that places suspects into a 'BAD GUY' category because of race, nationality, grooming, or mode of dress . . . [do not] reach any definite conclusions that may lead to irreversible police action because of a suspect's appearance. Looks can be deceiving and should not form the basis for action." See Peter Noel, "I Thought He Had a Gun," *Village Voice,* January 13, 1998, p. 44.

42. Jeffrey Goldberg, "The Color of Suspicion," *New York Times Magazine,* June 20, 1999, Section 6, p. 51.

43. Because it describes a criminal "type," a profile shares the same risks and flaws that status crimes like vagrancy do: they punish being, rather than doing. For a discussion of status offenses, see Anthony G. Amsterdam, "Federal Constitutional Restrictions on the Punishment of Crimes of Status, Crimes of General Obnoxiousness, Crimes of Displeasing Police Officers, and the Like," 3 *Crim. L. Bull.* 205 (1967); *Papachristou v. Jacksonville,* 405 U.S. 156 (1972).

44. Goldberg, "The Color of Suspicion."

45. If a policeman cannot visually distinguish between a Colombian and a Mexican-American, using this profile will not increase the percentages of success. Similarly, if Colombians are not in fact responsible for most of the target crimes, the profile will also be ineffective.

46. Seymour M. Hersh, "Missed Messages," *New Yorker,* June 3, 2002.

47. Race or national origin can legally be considered as one factor. See *United States v. Brigoni-Prince,* 422 U.S. 873, 886–87 (1975); *United States v. Martinez-Fuerte,* 428 U.S. 543, 563–64, n.16 and n.17 (1976); Kennedy, "Race, Law and Suspicion."

48. Recently, the Second Circuit validated police actions based on a profile of a "young black man with a cut on his hand," a profile the majority described this way: "this description included not only race, but also gender and age, as well as the possibility of a cut on his hand." See *Brown v. City of Oneonta,* 221 F.3d 329 (2nd Cir. 1999) (as amended August 8, 2000). This "description" was ineffective; the police asked black people in or passing through town to show their hands without success. The fact that the police made this inquiry of more than 200 people, including one woman, in a town where only 300 black people of any age or gender live—378 counting those on the adjacent SUNY campus—highlights the indiscriminate nature of the profile. These short inquiries, in almost all cases, did not rise to the level of a *Terry* stop, held the court, and thus the actions based on the "young black male" description were legal. Ibid. at 340. If the inquiries had been full *Terry* stops, said the court, then the police actions would have been illegal. Thus, the court acknowledged that "young black man with a cut on his hand" description does not create reasonable suspicion of any particular young black man.

49. See Kennedy, "Suspect Policy," p. 30.

50. See fn. 51–56, and text accompanying them, infra.

51. Data taken from a table published by the National Center For Health Statistics of the Centers for Disease Control and Prevention. The table, titled, "Table 62, Use of Selected Substances in the Past Month by Persons 12 Years of Age and Over, According to Age, Sex, Race, and Hispanic Origin: United States, Selected Years 1979–98," is available on line at www.cdc.gov/nchs/products/pubs/pubd/hus/tables/200/00hus062.pdf.

52. Ibid.

53. Ibid.

54. Stuntz, "Race, Class and Drugs"; David A. Harris, "The Stories, the Statistics, and the Law: Why 'Driving While Black' Matters," 84 *Minn. L. Rev.* 265, 294–97 (1999) (ACLU report).

55. Harris, "The Stories, the Statistics, and the Law," 265, 295–96, and n. 129.

56. Ibid.

57. See fn. 24–25 supra.

58. David Cole, "Discretion and Discrimination Reconsidered: A Response to the New Criminal Justice Scholarship," 87 *Geo. L. J.* 1059 (May 1999).

59. Ibid. at 1077–78, fn. 109.

60. Pretextual car stops were upheld by the U.S. Supreme Court in *Whren v. United States,* 517 U.S. 806 (1996). For a detailed analysis of how *Whren* changed courts' analyses of traffic stops, see Abraham Abramovsky and Jonathan I. Edelstein, "Pretext Stops and Racial Profiling after *Whren v. United States*: The New York and New Jersey Responses Compared," 63 *Alb. L. Rev.* 725 (2000). Currently, all jurisdictions except Washington state and two appellate districts in New York state have adopted *Whren.* Ibid. The Court recently announced an outer limit to *Whren*; pretextual roadblocks are not constitutional. See *Indianapolis v. Edmond,* No. 99-30, 2000 LEXIS 8084 (November 28, 2000).

61. *Terry v. Ohio,* 392 U.S. 1 (1968). As described in *Terry* at 8, the decision drew a line between an arrest and an investigatory stop and between a "frisk of the outer clothing for weapons and a full-blown search for evidence of a crime." At p. 10, the Court says that "[t]his scheme is justified in part upon the notion that a 'stop' and a 'frisk' amount to a mere 'minor inconvenience and petty indignity,' which can properly be imposed upon the citizen in the interest of effective law enforcement on the basis of a police officer's suspicion."

62. The targeted misdemeanors are quality-of-life crimes. Broken Windows theory, ostensibly embraced by the NYPD, postulates that focusing on such crimes indirectly reduces serious crime by changing the street environment. However, the NYPD has used the misdemeanors to *directly* target serious crime by legitimating the identification and searching of suspects. Kelling and Bratton first applied Broken Windows to the New York subway, and, despite

the postulated social dynamic of crime reduction, Kelling himself made clear that the "dividends" of arresting turnstile jumpers (discovering outstanding warrants and concealed weapons through the search legitimized by the fare-beating arrest) was critical for both decreasing the crime rate and increasing officer acceptance. Officers were pleased to use quality-of-life violations as a stepping stone to the arrest of serious criminals. See George L. Kelling and Catherine M. Coles, *Fixing Broken Windows* (New York: Touchstone, 1996), p. 134, and, more generally, pp. 108–56. See Newton, "The NYPD: Bigger Bolder —Is It Better?" p. 1 (Jack Maple, former NYPD commissioner and adviser to then-Commissioner Bratton, speaking about the impact of searching for and seizing guns; also discusses how misdemeanants are identified, searched and interrogated as part of strategy); James Ruttenberg and John Marzulli, "Crime Drop in Subway, Down 24% This Year, NYPD Says," *New York Daily News*, December 16, 1998 (quoting police, attributes crime decline both to discovery of criminals pretextually through order enforcement and to increased ridership's reducing of criminal opportunities). From 1995 to 1996, as New York's quality-of-life campaign intensified, arrests surged 21 percent, primarily for misdemeanors. See Michael Cooper "You're under Arrest," *New York Times*, December 1, 1996, Section 13, p. 1. New York's experience is relevant elsewhere, as quality-of-life movements are popular throughout the country. See Christine L. Bella and David L. Lopez, note, "Quality of Life—At What Price: Constitutional Challenges to Laws Adversely Affecting the Homeless," 10 *St. John's J. L. Comm.* 89, 90–92, fn. 7–12.

63. See *Terry*, 392 U.S. at 30.

64. There is evidence that the judicial standard is in fact very low, rendering *Terry* stops discretionary even if police obey the standard. See David A. Harris, "Particularized Suspicion, Categorical Judgments: Supreme Court Rhetoric versus Lower Court Reality under *Terry v. Ohio*," 72 *St. John's L. Rev.* 975 (1998); Cole, "Discretion and Discrimination Reconsidered," 1059, 1071–74. Two Supreme Court cases that treat the *Terry* threshold as a minimal one are *Illinois v. Wardlow*, 120 S.Ct. 673 (2000) and *United States v. Sokolow*, 109 S.Ct. 1581, 1585. In *Wardlow*, the Court held that "unprovoked flight" at sight of police officer, combined with "high-crime area," equals reasonable suspicion. The facts of *Wardlow* reveal the weakness of the standard; Justice Stevens notes in dissent that Wardlow's "unprovoked flight" may not have had anything to do with perceiving police. For example, the arresting officer could not remember whether the car he was in, which Wardlow ostensibly ran from, was marked or unmarked. Ibid. at 683–84. For a more detailed look at the impact of this case on *Terry* stops, see Terry L. Goddard Jr., "Current Event: *Illinois v. Wardlow No. 98-1036*, 2000 WL 16315 (U.S. January 12, 2000)," 8 *Am. U.J. Gender Soc. Pol'y and L.* 217 (2000). In *Sokolow*, the Court noted that a *Terry* stop requires some minimal level of objective justification.

65. Only 50–60 percent of NYPD stops and frisks were clearly constitutional. See Spitzer, "The New York City Police Department's 'Stop and Frisk' Practices" (hereinafter "Spitzer Report").

66. Ibid., p. ix, in the Executive Summary. The report acknowledged that not all frisks are recorded on forms, but statistical analysis of the data verified that the sample was sound. See pp. 91–92. While the study may not have been compromised by the absent forms, their absence suggests the absolute number of people suffering false positives may be much greater than the recorded data show. New York Attorney General Spitzer claimed that officers had told him that they fill out forms as rarely as "one in five, or one in ten" stops. See Richard Perez-Pena, "Police May Have Understated Street Searches, Spitzer Says," *New York Times,* March 23, 1999, p. B5. Spitzer's off-the-cuff remark may have been an overstatement; New York's Civilian Complaint Review Board (CCRB) found that, in the nonarrest cases it fully investigated, the forms were filled out about 52 percent of the time they were required. See William K. Rashbaum, "Review Board Staff Faults Police on Stop-and-Frisk Reports," *New York Times,* April 28, 2000, p. B1. Unsurprisingly, the NYPD, through Commissioner Safir, challenged the validity of the attorney general's report, critiquing the data and the methodology. See Kit R. Roane, "Safir Attacks State Finding of Racial Inequity in Searches," *New York Times,* December 2, 1999, p. B3. Professor Jeffery Fagan of Columbia's Center for Violence Research and Prevention did the empirical research underlying the Spitzer report. Fagan has just published a very detailed follow-up analysis of the data, which documents that the NYPD stops and searches are racially disparate, amount to "policing poor people in poor places," and have little to do with urban quality of life or crime. See Jeffrey Fagan and Garth Davies, "Street Stops and Broken Windows: *Terry,* Race, and Disorder in New York City," *Fordham Urban Law Journal,* vol. 28, p. 801.

67. Spitzer Report, p. 93, fn. 7 and accompanying text.

68. Ibid., pp. 117–22

69. Ibid., p. 102, table I.A.2.

70. The methodology is explained in detail at pp. 145–60 of the Spitzer Report.

71. Spitzer Report, p. 165, table II.B.2.

72. Unfortunately, unconstitutional stops were not rare: only approximately 60 percent of the NYPD's and the SCU's stops were clearly constitutional. Spitzer Report at II.B.3.

73. Debra Livingston, "Police Discretion and the Quality of Life in Public Places: Courts, Communities, and the New Policing," 97 *Colum. L. Rev.* 551 (1997). See, e.g., *Papachristou v. Jacksonville,* 405 U.S. 156 (1972).

74. See fn. 49 supra.

75. The most recent census data are available at http://www.census.gov/

276 JEROME H. SKOLNICK AND ABIGAIL CAPLOVITZ

hhes/poverty/povmeas/exppov/suexppov.html; as of 1999, nationwide, blacks and Hispanics were 2.5 times as likely to be poor as whites.

76. William J. Stuntz, "*Terry* and Legal Theory: *Terry's* Impossibility," 72 *St. John's Law Review* 1213, 1218 (1998); (internal cite omitted) Professor Stuntz is not the only academic who supports police practice but who acknowledges harm from them. Michael Tonry, who has argued that racial disparities in arrests and prison populations are not the result of bias in the criminal justice system, nonetheless has conceded that black men of all ages have suffered as a result of race-based police suspicion. See Michael Tonry, *Malign Neglect* (New York: Oxford University Press, 1995), pp. 50–51.

77. Harris, "The Stories, the Statistics, and the Law," 265, 269–75, 288–310 (relating personal harms through interviews of three DWB victims and discussing broader social harms of profiling). See Joseph F. Sullivan, "New Jersey Police Are Accused of Minority Arrest Campaigns," *New York Times,* February 19, 1990, p. B3 (interviews a couple who were stopped and upset).

78. Police practices were identified as the precipitating cause of the 1960s race riots. See Report of the National Advisory Commission on Civil Disorders (the Kerner Commission), March 1, 1968, at 161 (discussing underenforcement of law in minority communities and raising three issues: the toleration of higher levels of criminality, particularly vice; differential response to emergency calls from whites and from blacks; and a relative lack of police personnel assigned to minority areas), and at p. 302 (discussing perception by blacks that police are more brutal to blacks). More recently, the NYPD was so frightened by threat of riots after the brutalization of Abner Louima that it transferred minority officers into that precinct to calm tensions.

79. Wilson, "Just Take Away Their Guns," p. 47.

80. Surveillance has become a widespread, if controversial phenomenon. Photos were taken of everyone entering the stadium to watch the Super Bowl (see "Super Bowl Snooping," *New York Times,* February 4, 2001, Section 4, p. 16); and cameras are increasingly used in public spaces throughout New York City (and elsewhere). See Richard Weir, "Neighborhood Report: Greenwich Village: Candid Camera, Some Smile, Some Frown," *New York Times,* February 28, 1999, Section 14, p. 6 (cameras in Washington Square Park); Bruce Lambert, "Secret Surveillance Cameras Growing in City, Report Says," *New York Times,* December 13, 1998, Section 1, p. 61 (block-by-block voluntary survey found more than 2,300 cameras watching public spaces); David Halbfinger, "As Surveillance Cameras Peer, Some Wonder If They Also Pry," *New York Times,* February 22, 1998, Section 1, p. 1 (discussing use of cameras in housing projects throughout city and nationally).

81. A similar, highly controversial technology is a device that enables police to detect remotely whether someone has a home-based marijuana farm by analyzing the heat patterns of the house. The Supreme Court recently agreed

to decide whether such searches require a warrant and has heard oral argument on the issue. See Linda Greenhouse, "Search Warrant Case Prompts Lively Debate at Supreme Court," *New York Times,* November 2, 2000, p. A20.

82. Wilson, "Just Take Away Their Guns," p. 47.

83. Indeed, at least one police department—that in Dallas, Texas—is actively resisting this type of data collection. See Dave Michaels, "Racial Profiling Debated: Chief Opposing Data Collection," *Dallas Morning News,* January 4, 2001, Metro Section.

84. Indeed, one of the big problems for police managers can be getting police to take action. New York's Knapp Commission revealed that officers would avoid action while on duty so often that the practice had a name: "cooping." The Knapp Commission Report on Police Corruption (New York: G. Braziller, 1973). Chicago's police were apparently very unresponsive to citizen calls about gangs before the passage of the antiloitering statute, according to testimony by residents before the City Council considering the statute. See Roberts, "Foreword: Race, Vagueness and the Social Meaning of Order-Maintenance Policing," 775, 823; *City of Chicago v. Jesus Morales* No. 97-1121, *1997 U.S. Briefs 1121* October Term, 1997, September 11, 1998, Rep. Brief at *2. More recently, the NYPD was heavily criticized for its inaction in the "Central Park wilding." See Andy Geller et al., "Ax Hangs Over Cops Who Ignored Wilding," *New York Post,* June 17, 2000, p. 4.

85. Robert Davis and Pedro Mateu-Gelabert, "Respectful and Effective Policing, Two Examples from the South Bronx," Vera Institute of Justice, March 12, 1999.

86. United States General Accounting Office, Report to the Honorable Richard J. Durbin, United States Senate, "U.S. Customs Service Better Targeting of Airline Passengers for Personal Searches Could Produce Better Results," March 2000, GAO/GGD-00-38, 87.

87. For the search data, see ibid., pp. 10, 12–15 (tables 2 through 6 and accompanying text). White men and women, and black women, were targeted for intrusive strip/x-ray/body cavity searches out of proportion to the rate of contraband discovery for them. Black women by far faced the worst treatment; they were nine times as likely to be intrusively searched as were white women, but only half as likely to be carrying contraband.

88. The Supreme Court has held that Customs need not have any suspicion to do a routine border search; it has not ruled on what suspicion, if any, is necessary for a more thorough search. Some courts have suggested that the *Terry* reasonable suspicion standard is appropriate. By policy, Customs uses mere suspicion for frisks and the *Terry* reasonable suspicion standard for more intrusive searches. Ibid., pp. 3–5. The changes to the handbook are detailed at 5–6, 16, in the report.

89. Ibid., p. 29.

90. Ibid., pp. 23–25. Supervisor approval is now needed for all searches except for weapons frisks. Supervisors must also complete and sign a check sheet for each false positive, certifying that the search criteria have been reviewed and approved and that the supervisor has reviewed the process with the inspector for lessons learned.

91. Ibid., pp. 25–27. A document review revealed that complaints had been handled inadequately, and the standardization and systematization of complaints handling attempted to solve this problem.

92. Customs report at 28, Table 7.

93. In the thousands of pages of profiling data that New Jersey recently released was the statistic that searches of minority drivers discovered contraband 30 percent of the time, a rate touted as quite good. However, as the New Jersey attorney general noted, seven of every ten searched motorists were in fact innocent. Consequently, over a long period of time, an enormous number of black motorists were subjected to the humiliation of an unsuccessful search. See David Koceniewski and Robert Hanley, "Racial Profiling Was the Routine, New Jersey Finds," *New York Times,* November 28, 2000, p. A1.

94. See fn. 18 supra. Defense attorneys are also appealing convictions based on profiling. See David M. Halbfinger, "Defendants May Appeal Convictions Based on New Profiling Data," *New York Times,* December 7, 2000, p. B5.

95. See Lisa Walter, "Comment: Eradicating Racial Stereotyping from Terry Stops: The Case for an Equal Protection Exclusionary Rule," 71 *U. Colo. L. Rev.* 255 (2000). Some judges have shown a willingness to examine critically police testimony when applying the standard. The Sixth Circuit recently reversed a trial court and suppressed drugs seized from a truck because it did not find the officer's justification for the stop to be more than a hunch. See *United States v. Goodwin,* No. 98-6415, 2000 U.S. App. LEXIS 570, *7–9 (6th Cir. January 12, 2000). Two years earlier, the Sixth Circuit upheld a suppression motion because the defendant had been targeted solely or primarily because he was a Hell's Angel. See *United States v. Robinson,* No. 97-3142, 1998 U.S. App. LEXIS 10730 (6th Cir. May 22, 1998). Over a sharp dissent, the Seventh Circuit suppressed evidence seized from a person frisked upon exiting a suspected drug location because it did not believe an officer's testimony. See *United States v. Johnson,* 170 F.3d 708 (7th Cir. 1999). An Ohio state court also recently discredited an officer's testimony when it reversed the trial court and suppressed evidence. See *Ohio v. Clark,* Case No. 75827, 2000 Ohio. App. LEXIS 3814 (Ct. App. Ohio, August 24, 2000). For a judge's perspective, see the Honorable Jack B. Weinstein and Mae C. Quinn, "*Terry,* Race, and Judicial Integrity: The Court and Suppression during the War on Drugs," 72 *St. John's L. Rev.* 1323 (1998).

96. A New Jersey judge's discovery order forcing production of policing records enabled the plaintiffs to prove selective prosecution on the basis of

race and may have been the key to revealing racial profiling there. The judge found that profiling existed. The case was *State v. Soto,* 734 A.2d 350 (N.J. Super. Ct. Law Div. 1996). After documenting profiling, the New Jersey attorney general dropped his appeal of the *Soto* case. See Peter Verniero, "Interim Report of the State Police Review Team on Allegations of Racial Profiling," April 20, 1999, available on the Web at www.state.nj.us/lps/. Similarly, U.S. District Court Justice Scheindlin ordered discovery for defendants in a lawsuit against the NYPD's Street Crimes Unit that included statistical analyses of personnel information and arrests by SCU officers. See "Analysis of Personnel Information and Arrests by Street Crime Unit Is Not Privileged; *National Congress for Puerto Rican Rights v. The City of New York,*" *New York Law Journal,* May 12, 2000, p. 25.

97. See Debra Livingston, "Special Issue: Police Reform and the Department of Justice: An Essay on Accountability," 2 *Buff. Crim. L. R.* 815 (1999).

C. The *Brady* Approach

Chapter 12

The Effects of the Brady Act on Gun Violence

Philip J. Cook and Jens Ludwig

A. Introduction

In February, 1994, the federal government implemented the Brady Handgun Violence Prevention Act (PL 103-159) (hereafter *"Brady"* or "Brady Act"), arguably the most important new federal firearms law in the United States since the 1968 Gun Control Act. With the Brady Act, Congress established a minimum requirement on federally licensed firearms dealers (FFLs) in all states to conduct background checks on handgun buyers and to wait five days before transferring a handgun. A total of eighteen states already met this requirement, but dealers and law-enforcement officials in the other states (hereafter *"Brady* states") had to institute new, more stringent procedures.

On March 2, 2000, President Bill Clinton declared at a news conference that "the Brady Bill is saving people's lives and keeping guns out of the wrong hands,"[1] a claim motivated in part by the substantial number of people who have been denied handguns as a result of the law. In 1996 alone, 44,000 applications to purchase a handgun in the *Brady* states were rejected because the prospective buyer had a felony record or other disqualifying characteristic.[2] Other would-be buyers with criminal records may have been deterred from even applying. Since guns are more lethal than knives and other likely substitutes,[3] any reduction in criminal gun use due to *Brady* would translate into a net reduction in homicides.

Yet, this view of the Brady Act and its effects is not uncontroversial. One skeptic notes that many of those who are denied handguns by

FFLs because of *Brady* "subsequently may have obtained a handgun by submitting a false application to another FFL, by having a 'straw man'—an eligible friend or relative—purchase the handgun for him, or by purchasing a handgun on the secondary market."[4] (The secondary market includes the 30 to 40 percent of gun sales and other transfers each year that do not involve FFLs and are thus exempt from *Brady*'s background-check requirements.)[5] Still, the *Brady* requirements may have discouraged some dangerous people from obtaining a handgun, because acquiring guns from the secondary market may be more costly or risky or time consuming than acquiring them from FFLs. In any case, the number of handgun denials made by licensed dealers will not be the same as the number of people who are prevented from acquiring guns.

Whatever the true number of people who do not acquire handguns because of *Brady*, data from California suggests that the effects on violence of screening out some would-be handgun buyers are likely to be small. By one estimate, individuals who are denied purchase of a handgun because of a felony record have 23 percent fewer violent-crime arrests than those who have been arrested but not convicted for a felony and thus were able to successfully purchase a handgun from an FFL.[6] However, the follow-up arrest rates for both groups are fairly low, and "only" around 3 percent of violent-crime arrests are for homicide.[7] Projecting the California data to the nation suggests that those 44,000 convicted felons who were denied a handgun in *Brady* states in 1996 would have committed around eight fewer homicides as a result.[8]

The Brady Act may have some effect on suicides, as well, although self-inflicted gunshot wounds have figured less prominently in policy debates. The waiting period requirement could have prevented some impulsive suicide attempts.[9] The prohibition on transferring a firearm to someone who has been adjudicated mentally ill might also have some effect on suicide rates, if it were effectively enforced; however, information on such court findings is not consistently available in databases used for background checks.

The present essay evaluates the effects of the Brady Act on gun violence. Our main outcome measure is the homicide rate; while other types of crime are also of interest, the data on homicides are more detailed and far more accurate than those for robbery and assault. We also analyze the effects of the *Brady* regulations on suicide rates. Our evaluation exploits the fact that the Brady Act's requirements applied to only a subset of all states in 1994. The result is a sort of natural experiment, with one group of states in the "change" or "treatment" condition and the no-change states serving as "controls." Comparing homicide and suicide patterns across the *Brady* change and control states helps control for confounding trends in the United States as a whole over this period.

Our findings can be briefly summarized. We do not find evidence that the background-check requirement of the Brady Act has reduced lethal violence or affected the choice of weapons by killers. The Brady Act may have reduced firearm suicides among older Americans, the population at highest risk for suicide, although this decline is at least partially offset by some increase in nongun suicides.

Of course, all statistical evaluations are subject to some uncertainty. There is some chance that there has been an effect, positive or negative, that our method was too imprecise to discern. Further, we note that the Brady Act may have affected the rate of gun violence through other mechanisms that cannot be assessed using the method we adopted. For example, *Brady* reduced illicit gun trafficking from states with lax regulations to those with more stringent regulations,[10] thus potentially producing an increase in the black-market price of guns in control states. To the extent that *Brady* did reduce gun availability to violent people in control states, our comparison may underestimate the act's effects on violence in the *Brady* states. However, evidence from a case study of Chicago's experience suggests that any bias along these lines may be quite small in practice.

B. Data and Methods

This section discusses the Vital Statistics data used in the analysis, the system of classifying *Brady* states, and the empirical strategy for evaluating the effects of the Brady Act on fatal injuries.

1. Statistical Data

The data used in our analysis come from the Vital Statistics (VS) census of deaths to U.S. residents for the period 1990–1996. Key dependent variables are homicides, firearm homicides, suicides, and firearm suicides calculated as rates per 100,000 people. Each mortality rate is calculated separately by state and year for the United States during our sample period. Neither the numerators nor the denominators in these rates are subject to sampling variability.[11]

We also refine our analysis by focusing on homicide and suicide rates for adult victims, defined as those twenty-one years of age and older. Limiting the analysis to adults helps overcome potential biases introduced by the volatility of juvenile homicides during our sample period resulting from the rise and fall in crack-market activity.[12] A focus on adults is further motivated by the fact that *Brady* should have stronger effects on the commission of interpersonal violence by adults than by juveniles. People under twenty-one could not buy a handgun from an FFL even before *Brady,* and interviews with youthful criminals indicate that they rarely obtain their guns directly from FFLs.[13]

While we expect *Brady* to have a greater effect on adult than on juvenile gun misuse, reliable information on the age of the gun user is available only for suicide cases. For homicide cases, the Vital Statistics records the age of the victim but not the offender's age. The other possible data source for homicides is the Federal Bureau of Investigation's (FBI) Supplementary Homicide Reports (SHR). Because some local law-enforcement agencies fail to report crimes as part of this system, the SHR captures only 80 to 90 percent of all homicides.[14] The SHR provides information on the suspect's age for all cases where an arrest is made, but for only a subset of cases where there is no arrest. In any event, by limiting the analysis to adult victims, we ensure that we have included most cases in which there was an adult perpetrator; most adult victims are killed by an adult.[15]

We also control for state-level changes in the following factors that may influence rates of crime and violence: consumption of alcohol per capita (measured in gallons of ethanol), percentage of the population living in metropolitan areas, percentage of the population below the official poverty line and income per worker (in 1998 constant dollars), percentage African American, and the percentage of the population falling into seven different age groups (under 15; 15–17; 18–24; 25–34; 35–44; 45–54; and 55–64). Each of these state-level variables is measured annually with the exception of race and poverty, data for which come from the decennial Census and are interpolated for intercensal years.[16]

2. Classification of Brady States

When the Brady Act went into effect in February 1994, a total of thirty-two states were required to adopt the background check and five-day waiting period: Alabama, Alaska, Arizona, Arkansas, Colorado, Georgia, Idaho, Kansas, Kentucky, Louisiana, Maine, Minnesota, Mississippi, Montana, Nebraska, New Hampshire, New Mexico, North Carolina, North Dakota, Ohio, Oklahoma, Pennsylvania, Rhode Island, South Carolina, South Dakota, Tennessee, Texas, Utah, Vermont, Washington, West Virginia, and Wyoming. The remaining states were exempted because they already required a background check of those buying handguns from FFLs. In 1994, five states originally classified as *Brady* states met the act's exemption requirements (Colorado, Idaho, Minnesota, Tennessee, and Utah), while two more were granted exemptions in 1995 (New Hampshire and North Carolina) and another in 1996 (Washington State). Nevada was originally exempt but then later subject to the Brady Act's requirements.[17]

For our analysis, we classified all thirty-two original *Brady* states as the treatment group and the remaining states (including the District of Columbia) as the control group. In particular, we initially classified as treatment states the eight original *Brady* states that were later granted exemptions, since the effect of the act for that group was the same as for the other *Brady* states that instituted a background-check requirement in 1994. We did not count Nevada in the *Brady* treatment group, since this state had restrictions in place in February 1994 that were already strict enough to warrant a *Brady* exemption.

There is a minor issue about whether the Brady Act's "treatment" is still in effect in 1997, the last year of the time series used in this study. In June of that year, the Supreme Court invalidated the requirement that state officials conduct a background check,[18] on the Tenth Amendment grounds that it was a violation of state sovereignty. In practice, law enforcement officials in all but two of the *Brady* treatment states (Ohio and Arkansas) voluntarily continued to conduct background checks.

3. Evaluation Strategy

The Brady Act may in principle affect gun violence through two distinct mechanisms. First, by blocking sales to customers who are disqualified due to past felony convictions, current indictments, or other relevant conditions, *Brady* may have a direct effect on gun violence through a reduction in gun-ownership rates among violence-prone adults. Second, by increasing the difficulty traffickers face in obtaining guns from FFLs, there may be an indirect effect of reducing the supply of guns in the secondary market, which is where most youths and criminals acquire them. This indirect effect may be relevant for the *Brady* control states, as well as for the treatment states, as suggested by ATF data from traces of guns confiscated by the police. The crime guns in states with relatively stringent gun controls are in a majority of cases found to be imported from out of state, often from states with loose controls, including those that were affected by *Brady*.[19] Of course, if the Brady Act disrupts the flow of guns into secondary markets, then the indirect effect should also be relevant for the *Brady* treatment states, since a majority of crime guns in these states were first purchased in-state.[20]

Our evaluation approach exploits the natural experiment generated by the Brady Act by comparing changes in homicide or suicide rates in *Brady* treatment states with the changes observed in *Brady* control states. We define the pre-*Brady* period as 1990 through 1993, while the post-*Brady* period is defined as 1994 through 1997. If Y_{TPre} and Y_{TPost} represent the homicide rate per 100,000 for *Brady* treatment states during the pre- and post-*Brady* periods, respectively, and Y_{CPre} and Y_{CPost} represent homicide rates for the control states, our estimate for the direct effect of *Brady* on homicide in the treatment states is given by equation (1).

$$Brady\ \text{Impact} = [\ Y_{TPost} - Y_{TPre}\ ] - [\ Y_{CPost} - Y_{CPre}\ ]$$

Under what conditions will this "difference-in-difference" (DD) estimator yield unbiased estimates for the direct effect of *Brady* on gun violence? To the extent to which the indirect effect of *Brady* on secondary gun markets is of equal importance in the treatment and control states, this unmeasured impact of the law will be net out with our DD estimate. Our focus on comparing differences in trends across states helps control for unmeasured factors that cause some states to have persistently higher rates of violence than others. The central assumption behind the DD approach is that the treatment and the control states would have had similar trends in rates of lethal violence had *Brady not* been enacted. One check on the credibility of this assumption is to determine whether treatment and control states had similar trends before *Brady* went into effect.

We calculate our DD estimate by applying regression equation (2) to our state-level data, where Y_{it} represents some mortality measure for state (i) in period (t), and X_{it} represents the set of control variables already described. The model includes separate dichotomous indicator variables for each state, d_i, to capture unmeasured state-specific "fixed effects" that cause the level of violence to differ across states; a set of year indicator variables, g_t, that capture changes in the overall rate of violence in the United States conditional on the observed covariates; and the indicator variable T_{it} that is equal to 1 in the treatment states following implementation of the Brady Act and equal to 0 otherwise. With the Vital Statistics data, we have four years of post-*Brady* data (1994–1997). For comparability, we define the pre-*Brady* period as the four years prior to the law's implementation (1990–1993).

$$Y_{it} = b_0 + b_1 X_{it} + b_2 T_{it} + d_i + g_t + e_{it}$$

Since state fixed effects are included in the model, the key coefficient of interest (b_2) reflects the difference between the treatment and the control states in the change in violence rates from the pre- to the post-*Brady* periods.[21] The coefficient b_2 captures any one-time shift in the rate of gun violence in the treatment versus control states around the time of the Brady Act and should be negative if *Brady* reduces gun violence.

Equation (2) is estimated via weighted least squares, a technique that corrects for heteroskedasticity in the stochastic term by premultiplying the dependent and the explanatory variables by the square root of the state's population.[22] We calculate Huber-White standard errors to adjust for the nonindependence of observations from the same state.[23]

For policy purposes, it is important to isolate the association between waiting periods and gun violence. To do this, we exploit a second natural experiment embedded within the Brady Law. Of the original *Brady* states, five did not experience an increase in waiting periods either because they enacted an instant background-check requirement almost immediately following the implementation of *Brady* (Colorado, March 1, 1994; Utah, March 1, 1994) or because the state already had a waiting period of five days or more in effect prior to *Brady* (Minnesota, seven days; Rhode Island, seven days; Washington, five days). We reestimate equation (2) first comparing the *Brady* control states with the "partial-treatment" states that experienced no change in waiting periods and then compare the control states with the remaining "full-treatment"

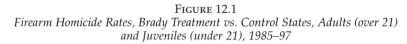

FIGURE 12.1
*Firearm Homicide Rates, Brady Treatment vs. Control States, Adults (over 21)
and Juveniles (under 21), 1985–97*

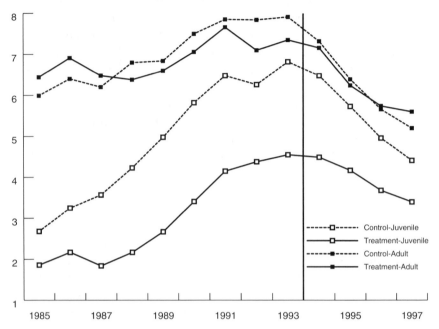

states. If waiting periods are effective in reducing mortality rates, then the estimated effect of instituting a waiting period together with background screening should be larger than the effect of background screening alone.

4. Results

We begin by developing our main findings—that the Brady Act had no detectable direct effect on homicides but may have had some effect on suicide rates among those over fifty-five. We then extend these results in a variety of ways to explore the underlying mechanisms behind the observed suicide effect, the sensitivity of our findings to our choice of outcome measures, and whether our estimates are biased by the possibility of "indirect effects" of *Brady* on gun trafficking, a mechanism that may be relevant for both the treatment and the control states.

Figure 12.1 presents the trend in gun homicide rates for the period

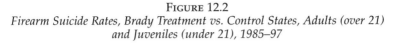

FIGURE 12.2
*Firearm Suicide Rates, Brady Treatment vs. Control States, Adults (over 21)
and Juveniles (under 21), 1985–97*

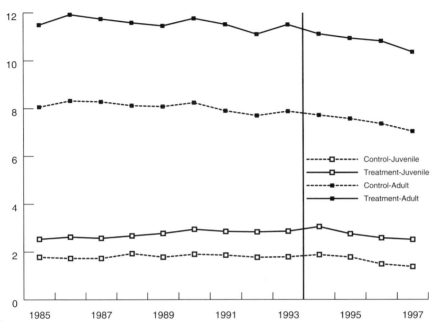

1985–1997 for *Brady* treatment and control states for victims under twenty-one years of age, as well as for those twenty-one and older. Two observations stand out from this figure. First, the *Brady* treatment and control states had very different trends for juvenile gun homicides even *before Brady* was implemented in 1994. Since the difference-in-difference estimation approach assumes that treatment and control states would have had similar trends in the absence of the Brady Act, our finding calls into question the reliability of DD estimates that draw on data on juvenile victims (or, by extension, victims of all ages). As a result, in the formal analysis that follows, we tend to focus on homicides and suicides to victims twenty-one and older. Second, the gun homicide rates for victims 21 and older in the treatment and control states track each other quite closely both before and after *Brady* goes into effect. A qualitatively similar picture emerges when we focus on all homicides, rather than just those committed with firearms (not shown), or on gun suicides (Figure 12.2).

TABLE 12.1

*Effects of the Brady Act on Homicide and Suicide Changes from Pre- to Post-*Brady *Period in Treatment Relative to Control States*

(Standard-error estimates in parentheses)

	Victims Age 21 and Older	Victims Age 55 and Older
Homicide (rate per 100,000)	−0.36	−0.09
	(0.64)	(0.27)
Gun homicide rate	−0.14	0.05
	(0.52)	(0.10)
Nongun homicide rate	−0.22	−0.14
	(0.15)	(0.20)
% homicides committed with gun	1.1	3.3
	(1.0)	(2.4)
Suicide (rate per 100,000)	−0.12	−0.54
	(0.27)	(0.37)
Gun suicide rate	−0.21	−0.92**
	(0.19)	(0.25)
Nongun suicide rate	0.09	0.38*
	(0.13)	(0.20)
% suicides committed with gun	−0.3	−2.2**
	(0.5)	(0.9)

The pre-*Brady* period is defined as 1990–1993 and post-*Brady* period as 1994–1997. Regressions are calculated by estimating equation (2) in text using state population as weights to adjust for heteroskedasticity.

** Statistically different from zero at the 5% p-value.

* Statistically different from zero at the 10% p-value.

Table 12.1 presents the results of estimating equation (2) using weighted least squares, making the same point more formally. As seen in the second column of Table 12.1, none of the differences between the treatment and control states in any of the homicide or suicide measures are statistically significant at the 95 percent level.

On the other hand, when we restrict the analysis to victims age fifty-five and over, there is some indication of an effect for suicide. The results in the third column of Table 12.1 indicate that firearm suicides by victims fifty-five and older declined by 0.92 per 100,000 population in the treatment states relative to the controls (p < .05), equal to around 6 percent of the gun suicide rate to those ages fifty-five and older in the control states during the post-*Brady* period. There is also an increase in nongun suicides to this population equal to 0.38 per 100,000 (p < .10). The net result is a statistically insignificant decline in the overall suicide rate for people age fifty-five and older that is only around half as large as the reduction in gun suicides.

It turns out that the reduction in firearm suicides among older residents is limited to those *Brady* treatment states that experienced changes in both waiting period and background-check requirements. Table 12.2 shows that the estimated effect is negligible in "partial-treatment" states, which experienced changes in background-check regulations but not waiting periods. In contrast, the *Brady* "full-treatment" states that also experienced increases in the waiting period for handgun purchases had a reduction in gun suicides to older residents equal to -1.03 per 100,000 relative to controls ($p < .05$).

The final issue that we explore is the possibility of bias to our estimates introduced by an "indirect effect" of *Brady* on gun violence. Our DD estimates may understate the direct effect of the Brady Act on violence in the treatment states if the Act helps stem the flow of guns from treatment-state gun dealers into the secondary market and if the consequences of this change for criminal gun use are more pronounced in the control than the treatment states. But based on one bit of evidence, a case study of Chicago, we believe that this indirect effect may be of minor consequence to gun use in crime.

Elsewhere in this volume, Philip Cook and Anthony Braga discuss

TABLE 12.2

Effects of the Brady Act on Suicide Victims Age 55 and Over: Changes from Pre- to Post-Brady Period in Treatment Relative to Control States

	Treatment states with no change in waiting periods vs. controls	Treatment states with extension of waiting periods vs. controls
Suicide (rate per 100,000)	−0.09	−0.60
	(0.57)	(0.39)
Gun suicide rate	−0.17	−1.03**
	(0.47)	(0.29)
Nongun suicide rate	0.08	0.43
	(0.30)	(0.28)
% Suicide with gun	−1.2	−2.4**
	(1.5)	(1.0)

The pre-*Brady* period is defined as 1990–1993 and post-*Brady* period as 1994–1997. Regressions are calculated by applying weighted least squares to equation (2) in text using state population as weights to adjust for heteroskedasticity.
** Statistically different from zero at the 5% p-value.
* Statistically different from zero at the 10% p-value.

FIGURE 12.3
Percent Homicides with Guns in Chicago, Victims 21+

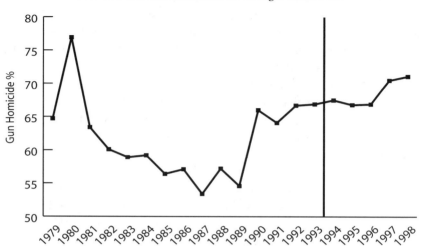

the flow of guns into Chicago around the time of the implementation of the Brady Act. Of the guns confiscated by the Chicago Police Department in 1999, about one-third of those that were first sold at retail prior to 1994 came from Mississippi and other *Brady* treatment states. But the flow of guns from the deep South dropped abruptly in 1994, apparently because traffickers found those states to be a less attractive source of guns following *Brady*. Since then, downstate Illinois has supplied most of the guns that end up in the hands of Chicago criminals.

What effect did the change in gun-trafficking patterns have on gun availability to dangerous people? Unfortunately, there are no data available on the prices or availability of guns "on the street" in Chicago. But, by one measure, the answer appears to be that gun availability changed very little as a result of *Brady*; as shown in Figure 12.3, there was little change in the fraction of homicides that involved firearms in the city over this period.[24]

C. Concluding Thoughts

It appears that the Brady Act had little effect on homicide rates. Our best point estimates for the effect of the act on homicide and gun homicide are small relative to the standard errors and also relative to the normal year-to-year fluctuation in homicide and suicide rates.

Our findings do not imply that regulating primary-market sales is worthless. Even before *Brady* went into effect, federal law required FFLs to ask buyers for identification and to deny anyone who was underage or admitted some other disqualifying condition. FFLs also were required to record the identity of each buyer and to make these records available to law-enforcement investigators. Those modest requirements may have had some effect on gun access. In any event, we know that the large majority of juveniles and criminals obtained their guns from the secondary market even before *Brady*.[25] The secondary market in guns, which is currently almost completely unregulated, is thus an enormous loophole that works to limit the effectiveness of primary-market regulations. Our analysis of the Brady Act highlights the difficulty of reducing gun violence in America through regulation of the primary market without some change in policy toward secondary-market transfers.

NOTES

The research reported in this chapter was supported by a grant from the Joyce Foundation. Thanks to Bob Malme, Chris Clark, Heath Einstein, Meghan McNally, and Esperanza Ross for valuable research assistance, and to Roseanna Ander, Steve Hargarten, David Hemenway, Arthur Kellermann, Debby Leff, Willard Manning, James Mercy, John Mullahy, William Schwab, Daniel Webster, Garen Wintemute, Mona Wright, and Franklin Zimring for useful comments. All opinions and any errors are our own.

1. Brady Campaign to Prevent Gun Violence, "Saving Lives by Taking Guns Out of Crime: The Drop in Gun-Related Crime Deaths since Enactment of the Brady Law," Executive Summary, downloaded from www.bradycampaign.org/facts/research/savinglives.asp, accessed on April 17, 2002.

2. D. A. Manson and D. K. Gilliard, *Presale Handgun Checks, 1996: A National Estimate* NCJ 165704 (Washington, D.C.: U.S. Department of Justice, Bureau of Justice Statistics, 1997).

3. See Franklin E. Zimring, "Is Gun Control Likely to Reduce Violent Killings?" *University of Chicago Law Review* 35 (1968): 721–737; Franklin E. Zimring, "The Medium Is the Message: Firearm Caliber as a Determinant of Death from Assault," *Journal of Legal Studies* 1 (1972): 97–124; Philip J. Cook, "The Technology of Personal Violence," in *Crime and Justice: An Annual Review of Research* (Michael Tonry, ed.) (Chicago: University of Chicago Press, 1991), 1–71.

4. James B. Jacobs and Kimberly A. Potter, "Keeping Guns Out of the 'Wrong' Hands: The Brady Law and the Limits of Regulation," *Journal of Criminal Law and Criminology* 86(1) (1995): 101–130.

5. Philip J. Cook, Stephanie Molliconi, and Thomas B. Cole, "Regulating Gun Markets," *Journal of Criminal Law and Criminology* 86(1) (1995): 59–92; Philip J. Cook and Jens Ludwig, *Guns in America: Results of a Comprehensive National Survey on Firearms Ownership and Use* (Washington, D.C.: Police Foundation, 1996).

6. Mona A. Wright, Garen J. Wintemute, and Frederick P. Rivara, "Effectiveness of Denial of Handgun Purchase to Persons Believed to Be at High Risk for Firearm Violence," *American Journal of Public Health* 89(1) (1999): 88–90.

7. Mona A. Wright and Garen J. Wintemute, unpublished calculations (Davis: Violence Prevention Research Program, University of California at Davis Medical Center, 1999).

8. Of course, those who have been arrested for a felony but not convicted may be somewhat less violence prone than those with an actual felony conviction; if this is true, then denying purchase for those with a conviction may reduce homicide rates by more than that, but the California data suggest that the effect is nevertheless likely to be quite modest.

9. Matthew Miller and David Hemenway, "The Relationship between Firearms and Suicide: A Review of the Literature," *Aggression and Violent Behavior* 4(1) (1999): 59–75; Mark Duggan, "Guns and Suicide: Correlation or Causation?" in *Evaluating Gun Policy* (Jens Ludwig and Philip J. Cook, eds.) (Washington, D.C.: Brookings Institution Press, 2003).

10. Douglas S. Weil, *Traffic Stop: How the Brady Act Disrupts Interstate Gun Trafficking* (Washington, D.C.: Center to Prevent Handgun Violence, 1997); Philip J. Cook and Anthony A. Braga, "A Comprehensive Firearms Tracing: Strategic and Investigative Uses of New Data on Firearms Markets," *Arizona Law Review* 43(2) (2001): 277–310.

11. Sherry L. Murphy, *Technical Appendix from Vital Statistics of United States, 1994, Mortality* (Hyattsville, Md.: National Center for Health Statistics, Mortality Statistics Branch, 1994).

12. Alfred Blumstein, "Youth Gun Violence, Guns, and the Illicit-Drug Industry," *Journal of Criminal Law and Criminology* 86 (1995): 10–36; Daniel Cork, "Examining Time-Space Interaction in City-Level Homicide Data: Crack Markets and the Diffusion of Guns Among Youth," working paper (Pittsburgh: Carnegie Mellon University, 1999); Philip J. Cook and John H. Laub, "After the Epidemic: Recent Trends in Youth Violence in the United States," in *Crime and Justice: A Review of Research* (Michael Tonry, ed.) (Chicago: University of Chicago Press, 2002), 117–153.

13. Joseph F. Sheley and James D. Wright, *Gun Acquisition and Possession in*

Selected Juvenile Samples (Washington, D.C.: National Institute of Justice, 1993); Cook, Molliconi, and Cole, "Regulating Gun Markets."

14. Philip J. Cook and John H. Laub, "The Unprecedented Epidemic of Youth Violence," in *Crime and Justice: An Annual Review of Research* (Michael H. Moore and Michael Tonry, eds.) (Chicago: University of Chicago Press, 1998), 26–64.

15. Ibid.

16. C. Moody, The Research Materials Web Site. Available at faculty.cm .edu/cemood/research.html. Accessed March 8, 2000; Steven Raphael, "The Deinstitutionalization of the Mentally Ill and Growth in the U.S. Prison Populations: 1971 to 1993," working paper (Berkeley: Goldman School of Public Policy, University of California, 1999); Bureau of Justice Statistics, *Prison and Jail Inmates at Midyear 1998* (Washington, D.C.: U.S. Department of Justice, Office of Justice Programs, 1999); U.S. Census Bureau, *Statistical Abstract of the United States 1999*, 119th ed. (Washington, D.C.: U.S. Government Printing Office, 2000).

17. See General Accounting Office, *Gun Control: Implementation of the Brady Handgun Violence Prevention Act* (Washington, D.C.: GAO Report 96-22.1996); Bureau of Alcohol, Tobacco, and Firearms, *Firearms State Laws and Published Ordinances, 1994 B, 20th ed.* (Washington, D.C.: U.S. Department of the Treasury, Bureau of Alcohol, Tobacco, and Firearms, 1994); Bureau of Alcohol, Tobacco, and Firearms, *Firearms State Laws and Published Ordinances, 1998 B, 21st ed.* (Washington, D.C.: U.S. Department of the Treasury, Bureau of Alcohol, Tobacco, and Firearms, 1998).

18. *Printz v. U.S.*, 117 S. Ct. 2365, 1997. See L. Greenhouse, "Justices Limit Brady Gun Law as Intrusion on States' Rights," *New York Times,* June 28, 1997.

19. Cook and Braga, "Comprehensive Firearms Tracing."

20. For example, at least 80 percent of all crime guns in Birmingham, Houston, and San Antonio were first purchased in state (Cook and Braga, "Comprehensive Firearms Tracing"). Each of the cities mentioned here participates in the Youth Crime Gun Interdiction Initiative, so that all crime guns recovered by the police are submitted to ATF for tracing.

21. This is easy to see by noting that the inclusion of dummy variables for each state is equivalent to measuring all of the dependent and explanatory variables as deviations from the state's average value of the variable over the sample period.

22. W. H. Greene, *Econometric Analysis,* 2nd ed. (New York: Macmillan, 1993).

23. In order to examine the robustness of our findings to alternative model specifications, we reestimated the basic model using the natural log of the dependent variable and using a negative binomial model. In addition, we replicated our estimates excluding 1993 and 1994 from the sample, since these

years could be "contaminated" by either the expectation of *Brady* during 1993 or an implementation lag during 1994. The results from these alternative estimates are reported in Jens Ludwig and Philip J. Cook, "Homicide and Suicide Rates Associated with Implementation of the Brady Handgun Violence Prevention Act," *Journal of the American Medical Association* 284(5) (2000): 585–591.

24. Figure 12.3 shows the results for victims twenty-one and older, although focusing on homicides to victims of all ages yields nearly identical findings.

25. James D. Wright and Peter H. Rossi, *Armed and Considered Dangerous: A Survey of Felons and Their Firearms* (New York: Aldine de Gruyter, 1986); Cook, Molliconi, and Cole, "Regulating Gun Markets"; Sheley and Wright, *Gun Acquisition*; Peter Ash, Arthur L. Kellermann, Dawna Fuqua-Whitley, and Amri Johnson, "Gun Acquisition and Use by Juvenile Offenders," *Journal of the American Medical Association* 275(22) (1996): 1754–1758.

Chapter 13

Gun Shows and Gun Controls

James B. Jacobs

In 1998, there were 4,442 gun shows in the United States, usually held in arenas, civic centers, fairgrounds, or armories.[1] There are scores of gun show promoters, who usually operate on a state or regional basis—for example, Bill Goodman's Gun and Knife Show (Ohio, Tennessee), Crossroads of the West Gun Shows (Arizona, California, Colorado, Nevada, Utah), Mid-Atlantic Arms Collectors (Pennsylvania, West Virginia), and R K Shows (Kansas, Missouri, Nevada, Oklahoma, Tennessee, Texas).[2] Most of these promoters are members of the National Association of Arms Shows, which provides extensive information about upcoming shows as well as representing the promoters' interests before Congress and state legislatures. On any given weekend, there is likely to be at least one gun show somewhere in practically every state. For example, Table 13.1 lists gun shows in Indiana, just for the month of January 2002.

Gun shows are usually held on weekends, drawing 2,500 to 5,000 attendees, who pay a small admission price to browse through the exhibits and to examine and purchase firearms that catch their fancy.[3] The vendors of guns and gun-related merchandise rent table space from the promoter. Some vendors/exhibitors sell or give away literature promoting hunting, shooting sports, gun safety, and gun ownership. Gun shows serve as a meeting ground for people who participate or are just interested in shooting sports or collecting firearms. Millions of people attend such shows each year.

While gun shows probably account for only a very small fraction (perhaps 2 percent) of total U.S. gun sales, they are a convenient venue for transferring guns from law-abiding owners to criminals, and vice

TABLE 13.1

January 2002 Indiana Gun Shows

DATES	HOURS	SHOW	CITY	VENUE	PROMOTER	OTHER
Jan. 5 Jan. 6	9–3 9–5	Vincennes Gun & Knife Show	Vincennes	Indiana National Guard Armory 1514 Emison St.	ProTEQ Firearms Training Academy & Gun Shows www.proteqguns.com 812-443-5435	Admission $5 Spouses 1/2 price Kids 12 & under free Tables $25.00
Jan. 5 Jan. 6	9–5 9–5	Central Promotions Muncie Gun Show	Muncie	Indiana National Guard Armory 401 Country Club Road	Daniel Hedger 765-855-3836 acmegun@aol.com	$4 adults, kids under 12 free
Jan. 5 Jan. 6	9–5 9–4	CPI Fort Wayne Gun Show	Fort Wayne	Memorial Coliseum IN 930 & Parnell Ave.	CPI, Inc. 219-483-6144	
Jan. 12 Jan. 13	9–5 9–3	Brazil Gun & Knife Show	Brazil	Clay County 4-H Fairgrounds 6650 N State Road 59	ProTEQ Firearms Training Academy & Gun Shows www.proteqguns.com 812-443-5435 ddb40@aol.com	Admission $5 Spouses 1/2 price Kids 12 & under free Tables $25.00
Jan. 18 Jan. 19 Jan. 20	2–8 8–6 9–4	Indy 1500 Gun & Knife Show	Indianapolis	Indiana State Fairgrounds Marsh South Pavillion	World Class Gun Shows P.O. Box 14194 Oklahoma City, OK 73113 405-340-1333	$7 adults, $2 under 12
Jan. 26 Jan. 27	9–3 9–5	Franklin Gun & Knife Show	Franklin	Johnson County 4-H Fairgrounds South East Building	ProTEQ Firearms Training Academy & Gun Shows www.proteqguns.com 812-443-5435 ddb40@aol.com	Admission $5 Spouses 1/2 price Kids 12 & under free Tables $25.00
Jan. 26 Jan. 27	9–5 9–3	Firearms Expo	Schererville	Villa Cesare 900 Eagle Ridge Drive	Village West Enterprises 219-394-4829	Admission $5
Jan. 26 Jan. 27	9–5 9–4	Annual Gun & Knife Show	Ferdinand	Ferdinand Community Center	812-678-3899	Admission $4, under 12 free. 130 tables. Concessions, gun raffle.

300

versa.[4] Thus, it is not surprising that gun control proponents have their sights on gun shows. This attention heightened after the April 20, 1999, shooting rampage at Columbine High School because the two teenage perpetrators obtained their weapons from gun shows. This chapter examines the feasibility of subjecting gun show firearms sales to more stringent regulations. In particular, it focuses on two Congressional bills—the Gun Show Accountability Act (GSAA) and the Gun Show Loop Hole Closing and Gun Law Enforcement Act—that lawmakers have put forward to "close the gun show loophole."[5]

Regulating Gun Shows

The Gun Control Act of 1968 (GCA) provided that a person "engaged in the business of selling firearms" had to obtain a federal license; federally licensed firearms dealers (FFLs) could sell firearms only at their place of business.[6] Almost twenty years later, the Firearm Owner's Protection Act of 1986 (FOPA), passed at the urging of gun owners' rights advocates, weakened the 1968 law by permitting FFLs to sell firearms at gun shows according to the same obligations and procedures as apply at the FFL's business premises.[7] This generated a great deal of FFL participation at gun shows and thus contributed to more and larger shows.

With a limited exception, the 1993 Brady Law required FFLs to initiate *Brady* background checks on gun purchasers, whether the purchase takes place at stores, at a gun show, or anywhere else. An FFL can forgo the purchaser background checks if the firearm being sold is part of the FFL's personal collection. However, casual sellers (non-FFLs) can sell or exchange their firearms without initiating any kind of purchaser background check or doing any paperwork. (They do have to see proof of the purchaser's in-state residency and age, since it is unlawful to transfer a firearm to an out-of-state resident, a handgun to anyone under twenty-one, and a long gun to anyone under eighteen.) A typical gun show might have a hundred or more tables, mostly rented by dealers. Some unlicensed gun owners offer their guns for sale or barter, either at a table or "by hand" as they walk around the show. Criminals or anyone else seeking to acquire handguns without a background check or paper trail can stroll into a gun show and purchase as many guns as they like from unlicensed sellers.

The Bureau of Alcohol, Tobacco, and Firearms (located in the U.S. Department of Treasury) has responsibility for enforcing U.S. gun laws at gun shows and everywhere else. Still, there are a limited number of agents and a vast number of FFLs, black-market gun traffickers, and gun shows. Thus, there is unlikely to be a federal regulatory presence at any particular show. According to Bill Bridgewater, executive director of the National Alliance of Stocking Gun Dealers:

> The BATF has established rules and regulations for these things they call "gun shows." The opportunity for the black marketers is that the BATF doesn't enforce those regulations and there isn't anyone else to do so. Consequently, there are literally hundred of "gun shows" scattered around the country where you may rent tables, display your wares, sell what you please to whomever you please; the sale that is made with no records, no questions and no papers, earns the highest sales price. There are wide-open "gun shows" the length and breadth of the United States, wherein anyone may do as he chooses, including buy firearms for children.[8]

The BATF's supervision of gun shows is limited to investigations of "situations where there are specific allegations that significant violations have occurred and where there is reliable information that guns sold at the specific gun show or flea market have shown up in crimes of violence with some degree of regularity."[9] Ironically, perhaps, BATF focuses more on the sales practices of FFLs than on those of non-FFLs because the former are subject to regulation.

On occasion, such investigations have revealed federal firearms violations such as FFL sales to "straw purchasers" (sales to persons who are acquiring the gun on behalf of an ineligible person), FFL sales to out-of-state residents, FFL sales without background checks, and sales by both FFLs and non-FFLs of illegal kits used to convert semiautomatic weapons to fully automatic weapons.

The GSAA

The fact that non-FFLs can sell firearms at gun shows without submitting their purchasers to background checks that might detect a prior criminal record or other disqualifying characteristic is sometimes referred to as "the gun show loophole."

On November 6, 1998, President Clinton charged a task force, made up of Attorney General Janet Reno and Secretary of the Treasury Robert Rubin, to come up with a proposal that would close "the gun show loophole."[10] The Attorney General and the Secretary of the Treasury conferred with U.S. Attorneys, law enforcement organizations, the BATF, and other individuals and agencies.

In January 1999, the task force recommended that all gun transfers (sales, barters, loans) at gun shows be made subject to *Brady* background testing; this would be accomplished by requiring that all gun transfers "go through" an FFL, who would call the National Instant Check System (NICS) with the purchaser's name and other identifiers. NICS has been able to clear the large majority of purchasers as eligible for sale in less than one hour, usually in just minutes; a small number of searches, however, indicate a "hit" in the database and must be investigated.[11] In other words, a non-FFL seller would have to find an FFL at the gun show who, for a fee, would initiate the background check and keep the paperwork on the sale. President Clinton endorsed the proposal. On February 23, 1999, Senator Frank Lautenberg (D-NJ) and Representative Rod R. Blagojevich (D-IL), introduced the Administration's proposal into the 106th Congress as the "Gun Show Accountability Act" (GSAA).[12] Two months later, the Clinton Administration put forward the GSAA as its principle response to the Columbine massacre.

The GSAA defined gun shows as (a) "any event where 50 or more firearms are offered or exhibited for sale, transfer, or exchange, if one or more of the firearms has been shipped or transported in, or otherwise affects, interstate or foreign commerce; and (b) at which 2 or more persons are offering or exhibiting 1 or more firearms for sale, transfer, or exchange." The Craig/Hatch bill, put forward by Republican legislators friendly to the gun lobby, defined gun shows more narrowly, excluding events with fewer than 10 "exhibitors" (undefined). Both bills required gun show promoters to register with the Secretary of the Treasury and assigned them certain responsibilities. The promoter would have to notify the Secretary of the Treasury when and where a gun show would be taking place, check the photo identification of each vendor, and keep a list of firearm vendors who display firearms at the show, indicating whether each vendor is an FFL. The promoter would also have to provide all vendors with information about federal and state gun laws and maintain copies of all the records mentioned at the FFL's permanent place of business. The Secretary of the Treasury would be authorized to review the records and the inventory of any promoter conducting a gun show, either at the show or at the promoter's permanent place of business, without a warrant or probable cause.

The GSAA stated that if any part of a firearm transfer took place at a gun show, it would be subject to an FFL-initiated background check. However, the bill did not define "part" of a transfer. This opened a potentially huge loophole. If a purchaser seeking to avoid a background check negotiated a purchase for the next week or the week after, would the transaction be covered? Did "part of the sale" cover sales *first negotiated? discussed? conceived?* at a gun show? The answer would depend upon regulations to be issued by the Secretary of Treasury. To make a gun show law even plausibly effective, those regulations would need to specify that *communications* leading to a firearm sale constitute "part of a sale," so the transfer must go through an FFL. But such a rule would be impossible to enforce. If both parties denied it, how could law enforcement officials prove that a firearm sale between two private (non-FFL) individuals had originated in a conversation at a gun show?

What if the purchaser first saw the gun at the gun show but didn't talk to the seller? Suppose the transfer occurred a day, a week, or a month after the gun show concluded? Would all transfers negotiated, discussed, conceived, or considered at a gun show be subject to the GSAA's requirements? Treasury Department regulations would have to address this issue, but there is no easy solution. The broader the meaning of "part of a sale," the greater the enforcement challenge. How would a law enforcement agency be able to trace a particular firearm sale back to a meeting of the minds at a particular gun show?

The GSAA did not include an independent waiting period but simply mandated compliance with the *Brady* law, which allows NICS up to three business days to block a sale on the basis of the purchaser's criminal record or other disqualification. The FFL brokering the sale would be required to maintain records of the manufacturer, model, and firearm's serial number, as well as identifying information about the buyer and the seller. Only information about the firearm would be sent to the BATF's National Tracing Center. However, the FFL would keep the information about the buyer and seller on file and release it to the BATF if requested for a bona fide trace in the event the gun was linked to a crime. If, in a five-day period, the FFL brokered more than one sale involving the same seller and buyer, the FFL would have to file a multiple sale form with the BATF. A person who transferred a gun without initiating a background check would be committing a federal felony carrying a maximum five-year prison term.[13] Moreover, an FFL who violated the law would be subject to having his FFL license suspended or canceled and to a $10,000 civil fine.

The GSAA enjoyed the support of President Clinton, Vice President Gore, Attorney General Reno, and a host of gun control groups, including Handgun Control Inc. and Americans for Gun Safety (AGS), a new gun control organization that made gun show regulation the centerpiece of its political debut. The National Alliance of Stocking Gun Dealers (NASGD), whose members resent the competition of non-FFL sellers, also enthusiastically supported the bill.[14]

A few gun control organizations urged more stringent regulation. For example, The Trauma Foundation of San Francisco argued that only FFLs should be permitted to sell firearms at gun shows and that there should be a limit on the total number of firearms sold at a single gun show. The Violence Policy Center (VPC) proposed (1) prohibiting non-FFLs from selling firearms at gun shows, (2) limiting the type of firearms sales that could be made by a non-FFL, and (3) prohibiting the sale of certain types of military hardware.

The Massacre at Columbine

On April 20, 1999, the massacre at Columbine High School, in suburban Littleton, Colorado, rocked the nation. Eric Harris, age eighteen, and Dylan Klebold, age seventeen, fatally shot twelve classmates and one teacher, as well as themselves; they wounded many others. Three of the four firearms used in the attack were long guns that a girlfriend purchased for them at a Denver gun show.[15] The killers also obtained a semiautomatic handgun from an adult who purchased the gun for them at a gun show.[16] (He later pled guilty to knowingly transferring a firearm to underage boys and was sentenced to a six-year federal prison term.)[17] Because the two boys obtained their guns indirectly from gun shows, there was a chorus of demand for effective federal regulation of gun shows.[18] Nevertheless, Congress has been unable to agree on a new regulatory regime.

As a presidential candidate, George W. Bush supported a background check for all firearms transfers at gun shows; however, he opposed applying the Brady Law's three-day waiting period on the ground that the show would be over and dismantled before the three days expired; some purchasers might not be willing to travel to the vendor's principle place of business to complete the sale. On June 18, 1999, Representative John Dingell (D-MI) offered an amendment allowing NICS only twenty-four hours to conduct a background check on a gun show firearm sale. It was defeated because of the opposition of Democrats, who believed this time limit insufficient to investigate questionable purchasers.[19]

Senators Orin Hatch (R-UT) and Larry Craig (R-ID) introduced an amendment similar to Dingell's House bill but narrowing the definition of gun shows.[20] For example, the Hatch/Craig bill would permit gun show vendors to pool their firearms, reducing the number of individual vendors, thus removing the event from the definition of a gun show. The Democrats opposed Hatch/Craig on the ground that it did not include a requirement that pawnshop operators conduct a background check on customers who redeem their own guns. The Senate passed the Hatch/Craig bill by a vote of 53–47, but the House version did not pass.[21] The dispute over the one-day versus a three-day waiting period brought the bill's progress to a standstill.

Gun Show Loophole Closing and Gun Law Enforcement Act of 2001 (GSLC)

With the GSAA hopelessly bogged down in Congress, Senators John McCain and Joe Lieberman presented a compromise bill to the 107th Congress.[22] The Gun Show Loophole Closing and Gun Law Enforcement Act of 2001 (GSLC), like the GSAA (reintroduced into the 107th Congress as the Gun Show Background Check Act) requires gun show promoters to collect and report to the Secretary of the Treasury basic information about vendors at their gun shows and to inform vendors of their legal responsibilities. However, the GSLC requires that only "frequent gun show operators" (those who supervise two or more gun shows within any six-month period) obtain an annual license; "infrequent operators" must notify the Treasury secretary of their intent to stage a gun show but do not need a license. Moreover, McCain-Lieberman defines a gun show as a public event at which seventy-five or more guns are offered for sale, in comparison to the GSAA, whose definition of gun show kicks in at an event where there are only fifty guns. McCain-Lieberman specifically exempts people who sell their own guns from their own homes and people who sell their weapons to an immediate family member. More important, the GSLC allows a state, after the passage of three years, to reduce the time limit for blocking a proposed sale from three days to one day if the state can certify that its criminal record system is automated to the extent that the shorter time limit will be sufficient to permit identification of ineligible purchasers. The McCain-Lieberman bill also provides sweeteners for gun control proponents, including funding for more crime gun tracing, implementation of Project Exile programs, research on "smart gun" technology, and the addition of gun crime prosecutors and 200 ATF agents.[23]

The Americans for Gun Safety immediately announced its support for this compromise gun show bill and committed $1 million to passing it. NAPO, an association of police unions and the National League of Cities (which also urges federal regulation of "Internet-facilitated firearms commerce" also provided swift endorsements.[24] But some pro–gun control organizations registered opposition. For example, the Violence Policy Center issued a press release stating:

> The goal of closing the gun show loophole is to ensure that felons, domestic abusers, and other prohibited persons cannot purchase firearms from private individuals at gun shows without background checks. Unfortunately, the McCain-Lieberman bill draws on gun lobby proposals from 1999 that actually undermine and weaken the federal Brady law. . . . The McCain-Lieberman bill would create a weaker background check at gun shows for unlicensed sellers, while at the same time giving priority to checks at gun shows. In addition, the bill creates a new class of gun seller, "special firearm event licensees," based on a concept first promoted by NRA Board Member and U.S. Senator Larry Craig (R-ID). This idea was soundly and uniformly rejected by gun control organizations and Congressional gun control leaders in 1999. In addition, the bill could weaken state laws that

currently rely on the federal background check provision for all gun show sales. . . .[25]

While there are minor differences between the GSAA and the GSLC bills, both treat gun show sales by non-FFLs differently from all other sales by non-FFLs. For that reason, both bills could be easily circumvented by anyone who wants to buy (or sell) a gun with no questions asked.

What the GSAA or the GSLC Would Likely Accomplish

If passed, would the GSAA or GSLC make it more difficult for criminals and other dangerous people to obtain firearms? Yes, but only marginally.[26] *A law that regulates secondary transfers, but only those that occur at gun shows, makes little sense except as a step toward regulating all secondary transfers.* Otherwise, private sellers could use the gun shows to display their guns and give out business cards. They could complete the sales later in the privacy of their homes or cars or even on street corners. Much depends upon the motives and attitudes of gun show vendors. If they do not want to sell guns to ineligible persons, access to the background check system, through an FFL, would help them to act responsibly. If they are indifferent or hostile to the *Brady* machinery, they could easily ignore it, for example, by making the sale after the show closes. Unless they had the bad luck of selling to an undercover agent, it is very unlikely that their unlawful sale would ever come to light.

The GSAA and the GSLC, like the Brady Law, would be easy to circumvent. The easiest avoidance strategy for an ineligible purchaser would be to have a straw purchaser—a friend, relative, or gang comrade with no criminal record—buy the gun for him. A vendor who is selling a stolen gun or who just wishes to avoid the time and expense of finding an FFL to contact NICS could walk around a gun show with a placard that reads ".44 Magnum for sale; no questions asked." Upon inquiry, the seller with an eye on the GSAA or GSLC might explain that he does not have the firearm with him but that he can show and sell it that evening or some evening the next week at a designated location.

Only a small percentage of non-FFL gun sales and transfers take

TABLE 13.2
Gun Classified Ad Policies for 184 Major City Newspapers

Will accept gun ads for all types of guns	53%	(98)
Will accept gun ads but not for assault weapons	4%	(7)
Will accept gun ads but not for semiautomatic guns	2%	(3)
Will accept gun ads but not for handguns	12%	(23)
Will accept gun ads but not for handguns or assault weapons	7%	(13)
Will accept gun ads but not for handguns or semiautomatic guns	2%	(3)
Will not accept gun ads	20%	(37)
Total	100%	(184)

SOURCE: Professor William Ruefle

place at gun shows. While bringing those sales under the Brady Law's regulatory umbrella might do *some* good, it won't do *much* good. A person who wishes to avoid a background check would still easily circumvent the regulatory regime. And a non-FFL who wishes to sell firearms without imposing paperwork and a background check on the purchaser could pass out business cards at a gun show.

Non-FFLs, of course, have many options, other than gun shows, for disposing of their firearms. Professor William Ruefle, of the University of South Carolina's College of Criminal Justice, conducted a fascinating field experiment.[27] He placed advertisements offering for sale a variety of handguns in a local newspaper and was able to sell two dozen guns in a short time without difficulty. Some purchasers from as far as 100 miles away agreed to make the purchase at Ruefle's home or at a convenient rest area along the interstate between their home and his. Professor Ruefle also found that the vast majority of newspapers had no qualms about accepting classified ads for guns even if the newspaper's editorial page supported more gun controls (See Tables 13.2 and 13.3).

Professor Ruefle's next field study cast further doubt on the likelihood that gun owners will comply with licensing and registration requirements. He called forty-two individuals who had taken out "gun for sale" newspaper advertisements. Explaining that he was from out of state, he asked if that would cause any problem in purchasing the advertised firearm. Although it is a crime knowingly to sell a firearm to an out-of-state purchaser, thirty-eight sellers told him it would be no problem.

TABLE 13.3

Guns Offered for Sale in One Year of Classified Ads in the Atlanta Constitution, San Francisco Examiner, Times-Picyune *(New Orleans),* The State *(Columbia, SC), and* The Carolina Trader

	Atlanta Constitution Sunday circulation 687,397	San Francisco Examiner Sunday circulation 633,513	Times-Picyune (New Orleans) Sunday circulation 316,977	The State (Columbia, SC) Sunday circulation 160,381	The Carolina Trader Weekly circulation 33,000
Semiautomatic handguns	30% (102)	Not Accepted	25% (166)	21% (16)	19% (396)
Other handguns	12% (40)	Not Accepted	13% (85)	12% (9)	14% (305)
Semiautomatic rifles	10% (33)	11% (7)	26% (171)	18% (14)	15% (313)
Other rifles	28% (95)	33% (21)	16% (104)	28% (21)	25% (528)
Semiautomatic shotguns	6% (20)	17% (11)	8% (50)	7% (5)	9% (200)
Other shotguns	14% (48)	39% (25)	13% (86)	14% (11)	18% (392)
Total annual guns offered for sale	100% (338)	100% (64)	100% (662)	100% (76)	100% (2,134)
Total annual guns offered for sale per 10,000 Sunday readers	4.9	1.0	20.9	4.7	646.7

SOURCE: Professor William Ruefle

State Regulation of Gun Shows

In a few years, we may be able to assess the potential impact of federal gun show regulation by evaluating several state and local gun show laws. For example, California has a significantly stricter gun show requirement than the GSAA, including a ten-day waiting period on sales, but gun shows continue to flourish there.[28]

On August 9, 2000, New York State passed legislation requiring gun show promoters to notify all gun show vendors, FFLs or non-FFLs, that they must subject purchasers to background checks prior to transferring a firearm.[29] Moreover, the New York law attempts to deal with background check avoidance by providing that "[no] person [shall] offer or agree to sell a firearm, rifle or shotgun at a gun show and then transfer or deliver such weapon at a location other than the gun show for the purpose of evading or avoiding the check."[30] Violation of this law is a class A misdemeanor. No data or studies of the law's operation and effect have yet appeared.

In the wake of the Columbine massacre, bills were introduced in some pro-gun states to regulate gun shows. Americans for Gun Safety campaigned for referenda in Oregon and Colorado (which, like the GSAA and GSLC) subjected all firearms purchasers at gun shows to background checks. Both proposals passed by substantial majorities.

The state-level gun show laws vary from one to another and, of course, will be implemented and enforced by state agencies that vary in competence, resources, and commitment. Moreover, all state schemes, like the proposed federal laws, can be circumvented by sellers and purchasers who wish to avoid a background check.

Some counties and cities have taken steps to regulate gun shows, when similar controls could not be passed at the state level. Such ordinances have invariably been challenged in court on grounds of state preemption and the First Amendment. Santa Clara County, California, sought to prohibit gun shows on county-owned or public property by requiring public entities to insert a clause into their leases that would prohibit lessees from sponsoring events at which vendors offered guns for sale. Otherwise, the county argued, people might think that the county supported an armed citizenry. The Ninth Circuit Court of Appeals held that offers to sell guns are protected commercial speech which the county supervisors could not ban at publicly owned fairgrounds.

> The County has not presented a shred of evidence that any County resident, or anyone else, has somehow gotten the mistaken impression that the County promotes gun usage. Even assuming that some people mistakenly believe that to be true, the County has offered no evidence to substantiate its claim that the practice of holding gun shows at the Fairgrounds either caused or reinforces that mistaken belief. Rather, the record suggests that the addendum is at best an inept response to pressure by residents who strongly support the cause of gun control.[31]

Los Angeles and Alameda counties also moved to prohibit gun shows on fairgrounds and other public property. The Alameda ordinance bans gun shows on public property. The Los Angeles ordinance permits gun shows but bans sale of guns at such shows. Neither ordinance deals with gun shows on private property. The Ninth Circuit referred challenges to these ordinances to the California Supreme Court for a ruling on whether local lawmaking on the subject of gun shows is preempted by state law. Twenty California counties and cities filed an amicus brief in support of Los Angeles and Alameda. In April 2002, the California court upheld the *power* of local governments to pass such ordinances.[32]

Montgomery County, Maryland, passed an ordinance prohibiting gun shows on public property by denying public funding to "any organization [e.g., a fairgrounds operator] that allows the display and sale of guns" on its property. It also prohibits gun displays and sales in gunfree zones, defined as any place within 100 yards of a "place of public assembly," including fairgrounds, conference centers, and exhibition halls. Since the enactment of the ordinance, the Board of Directors of the Montgomery County Agricultural Center canceled future gun shows rather than forfeit the large subsidies in funding that it receives from the county.

In October 2001, U.S. District Court Judge Marvin J. Garbis struck down the ordinance on the grounds that the county had no regulatory authority over privately owned fairgrounds located within the City of Gaithersburg, and that the council's funding restriction constituted "a gun sale regulation enacted by Montgomery County in the guise of a discretionary spending provision." He did not reach the First Amendment issue, but noted that the plaintiffs had made a strong argument.[33]

A lawsuit over the power of South Bend, Indiana, to ban gun shows at the city's civic center ventilated the same issues; once again, the gun show promoters prevailed. Northern Indiana Gun and Outdoor Shows, Inc. sued city officials, contending that the ordinance violated the First Amendment and the Equal Protection clause. Among its claims, the plaintiff argued that the ban on firearms and ammunition curtailed its ability to convey information about lawful products. Interestingly, the judge found the First Amendment issue to be a question of fact for the jury, which brought in a $300,000 damage judgment for the plaintiffs.[34]

Gun control at the county and the city level may have a much brighter future than gun control at the state and especially the federal levels for the simple reason that some cities contain very significant gun control majorities. It seems likely that a way will be found to prohibit gun shows without violating the First Amendment. Preemption is a more serious obstacle. Gun owners' rights groups have lobbied hard to pass state laws preempting municipalities from bringing tort suits against firearms manufacturers or outlawing gun shows.[35] But, even if the municipalities are successful in banning gun shows, it is hardly certain that fewer guns will get into the hands of ineligible persons.

Subjecting All Secondary Sales to Background Checks

Perhaps 40 to 50 percent of all handgun transfers, and a much higher percentage of transfers to criminals, are made by non-FFLs. Only a small fraction of these transfers take place at gun shows.[36] Thus, preventing gun sales at gun shows to persons with a criminal record would constitute only a *very small step* toward keeping guns out of criminals' hands. Regulating non-FFL sellers at gun shows but nowhere else would have little effect on the flow of guns into the hands of ineligible persons.

Could all secondary sales, no matter what venue, be channeled through FFLs? California has recently mandated just such a requirement.[37] This means that if S (seller) wants to give or sell his gun to B (buyer), both must appear before D (a licensed dealer), and fill out documents in order to consummate the sale. As under *Brady*, D must forward the would-be purchaser's name to the NICS for a background check. S and B would have to delay transferring the gun until D informs them that the NICS has approved the transaction or until three business days elapse.

Of course, if he feared flunking the background check, B could evade this scheme, just as he could avoid *Brady*, simply by having straw purchaser SP, a friend with no criminal record, buy the firearm from D. Let us assume that B has no eligible friends or relatives willing to act as straw purchaser, and further assume that, desperate to purchase a handgun, B makes the purchase from S, who has no license and no desire to run the transaction through a licensed dealer. Law enforcement officials would not know that S sold this gun to B. Since S is not an FFL, he is not obliged to maintain any records on his secondhand gun sales. There is no registry of the 250+ million firearms in private hands.[38]

Since there is no gun registry, S can discount the possibility that a police officer or BATF inspector will appear at his door demanding that he produce a particular firearm or, if he cannot produce it, explain satisfactorily what happened to it. Suppose one day, the police arrest B, an ex-felon, for possessing the handgun that S sold to him and that the police urge B to identify the person who sold him the gun. B might never have known S's full name or, having known it, might have forgotten it. B might remember S's name but refuse to divulge it. B might refuse to cooperate. He might lie, saying that he does not remember where he got the gun. If he had a devious sense of humor, B might say that he purchased the handgun from an FFL but has lost the receipt. *He could say anything.*

However, let us suppose that B, hoping for leniency, names S as the person who transferred the handgun to him. Assume, too, that the police locate S. Under interrogation, S might break down, admit having knowingly sold the handgun to an ineligible purchaser, and throw himself on the mercy of the police, prosecutor, and court. More likely, S would either lie or remain silent. No proof exists that S sold any handgun to B, much less this particular handgun. Even if there were witnesses to the sale, how could they identify a particular handgun as the one that S sold to B weeks, months, or years ago? In fact, if S is a street seller, he himself probably has no idea whether he sold *that particular handgun* to B. Indeed, he may have met B only briefly, months or years before, and have no recollection of dealing with him.

If S is deceitful and sophisticated, he could admit the transfer but say he made it lawfully through his friend C, who, as far as S knows, is or was an FFL (at least that's what C told him). S might claim that he believed that C had obtained NICS approval; he had no reason to demand a signed receipt or other proof. If he once had a receipt, he has not kept it all this time. "No, S doesn't know where C is now." Indeed, even if C is found and denies knowing anything about B's gun, S may call C a liar, a person who masquerades as an FFL in order to collect a broker's fee on every street sale of a handgun. These hypothetical scenarios demonstrate that the recent California law that extends the *Brady* background check to all handgun transfers is unenforceable, even if the police give it high priority, which is very unlikely, given competing demands on their time and resources.

Conclusion

Nothing better symbolizes American exceptionalism in the area of firearms regulations than gun shows. The fact that, even after the Columbine massacre, the United States Congress has not been able to pass a law requiring a background check on all firearms sales at gun shows demonstrates the status of gun control in American politics. Indeed, no state has gone farther than requiring that all gun purchases at gun shows go through a licensed dealer so that the purchaser's eligibility will be checked against federal and state databases. With just a few exceptions, no city or county, much less state, has banned gun shows altogether. No major gun control organization advocates the prohibition of gun shows.

Examining the GSAA and the GSLC illustrates the limited effectiveness of incremental gun controls in the twenty-first-century United States. What is the point of the Brady Law's requirement that purchasers of firearms from FFLs be subject to a background check if purchasers can buy firearms from non-FFLs without a background check? What is the purpose of requiring non-FFLs to put their gun show customers through a background check but not customers who come to their homes or meet them at a street corner?

If the GSAA or the GSLC are ends in themselves, they hardly seem worth the effort. Admittedly, such laws would do little, if any, harm and might even prevent a dangerous person, here and there, from obtaining a firearm, at least for a short time. But it is difficult to see how such regulation can accomplish much good. A person who wished to purchase a firearm without undergoing a background check could pick up some business cards at a gun show and consummate the deal after the gun show closed. The would-be purchaser could forgo the gun show entirely and just put a "Gun Wanted" advertisement in the local newspaper or on an Internet Web site. A non-FFL who responded to the advertisement could make the sale without subjecting the purchaser to a background check.

Thus, subjecting all firearms purchasers at gun shows to a background check ought to be a step toward subjecting all firearm purchasers to a background check, regardless of whether the seller has a license and the place of sale. But the logistics of implementing and enforcing a universal background check for all firearms purchasers (much less all transferees) are daunting, indeed impossible in the absence of a comprehensive firearms registry. Without a registry, there is no way to determine whether an unrecorded gun transfer has taken place. Law enforcement officials would not be able to prove that x obtained his gun from y or anyone else. Yet, creating a comprehensive gun registry at this point in American history, with some 250 million firearms in private hands, could not be accomplished, even if there was political support for it, which there is not.[39]

NOTES

Earlier versions of this article appeared as James B. Jacobs and Daniel M. Heumann, "Extending *Brady* to Gun Shows and the Secondary Market," 37(3) *Criminal Law Bulletin* (May–June 2001): 248–262; James B. Jacobs, *Can Gun Control Work?* (Oxford: Oxford University Press, 2002), chapter 8.

1. Bureau of Alcohol, Tobacco, and Firearms, "Commerce in Firearms in the U.S." (Washington, D.C.: U.S. Department of Treasury, February 2000).

2. A comprehensive list of gun show promoters and links to their Web sites can be found on the Web site of the National Association of Arms Shows, Inc at: http://thomas.loc.gov/cgi-bin/bdquery.

3. *Gun Shows: Brady Checks and Crime Gun Traces* (Washington, D.C.: Bureau of Alcohol Tobacco and Firearms, 1999), 4.

4. David Kopel and Linda Gorman, "The Truth about Gun Shows," *Independence Institute*, September 11, 2000, available at: www.I2i.org/suptdocs/backgrounders/gunshows.htm.

5. GSSA, 106th Congress. 1st Session 1999. H.R. 902. It was reintroduced in the 107th Congress as Gun Show Background Check Act, S. 767. Senators John McCain and Joe Lieberman introduced the compromise Gun Show Loophole Closing and Gun Law Enforcement Act of 2001 into the 107th Congress, 1st Session.

6. Pub Law 90-618.

7. Pub Law 99-308.

8. Kristen Rand, "Gun Shows in America: Tupperware Parties for Criminals, July 1996." Violence Policy Center, Washington D.C., July 1996, 3.

9. Bureau of Alcohol, Tobacco, and Firearms, Statement of Richard J. Davis, Assistant Secretary of the Treasury, 1979, 360, available at: http://www.cs.cmu.edu/afs/cs.cmu.edu/user/wbardwel/public/nfalist/atf_hearing1a.txt.

10. Glenn H. Utter, *Encyclopedia of Gun Control and Gun Rights* (Phoenix, Ariz.: Oryx Press, 2000), 63.

11. See U.S. Department of Justice, Federal Bureau of Investigation, Criminal Justice Information Services Division, National Instant Criminal Background Check System (NICS), Operations Report, 2000.

12. H.R. 1903, S.B. 443.

13. An FFL's failure to carry out a *Brady* background check is a misdemeanor, 18 U.S.C. Sec. 922.

14. "Ten National Law Enforcement Groups Call on Congress to Close the Gun Show Loophole." *U.S. Newswire,* October 20, 1999.

15. Bill McAllister and David Olinger, "Clinton Wins Changes from Major Gun Maker," *Denver Post,* March 18, 2000, 25–26.

16. "Columbine Parents Atty. Predicts More," *United Press International,* May 27, 1999, 4.

17. News Services, *St. Louis Post-Dispatch,* May 9, 2000, 11.

18. James Dao, "In Turnaround, McCain Does Ad Urging Background Checks for Buyers at Gun Shows," *New York Times,* October 4, 2000, 18.

19. "Ten National Law Enforcement Groups Call on Congress to Close the Gun Show Loophole," *U.S. Newswire,* October 20, 1999.

20. The Hatch/Craig Amendment to GSAA, CR (S5309, 106th Congress) fails to define the term "exhibitor," so vendors could pool their firearms to circumvent the background check requirement.

21. 145 Cong. Rec. S 5146.

22. S.890, 107th Congress, 1st Session, 2001. Congressmen Castle and McCarthy introduced the same bill into the House of Representatives. H.R. 2377, 107th Congress, 1st Session, 2001.

23. For an overview of Project Exile, see U.S. Attorney's Office for the Eastern District of Virginia, Project Exile Executive Summary, available at: http:// www.law.richmond.edu/RJOLPI/COMB.htm.

24. http/ww2.americansforgunsafety.com/press_nlc.html.

25. http://www.vpc.org/press/0105show.htm.

26. James B. Jacobs and Kimberly Potter, "Keeping Guns Out of the Wrong Hands," 86 *Journal of Criminal Law and Criminology* (1995): 93.

27. Paper delivered by Professor William Ruefle at the Conference on Guns, Crime, and Punishment in America, University of Arizona College of Law, January 26–27, 2001.

28. The Hatch/Craig Amendment to GSAA, CR S5309, 106th Congress.

29. New York State Division of Criminal Justice 200, "Closing the Gun Show Loophole," available at: htp://criminaljustice.state.ny.us/pio/gunbill.htm.

30. Chapter 189, Laws of 2000, NYS (August 9, 2000).

31. *Nordyke v. Santa Clara County,* 110 F. 3d 707 (9th Cir. 1997).

32. *Great Western Shows Inc. v. County of Los Angeles,* 02 C.D.O.S., 3455 (April 2002); *Nordyke v. King,* 02 C.D.O.S. 3460 (April 2002).

33. *Frank Krasner Enterprises v. Montgomery County,* 166 F. Supp. 2d 1058 (2001).

34. *Northern Indiana Gun and Outdoor Shows, Inc. v. Hedman,* 111 F. Supp.2d 1020 (N.D. Ind. 2000). See the Supreme Court's commercial speech decision

in *Central Hudson Gas and Elec. Corp. v. Public Serv. Comm'n,* 447 U.S. 557 (1980).

35. The American Legislative Exchange Council has proposed a model "Consistency in Firearms Regulation Act," which would prohibit local jurisdictions from independently enacting restrictions on the possession of firearms.

36. Philip J. Cook, Stephanie Molliconi, and Thomas B. Cole, "Regulating Gun Markets," 86 *Journal of Criminal Law and Criminology* (fall 1995): 59, 69.

37. Cal. Pen. C. 12071 (b) (3) bans the sale of any firearm except through licensed dealers.

38. For an analysis of the massive administrative and enforcement challenge that would be involved in registering all firearms, see James B. Jacobs and Kimberly Potter, "Comprehensive Handgun Licensing and Registration: An Analysis and Critique of Brady II, Gun Control's Next (and Last?) Step," 89 *Journal of Criminal Law and Criminology* (1998): 81–110.

39. Ibid.

D. Federal Enforcement of Gun Laws

Chapter 14

Project Exile and the Allocation of Federal Law Enforcement Authority

Daniel C. Richman

I. Introduction

With each report of violent crime statistics or the latest firearms outrage, we hear the antiphony of the gun control debate.[1] Advocates of increased federal regulation decry the inadequacies of a regime that permits relatively free access to firearms and argue that the availability of guns is itself a spur to more deadly violence. Advocates of minimal regulation condemn measures that, they say, primarily penalize law-abiding citizens and instead call for more vigorous enforcement of existing laws, targeting "criminals," not their weapons.

These themes echoed (albeit in muted form) in the 2000 presidential and congressional campaigns and in Attorney General John Ashcroft's confirmation hearings and will surely be heard in the future. There is one unison note, however: The Eastern District of Virginia United States Attorney's Office's Project Exile has been a stupendous success and ought to be replicated (to one degree or another) wherever gun violence threatens the social fabric.

Conceived late in 1996, Project Exile targeted gun violence in the Richmond area by funneling all gun arrests made by state and local authorities to federal court, where, if at all possible, defendants were to be prosecuted under federal firearm statutes.[2]

Politically, Project Exile soon began receiving rave reviews from every side. In the spring of 1999, President Bill Clinton and Attorney General Janet Reno both touted the program.[3] Yet, Republican cheers were even louder. In June 1999, George W. Bush appeared in

Richmond to endorse Exile and to call for its implementation nation-wide.[4] And in the debates between the two candidates, it was Bush, not Gore, who singled out Exile for special praise.[5] Both the NRA[6] and its nemesis, Sarah Brady,[7] also endorsed the program.

Part of the story, of course, is that no one wants to come out against the prosecution of armed violent criminals. But the bipartisan unanimity on the virtues of Project Exile has masked deep differences about its lessons. Indeed, the political saga of Exile has related more to the negative implications of an Exile-based strategy than to the project's achievements. While the federal officials who established the program simply addressed a local emergency, Exile has carried far more freight in the legislative arena, where the real issue has been whether federal firearms enforcement efforts should go *beyond* such programs.

The implications of Exile politics go beyond the gun control debate, for they may well mark a new stage in the devolution of federal enforcement power. An inevitable consequence of the now longstanding presidential interest in episodic (as opposed to organized) violent crime has been to shift control over federal enforcement assets from Washington to U.S. Attorneys' Offices—the entities best suited to assess and target local problems and to obtain the cooperation of local authorities in the effort. The devolution, however, has not gone much further than this, and the federal commitment of resources in this area has been highly discretionary, varying by district, and balanced against the needs of more national programs. Now comes Project Exile and, more significant, the legislative movement it has spawned—a movement that would encourage and institutionalize the elimination of federal prosecutorial gatekeeping.

The purpose of this essay is to recount this saga and pursue its implications. The story is far from complete—particularly in the wake of September 11. But I've tried to capture its flavor and highlights.

II. Project Exile: Origins, Components, and Political Uses

A. Triggerlock

On April 10, 1991, against the backdrop of the (first) Bush administration's effort to block passage of the Brady bill,[8] Attorney General Richard Thornburgh announced Project Triggerlock.[9] The idea was to have federal prosecutors work with local police agencies to identify repeat and violent offenders who used guns and then to prosecute them in federal court.[10] The program continued into the Clinton administration, but Republicans soon charged that it was being pursued with insufficient zeal.[11] Responding at a September House hearing, Assistant Attorney General Jo Ann Harris, chief of the Criminal Division at the Department of Justice ("DOJ"), avowed that Triggerlock remained "in full force" as an "important component" of Attorney General Reno's Anti-Violent Crime Initative.[12] Conceding that federal firearm prosecutions had recently declined, she explained that "it is a much wiser and more productive approach to focus our attention and resources on the quality of the investigations initiated and prosecutions undertaken to identify and target those armed and violent offenders responsible for the greatest amount of crime," particularly those connected with gangs. In any event, Harris testified, prosecutions alone would not solve the problem of violent crime: "[W]e all know that the best way to prevent crime with guns is to stop criminals before they get the guns."[13]

B. Project Exile

The Criminal Division chief candidly admitted that the Anti-Violent Crime Initiative would have to be implemented by the U.S. Attorney in each district and that these officials, responding to local problems and personalities, "must of necessity make their own policies with respect to where they put their resources."[14] This was something of an understatement. Although the extent of U.S. Attorneys' independence from Washington varies,[15] most, if not all, have traditions of autonomy, fortified by the relationships between their leaders and the political powers within their respective districts.[16] This autonomy is particularly great when the federal government turns to violent street crime, because, in this area, U.S. Attorneys are best suited to negotiate relationships with the local police departments that are the best sources of information about such activities. Equally well suited to an initiative that, quite self-consciously, plunged into an area of traditionally local responsibility was the agency that was to play a leading role in bringing firearms cases to prosecutors. These cases, of course, fell squarely within the statutory bailiwick of the Federal Bureau of Alcohol, Tobacco, and Firearms (ATF). Moreover, perhaps more important, ATF had for some time responded to its political vulnerability in Washington by working particularly hard on its relationships with local enforcers.[17]

From out of these political and institutional currents came Project Exile. In February 1997, responding to a plague of gun violence that gave Richmond one of the top five per capita murder rates in the country, the Eastern District of Virginia U.S. Attorney's Office unveiled the program. Exile's law enforcement component, initiated in coordination with the local police and prosecutors, was quite straightforward: When a police officer found a gun, he would page an ATF agent. If a federal statute applied, the case would be prosecuted federally.[18] The benefits of taking cases federally, according to the U.S. Attorney's Office, flowed from the federal bail statute, which allowed pretrial detention on the ground of dangerousness; the federal system of mandatory minimums and sentencing guidelines, which limited sentencing discretion and resulted in predicable and substantial sentences; and the federal prison system, which made it likely that any sentence would be served far away (hence the idea of "exile").[19]

The effects of the Project were impressive (or at least were uniformly perceived as such).[20] Firearms seizures by the Richmond Police Department were soon down by 48 percent.[21] By March 1999, the U.S. Attorney's Office could give at least partial credit to the Project for reducing the homicide rate by 33 percent between 1997 and 1998, giving Richmond its lowest rate since 1987.[22]

C. Political Responses to Project Exile

Precisely how Project Exile gained such prominence in national policy circles is difficult to determine. The program's advertising and educational components ensured it a high profile around Virginia. And perhaps federal, state, and local authorities in Virginia were particularly assiduous in drawing national media attention to the program's (and their own) success. However, the main story lies elsewhere. One could easily imagine a scenario in which the Clinton administration, while pursuing its gun control agenda of expanding the *Brady* regime and policing the gun markets, seized upon Project Exile as evidence of its continued commitment to Triggerlock's goal of getting armed criminals off the streets. But the race to embrace Exile was won by the administration's opponents.

In June 1998, the newly elected NRA president Charlton Heston touted Exile's success, and executive director Wayne R. LaPierre followed up, proclaiming that Exile "ought to be in every major city where there's a major gun problem."[23] The Clinton Justice Department even appeared willing to cede political control of Exile's symbolism to its adversaries. An August 31, 1998, *Wall Street Journal* article told of the inadequate support Exile was getting from Washington. It also reported that the person who until recently had been Attorney General Reno's "top aide on gun violence" had "dismisse[d] Project Exile as 'assembly line' prosecutions that bleed resources from other law-enforcement priorities" and had doubted that there was "any empirical evidence that Richmond's falling murder rate is related to Project Exile."[24]

By the time the new Congress convened in early 1999, NRA and Republican attention had propelled Exile to even greater prominence, with glowing reviews in the national media.[25] But now President Clinton stepped in. On March 20, 1999, just two days before a Senate Judiciary hearing at which Republicans were expected to criticize the administration's record of gun prosecutions, the President sought to reclaim Exile. In his radio address, he announced his commitment to "use every available tool to increase the prosecution of gun criminals and shut down illegal gun markets."[26] Even as he gave equal emphasis to trafficking enforcement, the only program Clinton singled out was Exile (which lacked any significant trafficking component).

While President Clinton had stolen a bit of their thunder, Senate Republicans proceeded with the March 22 hearing. They were "pleased" that the Administration was finally trying to extend Exile, but the fact was that federal gun prosecutions had declined by 46 percent between 1992 and 1998.[27] In response, the U.S. Attorneys from Richmond and Boston strove mightily to situate Exile within the broader departmental strategy. ATF's assistant director for field operations, Andrew L. Vita, no doubt basking in rare (albeit misleading) bipartisan approval for his agency's work, also emphasized ATF's special role in targeting *both* gun trafficking and gun violence.[28]

The shootings at Columbine High School on April 20, 1999, gave the administration and its congressional allies new momentum in their push for broader regulatory regimes. Within a week, the President had proposed legislation to restrict the purchase of handguns to one per month, raise the minimum age for handgun possession, and require background checks for firearms purchases at gun shows.[29] While Republicans, pointing to the decrease in Triggerlock prosecutions, suggested that new laws would do little good if the administration failed to enforce them, the Senate ultimately passed some regulatory measures.[30] But Senate Republicans (including Senator John Ashcroft [R-Mo.]) made sure that the compromise legislation also enshrined Exile in the Criminal Use of Firearms by Felons (CUFF) Act.[31] After applauding Triggerlock, bemoaning the decline in federal firearms prosecutions between 1993 and 1998, and celebrating the success of Exile in Richmond, the bill required that, in twenty-five high crime jurisdictions,[32] the Attorney General and the Secretary of the Treasury were to "provide for the establishment of agreements with state and local law enforcement officials for the referral to the ATF and the United States Attorney for prosecution of person arrested" for firearms offenses and to ensure that at least one Assistant U.S. Attorney be assigned to prosecute gun cases.

The action then moved to the House, where, at a May 27 hearing, Representative Bill McCollum (R-Fla.) noted the "significant drop-off" in federal gun prosecutions.[33] Administration witnesses responded by asserting that its "strategy of increased collaboration among federal, state, and local law enforcement" had resulted in a sharp rise in the "combined number of federal *and state* firearms convictions" since 1992 and a 25 percent increase in the number of *federal* cases in which an offender received five or more years imprisonment.[34] The administration's testimony warned: "Substantial opportunity costs are incurred when federal resources that could be used to combat uniquely federal crimes—like interstate gun trafficking—are used instead on cases that could be handled effectively by state and local authorities."[35]

As summer approached, the action moved from Capitol Hill to the hustings. On June 22, George W. Bush went to Richmond to "embrace" the program and to tell how it should be adopted nationwide.[36] And the venue for Vice President Gore's response a few weeks later? Readers who have gotten into the spirit of the debate should be able to figure it out. Surrounded by Boston police officers, Gore called for broader gun control measures and pledged "to work with states that want to stop plea bargaining on gun crime."[37] On January 18, 2000 (in Boston, of course, not Richmond), President Clinton announced his National Gun Enforcement Initiative—a more concerted effort to use street-crime enforcement programs as a vehicle for selling a far broader firearms strategy, including a call for 500 new ATF agents *and inspectors* to "help us crack down on violent gun criminals, illegal gun traffickers, and bad-apple dealers."[38]

The task the House Republicans now faced was somewhat harder than before: It was not enough simply to tout Exile-like programs as a substitute for new gun legislation, since the administration was now using Exile's success as an argument for increasing ATF's budget. Congressman McCollum, backed by the House Republican leadership, had a ready answer, however: a bill, introduced March 22, that focused attention on the rigors of existing federal firearms laws but that steered funding for enforcement programs to state enforcers. This was Project Exile: The Safe Streets and Neighborhood Act of 2000,[39] which provided $100 million over five years to states that enacted firearms sentencing laws with five-year mandatory terms for use of a gun during a violent felony or serious drug crime and/or for possession of a firearm by a predicate felon. A state without such laws could obtain grant money by entering into "an equivalent federal prosecution agreement" that committed the state to refer such cases to federal prosecuting authorities.[40] Hearings on the legislation, gave the Republican governor of Virginia, James Gilmore III, a chance to tell how, in July 1999, his state had instituted "Virginia Exile."[41] By passing sentencing and bail statutes similar to the federal provisions, this program had "enhance[d] the sovereignty of the state in prosecuting gun crimes, and reliev[ed] it of the need to refer cases to federal courts."[42] A representative of Texas's attorney general told of "Texas Exile." Texas did not have gun laws like those proposed in McCollum's bill, but it was "considering the option" and, in any event, would be eligible for funding because it had entered into a "cooperative agreement with all four U.S. Attorneys to prosecute those criminals under federal law where appropriate."[43]

It was the Texas approach that most troubled the Justice Department. It urged Congress "not to create incentives that might lead to wholesale federal adoption of local gun prosecutions, which would significantly hinder the ability of federal authorities to enforce the other important federal laws and overwhelm the federal courts."[44] Congressional Democrats had their own response to McCollum's bill in their ENFORCE Act, which provided for 600 new ATF agents and inspectors with greater regulator authority, 114 new federal prosecutors to bring federal gun cases, and grants for local prosecutors.[45]

House Republicans had the votes, though. After they raced to get the bill to the floor before the anniversary of the Columbine High School shootings, it passed on April 11, 358 to 60.[46] Senator Mike DeWine (R-Ohio) introduced an identical bill in the Senate immediately thereafter, giving Republican senators another opportunity to tout the virtues of "this basic crime-fighting approach."[47]

Yet Clinton administration allies continued to push for a greater state role in gun enforcement. In May, some House Democrats introduced the Community Gun Prosecutor Act of 2000, which would have designated $150 million for state and local prosecutors to bring state gun cases.[48] If the Republicans thought existing gun laws were sufficient, one sponsor challenged, why not fund the enforcement of the state laws (as well as the federal ones) on the books?[49] And, at a June 2000 press conference, Clinton noted that a House appropriations committee was "on the verge" of rejecting his administration's "proposal for the largest gun enforcement initiative in history." He chided Republicans for failing to fund 1,000 new state and local gun prosecutors and thus "undermin[ing] our efforts to replicate the success of Richmond's Project Exile, another key initiative the Republicans have always said they support."[50]

In part because neither Bush nor Gore found it advantageous to press his position, and in part because no major gun tragedies required them to do so, gun control rhetoric ended up being rather muted in postconvention campaigning. In his final days after the Bush victory, however, Clinton signed budget legislation that provided the nearly $200 million that he had sought in his Gun Enforcement Initiative to fund 500 ATF agents and inspectors and more than 600 federal, state, and local prosecutors.[51] Had Gore become president, Clinton's budget victories might well have reduced the effect of Exile politics upon overall federal policy, giving ATF resources to pursue both supply-side cases and violent use and possession cases. But, of course, had Gore become president, there might not have been such budget victories. In any event, the election of Bush, and his selection of another leading Exile supporter, John Ashcroft,[52] as attorney general, vastly raised the likelihood that Exile-type programs would become the primary focus of federal gun enforcement efforts[53] and that most of the newly obtained federal resources would be deployed in this direction.[54]

III. Assessing Exile

Was Project Exile a good idea? Should it be implemented nationwide? In one way, these are easy questions. There is near unanimity that gun-toting drug traffickers or robbers ought to be prosecuted and substantial agreement that a convicted felon should face charges for possessing a firearm.[55] In other ways, Project Exile raises some extremely difficult policy questions. Its targets undoubtedly should be charged. But why federally? One need not invoke constitutional absolutes to make a good case for leaving state and local authorities primarily responsible for street crime.[56] Federal enforcers may have a more powerful arsenal, but, as many opponents of "overfederalization" have pointed out, federal intervention in this area may allow state and local authorities to dodge their responsibilities.[57]

Did this happen in Richmond? It's hard to say. After all, it did not take very long for Virginia to change its bail laws, increase its sentences, and commit significant police and prosecutorial resources to Exile-type cases. Perhaps state officials might have acted earlier, if left to their own devices or, alternatively, have been fittingly faulted for inaction in the face of Richmond's devastating homicide rate. But one can equally argue that the U.S. Attorney's Office simply piloted a project whose success catalyzed state processes—not a particularly egregious role for the federal government to play. In the face of a spiraling homicide rate that threatened the very fabric of a hard-pressed community, federal officials, lacking any direct political accountability but still tied to local power structures,[58] simply drew on the strategic reserve that discretionary enforcement has traditionally allowed them to amass.[59] As soon as possible, they shifted responsibility for the program to the state. One can also argue that, regardless of the moral hazard that federal intervention creates for state and local enforcers, the apportioning of federal versus state responsibilities should not be done on the backs of a besieged citizenry (particularly when they are urban residents of a primarily suburban or rural state).

The policy conundrum is not merely one about the federal-state divide, either. Even if one assumes that Project Exile is an appropriate exercise in "cooperative federalism,"[60] it still raises hard questions about federal firearms enforcement policy. Programmatic commitments always have opportunity costs, both in political attention and in enforcement resources. And the politics of Exile have really been about the project's negative implications. The paeans to Exile have not just been to the idea of locking up gun-toting criminals but to the idea that such a strategy should be the primary (even exclusive) federal response to violent crime, as opposed to broader regulatory approaches. Equally important to Exile's loudest champions may be the effect that such programs would have on ATF's ability to enforce existing laws against targets other than street-level criminals. Given ATF's limited resources, the unstated corollary of calls for ATF to expand its focus on street violence is to discourage the agency from targeting gun dealers and pursuing "technical" violations of the firearms laws.

An agency as politically vulnerable as ATF can be quite susceptible to such legislative signals. The elegance of the Project Exile approach for advocates of minimalist gun regulation, however, is that it does not rely simply on legislative fiat or suasion. While Congress often is hard pressed to monitor compliance with its enforcement priorities,[61] Exile provides the perfect monitoring mechanism in the form of state and local authorities, who, because they generate the cases, know whether federal authorities are following through on their commitment to pursue them. With a strong and independent motive to shunt enforcement costs over to the federal government, state officials can be counted on to complain to their local representatives if the feds renege.

This all explains the delicate dance that ATF officials have performed. Positive coverage of agency operations has been all too rare in recent years, and the temptation to bask in favorable coverage from traditionally unsympathetic corners has surely been great. But were Project Exile to be used as a template for nationwide antiviolence programs, the agency's ability to pursue large aspects of what it believes to be its core mission would be severely limited.

The Clinton administration and pro-control legislators shared these concerns. The constant references to "Boston" instead of, or at least in addition to, "Richmond"; the focus on state, not just federal, gun crime prosecutions; the efforts to highlight ATF's gun trafficking prosecutions—the theme running through all of these is that federal firearms enforcement must address supply as well as demand and that ATF must be allowed to strategically use its limited resources, special expertise, and unique national scope to work both sides of the market. The goals have been both to promote ATF's pursuit of supply-side cases and to prevent the wholesale legislative commitment of ATF assets to street-level possession and use cases. And if ATF had to be sad-dled with nationwide Exile-type programs, the agency needed more manpower.

Once one recognizes the likely, and intended, consequences of the Republican efforts to establish Exile nationwide, the question becomes whether this is good firearms policy. Yet, at this crucial juncture in my story I have the least to say. The extent to which such end-use enforce-ment programs should dominate our national antiviolence strategy is of course *the* critical issue in the gun debate—an issue over which the conflict often seems as much over expressive norms[62] as over empiri-cal evidence. And I will restrict myself to the understatement that this is a point on which reasonable minds differ.

IV. Exile Politics and the Control of Federal Enforcement Assets

Not taking a position on the broad firearms policy debate does not preclude one from critiquing the implications of Exile politics for the federal enforcement bureaucracy. On this score, the focus is less on the need for Exile-type programs than on congressional efforts to mandate them.

The story of federal criminal legislation in the twentieth century was one of steady encroachment into areas that once had been the ex-clusive province of state and local enforcers.[63] The pace has only in-creased in recent years, notwithstanding strong criticism by numerous judges and scholars.[64] Yet, while Congress has been quite aggressive in passing statutes that ignore, or even eliminate, traditional enforcement boundaries, legislators have been remarkably passive in dictating the actual terms of interaction between federal enforcers and state and local authorities. The minuscule size of the enforcement bureaucracy relative to the number of crimes that could be charged federally is undoubtedly a reflection of Congress's belief that the primary respon-sibility for fighting crime, particularly street crime, remains with the states. Beyond setting structural parameters, however, Congress has generally let federal enforcers negotiate explicit or tacit understand-ings with their counterparts about divisions of labor. Each element of the federal apparatus has thus played a part in setting the fed-eral agenda. Administrations have had national priorities, with Trig-gerlock being a prime example. But the decentralization of federal prosecutorial authority has given U.S. Attorneys discretion in implementing these priorities and considerable ability to pursue initiatives of their own—like Project Exile.

There are real advantages to letting federal, state, and local enforcers in each district negotiate the boundaries of their interaction without legislative interference. Without the formality of statutes, the modus vivendi within a district can respond to changing local conditions and to the expertise of those on the scene. Turf wars do occur, but, "[g]iven the degree of statutory overlap between the state and federal systems, and the absence of any formal division of authority, [] what is remarkable is not the occurrence of such disputes but their relative infrequency."[65]

Yet, "a system of low-visibility negotiated boundaries diminishes the accountability of the system's actors."[66] State and local officials can circumvent their jurisdictions' evidentiary rules, sentencing provisions, or forfeiture procedures by handing cases over to the feds. Local police can avoid the political controls ordinarily imposed by their need to take cases to locally elected prosecutors. State legislators can avoid being held responsible for the inadequacies of their enactments. U.S. Attorneys, for their part, can gain even more independence from Washington (and thus diminish their political accountability) by relying on state and local enforcers, instead of highly centralized federal enforcement agencies. U.S. Attorneys and their assistants may self-deal by selecting those cases that best further their careers.[67]

How, then, does one strike the appropriate balance between these advantages and disadvantages? Although many, including a majority of the Supreme Court,[68] think otherwise, it is futile to look for some a priori constitutional divide that, for example, puts street crime outside federal bounds. The best we can do is to increase transparency and accountability. These two values are well served by increasing the legislative involvement in line-drawing, encouraging Congress not merely to authorize federal enforcement activity but also to play a bigger role in setting enforcement priorities in this sensitive area. Without taking a position on the wisdom of the particular policies embodied in the Republican proposals to export Project Exile nationwide, one can thus defend them as appropriate congressional involvement in the deployment of federal enforcement assets in areas of traditional state and local authority.[69] On the other hand, the politics of Exile also highlight the institutional costs of extensive legislative involvement in these matters.

Direct political accountability is not an unalloyed good in law enforcement. With primary responsibility for public safety within clear geographically defined bounds, local authorities will often be hard pressed to save up resources for strategic use. Imagine the consequences if a police force stopped patrolling one neighborhood so as to better focus on crime in another. Yet this is precisely what federal enforcers—with the "luxury" of resources so plainly inadequate for addressing every crime on their "beat"—regularly do. At its best, the federal enforcement bureaucracy thus complements state and local systems nicely by providing the strategic reserve that local officials do not ostensibly control (and therefore lack political responsibility for) but that they can draw on when significant investigative (or adjudicative) investments are needed.[70]

The keys to this system, though, are discretionary gatekeeping by federal officials and the delicate balance between local and national federal authority. Against sometimes parochial local needs, a U.S. Attorney must consider broader national priorities, usually conveyed by Main Justice or expressed by the referrals of highly centralized enforcement agencies. One need not subscribe to an administration's particular national priorities to see how the dynamic equilibrium between local and national demands is perhaps the best guarantee that the strategic federal reserve will not quickly be dissipated into the bottomless pit of local needs.

Viewed from this perspective, legislative efforts to implement Exile nationwide—by directly pressuring federal enforcers to adopt such programs and encouraging state authorities to extract commitments from U.S. Attorneys to this end—are a troubling challenge to the notion of the federal government as a strategic resource. In the current political climate, in which politicians at the national level from both parties strive to outdo one another in targeting violence, it is inevitable (however regrettable to the Supreme Court and others) that federal enforcers will take cases that traditionally have fallen within the province of state and local governments. What Exile's fiercest legislative champions would do, however, is to make U.S. Attorneys' Offices the prosecutors of first resort in a broad range of these cases and to do so in a way that would be hard to reverse. As a technical matter, an Office would not be obliged to commit itself to an Exile-type arrangement. But a U.S. Attorney would be hard pressed to resist the calls of local officials for such a program, especially where violence was at a high level and federal grants proffered. Given that a critical source of a U.S. Attorney's autonomy lies in the counterbalance that her ties to local officials and to her district's congressional delegation provides to Washington's authority, the combination of these two forces would be potent.

Once an Exile-type program is in place, need the maximal federal commitment be permanent? Not necessarily. Virginia itself shows the possibility of progress, with the Commonwealth dramatically moving to take more responsibility for gun cases through its "Virginia Exile" program. By the summer of 2000, more than half of Richmond's gun cases over the past year had been prosecuted in state court.[71] But even here, federal withdrawal promised to be difficult, as reports of state inadequacies emerged. The conviction rate for defendants prosecuted under Virginia Exile between July 1, 1999 (when the program became law) and May 31, 2000, was 40 percent, compared to an 80 percent conviction rate for the Exile cases in federal court.[72]

The point is more general. In Richmond, and elsewhere, unilateral federal withdrawal would be hard, even in the absence of the Republicans' proposed Exile legislation. The U.S. Attorney would invariably face the prospect of yet another horrendous shooting that cried out for the same harsh treatment given to previous shootings.[73] Federal enforcers always have to consider the needs (and capabilities) of local enforcers on whose cooperation they must depend in other contexts. And legislators have never been shy about demanding federal cooperation with the state and local authorities in their home districts.[74] But any difficulties that a U.S. Attorney would already face in phasing out an Exile-type program would surely be magnified by intensive congressional supervision of the sort proposed. And the ultimate effect of congressional efforts to institutionalize Exile would be to give state and local authorities a virtual blank check on a range of federal enforcement assets and to shift control of these assets away from Washington.

Perhaps Exile politics will become more muted, under a president and an attorney general who have long championed Exile and can be counted on to promote it as a matter of executive policy. Even so, the real risk is that the congressional proposals will raise the bar for showing legislative outrage at criminal activity in areas of traditional state responsibility. Until now, Congress has spoken almost exclusively in the language of substantive law. Yet, it was understood, and probably intended, that enforcement of these provisions be highly discretionary. Perhaps the gun debate is unique—because regulatory minimalists feel they lack sufficient substantive outlets for expressing their condemnation of gun violence[75]—but the key development in Exile politics is that the language of condemnation has become a promise of maximal federal enforcement. Should legislators, with the encouragement of local officials wanting to shift costs and responsibilities to the federal government,[76] begin to make such promises with the same alacrity that they enacted substantive criminal provisions, they will severely threaten the continued vitality of federal criminal institutions.

V. Conclusion

The political saga of Project Exile may not make for a particularly significant chapter in the long gun control debate. The atmospherics may be a little different, but the story is the usual one: Gun control minimalists support offender-specific criminal enforcement as an alternative to broader regulation of trafficking and access. And advocates of broader regulation embrace such enforcement programs as well, both as a shield against minimalist criticism and because their regulatory scheme naturally includes this sort of criminal enforcement.

As a milestone in the accelerated devolution of centralized federal criminal enforcement power, the saga of Exile may prove quite important, though. Only time will tell whether Exile politics are just a peculiar brand of gun control rhetoric or whether they mark an new phase in efforts of legislators to put federal enforcement resources at the disposal of state and local authorities. If the latter proves true, then the legacy of Project Exile—itself an innovative federal initiative—may be a serious challenge to the idea of federal enforcement policy in the areas where federal, state, and local authority most overlap.

For nearly half a century, policymakers, courts, and academics have asked what role the federal government should play in criminal enforcement. To what extent should federal enforcers be supporting state and local authorities, as opposed to vindicating peculiarly federal interests or operating in areas where they have a comparative advantage? The politics of Exile are a reminder that for a great many policymakers, the answers to these broad allocation questions are often, and perhaps inevitably, driven more by preferences about which laws should be enforced (and to what degree) than by considerations of who should do the enforcing. However, while legislators may seek to deploy firearms enforcement resources on the basis of their conceptions of what gun control policy ought to be, their decisions may have lasting implications for federal criminal enforcement more generally.

Afterword

This essay was written before September 11, 2001. But Project Exile has been remarkably resilient (in all but its name). Indeed, recent milestones have more to do with the 2000 election than with any change in enforcement priorities.

- On May 14, 2001, President George W. Bush and Attorney General John Ashcroft announced "Project Safe Neighborhoods." All new U.S. Attorneys were asked to "work in partnership with federal, state and local authorities to create an aggressive attack on gun violence, seeking the most punitive remedies for each gun crime." In 2001, "113 new federal prosecutors [would] be dedicated to prosecute illegal gun use," with $75 million in grants to hire and train approximately 600 nonfederal gun prosecutors.[77]
- On November 30, 2001, President Bush nominated Assistant U.S. Attorney James B. Comey, the principal architect of Project Exile in Richmond, to be United States Attorney for the Southern District of New York.[78]
- On January 23, 2002, Attorney General Ashcroft announced that another 94 Assistant U.S. Attorneys would be hired to combat gun crime as part of Project Safe Neighborhoods, and state and local prosecutors' offices would get $70 million in grants.[79]
- On March 20, 2002, Representative John Conyers Jr. (D-Mich), the ranking Democrat on the House Judiciary Committee, introduced the Gun Show Background Check Act of 2002 and chided colleagues for "unwisely plac[ing] a great emphasis on enforcement programs such as 'Project Exile.'"[80]

NOTES

1. This chapter has been adapted from a piece in the *Arizona Law Review,* Vol. 43 (summer 2001): 369–411.

2. Review of Dep't. of Justice Firearm Prosecutions, *Hearing before the Subcomm. on Criminal Justice Oversight and the Subcomm. on Youth Violence, Senate Judiciary Comm.,* 106th Cong. 201 (1999) [hereinafter *Firearm Prosecutions*], at 36 (statement of Helen F. Fahey).

3. See Radio Address of the President to the Nation (Gun Violence) (Mar. 20, 1999); *Hearing before the Committee on the Judiciary United States Senate Concerning Justice Department Oversight* (May 5, 1999) (statement of Attorney General Janet Reno)

4. R. H. Melton, "Bush Favors Va.-Style Gun Control; Candidate Has National Hopes for Program Penalizing Felons," *Wash. Post,* June 23, 1999, at A8.

5. "Exchanges between the Candidates in the Third Presidential Debate," *N.Y. Times,* Oct. 18, 2000, at A26.

6. See Charlton Heston, Congressional Testimony on Project Exile, House Government Reform Subcomm. (Nov. 4, 1999), available at: http://www .nraila.org/news/19991104-CrimeControlJustice-002.html; see also *Hearing before the House Judiciary Comm. Subcomm. on Crime, Testimony of Wayne R. LaPierre, NRA Executive Vice-President* (May 27, 1999), available at: http:// www.house.gov/judiciary/lapierre.html (noting NRA's support for Project Exile—"the fierce prosecution of federal gun laws that has cut crime rates overnight in the few places it's been tried").

7. See *Firearms Prosecutions,* supra note 1, at 43.

8. See Osha Gray Davidson, *Under Fire: The NRA and the Battle for Gun Control* (Iowa City: University of Iowa Press, 1998), 247.

9. Tracy Thompson, "Gun Crimes Targeted by Prosecutors: National Effort Seen as Partly Political," *Wash. Post,* Apr. 11, 1991, at A14.

10. "Thornburgh Orders Drive on Gun Violence," *N.Y. Times,* Mar. 27, 1991, at A20.

11. See James A. Baker III, "Crime, Promises—Had Enough?" *Houston Chron.,* Mar. 6, 1994, at Outlook 1; Joyce Price, "2 Faces of Gun Control at Justice? Congressman Says It Isn't Enforcing Key Anti-Crime Law," *Wash. Times,* May 21, 1994, at A5.

12. See Prosecution of Federal Gun Crimes, Hearing Before the Subcomm. on Crime and Criminal Justice of the House Judiciary Comm., 103rd Cong., 2nd Sess. 4 (1994) [hereinafter *Prosecution of Federal Gun Crimes*]; see also 1994 *Annual Report of the Attorney General of the United States* 5–6.

13. Ibid.

14. Ibid., at 47–48.

15. See James Eisenstein, *Counsel for the United States: U.S. Attorneys in the*

Political and Legal Systems (Baltimore: Johns Hopkins University Press, 1978), 116–17.

16. See Daniel C. Richman, "Federal Criminal Law, Congressional Delegation, and Enforcement Discretion," *University of California, Los Angeles Law Review* 46 (Feb. 1999): 757, 781, 785.

17. See William J. Vizzard, *In the Cross Fire: A Political History of the Bureau of Alcohol, Tobacco and Firearms* (Boulder: Lynne Rienner, 1997), 89; William A. Geller and Norval Morris, "Relations between Federal and Local Police," in *Modern Policing,* ed. Michael Tonry and Norval Morris, vol. 15 of *Crime and Justice: A Review of Research* (Chicago: University of Chicago Press, 1992), 231, 247 n.8; Richman, supra note 16, at 796.

18. *Firearm Prosecutions,* supra note 1, at 5. James Comey, Managing Assistant U.S. Attorney and Chief Criminal Supervisor in Richmond—the "chief midwife" of Exile—described Exile as "Triggerlock on steroids." Get Out of Town!: Richmond's Project Exile Stems a Spiral of Violence with Its Focus on Gun-Toting Felons," *Law Enforcement News,* Dec. 15/31, 1999.

19. *See Firearm Prosecutions,* supra note 1, at 38 (statement of Helen F. Fahey).

20. Determining the degree to which any drop in crime can fairly be attributed to policing tactics is frightfully difficult. See, e.g., Jeffrey Fagan et al., "Declining Homicide in New York City: A Tale of Two Trends," *Journal of Criminal Law and Criminology* 88 (summer 1998): 1277. This essay thus makes no such empirical claims about Exile.

21. See Tom Campbell, "An 'Exile' for Firearms? Some Gun-Toting Criminals Face Federal Prosecution," *Richmond Times Dispatch,* July 7, 1997, at A1.

22. See ibid. at 14; see also Michael Janofsky, "Fighting Crime by Making a Federal Case about Guns," *N.Y. Times,* Feb. 10, 1999, at A12.

23. R. H. Melton, "Richmond Gun Project Praised: NRA Brady Group Laud Automatic Sentences for Armed Felons," *Wash. Post,* June 18, 1998, at A13.

24. See David S. Cloud, "Prosecutor's Strategy Scrambles Gun-Control Alliances," *Wall Street Journal,* Aug. 31, 1998, at 20 (reprinted in *Firearm Prosecutions,* supra note 1, at 71–73).

25. Michael Janofsky, supra note 22, at A12; Gary Fields, "City Makes Federal Cases of Gun Crimes," *USA Today,* Feb. 1, 1999, at A4; Chitra Ragavan, "A New Gun Plan Triggers a War between the Feds and the NRA," *U.S. News and World Report,* Mar. 1, 1999, at 18.

26. Radio Address of the President to the Nation (Gun Violence) (Mar. 20, 1999).

27. See *Firearm Prosecutions,* supra note 1, at 2–4.

28. Ibid. at 14 (written statement of Andrew L. Vita).

29. See Katharine Q. Seelye, "Terror in Littleton: The President's Plea; Clin-

ton Asks Hunters to Back His Proposals Curbing Guns," *N.Y. Times*, Apr. 28, 1999, at A26.

30. See S. 254, 106th Cong., 1st Sess. (passed May 20, 1999); Alison Mitchell, "Guns and Schools: The Politics; Democrats Gain Ground, an Inch, on Gun Control," *N.Y. Times*, May 21, 1999, at A23.

31. S. 254, 106th Cong., 1st Sess., tit. VIII, subtit. A (1999).

32. See ibid. § 803(d). The programs were to be established in: (1) the ten jurisdictions with a population equal to or greater than 100,000 persons that had the highest total number of violent crimes according to the FBI Uniform Crime Report for 1998; (2) the fifteen jurisdictions with such a population, other than the jurisdictions covered by paragraph (1), with the highest per capita rate of violent crime according to the FBI Uniform Crime Report for 1998. Ibid.

33. Hearing on Project Exile before the Subcommittee on Crime, House Judiciary Comm. (visited June 2, 2000) at: http:www.house.gov/judiciary/mcco0527.htm (statement of Rep. Bill McCollum).

34. Hearing before the Subcomm. on Crime, House Judiciary Comm., 106th Cong. 3 (May 27, 1999) (joint statement of Deputy Attorney General Eric H. Holder Jr. and Treasury Undersecretary for Enforcement James E. Johnson) (emphasis added).

35. Ibid. at 23–24.

36. Melton, supra note 4, at A8.

37. Melinda Henneberger, "Gore Unveils Crime-Fighting Plan, from Right and Left," *N.Y. Times*, July 13, 1999, at A10.

38. Remarks by the President at Announcement of National Gun Enforcement Initiative, (Jan. 18, 2000).

39. 106 H.R. 4051, 106th Cong. (Mar. 22, 2000).

40. Ibid.

41. Project Exile: The Safe Streets and Neighborhoods Act of 2000: Hearings on H.R. 4051 before the Subcomm. on Crime of the House Comm. on the Judiciary, 106th Cong. 41–73 (2000) (statement of Hon. James S. Gilmore III, Governor of Virginia).

42. See ibid.

43. See ibid. at 152–56 (statement of Michael T. McCaul).

44. Ibid. at 74–125 (statement of Walter Holton Jr., U.S. Attorney for the Middle District of North Carolina).

45. Act for Effective National Firearms Objectives for Responsible, Common-Sense Enforcement of 2000, 106 H.R. 4066 (2000).

46. See Sean Scully, "House Passes Bill Getting Tough on Guns; Measure Urges Mandatory Terms for Related Crimes," *Wash. Times*, Apr. 12, 2000, at A1.

47. See Sen. Jeff Sessions, "Guns: What Works, What Doesn't," *Wash. Times*, May 15, 2000, at A16.

48. H.R. 4456, 106th Cong., 2d Sess. (2000).

49. 146 Congressional Record H5017 (June 22, 2000) (statement of Rep. Carolyn McCarthy [D-NY]).

50. Remarks by the President on Prescription Drug Benefit (June 14, 2000).

51. See Consolidated Appropriation Act, 2001, Pub. L. 106-554, 114 Stat. 2763 (Dec. 21, 2000); *The White House: President Clinton: Expanding the Circle of Opportunity—Enacting a Budget That Invests in Education, Health Care, and America's New Markets* (Washington, D.C.: White House Press Office, Dec. 28, 2000).

52. See Time Bryant, "Ashcroft Would Boost Efforts Here to Fight Illegal Guns," *St. Louis Post-Dispatch,* Mar. 4, 2000, at 8 (reporting that Ashcroft "says more federal prosecutors are needed in St. Louis to convict and imprison those who use guns illegally"); Steve Kraske, "Senate Rivalry Deepens: Issue of Crime Comes to Forefront in Missouri Contest," *Kansas City Star,* July 5, 2000, at A1 (following criticism by his opponent in the Senate election for consistently opposing gun control measures, Ashcroft maintained that he had "zero tolerance" for gun violence and supported Project Exile).

53. At his confirmation hearing, Ashcroft noted: "I think the context of the gun purchase requirements are very important. And in a technical sense, those are against the law and they are criminal acts. But people who actually perpetrate crimes using guns obviously need to be a focus of our enforcement effort. And the most famous of these is the Project Exile—at least best known for me." Day II, Morning Session of a Hearing of the Senate Judiciary Committee: Nomination for Attorney General; Witness, John Ashcroft, at 35, available in LEXIS, Federal News Service file; see also Michael J. Sniffen, *John Ashcroft Blasts Clinton, Salon* (Feb. 8, 2001), available at: http://www.salon.com/politics/wire/2001/02/08/ashcroft/index.html (reporting that, in his first interview as attorney general, Ashcroft said he "wanted to expand a federal antigun effort used in Virginia known as Project Exile").

54. See Bob Kemper, "Bush Launches Strategy to Combat Gun Violence; Plan Would Push Prosecutions into the Federal Courts," *Chicago Tribune,* May 15, 2001, at 7 ("Taking a local Virginia gun-control program and expanding it into a national strategy to combat violence, President Bush on Monday pledged to spend more than $550 million over the next two years to prosecute local gun crimes in federal court.").

55. The breadth of the felon-in-possession statute could make for some sympathetic cases, however. See Daniel C. Richman, "*Old Chief v. United States*: Stipulating Away Prosecutorial Accountability?" *Virginia Law Review* 83 (Aug. 1997) 939, 953 n.50.

56. See Kathleen F. Brickey, "Criminal Mischief: The Federalization of American Criminal Law," *Hasting Law Journal* 46 (Apr. 1995) 1135; Daniel C. Richman, "The Changing Boundaries between Federal and Local Law En-

forcement," in *Boundary Changes in Criminal Justice Organizations, 2 Criminal Justice 2000* (Washington, D.C.: National Institute of Justice, 2000), 96–99.

57. See *New York v. United States*, 505 U.S. 144, 169 (1992) (noting that accountability diminishes when citizens cannot easily determine which level of government is responsible for a particular regulatory decision); see also Barry Friedman, "Valuing Federalism," *Minnesota Law Review* 82 (Dec. 1997): 317, 394–97 (1997); Richman, supra note 16, at 783–84; Ben Tinsley, "Program Punishes Firearms Offenders; Prosecutor Set on Getting Criminals More Jail Time," *Dallas Morning News*, Nov. 23, 2000, at A1 (commenting on Exile, a Wise County, Texas, district attorney noted: "Your state government is hiring prosecutors to take cases away from the local elected district attorneys and route them to the federal prosecutors and federal judges who do not answer to the voters. This should scare you to death.").

58. See Richman, supra note 16, at 785.

59. See Elizabeth Glazer, "Thinking Strategically: How Federal Prosecutors Can Reduce Violent Crime," *Fordham Urban Law Journal* 26 (Mar. 1999): 573.

60. See Daniel A. Braun, "Praying to False Sovereigns: The Rule Permitting Successive Prosecutions in the Age of Cooperative Federalism," *American Journal of Criminal Law* 20 (fall 1992): 1.

61. See Jonathan R. Macey, "Separated Powers and Positive Political Theory: The Tug of War over Administrative Agencies," 80 *Georgetown Law Journal* (Feb. 1992): 671, 671–72; see Richman, supra note 16, at 776–78.

62. See Dan M. Kahan, "The Secret Ambition of Deterrence," *Harvard Law Review* 113 (Dec. 1999): 413, 451–62.

63. See Richman, supra note 58, at 83–91.

64. See ibid., at 89–91.

65. Ibid. at 96.

66. Ibid. at 97; see also John S. Baker Jr., "State Police Powers and the Federalization of Local Crime," *Temple Law Review* 72 (fall 1999): 673, 702–7.

67. See Richman, supra note 58, at 102.

68. See *United States v. Morrison*, 120 S. Ct. 1740 (2000) (invalidating the Violence against Women Act's tort remedy); *United States v. Lopez*, 514 U.S. 549 (1995) (invalidating the Gun Free School Zones Act of 1990).

69. See Richman, supra note 58, at 101–3.

70. Explaining the appeal of Exile, Erie County (N.Y.) District Attorney Frank J. Clark (a former federal prosecutor) noted: "'It gives us more flexibility. . . . It brings in the FBI, ATF, more resources. . . . Let's face it . . . [t]he feds need the grist for the mill. We're the grist. They need the street-level crimes. They provide the resources, the extra jurisdiction.'" Michael Beebe, "Going after Guns; Project Exile Aims to Take Criminals Off the Streets," *Buffalo News*, Sept. 18, 1999, at A1.

71. Frank Main, "Virginia Gun Program Cuts Street Violence," *Chicago Sun-Times,* July 30, 2000, at 32. In May 2000, South Carolina's attorney general called for "Palmetto Exile" and proposed legislation providing for harsh mandatory penalties for gun possession offenses. See Pat Willis, "Official Touts Benefits of Gun Program; Attorney General Says Palmetto Exile Would Be Effective in Locking Up Criminals Who Carry Firearms," *Augusta (Ga.) Chronicle,* May 12, 2000, at C2.

72. Tom Campbell and Gordon Hickey, "Va. Exile Program Falls Short of Intent; Prosecutor Laments 40% Conviction Rate," *Richmond Times Dispatch,* Aug. 7, 2000, at A1; see also Arlo Wagner, "Get-Tough Program Lowers Richmond Homicide Rate; But Conviction Figures Are 'Very Bad'; Official Says Evidence Often Is Lacking," *Wash. Times,* Aug. 9, 2000, at C1.

73. See, e.g., Brett Lovelace, "U.S. Attorney Won't Prosecute Shootout Suspect," *Intelligencer Journal* (Lancaster, Pa.), June 29, 2000, at A1.

74. Richman, supra note 16, at 785.

75. But see Sean Scully, "Casualties Feared as Clinton, NRA Spar; GOP Lawmakers Avoid Skirmish," *Wash. Times,* Mar. 15, 2000, at A1 (noting Republican leaders' support for "measures aimed at combating violence in the culture, including authorizing a federal study of media violence and allowing states to post the Ten Commandments in public buildings, such as schools").

76. See Aaron Chambers, "Lawmakers Eye Fed Muscle on Gun Crimes," *Chicago Daily Law Bulletin,* Nov. 13, 2000, at 1 (urging state legislators to adopt measures requiring the state police to encourage federal prosecutions, one Republican legislator noted "that Project Exile should not cost the state any money because Congress was supposed to provide grants for Illinois and other states to fund the projects").

77. Press release, Department of Justice, President Bush and Attorney General Ashcroft Announce Project Safe Neighborhoods, May 14, 2001.

78. Benjamin Weiser, "Bush Picks Virginia Prosecutor for U.S. Attorney," *N.Y. Times,* Dec. 1, 2001, at D3.

79. Press release, Project Safe Neighborhoods, Office of Justice Programs, U.S. Dep't. of Justice, Justice Department Provides $70 Million in Funds to Promote Gun Violence Prosecution, Jan. 23, 2002.

80. Press release, Congressman John Conyers Jr., Conyers Introduces the "Gun Show Background Check Act of 2002," Mar. 20, 2002.

Chapter 15

The Unintended Consequences of Enhancing Gun Penalties

Sara Sun Beale

To deter gun violence and punish gun offenders, Congress—like state legislatures—has repeatedly increased the penalties for illegal gun possession and the use of guns in the commission of other crimes. After several rounds of statutory increases, the penalties are now much higher than penalties for criminal conduct that accompanies gun possession and also very high relative to penalties for other serious offenses. By designating separate penalties for gun use that are as high as or higher than the penalties for many of the most serious traditional offenses, Congress has sent a deterrent message to would-be offenders (and sought to incapacitate those who would not be deterred). Whether this message has been successful in altering the behavior of those who might otherwise commit gun offenses is an empirical question that other researchers are attempting to answer.[1]

Although Congress intended to incapacitate or alter the behavior of would-be criminals, it has created behavior-altering incentives for other actors in the criminal justice system, as well. This essay explores how the legislative attempts to crack down on gun violence have affected the behavior of judges and prosecutors and what legal issues, outcomes, and concerns these attempts have generated.

In this essay, I explore how the pressure to enhance gun penalties has affected the boundary between federal and state law, raising both constitutional and prudential issues. This pressure was a critical factor leading to a historic ruling that limited the scope of federal jurisdiction under the Commerce Clause, as the Supreme Court responded to potential institutional damage to the federal courts. At the

344 SARA SUN BEALE

administrative (or prosecutorial) level, there has been pressure on the definition of the offenses in question, as federal prosecutors have sought to construe these firearms statutes broadly to secure enhanced sentences in a wider range of cases. As the example of Richmond's Project Exile reveals, these pressures also have the potential to reshape the character of federal law enforcement.

The pressure on the boundary between federal and state law is important, but it is not the only consequence of federal efforts to increase gun penalties. As I have argued elsewhere,[2] gun-related penalties have also placed pressure on a different boundary, the line defining the elements of an offense. Prosecutors have pressed vigorously for expansive interpretations of the elements of the most commonly prosecuted federal firearm offense, the felon-in-possession statute, to expand the range of cases in which the enhanced penalties may be imposed. In an unusual volume of litigation, prosecutors have successfully expanded the effective scope of the statute. A review of prosecutorial practices also reveals an apparently conflicting trend: Federal prosecutors bargain away or decline to bring charges under the enhanced penalties in the majority of cases. Thus, enhancing the penalties available under federal law and expanding the range of cases to which those penalties apply also has enhanced the prosecution's bargaining power and its unchecked discretion in a wide range of cases.

I. Pressure on the Boundary between Federal and State Law

One of the most obvious boundary lines affected by the pressure to increase the punishment for gun crimes is the boundary that separates federal and state criminal law. The general police power is reserved to the states; both constitutional design and tradition have narrowly limited the scope of federal criminal law. Local crime has traditionally been regarded as the province of the states, and federal criminal jurisdiction has been the exception, rather than the rule. In the last third of the twentieth century, however, a plethora of new federal criminal statutes strained the general principle of leaving local crime to state prosecution. Some of the most significant statutes that extend the scope of federal criminal jurisdiction involve firearms offenses—and some legislative proposals would expand jurisdiction even further. These new laws, which make federal crimes of conduct already illegal under state law, have generally been intended to impose harsher penalties than those currently available under state law.

Section A begins by describing the legislative initiatives. Since 1968, Congress has pressed the policy and the constitutional limits of federal jurisdiction in efforts to extend federal firearms provisions to a broader range of violent crime under the Commerce Clause. The Supreme Court has responded to these legislative changes and has repeatedly read federal firearms legislation narrowly, thereby reducing its scope and impact. More important, the Court also issued its most important Commerce Clause opinion in fifty years in a federal firearms case.

Although each of these decisions may be explained on other grounds, together they suggest an institutional response by the Court to the threat that federalizing gun-related crime could swamp the federal courts and alter their fundamental character.

As discussed in Section B, federal prosecutors also have pushed the envelope by interpreting the firearms statutes expansively and by using their charging discretion to accommodate a larger number of firearms cases. Both legislative and executive activity directed at enhancing the sentences for gun offenders have expanded—and arguably distorted—the traditional territory of federal criminal law.

A. Legislative Initiatives and Judicial Responses

The modern era of federal firearms legislation began in 1968 after the assassinations of Robert Kennedy and Martin Luther King Jr. That year, Congress expansively employed its authority under the Commerce Clause to reach a wide range of gun-related crime. For present purposes, the most important provision of the 1968 legislation made it a federal crime for a previously convicted felon to possess a firearm.[3] The Department of Justice interpreted the statute as extending federal jurisdiction to any felon who possessed a firearm—with no required showing of any connection to interstate commerce or other basis for federal jurisdiction—and the lower courts accepted this interpretation.[4] So interpreted, the federal felon-in-possession statute and the loan-sharking statute[5] were the first federal criminal statutes to employ the class-of-activities model to assert criminal jurisdiction under the Commerce Clause. In a pair of decisions in 1971, the Supreme Court upheld the class-of-activities approach in the loan-sharking

statute,[6] but it finessed the issue in a case involving the felon-in-possession statute. Noting that the lower courts' interpretation of the
felon-in-possession statute would work a major change in the boundary between federal and state law, the Supreme Court sidestepped the
constitutional and policy issues posed by this expansive reading of the
statute. Finding the statutory language and the legislative history ambiguous, the Supreme Court applied the rule of lenity and declined to
"assume that Congress meant to effect a significant change in the sensitive relation between federal and state criminal jurisdiction."[7] The
1968 legislation thus illustrates either Congress's willingness to press
its authority under the Commerce Clause to reach felons who possess
firearms or the Justice Department's zeal to interpret an ambiguous
statute in these terms.

The Supreme Court's interpretation of the 1968 legislation typifies
its response to many of the federal firearms statutes. Despite the
Court's strong law-and-order orientation in the past twenty-five years,
it has interpreted the various federal firearms statutes to restrict their
scope and impact.[8]

More recently, Congress authorized federal criminal jurisdiction
over another class of activities—gun possession in a school zone—
pursuant to its power to regulate interstate commerce. The Gun-Free
School Zones Act of 1990 made it a federal offense "for any individual
knowingly to possess a firearm at a place that the individual knows,
or has reason to believe, is a school zone."[9] The Supreme Court's decision in *United States v. Lopez*[10] was the first Commerce Clause decision
in more than half a century to strike down a federal statute. *Lopez* sent
a shock wave through both the judiciary and the academy and set off
a wave of litigation challenging a wide variety of other federal criminal statutes on constitutional grounds. At first it appeared that *Lopez*
might be a derelict on the waters of the law, as the lower courts generally read the Supreme Court's decision narrowly and upheld the challenged laws. But five years later the Supreme Court, following *Lopez*,
struck down a key provision of the Violence against Women Act
(VAWA) in *United States v. Morrison*.[11] *Lopez* and *Morrison* provide a
doctrine with which the Supreme Court can prune back federal criminal jurisdiction, particularly in cases involving conduct the Court
deems noneconomic.

In light of Congress's efforts to saddle the federal courts with many
new criminal cases, positive political theory[12] provides a convincing

explanation for a series of Supreme Court decisions that culminated in *Lopez* and *Morrison.* From the viewpoint of positive political theory, the Supreme Court can be understood as a rational, self-interested actor interacting with the other branches of government.[13] Indeed, prior to the decision in *Lopez,* scholars tracking the Supreme Court's interpretation of various federal statutes identified two criminal cases that departed from the Court's normal rules of statutory interpretation and interpreted these decisions as signal of the Court's displeasure with the expansion of federal criminal jurisdiction. Writing one year before *Lopez,* they summed up the Court's response to the increasing federalization of crime:

> In this area, the Court and Congress are at loggerheads, and the Court may feel that it must communicate its concern to Congress clearly. . . . [I]n this area the Court is an active opponent of Congress and seems to be throwing up what roadblocks it can. In addition, because there are few interest groups to derail feel-good, do-something federal crime bills, the Court may sense that it alone is left to confront Congress.[14]

The federal courts had a second institutional interest at stake when Congress sought to enlarge the scope of federal criminal jurisdiction: status and dignity. These dignity concerns caused the federal judiciary to distinguish sharply between the cases of national import that should be heard in the federal courts and the ordinary street crimes historically prosecuted in the state courts.

Workload and dignity concerns combined in claims that the federal courts would become police courts. Use of the term "police court" raised the specter of high-volume urban courts where vast numbers of cases are processed in an assembly-line fashion reminiscent of traffic court.[15] Thus, dignity concerns, intertwined with workload concerns, gave the Supreme Court an institutional interest in opposing congressional federalization of crime, particularly low-status, high-volume crimes.

These concerns came to a head in 1994 when Congress came within a hair's breadth of adopting a proposal to expand federal jurisdiction over gun-related crime to unprecedented levels. In the early 1990s, Senator Alfonse D'Amato proposed making every crime committed with a gun that had crossed state lines a federal offense.[16] This proposal would have extended federal jurisdiction to nearly every one of the 900,000 gun offenses that occur each year in the United States, dwarfing the current federal criminal caseload of fewer than 50,000 cases. Senator D'Amato also proposed legislation that would have made it a federal crime punishable by death to commit a murder with a handgun that had traveled in interstate or foreign commerce.[17] In 1994, it appeared these provisions would become law. They were approved by both houses but were not included in the conference bill that became law.[18]

The federal judiciary vigorously opposed Senator D'Amato's proposals. In 1991, Chief Justice William Rehnquist wrote to Congress to express the Judicial Conference's opposition. The Chief Justice also highlighted his opposition in his 1991 report on the federal courts, arguing that to federalize these crimes would be contrary to fundamental concepts of federalism, would swamp federal prosecutors, and would ensure that the already overburdened federal courts could not provide a timely forum for civil cases.[19] The Chief Justice made similar comments in various public statements throughout the period that the D'Amato proposals were under consideration in Congress.[20] Other justices who testified before Congress in 1994 also expressed concern that the D'Amato proposals and the extension of federal jurisdiction would incapacitate the federal courts or turn them into "police courts."[21] The Administrative Office of the U.S. Courts, which opposed the D'Amato proposals, estimated that their enactment would generate 200,000 new cases in the federal system.[22]

Since majorities in both houses appeared to support the D'Amato proposals when *Lopez* was decided, the Supreme Court could anticipate that similar proposals would be introduced in the future with a good chance of enactment. From the Court's perspective, these proposals threatened to overload the federal courts and undermine their prestige. Although the efforts to expand federal jurisdiction over gun-related crime were not the only factor, they played a significant and critical role in motivating the Court to announce the first modern judicial limitations on federal authority under the Commerce Clause.

The Chief Justice's opposition to the D'Amato proposals was a harbinger of his opinion for the Court in *Lopez*,[23] as well as of his later opinion in *Morrison*.[24] Writing for the *Lopez* majority, the Chief Justice emphasized the need to keep the traditional balance between federal and state law, "between what is truly national and what is truly

The Unintended Consequences of Enhancing Gun Penalties 349

local."[25] The majority declined to follow a chain of attenuated effects on commerce that would allow Congress to regulate "all violent crime," as well as "activities that might lead to violent crime."[26] The Chief Justice returned to this theme in *Morrison*, in which it followed and extended *Lopez* to hold that the civil provisions of VAWA exceeded Congress's power under the Commerce Clause (and under the Fourteenth Amendment).[27] *Morrison* was not a firearms case, but the domestic violence focus of VAWA (often associated with low-status family and police courts) triggered the same institutional response that motivated the *Lopez* decision. The Chief Justice's opinion in *Morrison* emphasized that VAWA as a whole was an attempt to encroach on the traditional power of the states to regulate criminal conduct under their police powers. Speaking for the Court, Rehnquist wrote that there is "no better example of the police power, which the Founders denied the National Government and reposed in the States, than the suppression of violent crime and vindication of its victims."[28]

In *Lopez* and *Morrison*, the Rehnquist-led majority served notice that the federal courts cannot be transformed into police courts. From the viewpoint of positive political theory, *Lopez* and *Morrison* reshaped Commerce Clause doctrine to protect the traditional role of the federal courts from the irreparable damage that could be inflicted by "feel-good do-something federal crime bills."[29] Because gun-related crime makes up such a large portion of the state courts' caseload, a proposal to federalize a broadly defined class of crimes involving firearms would necessarily work a radical change in the federal courts. Such change would occur by either crowding out traditional federal court cases in favor of low-status police court cases or requiring an enlargement of the courts that might hamper their effectiveness and lower their prestige. Similar institutional interests were also present in *Morrison*. The subject matter of VAWA was a form of extremely common criminal activity associated with the low-status family courts or criminal courts. Indeed, the Judicial Conference and the Chief Justice had publicly opposed the provisions later struck down in *Morrison* on the ground that they "could involve the federal courts in a whole host of domestic relations disputes."[30]

Pressure from gun cases was not, of course, the only factor motivating the *Lopez* and *Morrison* decisions. These cases are also part of a broader effort by the Court's majority to restrict federal power in favor of state authority, as reflected in decisions limiting federal authority to subject states to suit in federal court or commandeer state officials.[31] But the Rehnquist majority's institutional concerns regarding the federalization of certain kinds of criminal cases explains the timing of the Court's first effort in half a century to limit the commerce power, the choice of the two cases in which those limitations were announced, and the limited application of those decisions. It makes sense of the Court's failure to follow *Lopez* in cases that do not raise the same concerns, including civil cases and criminal cases that fall within more traditional conceptions of federal criminal jurisdiction. For example, less than a week after the *Lopez* decision, the Court declined an opportunity to develop the themes initiated in that opinion. In *United States v. Robertson,* the Ninth Circuit had ruled that a small gold mine in Alaska lacked sufficient effect on commerce to support jurisdiction under the Racketeer Influenced and Corrupt Organizations Act (RICO).[32] The Court granted certiorari on the question of the necessary degree of effect on commerce but finessed this issue in a brief per curiam opinion holding that it was unnecessary to define the scope of the required effect on commerce because the gold mine was operating in interstate (as opposed to intrastate) commerce.[33]

Positive political theory provides a ready explanation for the Court's quite different response to this organized crime case decided just one week after *Lopez*, a garden-variety gun case. Organized crime prosecutions fall within the traditional conception of the distinctive federal role in law enforcement, and RICO has never generated a large number of criminal prosecutions. High-profile, complex organized crime prosecutions do not have the feel of police court cases.

Two interconnected questions arise in regard to the Court's resistance to expanding federal criminal jurisdiction. First, why does the self-interest of the Supreme Court—as opposed to the lower federal courts—favor reducing the volume of federal criminal litigation? An increased number of cases might overburden the lower federal courts and reduce the prestige of judgeships on those courts, but the Supreme Court has virtually unlimited authority to determine the size of its caseload. Whatever the impact on the lower courts, the Supreme Court cannot be overburdened by an expansion of federal criminal (or civil) jurisdiction. Nonetheless, as illustrated by their reaction to the D'Amato proposals, the Justices (and particularly the Chief Justice) have adopted the perspective of the federal courts as a whole, rather than that of the Supreme Court.

The second question is why, in favoring its own institutional interests and prestige, the Court does not seek to expand the caseload of the federal judiciary? In general, institutional actors seek to expand their authority, or turf.

Two possible explanations have occurred to me, one based on prestige and one on policy preferences. One form of prestige involves not extending turf but rather remaining small and exclusive. An increased number of cases might overburden the lower federal courts and reduce the prestige of judgeships on those courts. Although the Supreme Court has virtually unlimited authority to determine the size of its docket, the Supreme Court may have adopted exclusivity over expansive jurisdiction in part because of the Chief Justice's role as the head of the Judicial Conference. In this position, the Chief Justice presents to Congress the views of the federal judiciary as a whole, rather than the views of the Supreme Court. Since lower federal court judges make up the Judicial Conference, the Chief Justice is heavily influenced by their experiences and preferences. To the extent that the Chief Justice played a dominant role in *Lopez* and *Morrison*—in which he wrote both opinions—his role as head of the Judicial Conference might have been quite significant.

Perhaps more important, the institutional perspective of each branch coexists with individuals' policy preferences. As manifested in many other cases, the Justices who made up the majority in *Lopez* and *Morrison* prefer to restrict the size and influence of the federal government in favor of the states. Some or all of these Justices also may have little sympathy for the groups seeking redress under VAWA,[34] or they may oppose federal regulation of firearms.[35] Individual Justices' policy preferences would likely make them receptive to concerns of overburdening the lower courts and diluting their elite role.

Positive political theory also raises the question whether there should be additional restraints on the courts' self-interested actions. The Chief Justice's opposition to the D'Amato proposals was not an isolated occurrence. The Judicial Conference has become increasingly involved in lobbying Congress in favor of institutional recommendations about the scope of the federal courts' jurisdiction.[36] These institutional recommendations inevitably involve not only caseload considerations but also policy judgments about competing groups that seek access to the federal courts. The norms advocated by the Judicial Conference can become background assumptions that can shape the adjudication of cases, determining the rights of the groups in question.[37] Positive political theory reinforces concerns about the motives of the Judicial Conference and could support restrictions on the judiciary's role in lobbying regarding the scope of federal jurisdiction.

Separation of powers concerns, on the other hand, support self-interested judicial rulings (and perhaps even judicial lobbying), particularly when the political branches adopt policies that can seriously damage the courts and the public interest. The institutional roles of both prosecutors and legislators drive them to continually expand the criminal law, increasing the number and breadth of offenses, as well as the penalties.[38] Action is more politically popular than inaction, and at the federal level most anticrime legislation creates new federal offenses or provides new federal resources to prosecute federal offenses. This institutional design leaves the courts with relatively little ability to check the one-way ratchet wielded by the other branches.[39] Other research suggests that the media's focus on crime also creates strong public and political pressures in favor of ever-expanding criminal liability.[40]

If these accounts of the political economy of criminal law are correct, they argue for allowing the courts some leeway to enter the political arena. They certainly provide a reason to allow courts to consider institutional self-interest as a factor in their constitutional analysis. Indeed, the fundamental insight of positive political theory—that each branch acts in ways consistent with its institutional self-interest—is a fundamental tenet of the theory of separation of powers as espoused by the Founders. As *Federalist* No. 51 explains, the purpose of the division of powers among the executive, legislative, and judicial branches is for the branches to "be the means of keeping each other in their proper places."[41] The constitutional structure was premised upon the idea that each branch would be self-interested: "Ambition must be made to counteract ambition."[42] Thus, it is entirely proper for the judiciary, which bears the burden of extending federal jurisdiction in gun cases, to bring these values into play in its interpretation of the Commerce Clause, providing some counterweight to the political branches, which inevitably will press, over time, for enlarged criminal jurisdiction.

B. Executive Initiatives

The same expansive pressures also operate at the administrative level under the existing federal gun statutes. The United States attorney in Richmond, Virginia, developed a program called Project Exile.[43] Beginning in early 1997, Project Exile targeted gun violence in Richmond by funneling all gun arrests made by state and local authorities into federal court, where defendants were prosecuted under federal firearms statutes when possible. This was a radical departure from the ordinary practice, in which street crime is the general province of state and local police and prosecutors. As a result of Exile, gun homicides dropped substantially in Richmond, and Exile became one of the most highly publicized federal anticrime initiatives of the Clinton era.[44]

Project Exile gun prosecutions are now being handled by prosecutors detailed from state and local offices. Thus, although the United States attorney initially believed that the project would be a substantial burden on her office, a later review reported that the personnel resources required were "relatively limited" because state prosecutors had been designated to handle these federal cases.[45] Cross-designating state prosecutors to bring federal prosecutions is a well-established practice, and it can be used to cope with an expanded caseload of gun-related crimes. Indeed, Senator D'Amato argued that state prosecutors could be designated to bring the resulting federal prosecutions if his amendment making all gun crimes federal offenses were enacted.[46]

Project Exile demonstrates that efforts to expand federal jurisdiction over gun offenses can alter what federal jurisdiction means in practice. In gun cases, federal jurisdiction may routinely mean that a state, rather than a federal prosecutor, will exercise charging and bargaining discretion and will represent the United States in court. Statutory authority clearly allows individuals to act as federal prosecutors in particular cases.[47] But programs like Project Exile may transform case-by-case cross-designation into a semipermanent, wholesale incorporation of a group of junior varsity federal prosecutors. These prosecutors will not undergo the same selection process as "real" federal prosecutors,[48] and they will not have the same training. Moreover, most state prosecutors work in offices headed by an elected district attorney, and state prosecutors' offices are typically more politicized than their federal counterparts. Although the federal system is quite decentralized, with most prosecutorial decisions controlled by the United States attorney in each federal judicial district, but all federal prosecutors receive a degree of centralized control, training, and oversight from the Department of Justice, and they benefit from centralized legal and policy resources. The present federal system keeps politics in check and strikes a careful balance between uniformity and diversity. The centralizing effects of the authority of the attorney general and the Department of Justice are balanced by the authority conferred on the presidentially appointed United States attorneys who are responsible for federal law enforcement in their judicial districts. When cross-designated state prosecutors are given responsibility for a part of the federal criminal docket, do they exercise their authority in the same fashion as "real" federal prosecutors? How does this affect the balance between uniformity and diversity? Does it inject a greater political emphasis in prosecutorial decisions? Given the enormous discretion wielded by federal prosecutors, a good deal rides on the decision to consistently use such hybrid federal-state prosecutors.

Project Exile has had a different effect on the courts. Prosecutorial discretion and cross-designation give the Justice Department and federal prosecutors the means to deal with legislative efforts to expand federal jurisdiction to reach gun-related crime. If federal prosecutors lack sufficient resources to prosecute these cases, they may choose not to bring the prosecutions or may cross-designate state prosecutors to present the cases in federal court. In contrast, the federal courts have no capacity to cross-designate state judges, and they have no discretion to dismiss criminal prosecutions that exceed their resources. Thus, the federal courts are more likely to feel the pinch of legislation that extends federal criminal jurisdiction and may have a greater stake in reading such statutes narrowly.[49] It is unsurprising that the chief judge of the United States District Court in Richmond has complained that Project Exile has turned the federal district court into a "a minor-grade police court."[50] This objection underlines the point made earlier regarding the federal courts' self-interested behavior.

Pressure also may be building on another traditional boundary, the boundary between legislative and executive authority in the decision to bring federal criminal prosecutions. Project Exile demonstrates that existing federal firearms provisions are already broad enough, if used aggressively, to flood the federal courts with cases traditionally heard in state courts. At present, each United States attorney's office decides how many gun cases to bring. Congress traditionally has accorded federal prosecutors virtually unregulated discretion to determine whether and when to bring prosecutions under the existing federal criminal statutes. Prosecutors use their discretion to tailor caseloads to resources, accommodate local circumstances, set priorities, and take account of the equities and evidentiary strengths of individual cases. Although prosecutors exercise much of their discretion in a decentralized fashion, the attorney general establishes some priorities at a national level. White-collar and organized crime have been designated as national priorities, and Attorney General Richard Thornburgh announced Operation Trigerlock, an effort to use federal laws to prosecute the most serious violent offenders.[51] Although these prosecutorial priorities have been set by the attorney general, the United States attorneys, and the heads of other units within the Department of Justice, those priorities were subject to a continuing dialogue with Congress as it pursued its oversight responsibilities and considered the Department's appropriations.

Since Project Exile, however, Congress has proposed various nationwide mandates based on the Exile model. It would be a highly significant change if Congress were to mandate a national program requiring prosecutors to bring gun cases in the federal courts, instead of simply providing them with tools to bring such cases in their discretion. Some of the post-Exile legislative activity takes a step in that direction. For example, the Criminal Use of Firearms by Felons (CUFF) proposal provided that, in twenty-five high-crime jurisdictions, the attorney general and the secretary of the Treasury were to provide for the establishment of Exile-style agreements, in which state and local law enforcement officials would refer firearms prosecutions to the Bureau of Alcohol, Tobacco, and Firearms and the United States attorney.[52] CUFF also required that the United States attorney in each district designate at least one assistant to prosecute these cases, and, most important, that each person referred to the United States Attorney's Office under these programs be charged with a violation of the most serious federal firearms offense committed.[53]

The recent experience with Project Exile demonstrates that the efforts to impose harsh federal penalties on gun criminals may have a major effect on federal prosecutorial practices by weakening the traditional assumption that federal prosecutors will prosecute federal crimes and by giving Congress an incentive to regulate prosecutorial practices more closely.

Conclusion

Congress's efforts to respond to gun violence have had far-reaching effects within the federal system. The legislative efforts to expand the boundaries of federal criminal jurisdiction brought Congress to the threshold of a major shift in the federal-state boundary. The Supreme Court responded with its first decision in half a century limiting congressional power under the Commerce Clause. This historic decision seems to have been motivated to a significant degree by the Court's institutional concerns about a possible flood of federal gun prosecutions.

It is far from clear that enhanced gun penalties achieve their intended purposes of deterring crime and incapacitating dangerous criminals. Even if they have little effect on offenders, the federal gun laws have had a significant impact within the federal system, creating a backlash from the Supreme Court that may tie the hands of Congress in the future and creating perverse incentives for prosecutors that result in greater inequity among defendants as a result of mandatory sentencing provisions. More subtle changes also may have been set in motion, as federal prosecutors seek to handle the crush of new gun cases by wholesale cross-designation of state prosecutors, setting a precedent for the delegation of federal prosecutorial authority to local actors.

NOTES

Reprinted with permission from the *Duke Law Journal*.

1. For a helpful review of the research, see Paul J. Hofer, "Federal Sentencing for Violent and Drug Trafficking Crimes Involving Firearms: Recent Changes and Prospects for Improvement," *American Criminal Law Review* 37 (2000): 43–45.

2. Sara Sun Beale, "The Unintended Consequences of Enhancing Gun Penalties: Shooting Down the Commerce Clause and Arming Federal Prosecutors," *Duke Law Journal*, vol. 51 (March 2002) [hereinafter "Enhancing Gun Penalties"].

3. *Title VII of the Omnibus Crime Control and Safe Streets Act of 1968, U.S. Statutes at Large* 82 (1968): 236–37 (repealed 1986).

4. See *United States v. Bass*, 404 U.S. 336, 338 (1971).

5. *Consumer Credit Protection Act, U.S. Statutes at Large* 82 (1968): 159 (codified as amended at *U.S. Code*, vol. 18, secs. 891–896 (2000)).

6. *Bass*, 404 U.S. at 338; *Perez v. United States*, 402 U.S. 146, 154–57 (1971).

7. *Bass*, 404 U.S. at 349–50.

8. See, e.g., *Bailey v. United States*, 516 U.S. 137, 150 (1995); *Staples v United*

States, 511 U.S. 600, 619 (1994); *Busic v. United States,* 446 U.S. 398, 399–400 (1980); *Simpson v. United States,* 435 U.S. 6, 16 (1978).

9. U.S. Code, vol. 18, sec. 922(q)(1)(A) (1988 and Supp. V 1993).

10. 514 U.S. 549 (1995).

11. 529 U.S. 598, 627 (2000) (holding that Congress exceeded its authority under the Commerce Clause—and under Section 5 of the Fourteenth Amendment—in enacting the civil cause of action under the Violence against Women Act, U.S. Code, vol. 42, sec. 13981).

12. See Daniel A. Farber and Philip P. Frickey, "Foreword: Positive Political Theory in the Nineties," *Georgetown Law Journal* 80 (1992): 458–63 (describing varying views of positive political theory).

13. William N. Eskridge Jr. and Philip P. Frickey, "The Supreme Court, 1993 Term—Foreword: Law as Equilibrium," *Harvard Law Review* 108 (1994): 28–29 [hereinafter "Law as Equilibrium"].

14. Ibid., 71.

15. A sense of what the term "police court" implies can be gleaned from the Supreme Court's decision in *Argersinger v. Hamlin,* 407 U.S. 25, 34–35 (1972).

16. See *Cong. Rec.,* 103rd Cong., 1st sess., 1993, 139, 18223-24; *Cong. Rec.,* 102nd Cong., 1st sess., 1991, 140, 16830; *Cong. Rec.,* 103rd Cong., 1st sess., 1994, 140, 11178–81. For a more detailed review of the legislative history see Beale, "Enhancing Gun Penalties," 1648.

17. *Cong. Rec.,* 103rd Cong., 1st sess., 1993, 139, 28222–24.

18. See Beale, "Enhancing Gun Penalties," 1649.

19. William H. Rehnquist, "Chief Justice's 1991 Year-End Report on the Federal Judiciary," *Third Branch,* Jan. 1992, at 1, 3.

20. See, e.g., William H. Rehnquist, "Welcoming Remarks: National Conference on State-Federal Judicial Relationships, Address before the National Conference on State-Federal Judicial Relationships" (Apr. 10, 1992), in 78 *Virginia Law Review* 1657 (1992): 1660 (calling for "congressional self-restraint . . . in the federalization of crimes").

21. *Cong. Rec.,* 103rd Cong., 2d sess., 1994, 140, 11183. All of the reports of the hearings attribute the statement about police courts to Justice Kennedy, who picked up on Senator Hollings's use of that term (e.g., *Union Leader* [Manchester, N.H.], 4 Mar. 1994, 1).

22. *Cong. Rec.,* 103rd Cong., 2d sess., 1994, 140, 17234 (statement of Rep. Hughes).

23. *United States v. Lopez,* 514 U.S. 549 (1995).

24. *United States v. Morrison,* 529 U.S. 598 (2000).

25. 514 U.S. at 567–68.

26. Ibid., 564.

27. *Morrison,* 529 U.S. at 627.

28. Ibid., 618.

29. Eskridge and Frickey, "Law as Equilibrium," 71.

30. Judith Resnik, "The Programmatic Judiciary: Lobbying, Judging, and Invalidating the Violence against Women Act," *Southern California Law Review* 74 (2000): 271 [hereinafter "Programmatic Judiciary"] (quoting Rehnquist, see note 23, 3).

31. See, e.g., *Seminole Tribe of Florida v. Florida,* 517 U.S. 44 (1996); *Printz v. United States,* 521 U.S. 898, 933–34 (1997); *New York v. United States,* 505 U.S. 144, 177 (1992).

32. 15 F.3d 862, 868–69 (9th Cir. 1994).

33. See, e.g., Brief for Petitioner, at i, *United States v. Robertson,* 514 U.S. 669, 671 (1995) (No. 94-251).

34. Rehnquist is not known as a supporter of women's issues. See Donald E. Boles, *Mr. Justice Rehnquist, Judicial Activist: The Early Years* (Ames: Iowa State University Press, 1987), 6–7 (describing Rehnquist's views of Equal Rights Amendment).

35. Justice Thomas's opinion in *Printz v. United States,* 521 U.S. 889, 936–39 (Thomas, J., concurring), suggests that he is receptive to a robust interpretation of the Second Amendment that would limit the government's authority to regulate firearms. See also *Staples v. United States,* 511 U.S. 600, 611 (1994) (Thomas, J.).

36. Resnik, "Programmatic Judiciary," 278–82.

37. Ibid., 287–89.

38. William J. Stuntz, "The Pathological Politics of Criminal Law," *Michigan Law Review* 100 (December 2001): 528–39.

39. Ibid., 529.

40. See Beale, "Enhancing Gun Penalties," 1658.

41. *The Federalist* No. 51, at 320 (James Madison) (Clinton Rossiter ed., 1961).

42. Ibid., 322.

43. Daniel C. Richman, "'Project Exile' and the Allocation of Federal Law Enforcement Authority," *Arizona Law Review* 43 (2001): 370 [hereinafter "Project Exile"].

44. Ibid., 370.

45. See ibid., 380.

46. *Cong. Rec.,* 103rd Cong., 2d sess., 1994, 140, S6093 (statement of Sen. D'Amato).

47. U.S. Code, vol. 28, sec. 515(a) (1994).

48. For a variety of reasons, the federal hiring process is generally more selective than the state process. Two important factors are compensation and workload. Federal pay scales generally exceed those for state prosecutors, and federal prosecutors generally are responsible for a smaller number of cases.

Frank O. Bowman III and Michael Heise, "Quiet Rebellion? Explaining Nearly a Decade of Declining Federal Drug Sentences," *Iowa L. Rev.* 86 (2001): 1127–28.

49. It should be noted, however, that eventually the executive branch bears the cost of the incarceration of all federal offenders, and this expense has been growing very rapidly.

50. John S. Baker, "State Police Powers and the Federalization of Local Crime," *Temple Law Review* 72 (1999): 687.

51. See Text of Triggerlock Implementation Memo, *DOJ Alert,* vol. 1, No. 1, at 17 (July 1991).

52. S. 254, 106th Cong., sec. 803 (1999).

53. Richman, "Project Exile," 387–88 and nn. 132–35.

E. Civil Litigation against Gun Manufacturers

Chapter 16

The Cities Take the Initiative
Public Nuisance Lawsuits against Handgun Manufacturers

David Kairys

The easy availability of new, inexpensive, readily concealed handguns in urban areas, their role in violent and youth crime, and the enormity of the resulting harm visited on individuals, private and governmental institutions, and society as a whole have become common features of city life. Much would seem to be at stake: extraordinary levels of loss of life and personal injury, startling financial costs, a serious undermining of the quality and tenor of everyday life. For most of our large cities, armed criminal violence is the most devastating danger to public health and safety over the past few decades. Yet it all has an aura of regrettable normalcy, a deplorable but inevitable fact of life in urban America.

Until recently, little attention was paid to how these crime-friendly handguns find their way to urban streets, who benefits or looks the other way, or who might bear some moral or legal responsibility. Most of us assumed—if we thought about it at all—that something illegal must be going on, that, regardless of whether law-abiding people can have a rifle for hunting or a handgun at home for self-defense, sales of handguns are surely restricted and heavily regulated in ways that would minimize access to them for purposes of criminal activity. Further, we have usually assumed that handgun manufacturers, or at least the more established ones, have no active or knowing role in this. It must be the work of some shady characters operating an illegal, underground handgun market in dark alleyways.

Starting in 1998, more than forty cities and counties, and one state, including almost all of the major cities in the country, brought lawsuits against an array of handgun manufacturers. The facts alleged challenged the usual assumptions: Handgun manufacturers, including the biggest and most established, by their distribution and marketing policies and practices, knowingly and intentionally facilitate easy access to their products by criminals and youth. The predominant legal theory was also new: public nuisance.[1]

Handgun Manufacturers and Markets

The manufacturers' position, both publicly and legally, is that they just make handguns and then sell them exclusively to distributors or dealers licensed by the federal government. Others misuse them, but the manufacturers say they know nothing about that. Such misuses are a law enforcement problem, to be dealt with by the Bureau of Alcohol, Tobacco, and Firearms (ATF) on the federal level, local law enforcement, and other law enforcement agencies that have jurisdiction.

This is incomplete, to say the least.[2] First, we have become so accustomed to handguns and the damage they do that it is easy to ignore the context in which these manufacturers operate and the obvious differences between them and manufacturers of other products. The product made and marketed by these manufacturers is designed to kill. The salient characteristics of the product—and the features the manufacturers emphasize in advertisements—are the ease, speed, effectiveness, and low cost with which they are capable of actually or potentially killing a human being. This product is also the primary tool for street crime.

An extraordinary level of deaths and injuries is associated with the product: about fifty dead people per day. Another 150 to 200 per day are injured but not killed. These numbers are so large, and the loss of life and injury are so awful, in terms of the effect on individuals and on society, that they are difficult to deal with. This probably contributes to the denial and avoidance that characterize public debate on the issue. But, at the very least, society has every reason to expect, morally and legally, extraordinary diligence on the part of manufacturers who profit from sale of a product designed to kill that is associated with such enormous harm.

Second, a very small number of distributors and dealers are responsible for the overwhelming majority of handguns that wind up used in crimes, and the differences among distributors and dealers are not proportional to or explainable by sales volume. Only about 1 percent of the dealers are responsible for 57 percent of the guns traced because they were used in crimes. Similarly, a very small number of the distributors—the people to whom the manufacturers directly sell these products when they leave the factory door—are responsible for a very large proportion of the guns used in crime.[3]

Third, the manufacturers know which distributors are the culprits and know or could easily find out which dealers. In fact, they are provided specific notice by the ATF of which particular distributors feed the crime distribution channels.

The mechanisms and distribution channels used to distribute crime handguns are well known to researchers, government, the media, and the industry. The primary vehicles are multiple sales, straw purchases, gun shows, and "kitchen table" and "car trunk" dealers. Numerous studies show how quickly and easily—and, most often, legally—the manufacturers' new handguns move from the factories to the streets. The notions that crime guns are stolen or that multiple purchases of small, inexpensive handguns are made by "collectors" are overworn and destructive myths.

One study showed that most handguns are purchased by buyers who bought at least one other handgun within a fifteen-month period; 30 percent were bought by somebody who bought three or more; 17 percent were bought by somebody who bought five or more.[4] Buying more than one handgun—or as many as one can pay for—is not illegal under federal law or the laws of most states, nor is resale illegal or meaningfully regulated. For example, resale by someone who is not a licensed dealer is not even subject to the Brady Act record check. This is why "one-gun-a-month" laws—which restrict an individual to twelve a year—are proposed and enacted as a "reform." What legitimate reason is there for buying twelve small, inexpensive handguns in a year, or twelve more in each succeeding year? The one-a-month reform has some appeal and is sometimes enacted because individuals are buying even more. Most Americans would be horrified if the details of these practices and laws, or the lack of laws, were widely known and understood.

More handguns are produced than could conceivably be purchased by law-abiding customers, and some have features that facilitate criminal use and are so advertised. For example, in the 1990s, while the handgun market was relatively stagnant (until the Y2K and millennium scares), the manufacturers increased production of 9-mm handguns—although their own market research showed that the market for 9-mms among law-abiding purchasers was already saturated. Nine-mm handguns are popular in the illicit drug trade and are widely viewed as the gun of choice for criminals, particularly murderers. One manufacturer, Navegar, was so brazen as to state in its brochure for its Intratec line that a trademarked coating yields "excellent resistance to finger prints."

States with weak handgun controls and restrictions, such as, in the east, Pennsylvania and some southern states along the I-95 corridor, are oversupplied with substantially more handguns than their residents are expected to purchase, for the specific purpose of sales whose end purchasers are in states, like New Jersey, that have substantial handgun controls and restrictions. For example, a congressional study of ATF data, released in December 1999, found that an extraordinary proportion of crime guns bought from "high-crime" gun stores were probably straw purchased: of 35,000 crime guns traced to 140 "high-crime" gun stores, 87 percent were possessed by someone other than the buyer. The study also found that one-third of these crime guns were recovered in connection with a crime within just one year of purchase, and half were traced to crimes within two years of purchase.

The manufacturers receive actual notice of which distributors feed the crime channels from the ATF. ATF contacts the manufacturers to trace about 200,000 guns used in crime each year. This amounts to, on average, more than one crime gun trace call per minute during each workday. The manufacturer is informed of the model and serial number, and ATF requests identification of the initial distributor to whom the manufacturer sold the weapon, which is in the manufacturer's records. Thus, with each trace, the manufacturer is placed on actual notice by ATF that a gun from a particular distribution channel was used in a crime.

These traces, once they accumulate in substantial numbers, provide a clear picture for each manufacturer of the crime-producing tendencies of its various initial distribution channels. Nevertheless, the manufacturers do not use the data literally placed in their hands on a daily basis by the ATF to terminate, limit, or otherwise discipline distributors (or dealers) whose sales yield inordinate numbers or percentages of crime-traced guns.

Imagine, for purposes of seeing the magnitude of this on particular manufacturers, that a manufacturer got 5 percent of these calls or communications; he would then get one every fifteen minutes of every workday. If you look at market share figures to get an idea how often this occurs for particular manufacturers (without suggesting that traces are distributed as market share is), 5 percent describes an awful lot of the manufacturers. At 10 percent, Smith and Wesson, the biggest, would get a call, on average over the past five years and using market share as a rough way to get an order of magnitude, every seven minutes of each workday.

The former vice president for marketing of Smith and Wesson, Robert Hass, stated under oath,

> [T]he industry as a whole are fully aware of the extent of the criminal misuse of firearms . . . [and] also aware that the black market in firearms is not simply the result of stolen guns but is due to the seepage of guns into the illicit market from multiple thousands of unsupervised federal firearms licensees. In spite of their knowledge, however, the industry's position has consistently been to take no independent action to insure responsible distribution practices. . . . [N]one of [the manufacturers] . . . investigate, screen or supervise the wholesale distributors and retail outlets that sell their products to insure that their products are distributed responsibly.[5]

Discovery in a range of cases has confirmed this insider's criticism.

The manufacturers do not monitor or supervise distributors or dealers; their contracts with distributors provide for termination if minimum prices are undercut but not for practices that facilitate criminal access. There are no inventory or sales tracking systems like those that have long been routine elsewhere in American industry, nor any training or instruction of dealers. Other manufacturers of dangerous or potentially harmful products have restricted their sales and their profits to minimize harm. For example, spray paint manufacturers, whose products have been used for graffiti, adopted a "Responsible Retailing Program," through which they educated and trained retailers and retracted their opposition to, and cooperated with, bans on sales to minors. Similarly, manufacturers of all-terrain vehicles place stricter age limits on purchasers than the law requires because of statistics that show a high number of injuries among younger purchasers. Handgun manufacturers place no limits on purchases of five, twenty-five, one hundred, or any number of crime-friendly handguns, although they know that anyone who meets local and federal requirements—which usually means passing only an instant record check—can buy and immediately walk out of the door with any number of their handguns.

Fourth, handguns used in crime constitute a substantial but not very large proportion of defendants' handgun sales. This raises an interesting question: Why would the manufacturers continue to distribute and market in ways they know result in enormous suffering and costs for others, rather than tightening their distribution policies and practices? They want to avoid regulation, but self-restraint in this manner would further that goal and also improve their public image. Some of them talk like they are doing the nation's, the Constitution's, or even God's work, but they are, ultimately, businesses. Many or most are currently owned or controlled by individuals or corporations that have little history or stake in guns.

The answer lies, at least significantly, in the structure of demand in the handgun industry. Demand for handguns is driven by fear. The public health community thinks of it as an epidemic, which seems appropriate, but it is an epidemic that is spread not by a virus or a bacteria but by fear. And, unlike most epidemics, the agent or instrument of harm is also posed as the solution—more guns, which just further spread the epidemic.

Here is how, in my view, demand works in this industry. A gun is used in a crime, say a stickup. It is on the local news or included in crime statistics or accounts of violent crime; it scares people. They then go out and buy another gun to protect themselves because they are afraid. The guns that they buy are then left in the home and very infrequently used for self-defense. Most often, if they harm someone, handguns in homes wind up being used in the large number of handgun suicides—usually teenagers who are distraught over school, relations with their parents, or a relationship that broke up and who, because of their stage of life, lack perspective. There is a very easy vehicle for ending it right then and there in Dad's closet or in the safe that Dad does not think you know the combination to. Those guns also get used in spousal murders and by kids who pick up a gun and take it to school.

There is a connection, based on fear, between the significant but relatively small crime market and the very large home protection, self-defense market. In economic terms, you could think of it as a "multiplier effect." Each gun used in a crime creates an incrementally increased level of fear, which then generates the demand for a certain number of other sales. So there is a lot at stake in the crime market for the manufacturers. That the handgun market is open and easily accessed for crime enhances the home protection and self-defense market. Just about anything in society that creates fear increases sales for the handgun industry. Columbine, a serial killer—all are good for handgun sales. The millennium scare and the Y2K scare led to a huge boost in sales, and these events were played up by the industry and in the gun magazines. The aftermath of 9/11 was the same. Events and phenomena that are the most devastating and destructive for American society are usually quite good for handgun sales. Those handguns are now just sitting in homes, cars, lockers, and so on.

Public Nuisance

Public nuisance is a unique tort. The focus is on the rights of the general public, rather than the rights of particular people harmed; the usual plaintiff is a governmental entity or official seeking to protect the public; and the hallmark is the incompatibility of a defendant's conduct with the public's rights.[6]

The required elements of a public nuisance claim are well and long established. Defendant's conduct must *create or contribute to* a *substantial interference* with *rights common to the general public,* and the interference with such rights must be *unreasonable.* Four independent and sufficient grounds for establishing unreasonableness are recognized: (a) defendant's conduct significantly interferes with the public safety, health, or peace; (b) it is continuing conduct that has produced a permanent or long-lasting effect, and defendant knows or has reason to know that it has a significant effect upon the public right; (c) defendant's conduct is unlawful; or (d) defendant's interference with rights common to the public is unreasonable on the basis of the totality of the circumstances.

These traditional elements and standards for a public nuisance claim do not include some of the usual requirements for other torts, which deal with the liability of one person or entity to another. Public nuisance is the only tort that establishes a duty to the public, rather than to particular individuals harmed, and its elements, rules, and limited relief reflect the specific purpose and function of protecting the public from danger. Thus, executive officials who bring a public nuisance claim cannot recover damages, on behalf of the government or the individuals affected, for the harm done to particular members of the public; correspondingly, the causation standard is framed in terms of causation of the public nuisance ("create or contribute to"), rather than in terms of direct or proximate causation of the harm the public nuisance does to individual members of the public. And the focus is the reasonableness of the interference with public rights, rather than the nature or culpability of the conduct or the harm done to particular individuals.

These standards and the underlying purposes of nuisance law are also evident if one considers the early common-law origins of the tort. The leading authority on nineteenth-century nuisance law characterized it this way:

> [Nuisance is] that class of wrongs that arise from the unreasonable, unwarrantable or unlawful use by a person of his own property, real or personal, or from his own improper, indecent or unlawful personal conduct, working an obstruction of, or injury to, a right of another or of the public. . . . It is part of the great social compact to which every person is a party, a fundamental and essential principle in every civilized community, that every person yields a portion of his right of absolute dominion. . . .

> [P]ublic nuisance is a violation of a public right, either by direct encroachment upon public rights or property, or by doing some act which tends to a common injury, or by omitting to do some act which the common good requires. . . .[7]

Lawful businesses have often been defendants in public nuisance cases, probably because their materials, processes, products, and wastes have the potential for incompatibility with common public rights. In public nuisance law, unlawfulness of conduct is not required; it is only one of the four separate and independent grounds for establishing unreasonableness. Nor is it a defense that the business is licensed or regulated.[8]

Some businesses were considered nuisances per se; others could be judged nuisances, although lawful, on the basis of very fact-specific analyses. For example, a blacksmith shop or a factory that uses a steam engine, though performing useful functions, could be public nuisances in certain circumstances (e.g., proximity to hotels and residences), even if they preceded the other, incompatible uses.

Some courts and commentators view nuisance law as hopelessly vague and open-ended or without limits, perhaps because of the unusual tort rules and the loose use of the term "nuisance" in earlier decades. Nuisance was used in certain periods to connote interference with a broad range of interests and became almost synonymous with any civil wrong. The first *Restatement of Torts* in 1939 narrowed it to two claims, private and public nuisance, which are defined and limited torts, but these definitions create some confusion because they have "almost nothing in common" except the term "nuisance."[9]

The standards for establishing a public nuisance claim are as clear and limiting of the scope of the tort as those applied in the range of other torts, such as, for example, negligence. Nor is a fact-specific, flexible approach unusual in tort law, and this makes particular sense for this tort. A public nuisance claim is the vehicle provided by civil law for executive-branch officials to seek immediate relief to stop and remedy conduct that is endangering the public. Since protecting the public expeditiously from whatever danger may arise is the underlying goal and purpose of the tort—and because such danger can come in many forms, by way of many instrumentalities, and from many types of conduct—courts have wisely preferred a case-by-case, fact-specific approach.

Two parallel tracks for dealing with public nuisances developed at common law and throughout our history. State and local legislatures generally have the power to declare, prohibit, and provide a remedy for public nuisances. This used to be accomplished by literal declarations; more recently, the power is used without the public nuisance declaration. Thus, the range of environmental laws passed in recent decades can be seen as a series of traditional public-nuisance enactments.

Simultaneously, executive-branch officials—mayors, county commissions and boards, governors, attorneys general—have the power to assess and seek a remedy for public nuisances that arise in their jurisdictions. This power is often recognized in state constitutions or statutes; where it is not, courts have generally recognized it as a common-law power. Although this has been depicted by the manufacturers in the handgun cases as a judicial track and criticized as a form of inappropriate activism, it is an executive-branch power, initiated and pursued by that other majoritarian branch. To protect the public by monitoring dangerous or threatening activities or conduct, to determine what conduct constitutes a public nuisance, and to seek immediate relief in court—these are among the highest powers and duties of executive officials.

In terms of its placement in relation to other torts, public nuisance is not fault based, but neither is it strict liability. It is not fault based because the defendant's conduct need not be unlawful or otherwise tortious. It is not strict liability because the interference with public rights must be unreasonable and substantial.

These unusual characteristics make sense because the underlying policy is to protect the public from lawful and even productive activities that are substantially incompatible with the public's common rights. Public nuisance is the only tort designed and equipped to protect the public from activities or conduct that is incompatible with public health, safety, or peace. Hence the flexible, fact-specific approach, and the key phrase in public nuisance law: unreasonable interference.

Public Nuisance in the Handgun Cases

Handgun manufacturers who knowingly or intentionally facilitate easy access to handguns by criminals and youth are creating or contributing to a public nuisance, applying the traditional elements and standards. The conduct by the manufacturers at issue is not related to their manufacture of handguns, nor is the claim based on any defect in their products. The conduct that forms the basis of the claim is their *distribution* of handguns. The public nuisance is not handguns or criminals but those items in combination—criminals and youths *with* handguns—a combination that the manufacturers facilitate with full knowledge of what they are doing and of the consequences. This claim does not require any reform or change in the law; it is based on a straightforward application of the traditional, settled elements and rules of public nuisance to the new facts presented.

Three of the recognized independent grounds for establishing the unreasonableness of an interference with common public rights apply in these cases. First, the interference with the public safety, health, or peace is not insubstantial or fleeting but rather involves the death and injury of large numbers of people and a disruption of public peace and order so serious that it threatens the fabric and viability of the community. Second, the manufacturers continually engage in their reckless conduct, which for some of them extends back as far as several decades, as they are continually informed of the resulting substantial, permanent, and long-lasting harm—and even as they receive daily notice from the ATF of the distribution channels they use that are doing the most harm. They have reason to know—and actually know —of the disastrous, continuing, and long-lasting effects of their conduct on cities, counties, states, and the nation.

Finally, the manufacturers' interference with rights common to the public is also unreasonable on the basis of the totality of the circumstances. There is surely no legitimate interest in getting handguns to persons who intend to use them for crime or who are prohibited from purchasing them; the only interest on the manufacturers' side is their profits, which hardly renders this most significant interference with the public's rights reasonable.

Further, there are reasonable actions completely within the control of defendants that would at least ameliorate or minimize the harmful effects of their conduct, including using the gun-trace information supplied to them by the ATF to monitor, terminate, or supervise their distributors and dealers, refusing to sell through gun shows and "kitchen table" and "car trunk" dealers who have no store, and limiting multiple sales. Other industries have limited their sales and profits in similar ways in response to far less serious or extensive harms associated with their products.

While the particular facts are new, there is an established, analogous line of public nuisance cases. Throughout the country, owners of bars can be liable in public nuisance where their lawful, licensed distribution of a lawful and regulated product, alcoholic beverages, knowingly harms and unreasonably interferes with the surrounding public. These "tavern" or "disorderly house" cases find liability although the injury or harm is done by third-party patrons whose conduct is usually unlawful and whom the tavern owner cannot control, because the owner, by his or her knowing distributional conduct, has contributed to a public nuisance: inebriated, unruly patrons who pose a danger to members of the public.[10]

Early Developments and Decisions

While publicly claiming that public nuisance lawsuits are baseless and would be easily defeated in court, gun manufacturers sought relief in state legislatures in the form of statutes prohibiting the suits. Many state legislatures complied, as they and Congress have generally to the requests of gun manufacturers. These statutes do not change the rules of or regulate lawsuits against manufacturers or businesses generally or address excessive or frivolous lawsuits generally. Rather, their focus and terms single out one industry—firearms—for litigation immunity against one kind of plaintiff—local governments—and, according to the legislative histories, they are aimed at particular litigation between particular parties—the city handgun cases discussed here. This raises fundamental state and federal constitutional issues.

These statutes are a throwback to the preconstitutional history of our country in which legislatures regularly exercised judicial functions and interfered with accrued or vested rights. The leading historian of early American constitutional history, Gordon S. Wood, summarized these early legislative practices:

> [T]he [state] assemblies in the eighteenth century still saw themselves, perhaps even more so than the House of Commons, as a kind of medieval court making private judgments as well as public law. . . . The assemblies constantly heard private petitions, which often were only the complaints of one individual or group against another. . . .
>
> . . . [Legislatures were] reaching for uncontrolled dominion in the administration of justice: becoming a court of chancery . . . interfering in causes between parties . . . and *even prohibiting court actions. . . .*[11]

The framers of the federal Constitution were quite clear about their disdain for such encroachments on the judiciary and about the resulting unfairness to those who had little or no influence with the legislatures. In *Federalist* No. 48, Madison called it "legislative usurpation . . . [that] must lead to . . . tyranny." "Legislative power is exercised by an assembly," Madison continued, with "all the passions which actuate a multitude." He focused on the example of Pennsylvania, where the "Constitution had been flagrantly violated by the legislature in a variety of important instances . . . [including] cases belonging to the judiciary department frequently drawn within legislative cognizance and determination." Cooley summarized the principle:

> The legislature may suspend the operation of the general laws of the State; but when it does so the suspension must be general, and cannot be made for individual cases or for particular localities. [There must not be, quoting Locke,] "one rule for rich and poor, for the favorite at court and the countryman at plough." . . . Special privileges are always obnoxious. . . . [O]ne cannot be deprived [of vested rights] by the mere force of legislative enactment. . . .

Wood's often-cited book, quoted earlier, describes how the repudiation of such legislative practices led to our current understanding and constitutional limits regarding three fundamental issues: separation of powers, retroactive legislation, and special legislation. Nevertheless, most courts have upheld these statutes in the handgun cases.[12]

Putting aside the lawsuits ended by state statutes, the results of motions to dismiss the governmental public nuisance lawsuits have been about evenly split. The manufacturers' motions to dismiss and their supporting briefs and oral arguments generally do not focus on the elements, standards, and underlying policies of public nuisance law. Instead, they argue, for example, that the complaints do not establish causation, suggesting that there is no difference between causation in a public nuisance claim and causation in a negligence claim. They strenuously assert a broad immunity, claiming that manufacturers of a lawful product cannot be held civilly liable for their role in creating or contributing to a public nuisance, nor can a court require them to alter any of their distributional practices—even if they knowingly facilitate violent criminal conduct.

The decisions denying motions to dismiss focus on the facts alleged and the traditional elements and rules of public nuisance law and reject the range of immunities and defenses claimed by the manufacturers. The decisions dismissing the cases rest primarily on causation grounds and often ignore the facts alleged and the usual elements and rules. Some create a new immunity to public nuisance claims for manufacturers or mangle or discard centuries of public nuisance law. The Third Circuit's decision in the Camden County, New Jersey, case and the Ohio Supreme Court's decision in the Cincinnati case provide good examples of both lines of decision.[13]

In *Camden County v. Beretta,* the Third Circuit, purporting to apply New Jersey law in a diversity jurisdiction case, acknowledged the factual allegations—the manufacturers' knowing facilitation of access to handguns by criminals—but created an immunity from public nuisance liability because they also happen to manufacture the handguns. This decision lacks support in New Jersey law or policy, which has generally been, compared to that in other states, favorable to civil plaintiffs and tough on manufacturers generally and gun manufacturers specifically. For example, the New Jersey legislature has imposed unusually strict regulations on firearms, and the New Jersey courts have rejected the economic loss doctrine. There is no basis in New Jersey law to exempt *anyone* who distributes devices designed to kill in such reckless and irresponsible ways and with such known disastrous consequences. The only New Jersey court to rule in these cases denied the motion to dismiss the Newark case. The only pertinent citation offered by the Third Circuit in the *Camden County* case is to an Eighth Circuit opinion holding that a product liability claim cannot avoid the requirements of product liability law by using the guise of a public nuisance claim. But the claim is not a disguised product liability claim; it has nothing to do with manufacturing or defects in any product.

Further, the Third Circuit decision affirmed a district court decision that literally changed the accepted public nuisance causation standard in New Jersey, the *Restatement,* and throughout the country: *"created or contributed to"* became *"controlled or created."* Substituting "controlled" for the far less restrictive "contributed to"—which means at least that contributions by others do not defeat the claim—is a serious modification of state law. The Third Circuit's discussion of the issue noticeably left out "contributed to" in its own formulation and emphasized "control" throughout the opinion.[14]

This more restrictive standard has no support in New Jersey law or public policy and will make it more difficult in the future for executive-branch officials to use public nuisance claims as they are intended—to protect the public from dangers to public health, safety, or peace. It also misconceives the distinct rules and policies of public nuisance law discussed earlier. The limits on the allowable remedies are crucial to an understanding of the unique elements and rules that govern public nuisance liability. Executive officials cannot recover damages for the harm to the individual members of the public injured, either for the government or on behalf of those injured. Rather, executive officials may quickly obtain an injunction stopping the conduct, but the damages available must be related to abatement of the public nuisance and are limited to the government's actual costs related to the public nuisance. This was the basis for the same court's decision only a year before that "claims of public nuisance . . . do not require a showing of proximate causation."[15]

If one considers the public nuisance claim as pled, it is hard to understand why control would be an issue at all. The manufacturers have complete control over their distributional system and over their products when they place them in the hands of particular distributors. They have control of the products at the pertinent time and place. The manufacturers' relations with their distributors and dealers are voluntary and consensual. They have the power to set the terms and conditions of those relationships—which could include, for instance, bans on sales at gun shows or limits on multiple sales—or to substitute or create alternative distribution mechanisms. They have control over the distribution system in the sense that they could abate the public nuisance by obvious measures. Their public nuisance liability stems from their marketing and distribution policies and practices, over which they have complete control.

The panel's opinion on causation and control, like the district court's below, incorrectly focuses entirely on the harm to the members of the public injured and on the conduct immediately preceding that harm and dismisses the complaint because the causal link to those injuries is not sufficiently, in their view,[16] direct or proximate. But the appropriate causal link for a public nuisance claim—that defendants knowingly *created or contributed to the public nuisance*—is actually quite direct and clear on the basis of the detailed factual allegations of the complaint, which are, of course, the only relevant facts for purposes of a motion to dismiss. The manufacturers contributed to the public nuisance—and also had complete control over their relevant conduct—by supplying handguns to distributors that they knew—because, inter alia, the ATF continually informed them—were channeling those devices designed to kill to the crime and youth market.

This view of causation in public nuisance cases is supported by the authorities. It is also reflected in the common factual settings that go back to the earliest cases. Suppose a defendant is sued in public nuisance for blocking the public thoroughfare in front of a mall. Suppose further that the blockage inconveniences some passersby and that others are injured because of it, either in their own efforts to go around it or because some drivers speed around it and cause serious accidents. The causation issue is whether the defendant's conduct "created or contributed to" the blockage, not whether the defendant's conduct caused or was the proximate cause of the harm to passersby who were inconvenienced or injured, damages that are not, in any event, available to the executive officials bringing the public nuisance suit. Thus, the question is not whether defendant's conduct is the proximate cause of the injury to a passerby hit by a speeder going around the blockage, and the speeder's unlawful or negligent conduct is not a defense to the public nuisance claim. The defendant's conduct must create or contribute to the public nuisance, which then results in harm to particular members of the public. The harm to members of the public may be relevant to whether there has been interference with public rights, but being the proximate cause and related remoteness standards are not elements or relevant.

Finally, the Third Circuit suggests that the case might not satisfy the requirement for a public nuisance claim that there be an interference with a "public right." But the public rights interfered with here are as fundamental and pervasive as those in any prior public nuisance case. The public nuisance to which defendants knowingly contribute is armed criminal violence, which, in Camden County: kills and maims many; poses a danger to all residents and visitors; renders the public streets, sidewalks, and parks places of fear rather than enjoyment; imposes huge costs on individuals, health and insurance institutions, and the public purse; diminishes business and commerce (despite the profits for the defendant manufacturers); and undermines the sense of community and the fabric of daily life. It is hard to imagine a more serious or unreasonable interference with public rights.

In the *Cincinnati* case, the Ohio Supreme Court majority found that the allegations established a claim. Since the claim is based on the distribution and marketing, not the manufacture, of handguns, there is no causation problem, the court held, and it is of no import that the manufacturers do not "control the actual firearms at the moment that harm occurred." Nor does it defeat the claim that the product is lawful and regulated. Manufacturers are not immune but can be liable, like anyone else, if they create or contribute to a public nuisance.

It is too early to fully assess the impact of the governmental handgun cases on the industry, the cities, the law, public consciousness, or society generally. About half of the motions to dismiss in cases not barred by statute have been denied, and some of those dismissed in the lower courts probably will be, like Cincinnati's, reversed on appeal. There has not, as yet, been a trial in any of the cases. Discovery is proceeding. The main obstacle so far has been the refusal of ATF to provide its computerized records of the trace calls made to the manufacturers. There is no plausible or legitimate reason for ATF to continue to protect the industry, rather than, as a public agency, to serve the public. A recent decision by the Seventh Circuit in a Freedom of Information Act lawsuit brought by Chicago ordered ATF, in no uncertain terms, to provide these crucial data.[17]

Smith and Wesson's early settlement with some of the governmental plaintiffs—in which the largest manufacturer of handguns agreed to responsibly restrict, monitor, and supervise its distributors—at least validated the underlying claim.[18] The cases have entered the public debate on guns and, at least, brought the role of the manufacturers to the public's attention. Previous litigation against this industry has been uniformly unsuccessful (except in cases where a particular gun was defective), and the legal theories asserted previously usually have required expansion of principles and rules of civil liability in a period characterized by judicial and legislative preference for corporations and civil defendants. At a comparable early stage, the governmental tobacco lawsuits were almost all dismissed. A fuller assessment of the governmental handgun cases will have to await further developments.

NOTES

1. In 1996, I was introduced to the problem, started to question the usual assumptions, and conceived the city lawsuits and the public nuisance theory. The legal theory, underlying facts, and origin and development of the cases are set out in more detail in David Kairys, "Legal Claims of Cities against the Manufacturers of Handguns," *Tempe L. Rev.* 711 (1998): 1; "The Origin and

Development of the Governmental Handgun Cases," *Conn. L. Rev.* 32 (2000): 1163; "The Governmental Handgun Cases and the Elements and Underlying Policies of Public Nuisance Law," *Conn. L. Rev.* 32 (2000): 1175. This chapter is based on my presentation at the Guns, Crime and Punishment in America conference at the University of Arizona Law School on January 26–27, 2001; significant portions were drawn from these articles and from portions of briefs and complaints I wrote in some of the cases, particularly the lawsuit brought by Camden County, New Jersey (see note 13). I appreciate the contribution of the many attorneys who have worked on the governmental cases, particularly, for purposes of this chapter, Peter Nordberg, of Berger and Montague; Lawrence Rosenthal and Matthew Getter, of the Chicago Corporation Counsel's Office; Paul De Marco and Jean Geoppinger, of Wait, Schneider, Bayless and Chesley; Marianna Bettman, visiting professor at the University of Cincinnati Law School; Locke Bowman, of the MacArthur Justice Center; Michael Dowd, of Milberg and Weiss; and Josh Horwitz, Karen Kohn, Carolyn Morrisette, and Sayre Weaver, of the Education Fund to End Gun Violence. I am part of the city, county, and state legal teams in most of the cases; the views expressed here are my own, not those of the clients or other lawyers.

2. Following the general format of this book, the essay is not heavily footnoted. On the factual basis of the governmental lawsuits set out here, see generally the articles cited in note 1 and also Tom Diaz, *Making a Killing* (New York: New Press, 1999). The complaints, motions, and briefs that contain the specific factual allegations and supporting materials in particular lawsuits are available online at firearmslitigation.org.

3. See particularly Department of the Treasury, Bureau of Alcohol, Tobacco, and Firearms, *Commerce in Firearms in the United States* (released February 2, 2000).

4. "Legal Claims of Cities," at 8–9 n.22.

5. Affidavit of Robert Hass, *Hamilton v. Accu-Tek*, "Legal Claims of Cities," at 7.

6. On public nuisance law, see generally *Restatement (Second) of Torts* § 821A, et seq. (1965) (widely adopted and universally recognized); W. Page Keeton, *Prosser and Keeton on Torts* § 90, et seq. (1984).

7. H. G. Wood, *The Law of Nuisances* §§ 1, 17, 20–21, 76, 498–500 (3rd ed. 1893).

8. Lawful businesses have often been conducted in ways that make them public nuisances. *Restatement*, §821B (unlawfulness is one, not the only, ground for finding unreasonableness of the interference); see, e.g., *Andover v. Lake*, 214 A.2d 870, 874 (N.J. App. Div. 1965) ("because the operation of a junk yard or an automobile wrecking yard has been held to be a legitimate and useful business, it cannot legislatively be declared a nuisance per se, although it may be found to be a nuisance in fact."). Nor is it a defense that defendants'

business is regulated or licensed. See, e.g., *State of New Jersey v. Sommers*, 66 N.J. Super. 334, 169 A.2d 165 (App. Div. 1961) ("a permit does not authorize the conduct of a business in such a way as to create a public nuisance"); *State of New Jersey v. WOR-TV Tower*, 39 N.J. Super. 583, 121 A.2d 764 (Ch. Div. 1956) (can be a public nuisance "notwithstanding" a building permit and federal agency licensing). To provide a defense, regulations would have to specifically authorize the particular conduct that is the basis for the claim. See generally *Restatement* §821B, Comment f; *Prosser and Keeton* §88A. The distributional conduct at issue here is not regulated.

9. *Prosser and Keeton on Torts* § 86. Private nuisance concerns land and involves the usual tort context of one person's conduct that is claimed to have harmed another. The usual elements and rules of culpability and proximate causation apply. Some of the opinions in the city cases conflate the two and thereby eradicate the significant purpose and function of public nuisance.

10. See generally *Restatement* § 821B, comment a (particularly cases collected in Reporter's Notes under "interferences with the public peace"). See *State of New Jersey v. Koettgen*, 88 N.J.L. 51, 95 A. 747 (N.J. Sup. Ct. 1915), *aff'd*, 89 N.J.L. 678, 99 A. 400 (N.J. 1916) (conduct of patrons "in the immediate neighborhood" actionable on the basis of the conduct and knowledge of owner); *Reid v. Brodsky*, 397 Pa. 463, 469, 472, 156 A.2d 334 (1959) ("It is highly significant" that defendant took no preventative action; no defense that the business owner "could not control the conduct"), cited with approval of the public nuisance formulation in *Grove Press Inc. v. City of Philadelphia*, 418 F.2d 82, 87 (3d Cir. 1969); *Ember v. B.F.D.*, 490 N.E.2d 764 (Indiana Ct. App. 1986); *People v. Montoya*, 137 Cal. App. Supp. 784, 786, 28 P.2d 101 (Cal. App. 1933) ("Could the defendants be liable, if the quarreling, fighting, andc., were in the street where he could not control the offenders?" "If the defendant voluntarily raised the storm . . . , it is no excuse for him that he could not afterwards quell it." 137 Cal. App. Supp. at 786. It is not a defense that the offending patrons could get their alcohol elsewhere. See *Prosser and Keeton on Torts* § 88B, at 634 ("the fact that others" might do the same thing as defendant "will not be a defense"). Some of these cases are criminal. The civil public nuisance claim came from the public nuisance crime, and the elements are the same. See *Prosser and Keeton on Torts* § 90, at 645 n.33.

11. Gordon S. Wood, *The Creation of the American Republic, 1776–1787* (University of North Carolina Press, 1969), at 154–55, 407–8 (emphasis added and quotation marks omitted).

12. See *The Federalist Papers* (Mentor Books ed. 1961), Nos. 47 and 48; Thomas M. Cooley, *Constitutional Limitations Which Rest Upon the Legislative Power of the States of the American Union* (1874), at 391–93, 358. The handgun cases ruling on these statutes are available at: <http://www.firearmslitigation .org.>

One can see the passions of which Madison spoke in the legislative history of the Pennsylvania statute, as legislators, led by Philadelphia State Senator Vincent Fumo, set out in some detail their version of the facts, the law, and the motivations of the parties and made their ruling in favor of the firearms manufacturers on the floor of the State Senate. See particularly Dec. 6, 1999, *Senate Leg. Journal,* at 1141–43. The facts alleged in Philadelphia's complaint are nowhere to be found, and the legislators do not examine the law of public nuisance, offer any support for the conclusion that the municipal suits are frivolous, or explain on what basis the legislature can or should intervene.

13. The opinions and pleadings in all of the cases are available on the Web site of the Education Fund to Prevent Gun Violence, at: <http://www.firearmslitigation.org>. The claims in the lawsuits are not uniform. While the public nuisance claim based on marketing facts emphasized here is the most prominent and has had the most success, it has sometimes been combined or merged with, or subordinated to, other claims and facts. This compilation of the governmental cases was made in early November 2002; cases barred by statute are not included. I was part of the city and county legal teams in *Cincinnati* and in *Camden County,* and I argued the latter case before the Third Circuit (the transcript of that oral argument is available at: <http://www.firearmslitigation.org>).

Motions to dismiss were denied, in whole or in part, in: *Cincinnati v. Beretta,* 95 Ohio St.3d 416, 2002-Ohio-2480 (2002); *City of Chicago v. Beretta,* Appellate Court of Illinois, First Division, No. 1-00-3541 (Nov. 4, 2002); *City of Boston v. Smith and Wesson,* 2000 Mass. Super. LEXIS 352 (2000); *People of the State of California v. Arcadia,* Superior Ct. of Cal., Judicial Council Coordinated Proceeding No. 4095 (2000)(consolidated cases of 16 cities and counties); *White and City of Cleveland v. Smith and Wesson,* 97 F. Supp.2d 816 (N.D. Ohio 2000); *James and City of Newark v. Arcadia,* Superior Ct. of N.J., Essex Co., No. ESX-L-6059-99 (2001); *Sills and City of Wilmington v. Smith and Wesson,* 2000 Del. Super. LEXIS 444 (2000); *Archer and Detroit and Wayne County v. Arms Technology,* Cir. Ct., Wayne Co., Nos. 99-912658 NZ, 99-912662 NZ (2000).

Cases were dismissed in: *Camden County v. Beretta,* 273 F.3d 536 (3d Cir. 2001); *Ganim and City of Bridgeport v. Smith and Wesson,* 258 Conn. 313 (2001); *Penelas and Miami-Dade County v. Arms Technology,* 778 S.2d 1042 (Fla. Ct. of App. 2001); *People of the State of New York v. Sturm,* Ruger, N.Y. Sup. Ct., No. 402586/00 (2001). See also *City of Philadelphia v. Beretta,* 277 F.3d 415 (3d Cir. 2002) (ruling on substance, as in *Camden County* decision, despite bar statute).

14. There are many circumstances in which public nuisance claims have been sustained where the defendant did not have the kind of control required by the Third Circuit. Cases with similar or analogous facts include: *Adams v. NVR Homes,* 193 F.R.D. 243, 256-57 (D. Md. 2000) (homes built on a dump; defendant "may be held liable for creation of the public nuisance, even though it

no longer has control of the product creating the public nuisance"); *Selma Pressure Treating Co. v. Osmore Wood Preserving Co.,* 221 Cal. App. 3d 1601, 271 Cal. Rptr. 596 (1990) (challenge to sufficiency of defendants' "contribution to" a nuisance in which third parties participated; enough that he "knew or should have known" of the danger and how others would use it); *Shockley v. Hoechst Celanese Corp.,* 793 F. Supp. 670 (D.S.C. 1992), *aff'd in part, rev'd in part on other grounds,* 1993 U.S. App. Lexis 15518 (4th Cir. 1993) (Hoechst shipped barrels of hazardous chemicals to a chemical reclamation facility, where the chemicals contaminated the groundwater beneath adjoining property; Hoechst denied liability because third parties carried out the nuisance, but the court held it liable for the nuisance because it knew that the barrels in which it shipped the chemicals were "rusty, aging and leaking"); *Garvey v. Public Service,* 115 N.J.L. 280, 179 A. 33 (N.J. Sup. Ct. 1935) (no defense that defendant did not have control over the nuisance needed to abate it). See also *Direct Sales v. United States,* 319 U.S. 703 (1943) (upholding criminal liability of drug manufacturer on the basis of its distributional conduct; defendant supplied drugs to doctor although it had knowledge of the doctor's inappropriate distribution of drugs from the quantities he ordered and from government agency inquiries).

15. *Allegheny General Hospital v. Philip Morris,* 228 F.3d 429, 446 (3d Cir. 2000).

16. Other courts, including the Ohio Supreme Court in the *Cincinnati* case, have concluded that the usual proximate causation standard is also satisfied in these cases.

17. *City of Chicago v. United States Dept. of the Treasury,* 287 F.3d 628 (7th Cir. 2002), reh. denied, 297 F.3d 672 (7th Cir. 2002). See also *NAACP v. ACUSPORT,* _ F.Supp.2d _, 2002 U.S. Dist. LEXIS 19202 (Sept. 18, 2002) (providing the same ATF data to an association suing on behalf of its members based on the nuisance theory). ATF has provided some data to particular cities, including Chicago. Usually ATF has provided, after requiring considerable effort and time, the trace data for crimes committed in the particular jurisdiction making the request. This undercuts its claims that to provide the full data would undermine some legitimate law enforcement purpose. The nationwide data are necessary because the manufacturers are not told in the trace calls where the weapon was used; proof of notice and knowledge gained from the trace calls requires the data on all calls made to them, not just the calls that concern a crime in a particular locality.

18. The settlement was reached on March 17, 2000. Its terms are available at: <http://www.firearmslitigation.org>.

Chapter 17

Tort Law and Criminal Behavior (Guns)

Mark Geistfeld

I. Introduction

As history shows, tort actions based on the defendant's criminal conduct are not controversial. A more controversial issue is whether tort liability should be based on crimes committed by someone else. If a third-party criminal caused the plaintiff's injury, should the plaintiff be able to recover from a noncriminal defendant whose conduct facilitated or enabled the crime? Whatever the normative resolution of this matter, noncriminal defendants have incurred liability for these "enabling torts" in a variety of contexts, including the negligent distribution of guns.

Enabling torts have been recognized by the tort system for a long period, and courts have exhibited an increasing tendency to hold a defendant liable for the negligent or criminal acts of a third person. Nevertheless, the enabling torts have not been adequately analyzed, which may explain why courts have not taken a consistent approach to unlawful behavior. When applying the enabling torts, courts recognize that some individuals (the third-party criminals) act unlawfully despite the threat of criminal and tort sanctions. When applying the rule of strict liability for abnormally dangerous activities, courts assume the threat of negligence liability induces all individuals to act lawfully, even the criminally predisposed. The courts adopt a concept of unlawful behavior for the enabling torts that is inconsistent with the behavioral assumption they make when applying the rule of strict liability for abnormally dangerous activities.

Courts should eliminate the inconsistency by applying the rule of strict liability in a manner that accounts for unlawful behavior. The superiority of this approach is illustrated by the tort litigation involving handgun manufacturers. The approach to strict liability currently used by courts obfuscates the real issue posed by these cases. By assuming that negligence liability induces everyone to exercise reasonable care, courts unrealistically assume that there is no criminal misuse of handguns and therefore never address the social problem created by the manufacture and distribution of handguns—the foreseeable likelihood that criminals will obtain handguns and shoot people. To address this problem appropriately, courts must account for the social fact of unlawful behavior when applying the rule of strict liability.

Part II describes the enabling torts. Part III analyzes these torts, concluding that they often will be ineffective because of an inherent limitation of negligence liability. For situations in which negligence liability is ineffective, strict liability is the obvious alternative. Part IV argues that the rule of strict liability should account for unlawful behavior. Part V applies this rule of strict liability to the manufacture and distribution of handguns, identifying a persuasive rationale for not applying strict liability that is far superior to the rationales previously relied upon by the courts.

Although courts may have reached a defensible result in these cases, their poorly reasoned decisions have substantially undermined an important role of strict liability to enforce the duty of care. Even tort doctrine, it seems, has been harmed by handguns.

II. Tort Liability Based on Third-Party Criminal Behavior

The enabling torts typically involve cases in which the noncriminal defendant has a special relationship with the victim of the crime. The relationship is essential to the tort duty, because the nature of the relationship exposes one party to the risk of criminal harm while putting the other in a good position to prevent such crimes. Relationships of this type include carriers and passengers, landlords and tenants, and landowners and business visitors.

Enabling torts also involve contexts in which the noncriminal defendant has a preexisting relationship with the third-party criminal who caused the plaintiff's harm. The prior relationship typically gives the noncriminal defendant the opportunity to control the criminal impulses of the third party, thereby creating a tort duty to those fore-seeable individuals who might be harmed by the criminally disposed third party. Those in charge of persons with dangerous propensities, such as criminals or the insane, therefore have a duty to reasonably re-strain their charges from harming others.

This latter form of the enabling torts is illustrated by the lawsuits involving gun manufacturers and distributors. For example, a store that sells a pistol to an escaped convict in violation of gun-registration laws can be liable for the shooting deaths caused by the sale.[1] Simi-larly, handgun manufacturers have a duty to market and distribute their products in a manner that reasonably reduces the risk of criminal misuse.[2]

The enabling torts define duty, or the corresponding concept of tor-tious risk, in terms of the harm threatened by third-party unlawful be-havior. The "inability to effectively reach the putative wrongdoer him-self, either through criminal or tort sanctions," creates a "deterrence gap" that provides the basis for the tort duty.[3] "This is the crux of the matter and the link to creating responsibility for enabling behavior."[4]

By defining duty or tortious risk in terms of third-party criminal conduct, the enabling torts recognize that a segment of society is crim-inally disposed and predictably responds to certain types of situa-tions. This predictability makes the risk of criminal conduct foresee-able, the condition required of any tort duty.

Even if the defendant does not know who will commit the criminal act, the crime can be foreseeable because criminals often predictably re-spond to situations in a rational, self-interested manner. Anyone who rationally contemplates engaging in criminal conduct considers the costs of criminal and civil sanctions. Presumably those sanctions are high enough for deterrence purposes under situations of perfect en-forcement, so rational, would-be criminals will obey the law if they know they will be caught and sanctioned for acting unlawfully. Situa-tions of underenforcement, which involve any circumstance that re-duces the likelihood a criminal will be caught and sanctioned, reduce the cost of crime and can lead a self-interested person to act unlawfully.

This concept of criminal behavior is supported by numerous empir-ical studies that have found that a reduced likelihood of sanction is as-sociated with an increased incidence of crime.[5] Such behavior is char-acteristic of the Holmesian "bad man," someone who complies with the law only for reasons of self-interest, rather than moral obligation.

By making it possible to foresee or predict how circumstances can influence the likelihood of crime, the concept of rational, self-interested unlawful behavior is an integral component of the enabling torts.[6]

III. The Limitation of Negligence-Based Enabling Torts

To establish liability for an enabling tort, the plaintiff must show that the defendant's failure to provide reasonable protection enabled the third-party criminal to cause the harm. The causal question is counterfactual, asking whether the harm would have occurred had the defendant exercised reasonable care. In the simplest version of the counterfactual inquiry, the hypothetical world is constructed by altering only the defendant's wrongful conduct and nothing else.

Consider a defendant who failed to comply with the gun-registration laws and negligently sold a pistol to a criminal who subsequently shot the plaintiff during a robbery. The simple counterfactual inquiry alters the world by making the defendant gun distributor comply with the gun-registration laws, while holding everything else constant. In this hypothetical world, the criminal cannot buy the gun from the defendant. The gun actually used by the criminal to shoot the plaintiff is no longer in the criminal's hands. Causation might seem to be established, as it appears the plaintiff would not have been shot had the gun distributor acted with reasonable care. That conclusion, though, is premature.

If the counterfactual inquiry must hold everything constant except for the defendant's wrongful conduct, then the inquiry must hold constant the third-party criminal's motive for purchasing the gun. That motive does not necessarily change merely because the criminal cannot buy the gun from a particular dealer, such as the defendant. The criminal's desire to obtain a handgun means he would try to get a gun elsewhere, and typically he would succeed given the widespread availability of guns on the secondary (unregulated) market, including gun shows. The criminal's motives, if held constant, also would often lead him to use that gun in a robbery, as reflected by his actual conduct. Perhaps someone other than the plaintiff would have been shot. The identity of the victim can be a coincidence, though, and causation does not depend on coincidental factors that do not affect the underlying risk of harm. Causation, in other words, requires the reduction of risk, rather than the displacement of risk from one individual to another. Hence, the defendant's negligent distribution of the gun often is not the legal cause of the plaintiff's injury, because the criminal would have gotten a handgun anyway.

Indeed, the widespread availability of guns in the unregulated market is a predictable outcome produced by self-interested unlawful behavior. Given the demand for guns by criminals, there should be a ready supply from those who find it in their self-interest to skirt the law. Gun manufacturers are obvious candidates for feeding the unregulated market. The desire to maximize profits, coupled with the knowledge that they will often avoid tort liability for unreasonable marketing practices, predictably leads gun manufacturers to feed the unregulated market. One gun dealer, for example, is responsible for selling 20 percent of the traced guns used in crimes in Baltimore over the past ten years.[7] The store is still open for business. According to an affidavit from a former senior vice president of marketing and sales for the gun manufacturer Smith and Wesson:

> The company and the industry as a whole are fully aware of the extent of the criminal misuse of firearms. The company and the industry are also aware that the black market in firearms is not simply the result of stolen guns but is due from the seepage of guns into the illicit market from multiple thousands of unsupervised federal firearms licensees. In spite of their knowledge, however, the industry's position has consistently been to take no independent action to [e]nsure responsible distribution practices. . . .[8]

IV. Strict Liability and Criminal Behavior

The negligence-based enabling torts inadequately reduce the risk posed by third-party criminals, because the element of causation often bars recovery against a noncriminal defendant who failed to take reasonable precautions against such risk. The causal bar is eliminated by strict liability. As long as the defendant has a relationship with the plaintiff or third-party criminal, the defendant could be strictly liable for any criminal risks to which the plaintiff is exposed as a result of the relationship. A gun manufacturer has a relationship with a criminal who possesses one of its guns, providing a relational basis for making the manufacturer strictly liable for the criminal misuse of its guns. By applying strict liability to the relationship, the tort claim avoids the causal problem that limits the effectiveness of the negligence-based enabling torts.

Strict liability applies to abnormally dangerous activities.[9] Despite the high degree of risk created by the criminal misuse of handguns, courts have uniformly rejected the claim that strict liability should apply to the manufacture and distribution of handguns.[10] The courts' primary rationale for doing so is that "a prerequisite for strict liability . . . is not merely a highly significant risk in the defendant's activity itself, but a highly significant risk that remains even when all actors exercise reasonable care."[11] Guns pose no risk of criminal misuse when everyone exercises reasonable care, as there is no criminal conduct (unreasonable behavior) involving guns. By assuming that guns do not pose a significant degree of risk, courts can readily conclude that the distribution of guns is not an abnormally dangerous activity governed by strict liability.

The reasonable-care assumption, despite its importance, has not been justified by the courts. The assumption would be defensible if it were improper to impose tort liability on one for the criminal or tortious behavior of another. The propriety of such liability, however, is established by the enabling torts. Hence, the reasonable-care assumption must be defended descriptively, as a realistic depiction of actual behavior under the law.

As a descriptive matter, the assumption might mean that everyone always obeys negligence law out of a sense of moral obligation. That description, of course, fails. Social facts establish widespread self-interested, unlawful behavior. The threat of negligence liability has not eliminated the criminal misuse of handguns, so the reasonable-care assumption cannot be defended on descriptive grounds.

The rule of strict liability therefore should not assume that everyone necessarily exercises reasonable care. To see how such a rule of strict liability would work, first consider those individuals who "live by the rules" because it is the right thing to do. These individuals look to tort law for guidance on how they should conduct themselves when exposing others to a risk of harm. The rule of negligence tells these individuals they should exercise reasonable care, and they will strive to do so. For this group of individuals, tortious risk for purposes of strict liability can be defined in terms of reasonable care.

Now consider someone who acts like the Holmesian bad man. A self-interested individual will exercise reasonable care only if doing so is less costly than acting negligently. The cost of negligent behavior depends on the likelihood that such behavior will be detected by a plaintiff, proven in court, and subjected to an enforceable judgment for damages. When enforcement is sufficiently high, the cost of negligent behavior (the expected damages) typically outweighs the cost of reasonable care, so the threat of negligence liability gives the Holmesian bad man a sufficient incentive to exercise reasonable care.

In contexts of sufficient enforcement, then, negligence liability induces all actors, whether the law-abiding citizen or the Holmesian bad man, to exercise reasonable care. Tortious risk therefore can be defined in terms of reasonable care for purposes of strict liability.

In other contexts, however, enforcement problems in a negligence regime yield higher risk levels than would occur under strict liability. One such context involves injurers who avoid negligence liability only because they do not get caught or are insolvent. The other context involves identifiable, solvent injurers who avoid negligence liability due to difficulties of proof. The amount of care actually required by the negligence standard depends upon the evidence available to plaintiffs and courts concerning the benefits and burdens of feasible risk-reducing measures. If good evidence concerning desirable safety precautions is unavailable, a negligent injurer who fails to take such precautions will escape liability. Similarly, a negligent injurer can avoid liability by relying on evidentiary problems concerning causation, as illustrated by the negligent distribution of guns. The Holmesian bad man, aware of these avenues for escaping liability, predictably will disobey the tort duty to avoid the cost of exercising reasonable care.

Under strict liability, by contrast, the desire to minimize costs will lead the Holmesian bad man to take safety precautions to reduce the incidence of injuries and payment of tort damages. If the Holmesian bad man would not take such precautions under an imperfectly enforced negligence rule, then strict liability will increase precautions and reduce risk below the level attainable by a negligence regime.

The rule of strict liability therefore should account for the possibility that enforcement problems will induce self-interested actors to act negligently, a particular concern for contexts in which actors are motivated by profit maximization. Such an enforcement rationale for strict liability has been recognized by generations of tort scholars and is an express rationale for strict products liability.[12] Moreover, as I have argued elsewhere, the enforcement rationale provides the best interpretation of the rule of strict liability for abnormally dangerous activities promulgated in the Restatement (Second) of Torts.[13] The key to this interpretation, which has been missed by most courts, is to give the term "reasonable care" practical rather than ideal meaning in the rule of strict liability:

> In determining whether an activity is abnormally dangerous, the following factors are to be considered:
>   a. existence of a high degree of risk of some harm to the person, land or chattels of others;
>   b. likelihood that the harm that results from it will be great;
>   c. inability to eliminate the risk by the exercise of reasonable care [practically induced by the negligence regime];
>   d. extent to which the activity is not a matter of common usage;
>   e. inappropriateness of the activity to the place where it is carried on, and;
>   f. extent to which its value to the community is outweighed by its dangerous attributes.[14]

Strict liability has no enforcement rationale if negligence liability in practice induces all actors, including the Holmesian bad man, to exercise reasonable care. In these contexts, courts can consider only factors (a)–(d).[15] Other contexts may provide an enforcement rationale for strict liability. To decide whether that rationale applies, the court must first conclude that the negligence regime, in light of practical considerations involving enforcement, yields a significant level of risk (factors (a)–(c)). If so, the court must determine whether the risk is "abnormally dangerous" by applying the remaining factors (d)–(f). The appropriateness of such an inquiry can be illustrated by applying this rule of strict liability to the manufacture and distribution of handguns.

V. Is the Manufacture and Distribution of Handguns an Abnormally Dangerous Activity?

The rule of strict liability for abnormally dangerous activities depends critically on the definition of the relevant "activity." Most courts have reasoned that the manufacture and distribution of handguns is not an abnormally dangerous activity because the danger inheres only in the subsequent use or misuse of the product. The use of a handgun may be abnormally dangerous, but not its manufacture and distribution. However, as the enabling torts show, the distribution of handguns involves a duty to reasonably reduce the risk of foreseeable criminal misuse. Tortious risk is not defined exclusively in terms of distribution but includes foreseeable criminal misuse. Consistency seems to require that tortious risk be defined in terms of foreseeable misuse for purposes of strict liability, implying that the activity of gun distribution includes the risk of criminal misuse.

The courts' reasoning in this regard becomes even more problematic when considered in relation to products liability. The manufacture and distribution of a defective product poses little or no danger; the risk is created by product use. If tortious risk were defined exclusively in terms of manufacturing and distribution, with no consideration of foreseeable product use, there would be no basis for imposing tort liability on the manufacturers and sellers of defective products. Such a limited definition of tortious risk has been widely rejected.[16]

Some courts in the handgun cases have acknowledged the relation between products liability and the rule of strict liability for abnormally dangerous activities, concluding that it requires rejection of the strict liability claim. "[W]ere we to hold a manufacturer liable for gun marketing as an abnormally dangerous activity, we would improperly blur 'the distinction between strict liability for selling unreasonably dangerous products and strict liability for engaging in ultrahazardous activities by making the sale of a product an activity.'"[17] This concern is unfounded.

Products liability claims filed on behalf of gunshot victims against gun manufacturers have been rejected by courts because plaintiffs could not show the handguns were defectively designed.[18] Absent an identifiable defect, courts would have to impose categorical or generic liability on handguns, a legal conclusion that handguns pose an unreasonable risk no matter how designed. That conclusion troubles the courts. If a product is defective no matter how designed, then it will be driven from the market. Sales of a product known to pose an unreasonable risk are subject to punitive damages. The imposition of categorical liability on handguns would be tantamount, therefore, to a ban by judicial fiat. The courts conclude that the banning of handguns is a legislative matter, making the imposition of categorical liability inappropriate.[19]

A judicial ban would not occur, though, if courts found the manufacture and distribution of handguns to be an abnormally dangerous activity. As a matter of law, an abnormally dangerous activity involves reasonable risks.[20] Hence, this form of tort liability does not inevitably lead to punitive damages and a ban by judicial fiat. Courts have previously found activities, such as blasting, to be abnormally dangerous. Those activities have not been driven from the market.

The blasting cases illustrate another important aspect of the relation between products liability and the rule of strict liability for abnormally dangerous activities. If manufacturers and distributors of handguns can be subjected to strict liability for abnormally dangerous activities, why can't the manufacturers and distributors of dynamite be strictly liable for injuries caused by the use of dynamite? Absent a limiting principle that distinguishes these cases, the rule of strict liability for abnormally dangerous activities might unduly encroach upon products liability. Such a limiting principle inheres in the enforcement rationale for strict liability, which is why the rule of strict liability for abnormally dangerous activities would not inappropriately encroach upon products liability as the courts have feared.

When used as a method for enforcing the duty of care, the appropriateness of strict liability for abnormally dangerous activities necessarily depends on the nature of the duty. In the handgun cases, the duty is defined by the enabling torts. The basis of that duty lies in the "inability to effectively reach the putative wrongdoer himself, either through criminal or tort sanctions."[21] Because the plaintiff usually cannot recover from the third-party criminal who directly caused the harm, the threat of tort liability does not lead the third party to exercise reasonable care, nor does the availability of such a tort action provide a meaningful remedy for plaintiffs. In these contexts, the only effective recourse for the foreseeable risks stemming from product misuse involve an action directly against the manufacturer or gun distributor.

By contrast, plaintiffs face no unusual difficulty in recovering from the product user in the blasting cases and others involving abnormally dangerous product use. The ability of plaintiffs to recover regularly from the product user means that any duty regarding product use can be effectively enforced against product users, eliminating the enforcement rationale for proceeding directly against the product manufacturer or distributor. Consequently, the manufacture and distribution of dynamite is not abnormally dangerous, because that activity poses no significant risk to bystanders, who are effectively guaranteed compensation for their injuries from the strictly liable blaster.

Thus, in finding that the manufacture and distribution of handguns is not an abnormally dangerous activity, courts have relied on indefensible rationales, the weakest being the assumption of reasonable care. The enforcement rationale for strict liability rejects that assumption and recognizes the social fact of gun violence.

By adopting this rationale, a court would find that the activity of gun manufacture and distribution creates a highly significant risk of criminal misuse. Under the rule of strict liability in the Restatement (Second) of Torts, however, the appropriateness of strict liability depends on the social value of the activity. The social-value factor addresses the distributive issue of how the application of strict liability to the class of cases in question would affect interests other than those represented by the private parties involved in the lawsuit.[22] This factor, as applied to the manufacture and distribution of handguns, appears to be sufficient to defeat the strict liability claim.

If strict liability were to apply to the manufacture and distribution of handguns, then the price of handguns would rise for everyone, criminals and noncriminals alike. The interests of criminals are not socially valuable and can be disregarded, leaving the interests of law-abiding citizens who own guns for self-defense. Strict liability, via its impact on the price of handguns, would burden the individual interest in self-protection by making it more costly for law-abiding citizens to obtain handguns. The burden, by possibly reducing the criminal misuse of guns and providing compensation for gun-shot injuries, would protect the victims of such crimes. The appropriateness of strict liability therefore depends on how these competing sets of interests should be mediated against one another.

Tort law appears to have already decided in favor of self-defense. If someone reasonably uses a gun in self-defense and accidentally kills an innocent third party, the party acting in self-defense need not pay for the injury.[23] The interest in self-defense has priority, for purposes of tort liability, over the competing interest a third party has in her physical security. The same set of interests is involved in the manufacture and distribution of guns. The privilege to purchase a gun for self-defense requires the marketing and distribution of guns in the market-place, with the attendant risk of criminal misuse. Consequently, individuals who exercise this privilege of self-defense expose innocent third parties to the threat of being injured by the criminal misuse of guns. The tort cases involving self-defense suggest that the gun-owners' interest in self-defense has priority, for purposes of tort liability, over the competing third-party interest in bodily security, as long as the force used in self-defense is reasonable.[24] As discussed earlier, abnormally dangerous activities involve reasonable risks as a matter of law. Applying the rule of strict liability to the manufacture and distribution of handguns therefore seems to violate the well-established tort principle concerning self-defense. If so, then the social value of the activity is sufficient to defeat the strict liability claim against the manufacturers and distributors of handguns.

The impact of strict liability on self-defense has concerned some courts, but they were unable to explain why the interest in self-protection defeats the strict-liability claim.[25] Such an explanation requires the enforcement rationale for strict liability. To be sure, the foregoing explanation might not withstand further scrutiny. Maybe the individual interest in self-defense should not have legal priority over the competing security interests of those who do not own handguns.[26] The point, however, is that legal rules concerning handguns necessarily implicate this normative question, and courts have already addressed that question in other tort cases involving self-defense. Courts have never directly addressed that question in the handgun cases, relying instead on reasons that do not withstand scrutiny. At minimum, an enforcement rationale for strict liability would enable the courts to reach better-reasoned and more defensible results in the handgun cases.

VI. Conclusion

An inquiry into the relation between tort law and criminal behavior reveals an inconsistency that requires redress. Negligence doctrine acknowledges that the threat of criminal and tort liability does not induce perfect compliance with the law, whereas strict-liability doctrine assumes perfect compliance.

As illustrated by the handgun cases, courts should eliminate the inconsistency by applying the rule of strict liability in a manner that accounts for unlawful behavior. In light of the vast number of deaths and injuries caused by the criminal misuse of handguns, the manufacture and distribution of handguns unquestionably creates a high degree of risk for some members of society. Instead of acknowledging the risk and determining whether strict liability is an appropriate response, courts have assumed the problem away. Criminals do not misuse handguns, and in any event there is nothing risky about the manufacture and distribution of handguns. This resolution of the problem is highly unsatisfactory and largely disconnected from the public debate on gun control. As the debate so clearly reveals, the legal regulation of handguns poses a hard question of how to mediate the legitimate interests of handgun owners, particularly regarding self-defense, against the interests of those who do not own handguns and face the threat of being shot by criminals. This normative question is ignored by the current judicial approach to strict liability.

This failure of the tort system is unnecessary. In cases of self-defense, the courts have long recognized that the interest in self-defense has legal priority over the competing security interest of a third-party, as long as the force used in self-defense is reasonable. The same issue is involved in the strict-liability claims against the manufacturers and distributors of handguns.

To address the real issue posed by the handgun cases, courts can apply the rule of strict liability in the Restatement (Second) of Torts, interpreted as a rule capable of enforcing the duty of care in contexts where the negligence rule cannot be adequately enforced. This interpretation would make the rule of strict liability consistent with the enabling torts and social facts. By adopting this interpretation, courts would undo the damage that the handgun cases have wrought on the jurisprudence of strict liability.

NOTES

This is an abridged version of an article with the same title that originally appeared in 43 *Arizona Law Review* 311 (2001). I received helpful comments from Ellen Bublick, Robert Rabin, and Gary Schwartz. Eric Womack provided excellent research assistance. This research was supported by a grant from the Filomen D'Agostino and Max E. Greenberg Research Fund at New York University School of Law.

1. See *Franco v. Bunyard*, 261 Ark. 144, 547 S.W.2d 91 (1977).

2. Although many courts have held that manufacturers have no duty regarding the legal marketing of nondefective products to the general public, courts have been willing to find a more limited duty regarding reasonable restraints on marketing. See *City of Boston v. Smith and Wesson Corp.*, No. 1999-02590, 2000 WL 1473568 (Mass. Super. Ct., July 13, 2000). For example, plaintiffs could allege that gun manufacturers have a limited duty not to sell guns to distributors like Baltimore Gunsmith, which has sold a disproportionately large number of handguns used in crimes. See infra note 7 and accompanying text. A limited duty of this type is substantially more defensible than the more general duty to refrain from marketing handguns to the general public. See *Hamilton v. Accu-Tek*, 96 N.Y.2d 222, 237 (2001).

3. Robert L. Rabin, "Enabling Torts," 49 *DePaul L. Rev.* 435, 444 (1999).

4. Ibid.

5. See Erling Eide, "Economics of Criminal Behavior," in V *Encyclopedia of Law and Economics* 345, 355–64 (Boudewijn Bouckaert and Gerrit de Geest eds., 2000) (providing a survey of these studies).

6. See Restatement (Second) of Torts,§ 448 cmt. b.

7. See Fox Butterfield, *The Federal Gun Laws: The First Obstacle to Enforcement* (2001) (unpublished manuscript presented at Symposium on Guns, Crime, and Punishment in America, James E. Rogers College of Law, University of Arizona, Jan. 2001) (on file with author).

8. Affidavit of Robert I. Hass, *Hamilton v. Accu-Tek*, 935 F. Supp. 1307 (E.D.N.Y. 1996), quoted in David Kairys, "Legal Claims of Cities against the Manufacturers of Handguns," 71 *Temple L. Rev.* (1998): 1, 7.

9. Restatement (Second) of Torts, §§ 519–20.

10. See Restatement (Third) of Torts: General Principles 21, Reporter's Notes, cmt. h, at 110 (Council Draft No. 2, Sept. 26, 2000).

11. See ibid. 21, cmt. b.

12. In one of the first tort treatises, Frederick Pollock observed that "the ground on which a rule of strict obligation has been maintained and consolidated by modern authorities is the magnitude of danger, coupled with the difficulty of proving negligence as the specific cause, in the particular event of the danger having ripened into actual harm." Frederick Pollock, *The Law of Torts* 393 (1st ed. 1887). Similarly, Oliver Wendell Holmes has observed that, "as there is a limit to the nicety of inquiry which is possible in a trial, it may be considered that the safest way to secure care is to throw the risk upon the person who decides what precautions shall be taken." Oliver Wendell Holmes, *The Common Law* 117 (1881). Recently, the rationale has been relied upon in the economic analysis of tort law. See Steven Shavell, "Strict Liability versus Negligence," 9 *J. Legal Stud.* 1 (1980). The rationale has been accepted in the products liability context. See *Barker v. Lull Engineering Co.*, 573 P.2d 443 (Cal. 1978)

("[T]his courts' product liability decisions . . . have repeatedly emphasized that one of the principal purposes behind the strict products liability doctrine is to relieve an injured plaintiff of many of the onerous evidentiary burdens inherent in a negligence cause of action."); see also Restatement (Third) of Torts: Products Liability 2, cmt. a (1998).

13. See Mark Geistfeld, "Should Enterprise Liability Replace the Rule of Strict Liability for Abnormally Dangerous Activities?" 45 *UCLA L. Rev.* 611 (1998): 646–60.

14. Restatement (Second) of Torts, § 520.

15. See Restatement (Third) of Torts: General Principles § 21 (Council Draft No. 2, Sept. 26, 2000).

16. See Restatement (Third) of Torts: Products Liability, § 2, cmt. p.

17. *Delahanty v. Hinckley,* 564 A.2d 758, 761 (D.C. Ct. App. 1989) (quoting *Martin v. Harrington and Richardson, Inc.,* 743 F.2d 1200, 1204 (7th Cir. 1984)).

18. See Timothy D. Lytton, "Tort Claims against Gun Manufacturers for Crime-Related Injuries: Defining a Suitable Role for the Tort System in Regulating the Firearms Industry," 65 *Mo. L. Rev.* (2000): 1, 10–14 .

19. See, e.g., *Martin v. Harrington and Richardson, Inc.,* 743 F.2d 1200, 1204 (7th Cir. 1984).

20. An activity that creates unreasonable risks is subject to negligence liability, obviating the need for strict liability. Not surprisingly, then, an abnormally dangerous activity "is carried on with all reasonable care." Restatement (Second)of Torts, § 520 cmt. b. But even though the risks posed by such activities are reasonable as a matter of law, a legal finding of no negligence is not a legal finding that the negligence regime induces perfect compliance with the standard of care. Cf., e.g., *Cooley v. Public Serv. Co.* 10 A.2d 673 (N.H. 1940) ("It is not doubted that due care might require the defendant to adopt some device [that would have prevented the plaintiff's injury]. Such a device, if it exists, is not disclosed by the record. The burden was upon the plaintiff to show its practicability. Since the burden was not sustained a verdict should have been directed for the defendant.").

21. Rabin, "Enabling Torts," at 444.

22. Any risk reduction attained by strict liability could be undesirable for socially valuable activities. Even if strict liability does not reduce risk, it could have socially undesirable distributive effects. Both concerns were the primary motivations for the inclusion of the social-value factor in the Restatement (Second) of Torts. See Restatement (Third) of Torts: General Principles 21, Reporter's Notes, cmt. k, at 123 (Council Draft No. 2, Sept. 26, 2000).

23. See, e.g., *Courvoisier v. Raymond,* 47 P. 284 (Col. 1896); *Morris v. Platt,* 32 Conn. 75 (1864). The conduct in these cases involves risky behavior, because the party acting in self-defense does not intend to harm an innocent bystander.

24. See Restatement (Second) of Torts, § 75.

25. See *Caveny v. Raven Arms Co.*, 665 F. Supp. 530, 531–32, 534–35 (S.D. Ohio 1987) (rejecting abnormally dangerous claim for Saturday Night Special handgun without recognizing relation to self-defense and rejecting a different claim of strict liability because removing "cheap weapons from the community may very well remove a form of protection assuming that all citizens are entitled to possess guns for defense"); *Copier v. Smith and Wesson Corp.*, 138 F.3d 833 (10th Cir. 1998) (rejecting abnormally dangerous claim for handguns in part because the claim "ignores a number of legitimate uses, including self-defense, home protection, and use by law enforcement officers"); *Martin v. Harrington and Richardson, Inc.*, 743 F.2d 1200, 1204 (7th Cir. 1984) (arguing that products liability claim is the same as the abnormally dangerous claim and rejecting both claims in part due to concern that liability would inappropriately burden the right of private citizens to possess arms).

26. Compare supra note 20 (observing the difference between reasonableness as a matter of law and fact).

Chapter 18

Guns and Burglars

David B. Kopel

I. Introduction

In recent years, litigators have begun to displace legislators as American lawmakers. Recently, more than two dozen cities and counties, under the coordination of an antigun organization, have filed suits against handgun manufacturers.

While the effect of these suits may be to impose de facto handgun prohibition by driving manufacturers out of business or by making handguns affordable only to the wealthy, the suits claim that handgun manufacturers should be held accountable for the externalities imposed by their products. For example, since city government hospitals spend money treating the victims of gunshot wounds, it is argued that handgun manufacturers should be forced to reimburse city governments.

The handgun suits are not unique; they are the latest manifestation of a growing trend to have litigators and courts decide complex questions of social policy that had previously been reserved to the legislature. Alcohol, prescription drugs, high-fat foods, and automobiles have all been discussed as potential future lawsuit targets if the handgun cases succeed. The handgun cases, it should be noted, are funded partly with the plaintiffs attorneys' winnings from the tobacco cases.

This essay analyzes one specific reason why courts are ill suited to exercise legislative functions, as the handgun suits and similar cases ask the courts to do: Courts cannot properly assess the true socioeconomic costs and benefits of controversial products. To illustrate the point, this essay looks in detail at a very large positive externality that is overlooked in the handgun suits: the major role that widespread gun ownership plays in reducing the rate of home invasion burglaries (a.k.a "hot burglaries"). Because potential burglars cannot tell which homes possess guns, most burglars choose to avoid entry into any occupied home for fear of getting shot.

The entry pattern of American burglars contrasts sharply with that of burglars in other nations; in Canada and Great Britain, burglars prefer to find the residents at home, since alarms will be turned off, and wallets and purses will be available for the taking.

Consequently, American homes that do not have guns enjoy significant "free-rider" benefits. Gun owners bear financial and other burdens of gun ownership, but gun-free and gun-owning homes enjoy exactly the same general burglary deterrence effects from widespread American gun ownership.

II. International Comparisons

It is axiomatic in the United States that burglars avoid occupied homes. As an introductory criminology textbook explains, "Burglars do not want contact with occupants; they depend on stealth for success."[1] Only 13 percent of U.S. residential burglaries are attempted against occupied homes.[2] But this happy fact of life, so taken for granted in the United States, is not universal.

The overall Canadian burglary rate is higher than the American one, and a Canadian burglary is four times more likely to take place when the victims are home.[3] In Toronto, 44 percent of burglaries were against occupied homes, and 21 percent involved a confrontation with the victim.[4] Most Canadian residential burglaries occur at night, while American burglars are known to prefer daytime entry to reduce the risk of an armed confrontation.[5]

Research by the federal government's Office of Juvenile Justice and Delinquency Prevention found that, according to 1994 data, American youths ten to seventeen years old had much higher arrest rates than Canadian youths for almost every category of violent and property crime. The lone exception was burglary, for which Canadian youths were one-third more likely to be involved.[6] In cities such as Vancouver, home invasion burglaries aimed at elderly people have become endemic and murders of the elderly during those burglaries all too frequent.[7] Unfortunately, help from the government is not always available. In Québec, the provincial police (Sureté du Québec) are under orders from their commander to reduce arrests for burglary, because the jails are full.[8]

A 1982 British survey found that 59 percent of attempted burglaries involved an occupied home.[9] The *Wall Street Journal* reported:

> Compared with London, New York is downright safe in one category: burglary. In London, where many homes have been burglarized half a dozen times, and where psychologists specialize in treating children traumatized by such thefts, the rate is nearly twice as high as in the Big Apple. And burglars here increasingly prefer striking when occupants are home, since alarms and locks tend to be disengaged and intruders have little to fear from unarmed residents.[10]

In Britain, 77 percent of the population was afraid of burglary in 1994, compared to 60 percent in 1987.[11] The *London Sunday Times,* pointing to Britain's soaring burglary rate, calls Britain "a nation of thieves."[12] In the Netherlands, 48 percent of residential burglaries involved an occupied home.[13] In the Republic of Ireland, criminologists report that burglars have little reluctance to attack an occupied residence.[14]

Of course, differences in crime-reporting and crime-recording behavior between nations limit the precision of comparative criminal data. Nevertheless, the difference in home invasion burglary rates between the United States and other nations is so large that it is unlikely to be a mere artifact of crime data quirks.[15]

Why should American criminals display such a curious reluctance to perpetrate burglaries, particularly against occupied residences? The answer cannot be that the American criminal justice system is so much tougher than the systems in other nations. During the 1980s, the probability of arrest and the severity of sentences for ordinary crimes in Canada and Great Britain were at least as great as in the United States.[16] Could the answer be that American criminals are afraid of getting shot? The introductory American criminology textbook states, "Opportunities for burglary occur only when a dwelling is unguarded."[17] Why is an axiomatic statement about American burglars so manifestly not true for burglars in other countries?

III. Risks to American Burglars

One out of thirty-one burglars has been shot during a burglary.[18] On the whole, when an American burglar strikes at an occupied residence, his chance of being shot is about equal to his chance of being sent to prison.[19] If we assume that the risk of prison provides some deterrence to burglary, it seems reasonable to conclude that the equally large risk of being shot provides an equally large deterrent. In other words, private individuals with firearms in their homes double the deterrent effect that would exist if government-imposed punishment were the only deterrent.

How frequently are firearms actually used in burglaries? The only comprehensive study of the subject was undertaken by five researchers from the Centers for Disease Control and Prevention ("CDC").[20] In 1994, random-digit-dialing phone calls were made throughout the United States, resulting in 5,238 interviews. The interviewees were asked about their use of a firearm in defending against a burglary during the past twelve months.

Thirty-four percent of the interviewees admitted to owning a firearm. This figure is low compared to the rate reported in many other national studies of household firearms ownership. Perhaps the telephone interviewers encountered an especially high number of people who were unwilling to disclose their ownership of a gun (and would therefore be unwilling to disclose, later in the interview, their use of that gun).[21] Thus, the burglary researchers are more likely to have underestimated antiburglar firearms use than to have overestimated it.

The researchers found that 6 percent of the sample population had used a firearm when threatened by a burglary during the past twelve months. Extrapolating the polling sample to the national population, the researchers estimated that in the past twelve months, there were approximately 1,896,842 incidents in which a householder retrieved a firearm but did not see an intruder.[22] There were an estimated 503,481 incidents in which the armed householder did see the burglar,[23] and 497,646 incidents in which the burglar was scared away by the firearm.[24] In other words, half a million times every year, burglars fled a home because they encountered an armed victim.

A much more limited study about home-invasion burglaries examined police reports of burglaries in Atlanta. Surveying police reports of 198 burglaries, Dr. Arthur Kellermann found only three cases in which the homeowner used a gun against the burglar. Kellermann stated that defensive gun use against burglars was rare.[25]

Yet Kellermann's study could not have been better designed to produce a gross undercount. Kellermann relied on burglary report forms compiled by the Atlanta police. Those report forms do not include any field for the police officer to report defensive gun use by the victim. Furthermore, Atlanta police officers are not trained to solicit information about defensive gun use from the victims.[26] Thus, the only time that a defensive gun use ("DGU") would be recorded on the offense report would be when an officer spontaneously decided to record it on the free-form section of the burglary offense report. In other words, Kellermann used a data set (burglary offense reports) that was not designed to record DGUs, and on the basis of this data set he concluded that DGUs were rare.

Besides the obvious inadequacy of the burglary offense reports, the Kellermann study was further flawed by its failure to account for the large number of cases in which a burglary victim scared away a burglar but did not report the incident. Fewer than half of all burglaries are reported to the police.[27] An armed citizen might perceive that, by making a report, he would take some risk of being charged with an offense (especially if he fired at the burglar) or of having his firearm confiscated. This perception might be particularly strong in Atlanta, where the mayor and his police chiefs are well known as advocates of severe gun control.[28] Even when reporting a burglary, a citizen might not disclose his use of a firearm.

The 1994 national CDC survey avoided all these problems. By making phone calls to a national random sample, the CDC study had a better chance of receiving information from burglary victims who chose not to call the police. Because the burglary victims were talking to a pollster, rather than to a police officer from a notoriously antigun administration, the victims would be more likely to admit defensive gun use. And, because the CDC pollsters (unlike the Atlanta police) were actually asking all burglary victims about DGUs in burglaries,[29] the pollsters were much more likely to find out about DGUs. Accordingly, the CDC study's figure of approximately half a million annual confrontations between armed citizens and home invasion burglars is plausible (although perhaps low), while Kellermann's assertion that such incidents are rare is not.

The most thorough survey of citizen defensive gun use in general (not just in burglaries) found that, in the large majority of incidents, the criminal is not wounded; apparently the mere display of a gun often suffices to end the attack.[30] The CDC study did not specifically ask whether a gun was fired.[31] It is reasonable to believe that burglary DGU is similar to DGU in general and that most incidents end with the burglar fleeing at the sight of the armed victim, rather than the victim killing or wounding the burglar.

IV. Target Selection and Planning by Burglars

According to the FBI Uniform Crime Reports, between 21 percent and 23 percent of American burglaries involve an entry into a residence at night.[32] American burglars tend to "work" at hours when persons are unlikely to be in the home. Consistent with the desire to avoid a personal confrontation, burglars prefer houses, such as those on corners, where the risks of being observed by a neighbor are reduced.[33] Two hours are spent on the average suburban burglary; most of that time is spent "casing the joint" to ensure that no one is home.

Rengert and Wasilchick's book about how burglars work reveals that fear of armed homeowners plays a major role in determining burglary targets. Burglars reported that they avoided late-night burglaries because "that's the way to get shot." Some burglars said that they shun burglaries in neighborhoods where most people are of a different race because "you'll get shot if you're caught there."[34]

The most thorough study of burglary patterns was a St. Louis survey of 105 currently active burglars. The authors observed, "One of the most serious risks faced by residential burglars is the possibility of being injured or killed by occupants of a target. Many of the offenders we spoke to reported that this was far and away their greatest fear." Said one burglar: "I don't think about gettin' caught, I think about gettin' gunned down, shot or somethin' . . . 'cause you get into some people's houses . . . quick as I come in there, boom, they hit you right there. That's what I think about." Another burglar explained:

> Hey, wouldn't you blow somebody away if someone broke into your house and you don't know them? You hear this noise and they come breakin' in the window tryin' to get into your house, they gon' want

to kill you anyway. See, with the police, they gon' say, "Come out with your hands up and don't do nothing foolish!" Okay, you still alive, but you goin' to jail. But you alive. You sneak into somebody's house and they wait til you get in the house and then they shoot you. . . . See what I'm sayin'? You can't explain nothin' to nobody; you layin' down in there dead![35]

In contrast, Missouri is one of only six states that has no provision allowing citizens to obtain permits to carry handguns for protection. Thus, a criminal in St. Louis faces a very high risk that the target of a home invasion may have a lawful gun for protection but minimal risk that the target of a street robbery will have a lawful firearm for defense. The same authors who studied active St. Louis burglars conducted another study of active St. Louis armed robbers. They found that "[s]ome of the offenders who favored armed robbery over other crimes maintained that the offense was also safer than burglary. . . ." As one armed robber put it: "My style is, like, [I] don't have to be up in nobody's house in case they come in; they might have a pistol in the house or something." On the streets, many of the St. Louis robbers "routinely targeted law-abiding citizens," who, unlike their counterparts in most American states, were certain not to be carrying a gun for protection. Law-abiding citizens were chosen as robbery victims because, as one robber noted, "you don't want to pick somebody dangerous; they might have a gun themselves."[36]

In addition to the St. Louis study, the Wright-Rossi National Institute of Justice surveyed felony prisoners in eleven state prison systems on the impact of victim firearms on burglar behavior. In that survey, 74 percent of the convicts who had committed a burglary or violent crime agreed that "One reason burglars avoid houses when people are at home is that they fear being shot."[37]

Surveys of prisoners may not be entirely representative of criminals as a whole, since prisoners constitute the subset of criminals who were caught and sentenced to prison.[38] Thus, nonprisoner criminals might be more "successful," perhaps because they are more skillful or more risk averse or are in some other way better at burglarizing. To the extent that prisoner bias would influence the results of the burglary question, it might be expected that nonprisoner burglars would be even more averse than imprisoned burglars to occupied-residence burglaries. After all, criminals who are not prisoners stay out of prison by avoiding unnecessary risks.

Fortifying the widespread presence of home defense firearms in the United States is a legal culture that strongly supports armed home defense. Colorado, for example, specifically immunizes the use of deadly force against violent home intruders from criminal and civil liability, regardless of whether lesser force would have sufficed.[39] The South Carolina attorney general recently instructed all prosecutors to refrain from bringing charges against "citizens acting to defend their homes," including citizens who use firearms.[40]

Although statistical evidence is hard to come by, it appears that homeowners who defend themselves against burglars in Canada and England face a substantial risk of criminal prosecution—even if the defense does not involve a firearm. A highly publicized 2001 case in England involved the successful murder prosecution of a farmer who shot a pair of career burglars.[41]

V. Real-World Tests of the Deterrence Model

It is possible to criticize the notion of armed deterrence to burglary (and, by implication, most other efforts to deter crime) by asserting that burglars are too irrational and impulsive to be deterred. But an English study of 309 burglars found that many burglars are careful and deliberate and that more than half of them perpetrate planned burglaries.[42] Another study found that burglary and auto theft were the two crimes most deterred by the potential offender's perceived risk of arrest.[43] Likewise, research on commercial burglars in the Netherlands found "more than eighty percent of the commercial burglars can be characterised as to some degree, rational."[44] A smaller survey of fifteen active residential burglars in the Philadelphia and Wilmington region found "the residential burglars in our sample respond to the risks and rewards associated with committing a burglary in line with expectations from deterrence theory."[45]

Real-world experiments yield results consistent with burglars' reports of their desire to avoid confrontations with armed victims. In Orlando, in 1967, the police responded to a rape epidemic by initiating a highly publicized program that trained women in firearms use.

While rape increased in the nation and in Florida over the next year, the rape rate fell 88 percent in Orlando, and burglary dropped 22 percent.

The same year, rising rates of store robberies prompted a similar (but smaller-scale) program in Kansas City, Missouri, to train store owners in gun use. The next year, while the robbery rate in Missouri and throughout the United States continued to rise significantly, the rate fell in the Kansas City metro area. The trend of increasing burglary in the area also came to an abrupt end, contrary to state and national patterns.[46]

In 1982, the town of Kennesaw, Georgia, passed an ordinance requiring every home to have a gun. Exceptions were made for conscientious objectors, people with criminal records, and people in various other categories.[47] In the seven months before the ordinance, there had been forty-five residential burglaries; in the seven months after the ordinance, residential burglaries declined 89 percent. Over the next five years, the residential burglary rate in Kennesaw was 85 percent below the rate before the enactment of the ordinance.[48]

The ordinance may not have actually changed gun ownership patterns much in Kennesaw. The mayor estimated that, even before the ordinance, about five of every six Kennesaw homes contained a gun. But the publicity surrounding the Kennesaw law may have served as a very powerful warning to persons contemplating a residential burglary in that town: Any homeowner confronted during a burglary would almost certainly be armed.

Consistent with the hypothesis of the deterrent effect of home firearms, lower-income neighborhoods have higher burglary rates,[49] while lower-income persons are less likely than the rest of the population to possess firearms.[50] Of course, there are likely other contributing explanations. Lower-income homes may be less likely to have sturdy locks. It is not unreasonable to expect that a combination of all the defensive weaknesses of lower-income homes plays some role in the higher burglary rates.

VI. Confrontations Involving Burglars

Some individuals may choose burglary because they dislike confrontations; however, not all burglars are nonconfrontational by nature. According to the Wright-Rossi prisoner survey, 62 percent of burglars had also perpetrated robberies.[51] The study of currently active burglars in St. Louis observed: "Most offenders in our sample . . . showed little concern for the well-being of their victims. In fact, several of them said they were prepared to use violence against anyone who got in their way during the commission of an offense."[52]

A. Confrontations with Armed Victims

What happens if a burglar does confront a family, and the family is armed? Gun prohibition advocates warn that the burglar will probably take the gun away and use it against the family. But "take-aways" occur in no more than 1 percent of defensive gun uses and are possible only if the gun owner is so indecisive that he holds the gun far away from his body and fails to act as the burglar comes near.[53]

B. Confrontation with Unprotected Victims

When burglars do encounter victims who cannot protect themselves, the results can be tragic. In 30 percent of these cases, the victim is assaulted or threatened. In 10 percent of these cases, the burglaries turn into rapes.[54] Over the ten-year period 1973–1982, this meant 623,000 aggravated (felony) assaults and 281,000 rapes. Overall, the victim rate of death from "hot" burglaries is six times the death rate from street muggings.[55]

C. The Reduction in Assault from Hot-Burglary Deterrence

The Florida State University criminologist Gary Kleck, in his award-winning book *Point Blank: Guns and Violence in America*, explains the implications of these assault statistics. Suppose that the percentage of "hot" burglaries rose from current American levels (around 12 or 13 percent)[56] to the average rate of Canada, Great Britain, and the Netherlands (around 45 percent).[57] Knowing how often a hot burglary turns into an assault, we can predict that an increase in U.S. hot burglaries to the levels of other nations would result in 545,713 more assaults every year. This by itself would raise the American violent crime rate 9.4 percent.

Put another way, the American violent crime rate is significantly lower than it would otherwise be, because American burglars are much less likely than Canadian burglars to enter an occupied home. Given that the average cost of an assault, in 1990 dollars, is \$13,490, and the cost of rape \$56,419,[58] the annual cost savings from reduced assault amount to more than \$7 billion (\$7,361,668,300). The savings from avoided rapes would be roughly similar.[59]

The \$7-billion saving from reduced assaults is, by the way, much larger than the revenue of the every American firearms and ammunition manufacturer combined.[60]

VII. Guns Compared to Other Antiburglary Devices

Gun ownership for home protection offers considerably more benefits to the community than do many other antiburglary measures. Burglars do not know which of their potential victims may be armed. Until a confrontation with a homeowner, the potential burglar generally has no idea whether any given homeowner has a gun.

Thus, careful burglars must (and most do) take care to avoid entering any home where a victim might be present. Because about half of all American homes contain a gun, burglars tend to avoid all occupied American homes. People who do not own guns—even people who belong to gun-prohibition organizations—enjoy free-rider safety benefits from America's armed homes.

In contrast to guns, burglar alarms appear to have no net community benefit. Burglar alarms have been shown to reduce burglaries for homes in which they are installed. However, the presence of many burglar alarms in a neighborhood does not appear to affect the burglary rate of unalarmed homes.[61] In addition, false alarms (which account for 94 to 98 percent of all burglar alarm activations) impose very large public safety costs through misappropriation of limited police resources. False-alarm signals travel over 911 lines and may crowd out genuine emergencies.[62] Thus, alarms impose substantial external costs on other homes in the community. Guns, of course, lie inert until someone decides to use them; they do not go off because a cat jumped into a beam of light.

Gun prohibitionists make all sorts of claims about the risks of "a gun in the home."[63] These claims have some validity if the gun is in the home of a violent felon, an alcoholic, or a person with suicidal tendencies. But, in responsible hands, guns are no danger at all, since the gun will shoot only in the direction in which it is pointed and will not fire unless the trigger is pulled. Whatever the risks of a gun in the home, the risks are borne almost entirely by the people in that home. The nongun owners in the community get the benefit of safety from home invasion burglars, while assuming no risks at all. (The most significant external danger of a gun in the home occurs if the gun is stolen by a criminal, a risk that also applies to any other device that could be stolen and used by a criminal, such as a car or a crowbar, or any valuables that could be sold and the profits used to buy crime tools.)

Guns stay quiet and unobtrusive until needed. They do not bark all night and wake up the neighborhood, as dogs often do. Nor do guns rush into the street to attack and sometimes kill innocent people, as some guard dogs do. In New Zealand, where defensive gun ownership is unlawful, a surge of home invasions has led to greatly increased sales of aggressive dog breeds.[64] It is not clear that New Zealand neighborhoods are better off with more Rottweilers and fewer shotguns.

Firearms, which are typically stored deep inside a home, do not make a neighborhood look ugly. Passive deterrents, such as window bars, give a neighborhood the appearance of a prison, and some can trap the occupants of a home during a fire.

Most people consider it rational for householders to have burglary insurance. Yet insurance premiums must (if the insurance company is to stay in business) be set at a level at which the cost of the premiums exceeds the probable payout by the insurance company over the long run. Insurance is, therefore, a bet on the wrong side of the odds for the insured. If it is reasonable for people to reduce the risks of burglary by buying insurance, it is also reasonable for people to reduce the risks of burglary by purchasing a gun for home protection. Over a ten-year period, the cost of insurance premiums far exceeds the cost of a good gun.[65] The gun, unlike the insurance premium, can actually prevent a victim from being injured. And, unlike insurance premiums, a gun helps benefit the entire community, since all American enjoy the 9.4 percent lower violent crime rate attributable to defensive gun ownership in the home.

Insurance companies, which already subsidize various home protection systems such as burglar alarms, should begin giving substantial discounts to policyholders who verify that they have a gun and have been trained in defensive gun use.

VIII. Policy Implications

A. Undersupply of Firearms

The "diffusion of benefits" is good news for people who do not own guns. They get the full free-rider benefit, while incurring neither the expense to buy a gun nor the time commitment necessary to learn to use the gun, practice with it, and clean it. But when free riding of a good is possible, then the good will be undersupplied.

Consider a recent study of a device called LoJack, designed to prevent auto thefts.[66] The LoJack is a radio transponder hidden in a car. When the car's owner reports that the car has been stolen, law enforcement can activate the transponder via radio signal. The LoJack transponder then begins emitting a radio signal, making it easier for police to locate the stolen car.[67] Like guns in the home, LoJack is unobservable to a criminal considering potential targets, unless he knows the victim personally.

Thus, LoJack (like guns in the home) benefits the entire community equally, rather than conferring a benefit mainly on the owner. A 1 percent increase in LoJack installation in an area led to a 20 percent decline in car thefts in big cities, and a 5 percent decline statewide. The total benefits of LoJack were fifteen times greater than the costs. But fewer than 10 percent of the total social benefits went to LoJack owners; the rest went to the free riders who did not install LoJack. As a result, LoJack was "dramatically undersupplied." The small insurance subsidies for LoJack installation were not sufficient to correct this problem.[68]

With guns, the undersupply problem would not be as severe. Besides preventing burglaries, guns have various benefits that are available only to the user (such as use in the shooting sports). On the other hand, many jurisdictions, such as New York City, impose severe externalities (expensive taxes and fees, complex licensing systems) to discourage gun ownership.[69] A few jurisdictions (Chicago, some Chicago suburbs, and Washington, D.C.) forbid possession of handguns, the gun most useful for defense in confined urban settings.[70]

Consider the scenario faced by burglars if the possibility that a victim would be armed were to increase to nearly 100 percent, that is, if almost every home had a gun that was readily deployable for home defense. It is not unreasonable to expect that the home invasion rate would drop to near zero. As noted earlier, as long as gun ownership did not increase among the small percentage of the population uniquely likely to abuse firearms (primarily substance abusers and violent criminals), an increase in defensive home gun ownership would have large social benefits and few social costs.

Thus, jurisdictions with prohibitory or repressive gun licensing laws should consider whether those laws, by depressing the rate of defensive gun ownership, may be imposing high costs on everyone in the jurisdiction. While a safer society is generally considered good, some firearms policy lobbyists morally oppose gun ownership for defensive purposes. As Mrs. Sarah Brady explains, "To me, the only reason for guns in civilian hands is for sporting purposes."[71] The antidefense view underlies a wide variety of gun control proposals, including laws similar to Canada's requirement that guns in the home be locked and stored so "safely" as to be inaccessible for defensive deployment during a break-in.[72]

B. Network Effects

In economics, an externality can be found where "an agent does not bear the full cost of his actions."[73] Although the concept of externality is most often used in cases where the agent inflicts costs on others (e.g., the agent's pollution falls on someone else's land), the concept can also be used when the agent reaps only part of the benefits of his actions. Firearms in the home appear to be the second type of case.

A network effect may be found when "the utility that a user derives from consumption of a good increases with the number of agents consuming the good"[74] or when "one consumer's value for a good increases when another consumer has a compatible good."[75]

The intensity of network effects varies along a continuum. At the highest end are actual communications networks. For example, a telephone would be of little use unless many other people were on the same telephone system. "At the other end of the continuum are a variety of phenomena in which provision of a good for service positively relates to some level of scale, but in which the scale economies themselves create the value rather than interactions among users of the good."[76]

In the context of home invasion burglary deterrence, firearms appear to be associated with network effects at the lower end of the continuum: The more homes with firearms, the greater the burglary deterrence. Thus, if one person in London were granted an exemption from English gun laws and were allowed to possess a firearm for home protection, there would be no improvements in burglary deterrence. From the burglar's point of view, more than 99.999 percent of London homes would still be unprotected. Conversely, high gun density in Kennesaw benefited all the homes. When burglars saw Kennesaw as an extraordinarily well-armed community, burglary deterrence increased.

One of the strengths of a free society is the potential for nonhierarchical coordination. Sophisticated social tools can be created without central planning. For example, "millions of people have incrementally helped shape the English language into an enormously ornate and valuable institution. Those who have contributed to this achievement have acted without the help of the state or any other hierarchical coordinator."[77]

Without central planning, firearms ownership in American homes has proliferated to the extent that important network effects now appear to be visible. These network effects seem to enhance community safety and to reduce burglary, especially home invasion burglary.

C. Courts and the Costs and Benefits of Firearms

Evaluating the total costs and benefits that firearms create is difficult. The fact that firearms ownership is protected by the U.S. Constitution and forty-four state constitutions suggests that firearms ownership (like the free exercise of religion, or freedom of the press, or other constitutionally protected acts) has already been set above the standards of cost-benefit analysis. Security in the home, like the right to attend the church of one's choice, has a value that cannot be quantified and is immune from any attempts at constriction based on a cost-benefit analysis.

The economic benefits of firearms are just being discovered. John Lott's research has gone a long way toward identifying societal benefits that accrue from laws that allow licensed citizens to carry firearms for protection in public. But very little has been done on the quantifiable benefits of firearms in many other contexts, such as protecting store proprietors from robbers, or protecting domestic violence victims from stalkers and similar predators. Criminologists and other social scientists will continue to study these topics, and legislatures will continue to make firearms laws based in part on this social science.

It seems doubtful that the function of making determinations based on criminology and econometrics should be transferred from legislatures to judges and juries. Figuring out aggregate costs and benefits becomes especially difficult for juries when the beneficiaries are not before the court—and may not even know they are beneficiaries. This is the case with home invasion burglary deterrence, in which most non-gun-owning households are not even aware that they are beneficiaries. While readers may agree or disagree about the exact degree to which U.S. firearms density deters hot burglaries, the very inability to come up with a precise answer suggests that resolution of the firearms cost-benefit issue is not appropriate for the judicial system.

NOTES

Reprinted by permission of the *Arizona Law Review.*

1. Freda Adler et al., *Criminology* (2d ed., 1995), 278.

2. U.S. Bureau of Justice Statistics, "Household Burglary," *BJS Bull.* (1985): 4.

3. See Lorne Gunter, "Canadians Suffer as Much Crime as Americans," *Edmonton J.,* Mar. 31, 1998 (citing International Crime Victimization Survey).

4. See Irwin Waller and Norman Okhiro, *Burglary: The Victim and the Public* (Toronto: University of Toronto Press,1978), 31.

5. For American burglars and daytime entry, see George Rengert and John Wasilchick, *Suburban Burglary: A Time and a Place for Everything* (Illinois: C. C. Thomas, 1985), 30, 62; John E. Conklin, *Robbery and the Criminal Justice System* (Philadelphia: Lippincott, 1972), 85. A study of an unnamed "northern city" in Ontario for 1965–1970 reported 12.2 percent of burglaries occurred during the day, 69.5 percent occurred at night, and the times of 18.3 percent were unknown. See Peter Chimbros, *A Study of Breaking and Entering Offenses in "Northern City" Ontario, in Crime in Canadian Society* (Robert A. Silverman and James J. Teevan Jr. eds., 1975), 325–26.

6. See Melissa Sickmund et al., "Juvenile Offenders and Victims: 1997 Update on Violence," *United Stated Department of Justice, OJJDP* (1997), 36.

7. See Peter Kennedy, "B.C. Home Invasions Claim New Victim; Woman, 82, Slain," *Globe and Mail* (Toronto), Nov. 15, 1999.

8. See "Sureté du Quebec Will Ignore Break-ins," *Journal de Montreal,* Jan. 9, 1997, 15.

9. See Pat Mayhew, *Residential Burglary: A Comparison of the United States, Canada and England and Wales* (1987) (citing 1982 British crime survey).

10. See Kevin Heilliker, "Pistol-Whipped: As Gun Crimes Rise, Britain Is Considering Cutting Legal Arsenal," *Wall St. J.,* Apr. 19, 1994, at A1. It might not seem intuitively obvious that New York City is a place where burglars need to fear armed residents. But the question is not whether New York City has a high rate of gun ownership compared to Texarkana but whether New York City has a high rate of household gun ownership compared to London. Although the New York City police licensing bureaucracy throws many obstacles in the way of a person who wants to own a handgun legally, it is relatively easy to obtain a permit to own a shotgun or rifle in New York City. In London, by contrast, legal ownership of any type of gun is very onerous. Moreover, New York City has a huge pool of unregistered firearms (up to three million by police estimates), most of which are potentially available to resist home invasions.

11. "See British Crime Fears Rise," *Wall St. J.,* Mar. 22, 1994, at A11.

12. See J. Ungoed-Thomas, "A Nation of Thieves," *Sunday Times,* Jan. 11, 1998, at Features Sec., p. 1.

13. See Richard Block, *The Impact of Victimization, Rates and Patterns: A Comparison of the Netherlands and the United States, in Victimization and Fear of Crime: World Perspectives* (Richard Block ed., 1984), 26 tbl. 3–5 (1977 Dutch National Crime Survey found 468 burglaries with someone home, 513 burglaries with no one home).

14. See Claire Nee and Maxwell Taylor, *Residential Burglary in the Republic of Ireland: Some Support of the Situational Approach, in Whose Law and Order? Aspects of Crime and Social Control in Irish Society* (Mike Tomlinson et al. eds., 1988), 143.

15. This essay does not suggest that differential rates of defensive gun ownership are the only explanation for the different hot-burglary rates among various nations—only that they are a major factor.

16. See Gary Kleck, *Point Blank: Guns and Violence in America* (New York: A. de Gruyter, 1991) 140.

17. See Adler et al., at 277.

18. See Rengert and Wasilchick, at 98.

19. See James Wright et al., *Under the Gun: Weapons, Crime and Violence in America* (New York: Aldine Publishing Co., 1983), 139–40; Gary Kleck, "Crime Control through the Private Use of Armed Force," 35 *Soc. Probs.* (1988): 1, 12, 15–16.

20. See Robert M. Ikeda et al., "Estiminating Intruder-Related Firearms Re-trievals in U.S. Households, 1994," 12 *Violence and Victims* (1997): 363.

21. See Gary Kleck, *Targeting Guns: Firearms and Their Control* (New York: A. de Gruyter, 1997): 64–69, 98–99 tbl. 3.2 (respondent nondisclosure in gun ownership surveys).

22. See Ikeda et al., at 366–67. The 95 percent confidence interval was a range between 1,480,647 and 2,313,035 such incidents—meaning that there is a 95 percent chance that the true national figure is somewhere in this range.

23. The 95 percent confidence interval was 305,093 to 701,870.

24. The 95 percent confidence interval was 266,060 to 729,231.

25. See Arthur L. Kellermann et al., "Weapons Involvement in Home Inva-sion Crimes," 273 *JAMA* (1995): 1759, 1762.

26. See Gary Kleck, "Degrading Scientific Standards to Get the Defensive Gun Use Estimate Down," 11 *J. Firearms and Pub. Pol'y* (1999): 77, 79–80 (based on interview with Atlanta police official).

27. See Bureau of Justice Statistics, *Criminal Victimization 1999* (Washing-ton, D.C., 2000) (NCJ 182734), 11.

28. Indeed, the Atlanta police chief was a co-author of Kellermann's article. See Kellermann, 36.

29. See Ikeda, 364.

30. See Kleck, *Targeting Guns,* 162 (1993 survey).

31. See Ikeda, 366.

32. About a third of burglaries involve nonresidences (such as offices or stores); between 25 percent and 29 percent involve burglaries of residences during the daytime; and 16–18 percent involve residential burglaries that took place at unknown times. See FBI "Uniform Crime Reports for 1976–1993," in *Sourcebook of Criminal Justice Statistics 1994,* tbl. 3.133. The nighttime residential burglary rate is not the same as the "hot" burglary rate. Some hot burglaries take place in the daytime, and many nighttime burglaries involve houses where no one is home due to vacation or other reasons.

33. Rengert and Wasilchick, 21–24, 84. Owners of corner houses are also typically more affluent and therefore make more lucrative targets.

34. Rengert and Wasilchick, 30, 62.

35. Richard T. Wright and Scott Decker, *Burglars on the Job: Streetlife and Residential Break-Ins* (Boston: Northeastern University Press, 1994), 112–13.

36. See Richard T. Wright and Scott H. Decker, *Armed Robbers in Action* (Boston: Northestern University Press, 1997), 52, 72.

37. See James D. Wright and Peter Rossi, *Armed and Considered Dangerous: A Survey of Felons and Their Firearms* (New York: A. de Gruyter, 1986), 146.

38. George W. McCall, *Observing the Law: Applications of Field Methods to the Study of the Criminal Justice System* (Bethesda, Md.: National Institute of Mental Health, 1975), 31.

39. See Colo. Rev. Stat. § 18-1-704.5 (1993).

40. Jon Dougherty, "Invade a Home and Invite a Bullet," WorldNet Daily (Jan. 26, 2001), available at: http://www.worldnetdaily.com/news/article .asp?ARTICLE_ID=21478.

41. Andrew Pierce, "Tories to Propose Action on Intruders," *The Times* (London) (Jan. 1, 2001), available at: http://www.thetimes.co.uk/article/ 0,,2-60623,00.html (describing opposition party proposal to allow use of "reasonable force" against home invaders).

42. Trevor Bennett and Richard Wright, *Burglars on Burglary* (Aldershot, UK: Ashgate Publishing Co., 1986), 47–48.

43. See Julie Horney and Ineke Haen Marshall, "Risk Perceptions among Serious Offenders: The Role of Crime and Punishment," 30 Criminology (1992): 575, 582.

44. Eric Wiersman, "Commercial Burglars in the Netherlands: Reasoning Decision-Makers?" 1 *Int'l. J. of Risk, Security and Crime Prevention* (1997).

45. Alex Piquero and George F. Rengert, "Studying Deterrence with Active Residential Burglars," 16 *Justice Q.* (1999): 451, 464.

46. See Kleck, *Point Blank,* 134–35; see also Kleck, *Targeting Guns,* 181.

47. See Code of Ordinances, City of Kennesaw, § 34-1.

48. See Kleck, *Point Blank,* 136–38. Follow-up work on Kleck's analysis of Orlando, Kennesaw, and Kansas City argues that the data, correctly interpreted, show no evidence of a deterrent effect from firearms. David McDowall et al., "General Deterrence through Civilian Gun Ownership," 29 *Criminology* (1991): 541. Kleck replies that the critique is flawed; for example, regarding Kennesaw, the McDowall article lumped residential and business burglaries together (even though the deterrent effect of home firearms would apply only to home burglaries, and burglars displaced from homes might attack unoccupied businesses) and used raw numbers instead of rates (the Kennesaw population rose 70 percent from 1980 to 1987, the years in question). See Gary Kleck, "Has the Gun Deterrence Hypothesis Been Discredited?" 10 *J. Firearms and Pub. Pol'y* (1998): 65.

49. See Garland F. White, "Neighborhood Permeability and Burglary Rates," 7 *Just. Q.* (1990): 64 (study controlling for effect of neighborhood instability and housing density).

50. See Kleck, *Targeting Guns,* 71.

51. See Kleck, *Point Blank,* 139.

52. Wright and Decker, *Burglars on the Job,* 111.

53. Kleck, *Point Blank,* 122 (citing National Crime Victimization Survey data).

54. See Bureau of Justice Statistics, "Household Burglary," *NCJ-96021* (1985): 4 tbl. 8, tbl. 9.

55. See Franklin E. Zimring and James Zuehl, "Victim Injury and Death in

Urban Robbery: A Chicago Study," 15 *J. Legal Stud.* (1986): 1; see also Franklin
E. Zimring, *Crime Is Not the Problem: Lethal Violence in America* (New York: Oxford University Press, 1997), ch. 10. Zimring argues that American sentencing
policy (such as California's three-strikes law) is misguided, because it treats
burglary as harshly as robbery. Since burglary is much less likely to lead to
victim death, Zimring argues, sentencing policies should encourages criminals to choose burglary over robbery. Zimring's point is valid as far as it goes,
but it fails to distinguish hot burglaries from other burglaries. Replacing robberies with cold burglaries could save lives; replacing robberies with hot burglaries would cost lives. See David B. Kopel, "Disarming the Victims," *Chronicles* (Apr. 1999): 46 (reviewing Franklin E. Zimring, *Crime Is Not the Problem*
(1997)).

56. See Bureau of Justice Statistics, "Household Burglary," 4 tbl. 8 (citing
12.7 percent).

57. See Kleck, *Point Blank*, 140.

58. Simon Hakim et al., "Estimation of Net Benefits of Residential Electronic Security," 13 *Just. Q.* (1996): 153, 161.

59. John Berlau, "Will Other Vices Be Targeted?" *Investor's Bus. Daily* (Feb.
12, 1998): A1.

60. Manufacturers are required to pay an 11 percent excise tax on the sale
of ammunition and long guns and a 10 percent tax on the sale of handguns.
Extrapolating from 1999 excise tax collections, one calculates that the gross
sales of American companies were $686 million for ammunition, $677 million
for long guns, and $369 million for handguns. Letter from Larry Ference, Na-
tional Shooting Sports Foundation, to David B. Kopel (Feb. 9, 2001) (on file
with author).

61. See Terance D. Miethe, "Citizen-Based Crime Control Activity and Victimization Risks: An Examination of Displacement and Free-Rider Effects," 29
Criminology (1991): 419, 429 tbl. 1.

62. Hakim et al., 157–60, 166. An analysis of burglar alarms in a police district in Dade County (Miami) found that, of 230 electronic alarms, only one
was the result of a real burglary. James J. Fyfe, "Police/Citizen Violence Reduction Project," *FBI L. Enforcement Bull.* (May 1989): 23.

63. See, e.g., *Handgun Control, Inc., Guns in the Home* (visited Feb. 7, 2001)
http://www.handguncontrol.org/facts/ib/gunhome.asp.

64. See "Invasions Prompt Inquiries for Guns," *The Press* (N.Z.), Nov. 10,
1999.

65. If one presumes that the annual cost of theft insurance for a home is
fifty dollars or more. The Beretta Model 3032 Tomcat Pistol carries a suggested
retail price of $333. See *Gun Digest 2001*, 242 (Ken Ramage ed., 2001). The Tau-
rus Model 85 Revolver is $286. See id. at 283. The least expensive handgun
listed in *Gun Digest 2001* is the Lorcin L-25, at $69. See ibid., 257.

66. See Ian Ayres and Steven Levitt, "Measuring Positive Externalities from Unobservable Victim Precaution: An Empirical Analysis of Lojack," 113 *Q.J. Econ.* (1998): 43.

67. See Shelly Feuer Domash, "Keeping Track with LoJack," *Police* (June 1999): 50.

68. See Ayres and Levitt, 47, 53, 58, 75.

69. See, e.g., Admin. Code of the City of N.Y., §§ 10-131, 10-301-306.

70. See, e.g., D.C. Code Ann. §§ 6-2312(a)(4) (1981). In Washington, D.C., use of a long gun for home defense is technically legal but in effect very difficult, since long guns must be kept unloaded and must also be locked up or disassembled.

71. Tom Jackson, "Keeping the Battle Alive," *Tampa Trib.,* Oct. 21, 1993.

72. See Department of Justice Canada, "Storage of Firearms by Individuals," Canadian Firearms Manual, available at: http://www.canadianfirearms .com/cfm/english/topics/14storag/1410300d.htm

73. Dennis W. Carlton and J. Mark Klamer, "The Need for Coordination among Firms, with Special Reference to Network Industries," 50 *U. Chi. L. Rev.* (1983): 446, 450, n.15.

74. Michael L. Katz and Carl Shapiro, "Network Externalities, Competition, and Compatibility," 75 *Am. Econ. Rev.* (1985): 424.

75. Joseph Farrell and Garth Saloner, "Standardization, Compatibility, and Innovation," 16 *Rand J. Econ.* (1985): 70.

76. Mark Lemley and David McGowan, "Legal Implications of Network Economic Effects," 86 *Calif. L. Rev.* (1998): 479, 609.

77. Robert C. Ellickson, *Order without Law* (Cambridge, Mass.: Harvard University Press, 1991), 5.

Contributors

Sara Sun Beale is Charles L. B. Lowndes Professor of Law at Duke University. She is the author of *Federal Criminal Law and Related Actions: Crimes, Forfeiture, the False Claims Act and RICO* (with Pamela Bucy and Sarah Welling) (West Group 1998), *Grand Jury Law and Practice* (with William C. Bryson, James E. Felman, and Michael J. Elston) (West Group 2d ed. 1997), and *Federal Criminal Law and Its Enforcement* (with Norman Abrams) (West Group 3d ed. 2000), as well as numerous articles dealing with various issues of criminal law and procedure. Beale has served as an associate reporter for the Workload Subcommittee of the Federal Courts Study Committee, as the reporter for a three-branch federal-state working group convened by Attorney General Janet Reno to consider the principles that should govern the federalization of criminal law, and as a member of an American Bar Association task force studying the federalization of criminal law. Before joining the Duke faculty, Beale worked in the United States Department of Justice, where she served as an Assistant to the Solicitor General and as an Attorney Adviser in the Office of Legal Counsel. Beale received her B.A. degree in English and her J.D. degree, magna cum laude, from the University of Michigan.

Jenny Berrien is an Analyst in the Housing and Community Revitalization Area of Abt Associates Inc. While at Abt, Berrien has worked on a number of program evaluation and technical assistance projects in the areas of workforce development, Section 8 housing, and homeless assistance programs. She served as Deputy Project Director for the evaluation of the Annie E. Casey Foundation Jobs Initiative and was a member of the qualitative research teams for Abt's evaluations of HUD's Moving to Opportunity Demonstration Program and Welfare to Work Voucher Program. Prior to joining Abt,

Berrien was a Program and Policy Analyst on Public/Private Ventures' faith-based initiative. Berrien entered a joint Master's in Public Policy/Master's in Business Administration program at Harvard University in Fall 2002. She received her A.B. cum laude in Sociology from Harvard University in 1998.

Carl T. Bogus is Professor of Law at the Roger Williams University School of Law. He is the editor of *The Second Amendment in Law and History* (New Press 2001) and the author of many articles about the Second Amendment, including "The History and Politics of Second Amendment Scholarship: A Primer," *Chicago-Kent Law Review* (2000), "The Hidden History of the Second Amendment," *U.C. Davis Law Review* (1998), and "Race, Riots and Guns," *Southern California Law Review* (1993). Professor Bogus has testified before Congress and spoken to groups around the country on the Second Amendment and is also recognized for his work in other areas. He is the author of *Why Lawsuits are Good For America: Disciplined Democracy, Big Business, and the Common Law* (New York University Press 2001). He received the Ross Essay Award from the American Bar Association for "The Invasion of Panama and the Rule of Law" (*The International Lawyer*). Professor Bogus received both his undergraduate and his law degrees from Syracuse University.

Anthony A. Braga is Senior Research Associate in the Program in Criminal Justice Policy and Management of the Malcolm Wiener Center for Social Policy, John F. Kennedy School of Government, Harvard University. His research focuses on developing problem-oriented policing strategies to control violent crime hot spots, disrupt drug markets, and reduce youth firearms violence. He has advised the U.S. Department of Justice, the U.S. Department of the Treasury, the Bureau of Alcohol, Tobacco, and Firearms, the Boston Police Department, the New York Police Department, and other state and local criminal justice agencies on these issues. Braga received his M.P.A. from Harvard University and his M.A. and Ph.D. in Criminal Justice from Rutgers University.

Abigail Caplovitz is an associate at the law firm of Chadbourne and Parke LLP in New York City. Before entering practice, she was a Leslie Glass Criminal Justice Fellow at New York University and the recipient of the Judge Abraham Lieverman Award for Outstanding Scholarship in Criminal Law. Caplovitz received her B.S. from the University of Connecticut and her J.D. from New York University School of Law.

Philip J. Cook is ITT/Sanford Professor of Public Policy at Duke University and research associate of the National Bureau of Economic Research. He joined the faculty at Duke University in 1973 after completing his economics Ph.D. at the University of California, Berkeley. He is the author of *Gun Violence: The Real Costs* (with Jens Ludwig) (Oxford University Press 2000), *The Winner-Take-All Society* (with Robert H. Frank) (Penguin Books 1995), and *Selling Hope: State Lotteries in America* (with Charles T. Clotfelter) (Harvard University Press 1989). His 1997 article on race and education (with Jens Ludwig) won the Vernon Prize for best article in the *Journal of Policy and Analysis and Management.* Cook is an elected member of the National Academies' Institute of Medicine and a fellow of the American Society of Criminology.

Garth Davies is a doctoral candidate in the School of Criminal Justice at Rutgers University. A former Excellence Fellow at Rutgers and winner of the Gene Carte Student Paper Competition, he has co-authored several reports and articles on crime and violence in New York City, including "Street Stops and Broken Windows: Terry, Race and Disorder in New York City" (with Jeffrey A. Fagan), *Fordham Urban Law Journal* (2000).

Christopher L. Eisgruber is Director of the Program in Law and Public Affairs at Princeton University, where he serves as the Laurance S. Rockefeller Professor of Public Affairs in the Woodrow Wilson School and the University Center for Human Values. He is the author of *Constitutional Self-Government* (Harvard University Press 2001) and many articles about the Constitution. He has co-authored a number of publications with Lawrence G. Sager, including *Law and Religion: A Critical Anthology; Religious Liberty and the Moral Structure of Constitutional Rights; Impeachment and Constitutional Structure; Punishing the President: The Use and Abuse of Impeachment; Good Constitutions and Bad Choices.* He received his M.Litt in Politics from Oxford University and his J.D. from the University of Chicago Law School.

Jeffrey A. Fagan is Professor of Law and Public Health at Columbia University. He is the editor of *The Changing Borders of Juvenile Justice:*

Waiver of Adolescents to the Criminal Court (with Franklin Zimring) (University of Chicago Press 2000) and author of numerous articles on crime, law, and social policy, including "Street Stops and Broken Windows: Terry, Race and Disorder in New York City" (with Garth Davies), in the *Fordham Urban Law Journal* (2000), "Guns, Youth Violence and Social Identity" (with D. L. Wilkinson), in *Youth Violence— Crime and Justice: A Review of Research* (1998), and "The Comparative Impacts of Juvenile and Criminal Court Sanctions for Adolescent Felony Offenders," in *Law and Policy* (1996). From 1995 to 2000, he served as the delegate from the American Society of Criminology to the American Association for the Advancement of Science. Fagan received his B.E. from New York University and his Ph.D. from the University at Buffalo.

Mark Geistfeld is Professor of Law at New York University School of Law. He has published extensively in the areas of insurance, products liability, and torts. His recent publications include "Negligence, Compensation, and the Coherence of Tort Law," in the *Georgetown Law Journal* (2002); "The Analytics of Duty: Medical Monitoring and Related Forms of Economic Loss," in the *Virginia Law Review* (2002); "Implementing the Precautionary Principle," in the *Environmental Law Reporter* (2001); and "Economics, Moral Philosophy, and the Positive Analysis of Tort Law," in *Philosophy and the Law of Torts* (Gerald J. Postema ed., Cambridge Univ. Press 2001). Before teaching at New York University, Geistfeld was an associate at the New York firms of Simpson, Thacher and Bartlett and Dewey, Ballantine, Bushby, Palmer and Wood. He also clerked for Judge Wilfred Feinberg, of the United States Court of Appeals for the Second Circuit. Geistfeld received his J.D. and his Ph.D. in Economics from Columbia University.

Bernard E. Harcourt is Professor of Law at the University of Chicago. He is the author of *Illusion of Order: The False Promise of Broken-Windows Policing* (Harvard University Press 2001) and of several articles on punishment, policing, and youth gun carrying, including "Measured Interpretation: Introducing the Method of Correspondence Analysis to Legal Studies," in the *University of Illinois Law Review* (2002), "After the 'Social Meaning Turn': Implications for Research Design and Methods of Proof in Contemporary Criminal Law Policy Analysis," in *Law and Society Review* (2000), and "Matrioshka

Dolls," in *Urgent Times: Policing and Rights in Inner-City Communities* (Joshua Cohen and Joel Rogers eds.) (Beacon Press 1999). Before joining the University of Chicago, Harcourt was a member of the law faculty and director of the Rogers Program on Law, Philosophy, and Social Inquiry at the University of Arizona and has been a visiting professor at Harvard Law School and at New York University School of Law. Harcourt received his A.B. from Princeton University and his J.D. and Ph.D. (Government) from Harvard University.

James B. Jacobs is Warren E. Burger Professor of Law and Director of the Center for Research in Crime and Justice at New York University. He is the author most recently of *Can Gun Control Work?* (Oxford University Press 2002) and of several articles on gun control as a regulatory and enforcement problem. He is also the author of numerous other books, including *Gotham Unbound: How NYC Was Liberated from the Grip of Organized Crime* (New York University Press 1999), and *Hate Crime, Law and Identity Politics* (with Kimberly Potter) (Oxford University Press 1998). He received his J.D. and Ph.D. (Sociology) from the University of Chicago.

Dan M. Kahan is Professor of Law at Yale Law School. His books and book chapters include *Urgent Times: Policing and Rights in Inner-City Communities* (1999) (with Tracey Meares), and "The Progressive Appropriation of Disgust" in *The Passions of Law* (Susan Bandes ed., New York University Press 2000). His publications on criminal law have appeared in journals such as the *Harvard Law Review,* the *Columbia Law Review,* the *Georgetown Law Journal,* the *Wall Street Journal,* and the *Washington Post.* Kahan clerked for Judge Harry T. Edwards, of the United States Court of Appeals for the D.C. Circuit, and for Associate Justice Thurgood Marshall, of the United States Supreme Court. He was a member of the faculty at the University of Chicago Law School between 1993 and 1998 and has been a visiting member of the faculties of Yale Law School and Harvard Law School. Kahan graduated magna cum laude from Harvard Law School in 1989, where he was President of the *Harvard Law Review.*

David Kairys is Professor of Law at Temple University. He is the author of *With Liberty and Justice for Some* (New Press, 1993) and editor of *The Politics of Law* (Basic Books 3d ed. 1998). He is a leading civil rights lawyer and has litigated landmark race discrimination and harassment cases. In 1996 he conceived the city lawsuits against handgun manufacturers and is now on the city teams in most of the pending cases. He set out the basis and theory of the suits in "Legal Claims of Cities against the Manufacturers of Handguns," *Temple Law Review* (1998). Professor Kairys started practice as a public defender on a fellowship at the University of Pennsylvania Law School after graduating from Columbia Law School in 1968 and was a founding partner of Kairys and Rudovsky, now Kairys Rudovsky, Epstein, Messing and Rau, in 1971. He began teaching constitutional law and civil rights at Temple in 1990. He has an LL.B. from Columbia University and an LL.M. from the University of Pennsylvania.

David B. Kopel is the Research Director of the Independence Institute, Associate Policy Analyst with the Cato Institute, and Director of the Center on the Digital Economy at the Heartland Institute. He is the author of *Guns, Who Should Have Them?* (Prometheus Books 1995) and the editor of *Gun Control and Gun Rights: A Reader and Guide* (with Andrew McClurg and Brannon Denning) (New York University Press 2002) and *Supreme Court Gun Cases* (with Alan Korwin and Stephen Halbrook) (Bloomfield Press 2002). He served as an Assistant Attorney General for the State of Colorado and as Adjunct Professor of Law at New York University School of Law. Kopel also writes for the *Colorado Springs Gazette, Liberty* magazine, *Chronicles* magazine, and *The National Review.* He graduated magna cum laude from the University of Michigan Law School.

Sanford Levinson is the W. St. John Garwood and W. St. John Garwood Jr. Centennial Chair in Law and Professor of Government at the University of Texas School of Law. He is author if *Constitutional Faith* (Princeton University Press 1988) and *Written in Stone* (Duke University Press 1998) and editor or co-editor of *Constitutional Tragedies* (New York University Press 1998), *Responding to Imperfection: The Theory and Practice of Constitutional Amendment* (Princeton University Press 1995) and *Interpreting Law and Literature: A Hermeneutic Reader* (Northwestern University Press 1988). His many articles have appeared in *Yale Law Journal, Harvard Law Review, Constitutional Commentary, Ethics, Philosophy and Public Affairs,* and elsewhere. He is currently working (with Paul Brest, Akhil Amar, and J. M. Balkin) on the fourth edition of their popular casebook *Proc-*

esses of Constitutional Decisionmaking (Aspen 2002). He has been a visiting professor at Harvard Law School and at New York University School of Law and is a member of the American Law Institute. He received his Ph.D. from Harvard University and his J.D. from Stanford Law School.

Jens Ludwig is Associate Professor of Public Policy at Georgetown University, an affiliated expert of the Johns Hopkins Center for Gun Policy and Research, and a member of the National Consortium on Violence Research. He has also served as a visiting scholar at the Brookings Institution and at the Northwestern University/University of Chicago Joint Center for Poverty Research. His research focuses on urban problems, particularly those related to poverty, education, and crime. He is the author of *Gun Violence: The Real Costs* (with Philip J. Cook) (Oxford University Press 2000) and the editor of *Evaluating Gun Policy* (with Philip J. Cook) (Brookings Institution Press 2002).

Daniel C. Richman is Professor of Law at Fordham University. He has published a number of articles about the federal criminal justice system, including *Personal Convictions* (forthcoming); *The Changing Boundaries between Federal and Local Enforcement* (July 2000); *Of Prosecutors and Special Prosecutors: An Organizational Perspective* (2000). From 1987 to 1992, he was an Assistant U.S. Attorney in the Southern District of New York. He clerked for Justice Thurgood Marshall, of the Supreme Court of the United States, as well as Chief Judge Wilfred Feinberg, of the Second Circuit Court of Appeals in New York. He received his J.D. from Yale Law School, where he was the Note Editor of the *Yale Law Journal*.

Jerome H. Skolnick is Adjunct Professor of Law and Co-Director of the Center for Research in Crime and Justice at New York University where he teaches seminars on police, law and society, and the regulation of vice. He retired in 1995 as Claire Clements Dean's Professor of Law, Jurisprudence, and Social Policy at the University of California, Berkeley, where he had for ten years been the Director of the University of California's Center for the Study of Law and Society. He is the author of numerous books and edited books, including *Above the Law: Police and the Excessive Use of Force* (with James Fyfe) (Free Press 1993), *Justice without Trial: Law Enforcement in Democratic Society* (Macmillan 1993), *Crisis in American Institutions* (with Elliot Currie) (Harper Collins College Publishers 9th ed. 1994), *Criminal Justice: Introductory Cases and Materials* (with John Kaplan and Malcolm Feeley) (Foundation Press 5th ed. 1991), and *The New Blue Line: Police Innovation in Six American Cities* (with David Bayley) (Free Press 1986). He has been awarded numerous distinctions, including the August Vollmer award of the American Society of Criminology.

Richard Slotkin is Olin Professor of American Studies at Wesleyan University. He is the author of an award-winning trilogy of scholarly books on the myth of the frontier in American cultural history, which includes *Regeneration through Violence: The Mythology of the American Frontier, 1600–1860* (1973), *The Fatal Environment: The Myth of the Frontier in the Age of Industrialization, 1800–1890* (1985), and *Gunfighter Nation: The Myth of the Frontier in Twentieth-Century America* (1992). Slotkin's scholarly articles and reviews have appeared in *American Literary History, American Quarterly, Berkshire Review, Journal of Popular Culture, Prospects 9, American Historical Review, Journal of the West, Western Historical Quarterly, William and Mary Quarterly, Radical History Review,* and *Representations.* In 1995, Mr. Slotkin received the Mary C. Turpie Award of the American Studies Association for his contributions to teaching and program building in American Studies.

Christopher Winship is Professor of Sociology and Senior Fellow at the Hauser Center for the Study of Nonprofits at Harvard University. From 1998 to 2001 he was chair of the Sociology Department at Harvard. Winship has done research on statistical models for qualitative dependent variables, latent class models, segregation indexes, and social networks. He has had a long-term interest in examining changes in the social and economic status of African Americans, examining changes in racial differences of youth unemployment, marriage patterns, and imprisonment rates. In the recent past, he has written a series of articles with Sanders D. Korenman that reanalyzed data in *The Bell Curve,* disputing key findings, and, in a series of papers with Martin Rein, examined the use of social science research in policy debates. His current research involves work on causal analysis with nonexperimental data, Bayesian approaches to classical model identification, the effects of education on mental ability, explanations for racial differences in educational performance in elite institutions of higher education, and an analysis of the importance of a police-ministerial alliance (The Ten-Point Coalition) for lowering crime rates and improving police-community relations in Boston.

Franklin E. Zimring is the William G. Simon Professor of Law and Director of the Earl Warren Legal Institute at the University of California at Berkeley. He has authored or co-authored twenty books, most recently *American Youth Violence* (1998) and *Crime Is Not the Problem: Lethal Violence in America* (1997) (with Gordon Hawkins) and a series of empirical studies on violence, on legal change, and on adolescent development. Professor Zimring currently serves on the National Academy of Sciences Panel on Juvenile Justice and on the federal expert panel on safe schools. He is the former Director of the Center for Studies in Criminal Justice at the University of Chicago, where he served as Karl N. Llewellyn Professor of Jurisprudence. Zimring is a Fellow of the American Society of Criminology and a member of the American Academy of Arts and Sciences.

Acknowledgments

This book grows out of the *Conference on Guns, Crime, and Punishment in America*, organized under the auspices of the University of Arizona Rogers Program on Law, Philosophy, and Social Inquiry and held in Tuscon, Arizona, in January 2001. A special debt of gratitude is owed to Toni Massaro and James E. Rogers, who helped envisage, create, and support the Rogers Program; to Vicki Fleischer and Donna Ream, at the University of Arizona, for exceptional assistance in organizing the conference; to Cara Conlin, at Harvard Law School, for her extraordinary assistance in putting this collection together; to the authors of this book for their stimulating contributions; and to the chairs, commentators, and other participants at the conference who contributed so much to these essays, especially Ellen Bublick, Fox Butterfield, Richard Carmona, James Coldren, Suzanne Dovi, Susan Ginsburg, Michael Gottfredson, Stuart Green, Scott Hattrup, Travis Hirschi, Fred Kay, John Lott, David May, Lois Felson Mock, Calvin Morrill, Michael Polakowski, Robert Rabin, Louise Marie Roth, William Ruefle, Henry Ruth, Carol Steiker, Bryan Stevenson, and Richard Unklesbay.

Index

431